ANALYZING THE PRESIDENCY

second edition

STAFF

Marguerite L. Egan   Program Manager
Brenda S. Filley   Production Manager
Charles Vitelli   Designer
Libra Ann Cusack   Typesetting Coordinator
Julie Arbo   Typesetter
Shawn Callahan   Graphics
Diane Barker   Editorial Assistant

Library of Congress Catalog Card Number: 89-081095
Manufactured in the United States of America
Second Edition, First Printing
ISBN: 0-87967-815-1

DPG

The Dushkin Publishing Group, Inc.
Sluice Dock, Guilford, CT 06437

Preface

Over the course of U.S. history, the office of the presidency has come to dominate the American political landscape. This development grew out of the handiwork of the Founding Fathers. They decided on a single rather than plural executive, and in doing so created the only institution in U.S. national government capable of speaking with one voice. In addition, the words they wrote into Article II of the Constitution, which established the presidency, were brief and often ambiguous, thereby providing the necessary opening for activist presidents who would one day seek to broaden the scope of the office. But changes and events—including the expanding role of the federal government, the growing involvement of the United States in international affairs, and the advent of mass communications—also combined with the constitutional structure to make the presidency the focal point of the U.S. political system and an energizing force.

I have taught a course on this fascinating institution during each of the last fifteen years. In assembling materials for the course, I routinely searched for a suitable collection of readings to assign students. None of the available readers left me wholly satisfied, however. Some fell well short of covering the major topics typically considered in a course on the presidency. Others provided the necessary breadth of coverage, but included only one selection under many of the topics considered. Still others were deficient on both counts.

This book represents an attempt to overcome these deficiencies. It does, I believe, cover those aspects of the presidency essential to a comprehensive understanding of the institution. Moreover, it seeks as well to achieve a greater degree of depth by providing at least two selections for each of the major topics. There is a total of 18 readings, which are organized into eight topic chapters (*Presidential Selection; Presidential Character; The President and the Public; The President and Congress; The President and the Bureaucracy; The President and the Media; The President and the Vice President; The President and the Policy-Making Process: Domestic and Foreign Policy*). Each topic chapter begins with a general examination and review of the topic as it is addressed in the readings in the chapter. Among the authors included, some are scholars; some are current or former public officials; and some combine experience in both academia and government. All have written essays that are both cogent and readable.

Changes to this edition   Since the first edition of this book, the press of events and more recent scholarship have necessitated changes for this second edition. Accordingly, in five of the eight chapters at least one of the selections has been replaced with a new article; and in chapters 4 (The President and Congress) and 5 (The President and the Bureaucracy), all the selections have been changed. As with the first edition, I made every effort to include articles that reflect the thinking of both scholars and practitioners of government.

Acknowledgments   I appreciate the useful suggestions from political scientists at colleges and universities who used the first edition and who communicated with The Dushkin Publishing Group. Throughout the completion of this project, I was most fortunate to have the assistance of Marguerite L. Egan of the DPG. Her formidable talents as a facilitator lessened my own burdens considerably.

Robert E. DiClerico
Morgantown, West Virginia

Contents

providing coherance to the policymaking process. He argues that the prevalence of divided government in the last thirty-six years has imperiled the nation's ability to address critical domestic and foreign policy issues.

Wilson is unpersuaded by those who claim that the separation of powers has become a serious hindrance to effective government, and he contends that the reasons for preserving this constitutional principle are as compelling today as they were over two hundred years ago.

Benda and Levine chronicle and evaluate the Reagan administration's unparalleled attempt to gain greater control over the bureaucracy via centralization, devolution, privatization, administrative modernization, and cost control.

Rockman notes that a mismatch of incentives makes some degree of tension between the president and career bureaucrats inevitable, and he maintains that the relationship has become more strained under recent presidents. Believing that such antagonism is not in a president's long term interest, he suggests how presidents can engage the bureaucracy more effectively.

Introduction

The modern presidency is vastly different from the administrations of earlier presidents. The mass media, the bureaucracy, political parties, public perceptions and Congress are all major actors on the modern presidential stage. In many practical ways the power of the president is limited. Congress has enacted legislation designed to restrict the freedom of presidential action in the area of military intervention abroad, and other entrenched interests can make change a difficult and slow process. In this environment, the ability of the president to persuade and communicate can often be of greater importance than his executive powers.

The chapters that follow examine the personal and institutional forces that shape a president's tenure. Because it is the most basic issue, in chapter 1 experts explore the ways in which we select our president. No further analysis is possible until we understand who the people are who become president and what the process is that selects them. Our process is demonstrably different from that of other Western democracies, and our entire political system is affected accordingly.

This theme is expanded upon in chapter 2 as a psychological model is applied to the presidency and the people who hold the office. Political success or failure can often be as dependent upon a president's personal character traits as upon the political environment in which he must operate. This personal component must be understood in order for us to make reasonable decisions concerning our political future.

Once in office, a president must contend with public perceptions of the job he is doing. As is made clear in chapter 3, we hold many expectations of our president, and many of them are contradictory. The ability of a president to deal with these conflicting expectations can determine public perceptions, which in turn can be translated into political power or political impotence.

It is in his dealings with the Congress that public perceptions are translated into practical victories or defeats. A president, such as Ronald Reagan, who was perceived as having massive public support, can create legislative programs that a less popular president could never achieve. This is one of the many senses in which perception becomes reality in the political world.

The implementation of legislative programs is the next obstacle to be faced by a president. Laws must be administered, and that can be done by career civil servants with enthusiasm or sullen acquiescence. In the Reagan administration, Americans witnessed a change of direction in many departments of the federal government.

Most of the perceptions that Americans hold concerning the character of their presidents are formed through the images presented by the mass media. Modern presidents, to a degree beyond the imagination of earlier leaders, can reach people in their own living rooms. The power to shape these impressions and perceptions in large part rests in the hands of the television, radio, and newspaper commentators who offer on-the-spot analysis of speeches and presidential initiatives. Since we have seen how perception can become reality, the media are in a position to wield great power. The approach that a president takes toward the media can determine much of the nature of his administration.

The presidency is, of course, intensely political in its nature. All of the aspects discussed above must ultimately be converted into governmental policy. Within this policy-making process, perceptions and political realities are weighed and examined. Just as the president must deal with external institutions, there are political struggles among advisers for access to the president, and there are different perspectives on policy issues that the president must resolve. In addition, Congress has dramatic influence that must be considered when formulating policy. In recent years, the role of the vice president has grown in these questions of policy formulation.

These are some of the questions that must be asked in order for us to gain an understanding of the presidency in America today. The essays presented here are the views of experts from inside and outside of government. We may agree or disagree with their assessments, but it is critical that we raise these questions in a democratic system.

 # Chapter One

Presidential Selection

Scholars and politicians have long recognized that the nominating process is the most critical stage in elections. As the eminent student of politics E. E. Schattschneider observed, "The definition of the alternatives is the supreme instrument of power."[1] Nor was this point lost on the notorious political practitioner Boss Tweed, who was fond of reminding his compatriots, "I don't care who does the electin', so long as I do the nominatin'."

Among the democracies of the world, America is unique in the extent to which its citizens are accorded a significant role in determining who the choices will be on election day. Such was not always the case, however. From 1800–1824, presidential candidates were nominated by the members of their respective parties in Congress. But the congressional caucus gradually fell into disrepute as criticism mounted against placing the nominating decision in the hands of so few people. After a brief transition period, during which time candidates were nominated by state legislatures or local conventions, the political parties instituted a new system—the national convention. Under this system, each state party established procedures for selecting delegates to represent it at the national convention. In certain states, some or all of the delegates were appointed by state party leaders. The most common practice, however, was for state parties to choose delegates through a multi-stage caucus/convention system, which began at the precinct level and progressed on up to the state party convention.

While the national convention certainly broadened participation beyond what had existed under the congressional caucus system, by the turn of the century it, too, came under fire for being subject to near-total manipulation by party bosses. As a consequence, reform-minded Progressives championed the idea of presidential primaries in which voters themselves would choose the delegates to represent their states at the national conventions. This method of selection gained in popularity, and by 1916 twenty-six states had adopted it. In subsequent years, however, enthusiasm for the primary waned for a variety of reasons. Party leaders were understandably opposed to this method because they could not exercise much control over it. In addition, the financial costs were high, voter turnout was disappointing, and many presidential candidates declined to enter them.

Up until 1972, any individual seeking the presidential nomination was confronted with one overriding reality—in order to win, he was compelled to gain the support of party leaders. This was so because a substantial majority of delegates were chosen not in the primaries, but rather by the appointment or caucus/convention methods, both of which were controlled by the party elites. Primaries, though not completely ignored by most candidates, were entered selectively and viewed principally as a means of demonstrating vote-getting ability to party elites.

1

The Democrats' 1968 nominating contest not only exemplified this reality but also served as a catalyst for changing it.

As the campaign season opened in 1968, President Johnson saw his Vietnam policy challenged by the little-known antiwar candidate, Eugene McCarthy. Initially given little chance of unseating an incumbent, McCarthy's surprisingly successful showing in the New Hampshire primary encouraged Robert Kennedy to enter the race also. The combined support for each of these candidates ultimately convinced Lyndon Johnson to withdraw. It was not until late April 1968 that Vice President Humphrey, with the blessing of the White House, threw his hat into the ring. Significantly, by this late date the filing deadlines for entering the primaries had passed in all but one state. The Democrats' presidential campaign, which had already been characterized by the unexpected, took another dramatic turn in early June when Robert Kennedy was assassinated just minutes after his big win in the California primary. With this untoward event, the field was now narrowed to McCarthy and Humphrey. This did not prove to be much of a contest, however. The vice president easily won on the first ballot at the Democratic National Convention—he garnered nearly three times the number of delegate votes as his opponent. That Humphrey was able to capture the nomination without having entered a single primary was dramatic testimony to the locus of power in the nominating process. He commanded the support of the party leaders. McCarthy did not.

The outcome of the 1968 convention left many McCarthy and Kennedy supporters bitter and disillusioned with the nominating process. Not only had the Democrats chosen a standard-bearer whose views on the Vietnam war differed little from President Johnson, but in contrast to McCarthy and Kennedy, Humphrey had not taken his case to the people in the primaries. In addition, McCarthy supporters charged that they had repeatedly been the victims of arbitrary rules and procedures used by some state parties in selecting delegates.

These complaints gave rise to calls for more democracy in the nominating process, and the Democratic party ultimately responded with a series of reforms that were implemented in 1972. These changes may be broadly characterized as follows:

1. establishment of uniform and detailed procedures for selecting delegates via the caucus/convention method;
2. a significant reduction in the number of delegates who could be appointed and a prohibition against reserving delegate slots for party and elected officials;
3. a requirement that state parties take immediate steps to increase the number of blacks, women, and young people in their state delegations;
4. the allocation of delegates on a proportional basis so as to ensure that caucus and primary results would more accurately reflect voter preferences.

Taking its cue from the Democrats, the Republican party also reformed its caucus/convention procedures and abolished reserved delegate slots for party and elected officials. It did not, however, require the allocation of delegates on a proportional basis and merely encouraged states to include more blacks, women, and young people in their delegations. Although some of these party reforms were modified in subsequent years, and others added, the overall goal of expanding participation in the nominating process has not been compromised.

These reforms were accompanied by a highly significant parallel development—an increase in the number of primaries. More specifically, in 1968 there were only seventeen Democratic party primaries and sixteen Republican ones. In both parties, moreover, only about third of the delegates were chosen in these primary contests. By 1980, however, the number of primaries had grown to thirty-five for the Democrats and thirty-four for the Republicans, and for each party, some seventy-five percent of convention delegates are now being chosen by this method. Although none of the reforms either urged or required states to choose their delegates in primaries, several factors appear to have fostered this increase. It seems likely that some states, perceiving a broad-based sentiment for greater participation in the nominating process, understandably saw the primary as the most democratic method for selecting delegates. Others felt that a switch from caucuses to primaries would bring their state greater media attention. Still others appear to have believed that the procedural reforms made by the Democratic party could be implemented more easily in primaries. Finally, to the extent that some of the procedural reforms curbed the ability of state and local party leaders to manipulate the caucus/conventions, these leaders now saw the primaries as less susceptible to control by insurgent elements within the party.

In any event, both the increase in primaries and the party reforms all but eliminated the once crucial role played by the party elites in choosing a nominee. To be sure, the Democratic party sought to restore some of their influence by reserving fourteen percent of the delegate slots at its 1984 convention exclusively for members of Congress and state and local party officials. This percentage was increased slightly to 15.5 percent for 1988. These changes, however, have not altered the fact that those seeking the presidency must now take their case to the people through the myriad primaries.

The reformed nominating process may allow for broader and more direct participation by the electorate; nevertheless, some critics seriously question whether it necessarily yields the best results. The two selections that follow give voice to these concerns. Anthony King contrasts the American and British selection processes with respect to the *type* of candidates running, *who* chooses them, and *how* they are chosen. He concludes that the American nominating process produces individuals lacking in the experience, political skills, and alliances necessary to govern effectively. Thomas Cronin and Robert Loevy are not happy with the existing system either. As an alternative, they propose that we adopt a national pre-primary convention that, they argue, would shorten the campaign, reduce media influence, enhance the deliberative nature of conventions, and tie candidates more closely to their parties.

Notes

1. E. E. Schattschneider, *The Semi-Sovereign People* (Holt, Rinehart and Winston, 1960), p. 68.

1.1

Anthony King

How Not to Select Presidential Candidates: A View from Europe

Anthony King is professor of government at the University of Essex in England and the author of The British Prime Minister: A Reader *and* The New American Political System. *In this essay he contrasts the American and British selection processes with respect to who the candidates are; who chooses them; and how they are chosen. By doing so, he presents an interesting perspective on the American process. He concludes that the American process yields individuals who lack the experience, political skills, and alliances necessary to govern effectively.*

All over Europe in the autumn of 1980, wherever people met to talk politics, there was only one topic of conversation: How on earth had a great country like the United States, filled with talented men and women, managed to land itself with two such second- (or was it third-?) rate presidential candidates as Jimmy Carter and Ronald Reagan?

Europe's political leaders had, of course, to be circumspect in what they said publicly; but the press had no such inhibitions. Newspapers like *Le Monde* of Paris and the *Neue Zurcher Zeitung* were tepid in their response to the two candidates. Leading British newspapers were more outspoken:

> In Europe, there is great bewilderment that the Americans should be landing themselves with a choice between two such mediocre figures. *(Financial Times)*

> It is no wonder that Americans feel that there has been some malfunction of their political system. The President talks perfectly good sense, but his reasonable words and good intentions are somehow converted into unsuccessful policies. Governor Reagan does not sound sensible at all. *(The Times)*

> In short, neither of the two main candidates gives much impression of knowing how they want to lead America in the complicated and difficult years ahead . . . One sighs for a man of stature. *(Daily Telegraph)*[1]

Asked to develop their views of the two men in more detail, the great majority of Euorpean politicians and public officials would probably have responded roughly like this:

From *The American Elections of 1980*, edited by Austin Ranney. (Washington D.C.: American Enterprise Institute, 1981.) Reprinted with the permission of the American Enterprise Institute for Public Policy Research.

Carter? a Nice enough chap in his way. Certainly well-meaning, undoubtedly intelligent—but, as we all know, hopelessly inept. Raises issues, claims to attach great importance to them, then unexpectedly drops them, often with the result that friends and allies are left out on a limb. No consistent goals or policies; no follow-through. Treats everything on a case-by-case basis: cannot seem to see that in politics everything is interconnected. A curious tendency to moralize everything: whoever heard of a *moral* energy policy!? Came to Washington knowing little about Europe; after nearly four years, has seemingly learned almost nothing. Surrounds himself with people who are as ignorant of the world as he is. In short, a decent man but hopelessly out of his depth.

Reagan? Probably no better than Carter, possibly a good deal worse. Like Carter, a man with no real experience of national-level politics; like Carter, too, a man with no previous experience of foreign affairs. An accomplished platform performer, but apparently without any real grasp of the complexity of economic and foreign-affairs issues. Evidently not very bright: seems actually to believe his simple-minded slogans! Said to be lazy. To be sure, a tolerable governor of California, but then that was hardly a difficult post to fill with the state's economy growing as fast as it then was. Most that can be hoped for: that Reagan would choose able people, then delegate a good deal of authority to them. In short, possibly a disaster, at best a sort of down-market Eisenhower.[2]

Such views may have been unfair; they may have been ill informed. But they were certainly widely—indeed almost universally—held in Europe in 1980. This chapter seeks to explain how two men who probably could not have been selected in any European country could become their parties' presidential nominees in the United States, and at the same time to point up certain contrasts between European methods of selecting party leaders and the methods currently being employed in America. Before we proceed, however, it is worth making the point that the views just expressed of Carter and Reagan were not confined to skeptical, world-weary Europeans; they were widely held in the United States itself.

American Views of Carter and Reagan

The available evidence suggests that the two main presidential candidates in 1980 were less well thought of by the American people than any other pair of candidates since at least the 1930s. To a remarkable degree, the year's political jokes were aimed not at Carter or Reagan separately but at the two together. A bumper sticker to be seen in the streets of New York read: "Your candidate is even worse than my candidate." The *Cincinnati Enquirer* published a cartoon showing a campaign committee room with two entrances. The sign outside one read, "Anybody but Carter Hdqtrs," the sign outside the other, "Anybody but Reagan Hdqtrs." The committee room was manned by John Anderson. The cover of *Public Opinion* magazine in June/July 1980 depicted a man wearing four campaign buttons on his lapel. The first three were for Carter, Reagan, and Anderson; the fourth said, "No thanks."[3]

Likewise, the views of newspapers and magazines in America were very similar to those of the European press. "The present prospects are dismaying," the *New York Times* commented in July. The *Washington Post* remarked somewhat later in the campaign:

Table 9-1

VOTERS GIVING "HIGHLY FAVORABLE" RATING TO MAJOR-PARTY PRESIDENTIAL
CANDIDATES, 1952–1980

	Percentage of Voters Giving Rating		
	Republican candidate	Democratic candidate	Total
1952	47	37	84
1956	59	33	92
1960	40	42	82
1964	16	49	65
1968	38	25	63
1972	41	21	62
1976	28	41	69
1980	23	30	53

Source: Gallup Poll, *New York Times*, October 31, 1980.

There is no way, given the nature of the two prime contenders for the office, that this country is going to elect a president in November who is especially gifted in or suited to the conduct of the office. And that is that.

On the eve of election day itself, *Time* magazine began its concluding story on the campaign:

For more than a year, two flawed candidates have been floundering toward the final showdown, each unable to give any but his most unquestioning supporters much reason to vote for him except dislike of his opponent.

A survey of more than 1,600 American daily newspapers found that, whereas in 1976 only 168 had refused to endorse any candidate, in 1980 fully 439 insisted on remaining neutral.[4]

The most important views, however, were the views of the American people themselves. Beginning in 1952, the Gallup poll has asked a sample of voters every four years to rate each of the presidential candidates on a ten-point scale ranging from very favorable to very unfavorable. If the two highest points on each candidate's scale (+5 and +4) are merged to form a single "highly favorable" rating, then the results for the last eight presidential elections are as shown in table 9-1. Carter individually, it appears, was not as unpopular as Hubert Humphrey in 1968 or George McGovern in 1972; similarly, Reagan individually was not as unpopular as Barry Goldwater in 1964. Taken together, however, the two 1980 candidates were given a "highly favorable" rating by fewer voters than in any of the previous seven Gallup surveys. To take the extreme cases, in 1956, 92 percent of the electorate thought highly of either Dwight Eisenhower or Adlai Stevenson, whereas in 1980 the proportion of voters holding Carter and Reagan in equally high esteem was a mere 53 percent. America's citizens manifested their lack of enthusiasm by turning out to vote on November 4 in smaller numbers than at any presidential election since 1948.[5]

In the rest of this chapter, we shall assume for the sake of argument that the instincts of the American people were right—that, compared with the other talent available, Carter and Reagan were (and are) pretty unimpressive political leaders. Such an assumption will clearly not please the minority of ardent Carter and Reagan enthusiasts; but even they may accept that there is some validity in the analysis that follows.

A European Contrast

No system of selecting political leaders can guarantee success. The ancient Athenians chose Pericles but also Alcibiades; the system that resulted in the nomination of Abraham Lincoln was essentially the same system that produced James Buchanan. All that a procedure for choosing leaders can do is make it more or less probable that men and women with certain characteristics, abilities, and aptitudes will emerge. America's presidential candidates in recent years have not, most people now believe, been altogether satisfactory. There may be a connection between this fact and the way in which presidential candidates are currently nominated.

One way of appreciating the peculiar features of America's way of selecting candidates for the country's highest office is to compare it with what happens in other countries. Britain provides an especially useful comparison, partly because it is better documented than most of the others but chiefly because it would be hard to imagine a system more unlike that of the United States; in most respects, as will become clear, the American and British systems are polar opposites. The British system is, moreover, not unusual. Party leaders in Australia, New Zealand, and Japan are selected in much the same way as in Britain, and the leadership-selection systems in most Western European countries certainly resemble the British system more closely than the American.[6]

At the time in 1980 when the Democratic and Republican presidential nominees were being chosen in the United States, the leaders of Britain's two largest parties, the Conservatives and Labour, were Margaret Thatcher and James Callaghan. The reader is asked to consider the process by which these two people rose to the leadership of their respective parties. (Both also became prime minister either immediately or later; but it is the process of *selecting* party leaders rather than of *electing* prime ministers that we are concerned with here.)[7]

Margaret Thatcher, a tax lawyer, fought her first parliamentary election in 1950 at the age of twenty-four. She finally entered the House of Commons nine years later at the age of thirty-four. After serving on the Conservative back benches for two years, she was promoted to junior ministerial office in 1961 at the age of thirty-six. She held the office of parliamentary secretary to the Ministry of Pensions and National Insurance until the Conservative party was defeated at the general election of 1964. For the next six years, while the Conservatives were in opposition, she spoke for her party in the House of Commons on housing, pensions, transport, energy, economic affairs, and, latterly, education. Edward Heath, then the Conservative leader, appointed her to his "shadow cabinet" in 1967. When the Conservatives were returned to power in 1970, she entered the real cabinet as secretary of state for education and science, a post she held until the Conservatives were again defeated in February 1974. In the new Parliament, she was first chief Conservative spokesman on housing and local government matters, then her party's shadow chancellor of the exchequer (that is, chief spokesman on economic and financial affairs).

By this time, Edward Heath's political star was sinking fast. The Conservatives had lost three of the four general elections that it had fought under his leadership, and the 1970–1974 Heath government was generally considered a failure. In October 1974 Margaret Thatcher decided to stand against him for the leadership. The election took place some four months later, in the first half of February 1975. All of the candidates were Conservative members of the House of Commons; so were all of the electors. No one outside the House of Commons participated in the election, except as observers. The various candidates' "campaigns," if that is the right word, consisted solely of canvassing and lobbying their fellow members of Parliament (MPs). Thatcher led on the first ballot, but not by quite enough to secure her election outright; on the second ballot, a week later, she won easily. The views of the mass public appear to have played little, if any, part in determining the outcome; opinion polls in 1975 indicated that at least two other prominent Conservatives were more highly regarded than Thatcher. Nevertheless, in becoming Conservative leader, she became automatically her party's candidate for prime minister.

James Callaghan, a minor trade union official, was elected to Parliament at his first attempt in 1945. He was then thirty-three, having served in the navy during the war. In the postwar Labour government, he served in two junior offices, first as parliamentary secretary to the Ministry of Transport, later as parliamentary and financial secretary of the Admiralty (a less important office than it sounds). Labour was defeated in 1951 and spent the next thirteen years in opposition. During this time, Callaghan became a member of the shadow cabinet and gradually a more and more prominent figure in his party; he served both as shadow colonial secretary and as shadow chancellor. When Labour finally returned to power in 1964, he became chancellor of the exchequer, remaining at the Treasury for three years before becoming home secretary in a sideways move in 1967. He was again a member of the shadow cabinet between 1970 and 1974, speaking mainly on foreign affairs; and when Labour was again elected in February 1974, Callaghan became foreign secretary and chief British negotiator with the European Community.

By 1976 Callaghan had probably abandoned his previous ambition of becoming his party's leader and prime minister; but in March 1976 the incumbent prime minister, Harold Wilson, suddenly resigned. Under Labour's rules, a new leader of the party had to be elected immediately. Callaghan stood, together with five other candidates. As in the case of the Conservative party, all of the candidates were MPs; so were all of the electors. Wilson resigned on March 16. The first ballot was held on March 22, the second on March 29, the third on April 5. Callaghan was runner-up on the first ballot but established a commanding lead on the second and finally won on the third. Unlike Thatcher, Callaghan was the most popular of the various contenders so far as the mass electorate was concerned. On becoming Labour leader, since his party was in power at the time, he immediately took over as prime minister.

Eight points need to be made about the British leader-selection process, if it is to be compared with the American. Several of them have been hinted at already.

1. *The winners had entered politics at an early age and had served for a considerable number of years in Parliament before becoming their party's leader.* Not only had Thatcher been an MP for sixteen years and Callaghan for thirty-one, but also most of their rivals had been around for just as long, in some cases even longer. William Whitelaw, Thatcher's main rival, was first elected to Parliament in 1955; Michael Foot, who finished second to Callaghan, was first elected to the House at the same time as Callaghan, in 1945.

2. *The winners had served in a number of different national-level offices.* Thatcher was somewhat unusual in having been a minister in only two departments (Pensions and National Insurance, and Education), but she had spoken for her party on a wide variety of other subjects. Callaghan was also unusual but in the opposite direction: he is the only prime minister in British history to have previously held all of the other principal offices of state: chancellor of the exchequer, home secretary, and foreign secretary. Most of the other contenders in 1975 and 1976 were at least as experienced as Thatcher, several of them more so.

3. *The candidates were assessed and voted upon exclusively by their fellow politicians.* All of the voters in the two leadership elections had had an opportunity to observe the various contenders at first hand—on the floor of the House of Commons, in committee, in party meetings, in some cases around the cabinet table. Most of them were on first-name terms with the people they were voting for; they were in an excellent position to know their strengths and weaknesses. More than that, they had a powerful incentive to arrive at the right decision since they personally would have to live with the consequences. They would have to work in the House of Commons with the new leader; if they made the wrong decision, they would suffer electorally and possibly also in career terms.[8]

4. *The leadership campaigns were very short.* In one sense, campaigns for the leadership of Britain's major parties are never-ending, since ambitious politicians, from the moment they first set foot in the House of Commons, are trying to establish their reputations, to have themselves noticed by their parliamentary colleagues; but the time taken for an actual leadership election is highly telescoped. Thatcher declared her candidacy in October 1974; the result was known by mid-February 1975, only twelve weeks later. The Labour contest lasted less than three weeks.

5. *The leadership campaigns involved very little wear and tear on the part of the candidates and their families.* Indeed the very term "campaign," as has already been suggested, is something of a misnomer. Public rallies and national tours have played no part in the election of British party leaders; even television appearances have mattered only insofar as they have influenced the occasional wavering MP. The arena in which the election has historically been fought has been almost entirely the House of Commons. In the weeks between October 1974 and February 1975, Thatcher probably accepted rather more speaking engagements in the country than she would have done otherwise; she undoubtedly appeared more often on television—though always being interviewed or addressing public meetings, never speaking straight-to-camera or trying to sell herself in "Thatcher commercials" (of which there were, and could be, none).[9] The only significant difference that the election probably made to Thatcher's life—apart from the emotional strains inherent in the occasion—was a much increased media interest in her comings and goings. Photographers congregated outside her house; she and other members of her family were pestered for interviews. The interest of the

press and television was increased by the fact that she was the first woman to be a serious contender for the leadership of either major party. Nevertheless, her life was not radically disrupted by the contest, except possibly during the last few days, and the House of Commons remained her main base of operations. In the case of Labour, the leadership contest made even less difference to the contenders. With Labour in power, all six candidates were already senior cabinet ministers. They all had big jobs to do; they were already in the public eye; they actually had to meet together several times a week to discuss government business. To be sure, they were photographed rather more often than usual; they were the subject of minibiographies on television; their wives were endlessly rung up by women's magazines. But that was about it.

6. *The leadership campaigns cost next to nothing*—largely for the reasons just given. Thatcher and her supporters undoubtedly had to do a certain amount of entertaining of their fellow MPs, and they must have run up considerable telephone and taxi bills. In the Labour party, entertaining has less part to play, but the telephone and taxi bills were probably about the same. At a guess, the Conservative leadership contest cost of all those involved a total of about £2,500—say, $6,000. It is doubtful whether the total cost of the Labour contest, to both the party and all of the participants, was more than £1,000—call it $2,500. Certainly there was no need to raise funds, and there were therefore neither fund raisers nor campaign contributors.

7. *The process of electing the leader in each case was entirely a party process.* The rules governing the internal affairs of political parties in Britain are, in effect, like the rules of a private club. Legislatures and courts neither determine what they should contain nor (except in very rare cases) decide how they should be applied. Thatcher was chosen by members of the Conservative party, Callaghan by members of the Labour party. The mass public played no part in the two contests; neither, except very marginally and indirectly, did television and the press. The parties made the decisions; outsiders merely watched.

8. *Electoral considerations did not loom large in the minds of most MPs as they decided how to cast their ballots.* Somewhat surprisingly, since the personality of the party leader is likely to have at least some bearing on how well the party does at the next general election, the evidence suggests that most MPs, in deciding whom to vote for, are not overly influenced by electoral considerations—or at least by opinion-poll findings. Thatcher was not the most popular Conservative in the country in 1975, but she won. Callaghan was the most popular Labour figure in the eyes of the electorate a year later, but it took him three ballots to defeat the much less popular Michael Foot. MPs appear to be chiefly influenced by considerations of policy and ideology and, probably to a lesser extent, by which of the contenders they think will make the better prime minister. This is a subtle, little-researched point, and there is no need to go into greater detail here.[10]

So much for how the people who led Britain's two major political parties in the summer of 1980 were originally selected. Now contrast the processes just described with the processes that resulted in Jimmy Carter's and Ronald Reagan's becoming the presidential nominees of the Democratic and Republican parties in the United States. To do so is to enter a different world.[11]

Carter, a small-town businessman and former naval officer, first ran for the governorship of Georgia in 1966. He was then forty-two and had already served two terms in the Georgia state senate. His first attempt at the governorship failed, but he then spent the whole of the next four years campaigning around the state, and in 1970 his efforts were rewarded; he won a runoff election by a handsome margin, defeating a previously popular incumbent. Although he lacked any experience of national politics and government, Carter's eyes were already on the presidency; and in 1972, halfway through the one term that Georgia's state constitution allowed him as governor, he and his advisers decided that he should make a bid for the Democratic presidential nomination in 1976. George McGovern had proved an appallingly bad candidate in 1972, and the race for the 1976 nomination looked as though it were going to be wide open. In order to make himself better known nationally, Carter volunteered to serve as the Democrats' campaign coordinator for the 1974 mid-term congressional elections. He announced his presidential candidacy in December of that year.

For the next eighteen months, the ex-governor of Georgia campaigned full time for his party's nomination. He began by dispatching 500,000 letters to potential campaign contributors. In the course of 1975, he traveled from coast to coast, spending time in forty-six states and the District of Columbia. To win the nomination, he needed, in some states, the support of state and local party leaders; but his main appeal had to be to the millions of ordinary citizens eligible to vote in the twenty-nine primary elections due to be held in 1976. The primaries would choose or bind nearly 75 percent of the 3,008 delegates to the Democratic National Convention in July. In the end, Carter's name appeared on the ballot in twenty-six states, and he campaigned actively in most of them. Altogether some 15.6 million people turned out to vote in the Democratic primaries; 6.3 million of them voted for Carter. He won the first primary in New Hampshire in February and had the nomination effectively sewn up by the beginning of June. His victory in the primaries and the state caucuses was ratified on the first ballot at the party's nominating convention in New York City. Democratic senators, congressmen, and governors played little part in the selection process—beyond, in most cases, casting their own primary ballots. In 1980, although he was president, Carter was forced to campaign again for the Democratic nomination.

Ronald Reagan, a retired film actor and professional after-dinner speaker, fought his first election in 1966 when he was already fifty-five years old. He was elected governor of California at this first attempt and was reelected to a second four-year term in 1970. He had had a certain amount of previous political experience, raising money and speaking for Barry Goldwater during the latter's ill-fated presidential campaign in 1964. Although, like Jimmy Carter, Ronald Reagan lacked firsthand experience of national government, Reagan's thoughts, like Carter's, soon turned toward the White House. He sought the Republican presidential nomination in 1968, though in that year he did little campaigning on his own behalf. Matters were quite different when it came to the 1976 nomination. By this time Reagan, no longer governor of California, was free to devote his whole time to his drive for the presidency—a circumstance that gave him a considerable advantage over the incumbent president, Gerald Ford. Reagan announced his candidacy in the summer of 1975 and, with the aid of crossover votes from conservative Democrats and independents, fared well in the Republican primaries in the following year, winning 50.7 percent of the vote to Ford's 49.3 percent. Ford, however, had a slight edge among delegates to the Kansas City convention and was able to win the nomination on the first ballot.

By the summer of 1976, Ronald Reagan had been working toward the presidency for nearly eight years—only part time between 1968 and 1975 but virtually full time in the months since then. For the next four years, throughout the lifetime of Jimmy Carter's presidency, he went on working. He visited nearly every state in the union, taping radio commentaries, giving thousands of speeches, shaking thousands of hands, traversing hundreds of thousands of miles. When in November 1979 he formally announced that he intended to run, he already had the support of most Republican leaders in states where such support counted; but his main objective, like Carter's four years before, was the amassing of votes in primary elections. As it turned out, Reagan's path was even smoother than Carter's in 1976 (and far smoother than Carter's in 1980). He drubbed his chief rival, George Bush, in New Hampshire in February and by the time of the Michigan primary in May had won enough delegates to secure the nomination. Of the 12.8 million votes cast in the Republican primaries, Reagan won 7.6 million (60 percent). In the Republican party, as in the Democratic, public officeholders played no formal role—and very little actual role—in the contest. When Reagan was finally acclaimed at his party's convention in Detroit in July 1980, he was sixty-nine years old. He had been campaigning for the presidency for the better part of a dozen years.

These events in the United States can easily be compared, point by point, with the events surrounding the selection of Margaret Thatcher and James Callaghan as party leaders on the other side of the Atlantic.

1. *The two winners in the United States had entered politics in middle age, and neither had very much experience of government.* Carter first ran for statewide office at the age of forty-two, Reagan at the age of fifty-five. By contrast, Thatcher first stood for Parliament when she was only twenty-four, Callaghan when he was thirty-three. At the time he won the Democratic nomination, Carter had spent four years in the Georgia state legislature and another four years as the state's governor; Reagan had spent eight years as California's governor in Sacramento. These two stints of eight years compare with Margaret Thatcher's sixteen years in the British House of Commons and James Callaghan's thirty-one.

2. *Neither winner in the United States had ever served in any capacity in the national government, whether in Washington or overseas. Moreover, at the time of their nomination neither held any public office whatsoever.* Indeed it is scarcely too strong to say that America's presidential nominees were drawn from the ranks of the unemployed. This was not true of all of the contenders for the two major parties' nominations in 1976 and 1980. Apart from the incumbent presidents in both years, in 1976 Democrats Henry Jackson (Washington) and Frank Church (Idaho) were both long-serving U.S. senators, and Democrat Morris Udall (Arizona) was a prominent member of the House of Representatives. Carter's chief rival in 1980, Edward Kennedy (Massachusetts), was also a U.S. senator. Among the Republicans in 1980, Howard Baker (Tennessee) was the Senate minority leader, and John Connally had served in the federal executive branch as secretary of the navy under John Kennedy and secretary of the treasury under Richard Nixon. George Bush had had the most varied experience, having served two terms in the House of Representatives and subsequently as ambassador to the United Nations, chief of the U.S. liaison office in Peking, and director of the Central Intelligence Agency. Bush, however, lost—and so did all of the others. Thatcher was relatively inex-

perienced by British standards when she became Conservative leader; but she had been a member of the Macmillan, Home, and Heath administrations for six and a half years and a member of the Heath cabinet for three and a half. Callaghan, as mentioned earlier, had held all three of the top posts in the British system. Moreover, at the time of their selection as party leaders both Thatcher and Callaghan were members of Parliament. Callaghan was also foreign secretary.[12]

3. *The candidates in the United States were assessed and voted upon by party activists in some states but mainly by voters in primary elections.* No special weight was attached to the views of public officeholders or to the views of those who had worked with the candidates or had had a chance to observe them at first hand. Senators, congressmen, governors, and others were in a position to endorse whichever candidates they preferred, and the candidates' own extensive travels enabled thousands of voters at least to catch a glimpse of them; but most activists and primary electors probably paid little attention to the endorsements, and of course the great majority had never been in the physical presence of any of the candidates, let alone done business with them. Instead they were forced to form impressions from what they could read in the printed media or see on television. The candidates' performances were all there was, and except for the incumbent presidents, Ford in 1976 and Carter in 1980, the performances that mattered were not in high office but on the small screen. Hence the large role played by the mass media in the selection of American presidential candidates; hence also the uneasiness of many people in the American media about the role that they play.[13] The contrast with the British system in this connection is complete. Thatcher and Callaghan were chosen by their fellow MPs—that is, by political insiders—and by no one else.

4. *The campaigns of would-be presidential nominees in the United States last for a very long time.* There is hardly any need to labor this point. Thatcher's campaign for the leadership of the Conservative party took twelve weeks; Reagan's campaign for the leadership of the Republican party took the best part of twelve years. The Labour party in March/April 1976 took three weeks to elect its new leader; Carter was on the campaign trail more or less continuously from the summer of 1974 until the summer of 1976. In the United States, staying power is at a premium.

5. *Campaigns for presidential nominations in the United States involve an enormous amount of wear and tear on the part of the candidates and their families.* "Wear and tear" is not easy to measure, and that which exhausts one person can be counted on to exhilarate another. Nevertheless, anyone reading accounts of would-be presidential nominees stumping the country must be impressed by the heavy toll that the whole process exacts: loss of sleep, loss of privacy, disrupted schedules, news conferences at which no one shows up, the endless room-service meals, the long, dreary hours in airport lounges. The same words keep cropping up: "grueling," "exhausting," "tiredness," "fatigue." Vignettes stick in the mind: Edmund Muskie weeping in the snows of New Hampshire, Jimmy Carter sprawled full-length on a sofa at LaGuardia Airport waiting for a long-delayed plane and seizing "an opportunity to at least make up for nights of lost sleep."[14] The essential point is that someone who wishes to compete for a major-party presidential nomination in the United States has to cast his life in an entirely new mold. Campaigning in primaries and caucuses is not something that one does part time, in the midst of other activities. It becomes, in itself, a way of life—"a severe test," in the words of Morris Udall, "of your stamina, your digestion, your marriage and your sense of

humor."[15] Among recent candidates, only Ronald Reagan seems to have been able to avoid some of the strain. Even when he first ran for the governorship of California at the age of fifty-five, he often managed a nap in the afternoon.[16] Again, the contrast between the all-consuming nature of American presidential nominating politics and the more low-key, contained way in which Thatcher and Callaghan were elected in Britain is striking.

6. *The campaigns in the United States cost enormous sums of money, and the candidates and their staffs have to devote a great deal of time and effort to raising money.* Jimmy Carter launched his campaign for the Democratic nomination by writing to potential campaign contributors, and raising money is one of the key tasks of American campaign organizations, even at the prenomination stage. Television and radio time have to be paid for; so do newspaper advertisements, direct mailings, travel facilities, staffers, consultants, opinion polls, and telephone calls. While the Federal Election Campaign Act has relieved some of the pressure on fund raisers by providing for federal underwriting of both primary and general election contests, at the same time the new legislation forces candidates to raise much larger numbers of small contributions. Quite apart from changes in the law, the costs of campaigning in the United States are high—much higher than in most other countries—and continue to rise. In 1976, the Democratic and Republican preconvention campaigns cost the participants and the federal government roughly $67 million; in 1980, the total was nearer $100 million.[17] If the rough estimates given above of the costs of Britain's two party-leadership elections in 1975 and 1976 are accepted as broadly accurate, then the costs of selecting American presidential candidates are some eight to ten thousand times greater than the costs of selecting party leaders in Britain.

7. *The process of selecting presidential candidates in the United States is by no means an exclusively party process.* On the contrary, as has often been pointed out, American political parties in the 1980s are not stable organizations, like parties in most other countries; they are rather prizes to be competed for. Most recent presidential aspirants have had long associations with the Democrat or the Republican party; but they need not have had. More to the point, those deciding who will be the party's standard-bearer in a presidential election include people who regard themselves as party regulars; but they also include, in far greater numbers, people with no continuing commitment to the party, people with no commitment to any party, and even people strongly committed to the opposition party. Such are the consequences of opening the candidate selection process to ordinary voters in primary elections. Yet again, the contrast with Britain is marked—indeed total.

8. *Electoral considerations may have loomed large in the minds of many of the party regulars who attended caucuses in 1976 and 1980, but they probably figured scarcely at all in the minds of most voters in the primaries.* American presidential nominating contests used to be concerned, in large part, with "picking a winner." The delegates to the quadrennial conventions wanted a man to head the ticket who would pull in the party's other candidates on his coattails. Those days are gone. Not only are presidential candidates' coattails badly frayed in an age of split-ticket voting, but those who select candidates for the presidency—chiefly voters in primaries—are hardly concerned with complicated tactical considerations. They seldom ask, Which of these candidates do I think other people would be most likely to vote for if he were the candidate of my party? Rather, they ask simply, Who would I like to be president? Even more important is the fact that those who

vote in primary elections are in no sense a microcosm of the electorate as a whole. Not only are they vastly fewer in number (32.3 million people voted in the primaries in 1980, 86.5 million in the November election), but all of the available studies indicate that they are a highly biased sample of the total population; they are more highly educated, more interested in politics, and considerably more likely than the electorate as a whole to hold extreme views.[18] In addition to all this, the system, as it now functions, makes it possible fo a contender to "win" the primaries and to go on to become his party's presidential candidate even though he has won substantially less than half of the votes cast in the primaries; for example, in 1976 Carter "won" the Democratic primaries with only 39.9 percent of the total vote.[19] In other words, under the present system a party's candidate can be the choice of a minority—and a biased minority at that. The bizarre outcome in 1980 was that the most open, most "democratic" leadership-selection system ever devised resulted in the nomination of the two least-respected and least-admired presidential candidates in modern American history. There should, however, have been no surprise about this, given the nature of the primary electorate. Even if there were a national primary, or a system in which would-be candidates had to secure 50 percent plus one of the primary vote in order to be nominated, it would still be perfectly possible for the minority of primary voters to plump for candidates whom the majority of the whole electorate did not want. More surprising, perhaps, is the fact that in Britain members of Parliament, who might be thought to have a personal stake in picking a winner, nevertheless frequently, like voters in primaries in the United States, choose a leader who is not the person that the voters at large prefer.[20]

Despite this last, rather unexpected similarity between the British and American systems for choosing party leaders and presidential candidates, the two systems are otherwise different in almost every particular: in who the potential candidates are, in who does the choosing, in how the choices are made. The contrast, in fact, is virtually complete.

Assessing the American System

The facts having been established, we now need to offer some assessment of them. Needless to say, it is not the purpose of this chapter to argue that "British is best." The British case was chosen, as we said earlier, partly because it is well documented, partly because it offers such a striking contrast to the American, but chiefly because the leadership selection systems in most liberal democracies resemble the British more closely than the American; the American system could equally well have been compared with, say, the Australian or the Swedish. In any case, the British system is neither perfect nor immutable. The Conservatives adopted their present arrangements as recently as 1965; the Labour party in 1980–1981 was taking active steps to adopt an entirely new system, one that would give a large say in the election of Labour leaders—and hence of potential Labour prime ministers—to the massed battalions of Britain's trade unions and to the party's activists in the constituencies.[21]

The contrast between the British system and the American does, however, serve to point up certain weaknesses inherent in the present American system, weaknesses of which many people in the United States are well aware.

To begin with, the length of the American nominating process and its grueling character undoubtedly have the effect of causing many able men and women to eliminate themselves from the race before it has even begun. Candidates in any system are, of course, compared with other candidates, but they should also be compared with non-candidates—people who might have run but chose not to. We ought to ask: Are there able and qualified persons who might make good presidents but are deterred from seeking their party's presidential nomination by the present arrangements? Suppose for the sake of argument that the pool of potential presidential candidates is taken to consist of serving U.S. senators and congressmen and state governors. Are there people in this pool who, contemplating the race as it now is, a combination of high hurdles and marathon, say to themselves, "I want no part of it?" It would be amazing if such people did not exist; rumor suggests that they do.[22] The most famous case of someone who did enter the race but abandoned it after completing the first lap is Walter Mondale, later vice-president under Carter. Mondale stumped the country between 1972 and 1974 with his eye on the 1976 Democratic nomination, but he did not like what incessant campaigning was doing to himself and his family, and he quit in November 1974, more than a year before the first primary. He announced in a public statement:

> I found I did not have the overwhelming desire to be President which is essential for the kind of campaign that is required . . . I don't think anyone should be President who is not willing to go through the fire . . . I admire those with the determination to do what is required to seek the presidency, but I have found I am not among them.[23]

How many other able men and women have, to the nation's cost, made the same discovery?

Mondale made his abortive bid for the presidency while a senator and a leading member of his party in the upper house. He knew perfectly well that, in his bid, he was handicapped as a candidate by being a senator and handicapped as a senator by being a candidate. So time- and energy-consuming has the pursuit of the presidency become that those who currently hold high public office are at a distinct disadvantage compared with those who do not. Not only can those who have left office behind them, or indeed never held it, devote more time and energy to campaigning, but they do not constantly have to choose between fulfilling their primary officeholding responsibilities and following the dictates of their personal ambition. "That was very clearly illustrated by Senator Jackson who in 1976 was continually torn between the needs of a presidential campaign and the needs of being in the Senate, especially for discussion of those issues on which he had the greatest expertise."[24] Howard Baker was probably putting it a little strongly in 1980 when he suggested that the current American system "requires you to be unemployed to be a successful candidate"; but the fact remains that, vice-presidents and incumbent presidents apart, three of the last four presidential nominees—Nixon, Carter, and Reagan—held no public office, major or minor, at the time of their nomination.[25] If those who hold no public office are indeed at an advantage over their officeholding rivals, it follows that future presidents of the United States, like the last two on the day of their inauguration, are likely to be individuals without, as Howard Baker put it, "current information about the problems that confront the country."[26]

Presidential candidates under the American system may well not be immersed currently in national and international problems; it is also true that they may never have been so immersed. Carter in 1976 had never been nearer Washington (let alone London, Paris, Bonn, Moscow, or Peking) than Atlanta; Reagan in 1980 had never been nearer than Sacramento.[27] In the British and most other leadership-selection systems, the formal rules, or alternatively the informal norms, require that would-be national leaders should have had substantial national-level political experience, typically in both the executive and the legislative branches of government. Even if the rules and norms in these countries did not so require, it is still likely that, in any system in which those who choose national party leaders include a significant proportion of people who are themselves national-level politicians, the results will tend to favor people from similar backgrounds; whatever the rules, national politicians will tend to choose other national politicians. In the United States, by contrast, neither the rules and norms nor the men and women who select presidential candidates—whether voters in primaries or delegates to state caucuses and conventions—appear to attach any great significance to high-level experience of government in Washington. On the contrary, both Carter and Reagan were able to make a virtue out of being their party's non-Washington, even anti-Washington, presidential candidate. They arrived in Washington the first two presidents since Woodrow Wilson wholly innocent of national-level governmental experience.[28] Most observers thought that the results were all too apparent in Carter's four-year term of office; it remains to be seen whether Reagan will learn more and faster.

More generally, a disjunction seems to have developed in the United States between the qualities required to win the presidential nomination of one's party and the qualities required to be a good president. To win the nomination, a person needs to be able to attract media attention, to be able to communicate easily with ordinary citizens, above all to be able to project an attractive image of himself on the small screen. He needs, in other words, to be someone who can convey a lot in a few words to a very large number of people. Some of these skills are required by an incumbent president, but some of them are not (presidents of the United States have no need to attract media attention: they have far too much already). More to the point, to win a presidential nomination in the age of caucuses and primaries, a person no longer has to do business with others, to build coalitions, or to bargain with people who possess things that he should acquire if he is to achieve his goals. It is enough that he be a supersalesman of himself. Before 1968 in the United States, a man who wanted to be president had to build a coalition out of the very same elements—members of Congress, big-state governors, big-city mayors, the leaders of major interest groups—upon which he would have to rely if and when he reached the White House. Not so in the 1980s:

In the present nominating system, he comes as a fellow whose only coalition is whatever he got out of the living rooms in Iowa. If there is one thing that Jimmy Carter's frustration in office ought to teach us, it is that the affiliation and the commitment that is made on Iowa caucus night and New Hampshire primary day is not by itself sufficient to sustain a man for four years in the White House.[29]

Such problems are, of course, short-circuited in a leadership-selection system like the British: The people with whom a party leader will have to work are the very people who elected him.

Underlying both the lack of experience exhibited by recent presidential candidates, and also doubts about whether they have the requisite political skills, is the fact, all but unique to the modern American political system, that the elected officeholders of a party play almost no part in selecting the party's presidential nominee. This fact has been mentioned before, but it needs to be emphasized again. In almost every political system but the American, the man or woman who wants to make it to the top needs to acquire the support of people who have been in the best position, usually over a considerable period of many years, to observe him or her at close range: namely, the individual's fellow national politicians. Such politicians are better placed than anyone else could possibly be to assess their colleague's strengths and weaknesses, many of which are likely to manifest themselves, not in front of the television cameras, but in the cut and thrust of legislative debate or behind the closed doors of committee rooms. In most political systems, these national-level politicians act as a sort of screening device or filter between the political parties and the mass electorate; they provide, in the American jargon, an element of "peer review." This element is entirely missing in the United States today.[30]

The primary-centered method of choosing presidential candidates is also part cause and part consequence of the general decline of American's political parties. Parties in the United States, as has often been pointed out, no longer provide cues to the electorate on the scale that they once did; they no longer even control their own nominations. The results are hard to disentangle from other important changes taking place within the American polity; but it seems reasonable to associate the decline of parties with the further blurring of lines of responsibility and accountability in the American system, the increasing alienation and frustration of the American electorate, the continuing assertiveness of interest groups, especially single-interest groups, the personalization of American politics, the seeming inability of Congress and the presidency to work together, and, more generally, a tendency in American government, reminiscent of the French Fourth Republic, toward immobilism and stalemate. If America's parties were to disappear completely—

> the candidate organizations, the women's caucuses, the black caucuses, the right-to-life leagues, and the like would become the only real players in the game. The mass communications media would become the sole agencies for sorting out the finalists from the original entrants [in presidential nominating politics] and for defining the voters' choices. And the societal functions of interest-aggregation, consensus-building and civil war-prevention would presumably be left to the schools, the churches, and perhaps Common Cause and Nader's Raiders.[31]

If such an outcome is to be avoided, changes will almost certainly need to be made in the way in which presidential candidates are selected. A larger strictly "party" element in the selection of presidential nominees will have to be reintroduced, if not on the British model, then on some other.[32]

Another consequence of the primary-centered method of choosing presidential candidates is to increase greatly the political vulnerability of first-term presidential incumbents. Once upon a time, a president of the United States, however disastrous, could count on being renominated by his party (always assuming that he wanted to be). To so great an extent did incumbency matter. It now matters a great deal less, and in an era of intractable international and economic problems may even be a handicap. Ford in 1976 and Carter in 1980 only just managed to fight off the challenges of rival candidates within their own parties; Reagan will be very lucky not to face a similar challenge in 1984. Opinions differ about the desirability of first-term presidents' being vulnerable in this way. On the one hand, it can be argued that the fear of formidable challenges in the primaries makes American presidents more sensitive to the wishes of the American people than they used to be; on the other, it can be alleged that, precisely because they are fearful of such challenges, they may conduct themselves from the moment of their inauguration with one eye on the electorate. Whatever the merits of this particular debate, it is clear that for the foreseeable future first-term presidents will spend enormous amounts of time and energy in their third and fourth years in office trying to make sure that they are renominated as well as reelected. Whether presidents can afford to spend quite such large quantities of time and energy in this way is open to question.

Finally, it is worth commenting on one rather strange consequence of the virtually total elimination of the element of peer review from American presidential politics. Peer groups, to be sure, have a way of becoming completely obsessed with their own internal dynamics, of becoming oblivious of the needs and desires of the outside world; but at the same time such groups often have the ability to make very accurate judgments about their own members—to overlook their superficial characteristics and to evaluate them at their true worth. In Britain in recent years, the Conservatives have been adventurous enough to choose a woman as their leader; similarly, the Labour party, in electing Michael Foot as James Callaghan's successor toward the end of 1980, showed itself prepared to elect a somewhat improbable-looking old man with untidy hair, thick spectacles, and a walk like Charlie Chaplin's. It is clear that in both cases their chances of selection were considerably greater among their fellow MPs, their peers, than if the choice had been made by millions of ordinary voters with no more to go on than what they could see on their television screens. One does not have to be an especial admirer of either Thatcher or Foot to acknowledge the possibility that a small-group, face-to-face system, containing a large element of peer review, may considerably widen the range of potential national leaders. "Presidents today," as Jeane Kirkpatrick has written concerning the post-1968 presidential nominating process," must be fit and not fat, amusing not dull, with cool not hot personalities."[33] She might have added that they must also be white and male. It is, however, not proven that great American presidents are to be found only in the ranks of the thin, the amusing, the cool, the white, the male, the glib, the invariably smiling, and the televisually presentable—even though the present arrangments for choosing American presidential nominees clearly assume that they are. By a strange but not uncommon irony, a system designed to maximize "openness" has probably had the unintended effect of barring the way to the top in American politics of a very large proportion of America's population.[34]

No system of selecting political leaders, as we said right at the beginning, can guarantee success; none is foolproof. Other countries, including Britain, have produced their duds; the old ways of nominating presidential candidates in the

United States yielded such second-raters, all within the same decade, as Warren G. Harding, James M. Cox, Calvin Coolidge, and John W. Davis. It may be that in 1984 the American people will be offered a more impressive choice than they were in 1980. It may be, too, that Ronald Reagan will turn out to be a better president than many people expect; it certainly behooves the rest of the world to suspend judgment. All the same, it must be said that America's friends abroad view with considerable apprehension the prospect of a long line of Carters and Reagans as presidential candidates. It does seem that recent developments in the American presidential nominating system have greatly increased the probability that men will be nominated who lack relevant experience and have no evident aptitude for one of the most demanding and powerful jobs on earth. Changes in the system that had the effect of reducing the role of primary elections and of providing for an increased element of peer review would be enormously welcomed by most of America's friends and allies in Europe and—dare one say it?—probably in the end by most Americans too.

Notes

1. For typical articles in *Le Monde* and the *Neue Zürcher Zeitung*, see "Un lourd processus," *Le Monde*, November 5, 1980, and "Jimmy Carter trotz allem," *Neue Zürcher Zeitung*, August 18, 1980. The three quotations from British newspapers are from, respectively, "A Hard Choice for the U.S.," *Financial Times*, July 31, 1980; "A Great and Noble Campaign," *The Times* (London), September 3, 1980; and "Presidential Antics," *Daily Telegraph*, September 12, 1980.
2. These are not real quotations but a sort of montage of the views of European politicians, journalists, and businessmen. It is doubtful whether any large number of informed Europeans would have dissented from them.
3. The New York bumper sticker was seen by the present writer. The *Cincinnati Enquirer* cartoon was reprinted in *Public Opinion*, June/July 1980, p. 25. The man with the lapel buttons appeared on the cover of the same issue of *Public Opinion*.
4. The survey was reported in *Newsweek*, November 10, 1980, p. 39. The other quotations are taken from "It's Still 'None of the Above,' " *New York Times*, reprinted in *International Herald Tribune*, August 1, 1980; "Using Presidential Power," *Washington Post*, October 20, 1980; and "Battling Down the Stretch," *Time*, November 3, 1980, p. 18.
5. The lowest previous turnout since 1932 was 51.5 percent in 1948. From 1920 to 1932 turnouts in presidential elections ranged from 44.2 percent (1920) to 52.9 (1932). In 1936 turnout rose to 57.5 percent and, except for 1948, has stayed above 54.0 percent until the 1980 election. For a brief discussion, see Richard A. Watson, *The Presidential Contest* (New York: John Wiley, 1980), chap. 4.
6. Unfortunately, no general comparative study of this subject exists; but see L. P. Crisp, *Australian National Government* (Melbourne: Longmans, 1974); Stephen Levin, *Politics in New Zealand* (Sydney: George Allen and Unwin, 1978); Robert E. Ward, *Japan's Political System*, 2d ed. (Englewood Cliffs, N.J.: Prentice-Hall, 1978); and Anthony King, "Executives," in Fred I. Greenstein and Nelson W. Polsby, eds., *Governmental Institutions and Processes*, vol. 5, *Handbook of Political Science* (Reading, Mass.: Addison-Wesley, 1975), pp. 183–94.
7 The ensuing account of how Thatcher and Callaghan were selected is largely drawn from Anthony King, "Politics, Economics, and the Trade Unions, 1974–1979," in Howard R. Penniman, ed., *Britain at the Polls, 1979: A Study of the General Election* (Washington, D.C.: American Enterprise Institute, 1981), and also from the sources listed there.
8. It should perhaps be explained for the benefit of American readers that voting in Britain since well before World War II has largely been party voting. That is, voters have been far more concerned with which party nationally would make the better government than with the personalities and voting records of their individual local candidates. It follows that members of

Parliament deciding how to vote in 1975 and 1976 had to consider what effect any given leadership candidate would have on the party's chances nationally and therefore on their own chances locally. Furthermore, whether the party won nationally would determine whether or not they had any chance of becoming government ministers. In short, their personal stakes were high—far higher than, say, the stakes of voters in primary elections in the United States.

9. There could be none because in Britain candidates for office are not permitted to buy time on television or radio to advertise themselves. At general elections, political parties are allotted a certain amount of free time; but this was not a general election. Even if the candidates had been able to buy time, it is doubtful whether they would have done so: a television spot seen by millions of people is not the most efficient way to reach some 250–300 people, whom one is anyway in a position to see almost every day.

10. British MPs, wisely or unwisely, behave as though they believe either that ideological and policy considerations are more important than electoral ones or that whomever they elect can be counted on, as the result of increased television exposure and such like, to become an acceptable national figure. Alternatively, they may be misinformed about opinion-poll findings or may simply not believe them. The point is discussed briefly at various points in King, "Politics, Economics, and the Trade Unions."

11. The ensuing account of the nominations of Carter and Reagan is based largely on Martin Schram, *Running for President: A Journal of the Carter Campaign* (New York: Pocket Books, 1977); James Wooten, *Dasher: The Roots and Rising of Jimmy Carter* (New York: Warner Books, 1979); Jules Witcover, *Marathon: The Pursuit of the Presidency, 1972–1976* (New York: Viking, 1977); Hedrick Smith et al., *Reagan: The Man, the President* New York: Macmillan, 1980); and Richard Harwood, ed., *The Pursuit of the Presidency 1980* (New York: Berkley Books, 1980).

12. Much of the best, indeed almost the only, comparative study of the selection of British prime ministers and American presidents is Hugh Heclo, "Presidential and Prime Ministerial Selection," in Donald R. Matthews, ed., *Perspectives on Presidential Selection* (Washington, D.C.: The Brookings Institution, 1973). Heclo, writing in 1973, emphasized the experience of American presidents and presidential candidates; in 1981 the picture looks somewhat different.

13. See, for example, David Broder's remarks about the "unhealthy and unnatural significance [of] the role of the mass media," in *Choosing Presidential Candidates: How Good Is the New Way?* (Washington, D.C.: American Enterprise Institute, 1979), p. 11, and also a large number of the comments in John Foley, Dennis A. Britton, and Eugene B. Everett, Jr., eds., *Nominating a President: The Process and the Press* (New York: Praeger, 1980).

14. Schram, *Running for President*, p. 118.

15. Quoted by Saul Pett, "Ex-Candidates, on Presidential Race: Mad, Mad Marathon," *New York Times*, August 30, 1980. The Pett article is full of good stories about the awfulness of campaigning for the presidency.

16. Adam Clymer, "A Star Is Born," in Smith et al., *Reagan*, p. 11.

17. For the 1976 figures, see Stephen J. Wayne, *The Road to the White House: The Politics of Presidential Elections* (New York: St. Martin's Press, 1980), p. 28. The 1980 figures are taken from Herbert E. Alexander, "Financing the Campaigns and Parties of 1980" (Paper delivered at Sangamon State University, Springfield, Illinois, December 3, 1980).

18. Voters in primary elections are still just about the most understudied major participants in American political life; but see Austin Ranney and Leon D. Epstein, "The Two Electorates: Voters and Non-Voters in a Wisconsin Primary," *Journal of Politics*, vol.28 (1966), pp. 598–616; Austin Ranney, "The Representativeness of Primary Electorates," *Midwest Journal of Political Science*, vol. 12 (1968), pp. 224–38; and Austin Ranney, "Turnout and Representation in Presidential Primary Elections," *Amerian Political Science Review*, vol. 66 (1972), pp. 21–37.

19. Gerald M. Pomper et al., *The Election of 1976: Reports and Interpretations* (New York: Longmans, 1977), pp. 14–15.

20. See section "A European Contrast" and n. 10.

21. At its regular annual conference in Blackpool in October 1980, the Labour party voted to extend the franchise in its leadership elections beyond the parliamentary party. At a special conference in Wembley in January 1981, it decided that trade unions should have 40 percent of the vote in Labour leadership elections, constituency activists 30 percent, and Labour members of Parliament, who had hitherto had 100 percent, only the remaining 30 percent. Hardly had the Wembley decision been taken, however, than there were moves afoot to try, at the next regular conference in Brighton in October 1981, to improve the parliamentary party's position. Whatever the outcome of that conference, it seemed all but certain in the summer of 1981 that

Labour's leadership-election system described earlier in this chapter had gone forever. The conservatives' system, however, was likely to remain the same.

22. The present writer is personally aware of at least one member of the House of Representatives, who, although he might well make an electable presidential candidate and a first-class president, decided long ago that the race was simply not worth running: the costs are too great, the chances of success too slight.

23. Quoted in Arthur T. Hadley, *The Invisible Primary* (Englewood Cliffs, N.J.: Prentice-Hall, 1976), p. 38. Portions of the Hadley volume concerning Mondale are reprinted in James I. Lengle and Byron E. Shafer, eds., *Presidential Politics: Readings on Nominations and Elections* (New York: St. Martin's Press, 1980), pp. 69–77. Michael J. Robinson has similarly observed: "The primary system has made it so that the nice guys, including the competent ones, stay out of the whole ordeal. Right from the start, the primary system means that only those who possess near psychopathic ambition and temperament will get involved and stay involved." These and other similar remarks are quoted in Herbert B. Asher, *Presidential Elections and American Politics: Voters, Candidates, and Campaigns since 1952*, 2d ed. (Homewood, Ill.: Dorsey Press, 1980), p. 307.

24. Jeane J. Kirkpatrick in Jeane J. Kirkpatrick et al., *The Presidential Nominating Process: Can It Be Improved?* (Washington, D.C.: American Enterprise Institute, 1980), pp. 9–10.

25. Baker is quoted in Pett, "Ex-Candidates, on Presidential Race."

26. Ibid.

27. The literal-minded may protest that both men had traveled widely and that Carter had played a prominent part in the so-called Trilateral Commission. But of course that is not the point: to visit Washington, even on business, is not the same as working there. Carter as president showed no real understanding either of politics in Washington or of how the world looked from the vantage point of foreign capitals.

28. See the table in Heclo, "Presidential and Prime Ministerial Selection," pp. 31–32.

29. David Broder in *Choosing Presidential Candidates*, pp. 7–8.

30. On the question of peer review, see David Broder in *Choosing Presidential Candidates*, p. 3; and Austin Ranney in Kirkpatrick et al., *The Presidential Nominating Process*, p. 6.

31. Austin Ranney, "The Political Parties: Reform and Decline" in Anthony King, ed., *The New American Political System* (Washington, D.C.: American Enterprise Institute, 1978, p. 247.

32. For a variety of suggestions on how the presidential nominating process might be reformed—or, rather, improved—see Kirkpatrick et al., *The Presidential Nominating Process*, pp. 15–27; Everett Carll Ladd, "A Better Way to Pick Presidents," *Fortune*, May 5, 1980, pp. 132–37; and Tom Wicker, "The Elections: Why the System Has Failed," *New York Review of Books*, August 14, 1980, pp. 11–15. Almost all the suggestions for improvement involve giving a larger say in the nominating process to a party's public officeholders and more generally to people with a continuing commitment to the party.

33. Jeane Kirkpatrick, *Dismantling the Parties: Reflections on Party Reform and Party Decomposition* (Washington, D.C.: American Enterprise Institute, 1978), p. 7.

34. This argument must not be pressed too far. A peer group may be extraordinarily conventional in its judgments if its members are guided not by what they think but by what they think others think. To take the obvious case, it took a primary election, in West Virginia in 1960, to persuade the leaders of the Democratic party that a Catholic could be elected president. Most European systems differ from the American in that voters are being asked to vote for a party as a whole, not for a single individual. Under these circumstances the personality of the leader is likely to be less important electorally.

1.2

Thomas Cronin and Robert Loevy

The Case for a National Pre-primary Convention Plan

Thomas Cronin is professor of political science at Colorado College. He has written extensively on the presidency and American politics—among his works are Rethinking the Presidency *and* The State of the Presidency. *Robert Loevy, a former congressional fellow, is professor of political science at Colorado College. In this selection Cronin and Loevy propose replacing the present nominating system with a new, three-stage process. They argue that the changes they recommend would shorten the campaign, increase voter interest, reduce media influence, enhance the deliberative nature of the conventions, and tie the candidates more closely to their parties.*

Our presidential nominating process has changed dramatically since the 1960s when John F. Kennedy entered just four contested state primaries. Once shaped mainly by state and national party leaders, it is increasingly shaped by single-interest groups and the media.

The formal nominating process begins with the Iowa caucus in January of an election year and lumbers through more state caucuses and conventions and thirty-six primary elections before candidates are finally selected at national party conventions in July and August.

Nobody, with the possible exception of Ronald Reagan, seems happy with the present nominating system—especially the patchworky maze of presidential primaries. The process strains patience and, critics say, eliminates good candidates. The current primary system plainly favors well-heeled out-of-office individuals who can devote their full attention to selected early state nominating battles. Thus Carter in 1976, and Reagan in 1980, could spend up to a hundred days in Iowa, New Hampshire, and Florida, while officeholders such as Udall, Baker, Anderson, Kennedy, and the sitting presidents had to remain on their jobs.

Our present nominating process has become a televised horse race focusing more on media appeal than on the competing ideas, programs, or character of the candidates. More voters, to be sure, take part in primary elections than in caucuses and conventions. But what about the *quality* of that participation? Primary voters often know little about the many candidates listed on the ballot. Popularity polls, slick spot ads, and television coverage of the early primaries offer episodes and spectacles, and the average citizen is hard pressed to separate significance from entertainment.

From *Public Opinion* (December/January 1983). Reprinted with the permission of the American Enterprise Institute for Public Policy Research

Momentum Fever

"Winners"—sometimes with only 20 percent of the vote—in the early small state nomination contests are given undue media coverage. For example, Jimmy Carter's victories in Iowa and New Hampshire in 1976 led to an outpouring of cover and human interest stories on him.

Voters in New Hampshire and a few other early primaries often virtually get the right to nominate their party's candidate. Candidates who do not do well in these early states get discouraged, and their financial contributors and volunteers desert them. In most presidential years, the nominees of both major parties are decided much too early in the process.

Critics are also concerned, rightly we believe, about the declining importance of the national conventions. Now that nominations are often "sewed up" by early primaries, the national conventions have become *ratifying* rather than *nominating* conventions. Most delegates, bound by various state and party election rules, have little more to do than cast their predetermined required vote, enjoy a round of cocktail parties, pick up local souvenirs, and go home. It is little wonder that the networks are moving away from gavel-to-gavel coverage.

A further complaint is that the current nominating system has diminished the role of party and public officials, and concomitantly increased the role of candidate loyalists and issue activists. Primaries bypass the local party structure by encouraging candidates and their managers to form candidate-loyalist brigades several months before the primaries. Elected officials generally are unwilling to become committed to one candidate or another until well along in the election year and hence they are often excluded from the process. But because most serious candidates for national office hold (or have held) elective office, the views of their peers can be particularly insightful. Because elected officials, especially members of Congress, have some obligation to implement the goals and platform of their party, they should participate in the development of party positions.

Elected officials plead to be brought back into the system; to be given incentives for involvement; to be given responsibility in selecting candidates and writing the platform. Let us integrate the national presidential party and the congressional party as one working unit where all the various components have some status and voice in the processes and outcomes.

Strengthening the party role in the nominating process does not require that elected or party leaders dominate or control nominations. Rather, it would encourage peer review and ensure that a reasonable number of elected officials are allowed to participate. Political scientist Everett Ladd suggests that the person who successfully "passes muster in a peer review process, if elected, comes into office with contacts and alliances that he needs if he is to govern successfully."

United States Senator Alan Cranston (D-Calif.) raises objections to the present system. He claims that few, if any, of the qualities that bring victory in primaries are the qualities the presidency demands.

> Primaries do not tell us how well a candidate will delegate authority. Nor do they demonstrate his ability to choose the best people for top government posts. . . . Primaries don't tell us how effective a candidate will be in dealing with Congress, nor how capable a candidate will be at moving the national power structure, nor how good an educator of the American public a

candidate would really be as president. . . . Primaries do not adequately test courage and wisdom in decision making—yet those are the ultimate tests of a good president.

The Alternative

We are more than a little aware that no procedure is neutral, that any system has various side-effects and unanticipated consequences. Further, we know that no method of nominating presidential candidates guarantees good candidates or good presidents. (The nominating method used in selecting Lincoln also gave us Buchanan. The methods that nominated Eisenhower and Kennedy nominated Richard Nixon as a member of the national ticket on five different occasions.) Plainly, no procedure can substitute for rigorous screening and the exercise of shrewd judgment at every step.

We think there is an intriguing alternative to the present system of nominating presidential candidates. Known as the National Pre-primary Convention Plan, it would reverse the present order of things. It would replace thirty-six individual state primaries with a caucus and convention system in all states, to be followed by a national convention, which in turn would be followed by a national Republican presidential primary and a national Democratic presidential primary to be held on the same day in September.

Although this proposal challenges the prevailing notion that the presidential primary should occur before the convention, there are working precedents at the state level. The proposal is new only when applied at the national level. At the state level, it has been well tested. Colorado, for example, has used this system since 1910 and has found it a good way to retain the strengths of both the party convention and the party primary election.

Delegates Bound and Unbound

A National Pre-primary Convention Plan starts with nationwide party caucuses on the first Monday in May of the presidential year. Any citizen would be eligible to attend a particular party caucus, but, in order to vote there, he would have to register at the caucus as a member of that political party. By national law, those who register in a political party at the precinct caucus could vote only in that particular party's national primary the following September.

Party members at the party caucus would be eligible to run for delegate to the county party convention. Those candidates for delegate who wished to identify themselves as supporting a particular candidate for president could do so, and they would be bound to vote for that candidate when they attended the county convention.

The county conventions would be held on the second Saturday in May. County convention delegates would elect delegates to the state party conventions, which would be held on the first Saturday in June. The state conventions would elect the state delegations to the national party conventions, which would be held in July.

Similar to the procedure at the precinct caucuses, candidates for delegate at the county and congressional district conventions would state their preferences among competing presidential candidates, or state their preferences to remain uncommitted. Those stating a preference would then be committed or "bound" only on the first ballot at the national conventions.

We propose, and the National Pre-primary Convention Plan would readily accommodate, the selection at the state party convention of 25 percent of the state's delegation to the national convention as "unbound" delegates. These persons so designated might be nominated by the state central committees from available state elected and party leaders who have demonstrated strong commitment to their party. Such officials might include several members of the state's congressional delegation, statewide elected officers such as governor and attorney general, a few big city mayors, and state legislators as well as state party leaders. These unbound delegates would sometimes mirror local and state caucus results. They would have an obligation to exercise their best political judgment, not simply to abide by public opinion and the temporary wishes of their supporters. Their presence and their perspective should help make national conventions more deliberative and more occasions for party renewal than has been the case in recent years. These officials could also take into consideration late breaking events or reflect current opinion in July as opposed to the public moods earlier in the spring.

The Rules of the Game

States would be prohibited by national law from holding any form of official preconvention presidential primary election. Throughout the entire process, the emphasis would be on selecting party members as delegates.

Voting procedures and other operational details at the party caucus, the county convention, congressional districts, and the state conventions would be left to individual state laws and national political party rules. The structure, organization, and scheduling of the Democratic and Republican national conventions would be the same as they are now, with the exception that both conventions would be held in July instead of one in July and the other in August.

The major task, as always, of the national convention would be to nominate candidates for the national party primary the following September. On the first of two ballots, bound delegates would vote for their declared choice, and unbound delegates could vote for any candidate. After the first ballot, all candidates except the top three finishers would be eliminated. The top three candidates would then run against each other on the second ballot, at which time *all* delegates would be unbound and could vote their preference.

The authors are of two minds about what should happen at this point. One of us believes that only the top two remaining candidates (so long as each receives a minimum of 30 percent from the convention) should be placed on the national primary ballot.

The other one believes that the endorsement threshold should be lowered to 25 percent, with the possibility that three candidates be allowed on the national primary ballot. If three candidates are placed on the primary ballot, a procedure called "approval voting" would come into effect. Under approval voting, voters can vote for as many candidates as they like. Thus if Reagan, Bush, and Baker were on the national Republican primary ballot in September 1984, a moderate Republican might vote for both Baker and Bush, while a conservative Republican might decide to vote for Reagan, or to vote for both Bush and Reagan. Approval voting is, in part, an insurance plan preventing an unrepresentative or least preferred candidate from winning in the three-person race.

Regardless of which formula is used to get two or three candidates in the party's national primary, only those candidates among the top three who received 25 percent of the vote or more on the second ballot would appear on the September primary ballot.

In certain presidential years, a candidate might be so strong at the convention that he would not have to face a national primary election. This would occur when, on the second ballot, neither the second-place nor the third-place candidate had 25 percent of the convention vote (or under our other alternative, when the second of two top finishers had less than 30 percent). Some states which use the Pre-primary Convention Plan also declare that a candidate who receives 70 percent of the state convention automatically receives the party's nomination. This same stipulation should apply at the national level. It would be expected, for instance, that a popular incumbent president with strong support from his own party could avoid the strain of a September primary.

The final duty of the national party convention would be to create a pool of acceptable vice-presidential prospects from which the eventual presidential nominee could make a choice following the national primary in September. All of the candidates who qualify for the second ballot at the convention would automatically be in this vice-presidential pool. The convention could add up to three more vice-presidential candidates. Immediately following the party presidential primary election in September, the winning candidate would select his vice-presidential nominee from the candidates in the pool.

The National Democratic Presidential Primary and the National Republican Presidential Primary would both be held on the same day, the second Tuesday after the first Monday in September (after August vacations and Labor Day weekend).

Any voter who was registered in a particular party by July 1 of the presidential year would be eligible to vote in that party's national presidential primary. The date of July 1 is suggested because it is late enough that those citizens who have had their partisan interests stimulated by the local precinct caucuses and state and county conventions, still will be able to register in a particular political party. The goal here is to prevent partisan voters whose party is not having a presidential primary in a particular year from switching their registration in order to vote for the weakest opposition candidate.

If there are, or should be in the future, states that do not provide under state law for voter registration in the two major political parties, the United States Congress should pass any necessary national laws to guarantee that all United States citizens have the right to register in a particular political party and vote in the September presidential primary.

The one candidate who gets the most votes in the September primary would be the party candidate in the November general election. A plurality of votes rather than a majority would be sufficient to declare the winner. In case of a tie, or in case of a close race where large numbers of ballots were contested, or if the winning candidate dies or becomes functionally disabled, the party national committee shall decide the official party candidate for the November election.

As noted above, the first official event following the national primary would be the selection of the vice-presidential candidate by the presidential nominee. Note that the presidential candidate will have considerable latitude in selecting his party running mate. If it appears propitious to select one of his defeated opponents and thereby mend party fences, he is free to do so. If he wishes not to choose a defeated opponent, however, he has three candidates available who have been officially approved by the convention.

Some Advantages of the Pre-Primary Convention Plan

The National Pre-primary Convention Plan is designed to eliminate the more criticized characteristics of the present presidential nominating system and also to provide some positive additions not found in the present system:

- Replacement of the present six-month series of thirty-six individual state primaries by a single national primary election campaign that would last only six to eight weeks
- Increased voter interest (and turnout) generated by a single national party primary election
- Reduction of the media's tendency to concentrate on political "momentum" rather than a candidate's character and issue positions in the early small state primaries
- Elimination of regional advantages for those candidates who are lucky enough to have strong support in early state primaries
- A return to the *nominating* rather than *ratifying* convention
- Re-emphasis on the importance of party membership and influence of party caucuses and conventions
- A strengthening of the average voter's role in the final decision
- Increased incumbent responsibility to his own party
- Increased role for party and elected officials

Possible Objections

No plan is perfect, and there are some possible defects in the National Pre-primary Convention Plan. Here are likely concerns and our discussion of them.

- Having all the local caucuses and state conventions taking place at the same time would make it more difficult for less known and less well-financed candidates to attract attention (and money). Our response in favor of the Pre-primary Convention Plan is that the cost of entering state caucuses is significantly, perhaps four times, lower than entering state primaries as a serious candidate. Second, a candidate need do well in only a handful of states to prove his or her abilities and capture at least some national delegates. Since the nomination would not usually be decided on the first ballot, a number of worthy candidates would be able to survive and thus obtain peer review and political scrutiny before the convention makes its final determination.

- Some will contend that the National Pre-primary Convention Plan is too national, too rigid, and too mechanistic. They might add that it diminishes federalism, at least to the extent it tells states when and how they will select delegates.

  Our response is that the presidency is a national office. Further, it is clear that the national parties have both the responsibility and the authority to decide on the procedure for the nomination of a presidential candidate. Finally, this new plan will strengthen the party at the state level, and it treats all states as equals.

- Critics are likely to say that the national primary feature of this new plan will encourage television and media events of the worst possible kind.

  Our plan will actually diminish much of the negative influence of television in the preconvention stage of a campaign. It will require presidential candidates to meet with party and elected local leaders and to build coalitions at the grass-roots level—not just appear in television spot ads.

- Some critics may fear this will diminish the role of minorities and lessen the affirmative action gains of the past decade—especially gains made in the Democratic party.

  We do not think this will be the case. Existing affirmative action rules may just as easily apply. Indeed, the increased turnout at the national primaries should enhance minority participation.

- What about its effect on third or minor parties? Third parties would still have their national conventions, but they would seldom need a national primary. A rule could be devised so that any national party receiving at least 5 percent of the vote in the past presidential election could participate in the national primary arrangements.

- Wouldn't the national primary be an even greater expense to the states? Perhaps. But conducting the national primary in fifty states in the fall as opposed to thirty-six in the spring is not really much different.

Here is a plan, we think, that shortens the formal election season and simplifies it so the average voter can understand its operations. More than the present system, it will test the political coalition-building skills of serious candidates—those skills so needed to win the general election and to govern; allow for sensible participation from all segments of the party; promote revitalized parties that are subject to popular control; facilitate and encourage the best possible candidates, including busy officeholders, to run for the presidency; encourage participatory caucuses and conventions at all levels of our system; and finally, it will go a long way toward rescuing the all but doomed national conventions and help make them more of an occasion for reflective societal leadership.

 # Chapter Two

Presidential Character

In the last fifteen years or so, scholars have become increasingly concerned with how an understanding of a president's personality can help us to explain his behavior in office.[1] This line of inquiry, as many pointed out, is not without its limitations. After all, psychoanalytic theory posits that the most decisive forces shaping personality occur during the formative years of an individual's life, and reconstructing the childhood experiences of a president is scarcely an easy task. No president has ever submitted to extended probings on this period of his life; nor, with rare exception, has any president written about it. The researcher may, of course, resort to interviews with family and friends, but even here one faces the problem of recall. Biographies may be of assistance as well, but there is no way of knowing that a biographer has recorded all the facts and events that a psycho-analyst might deem important. Finally, there is also the problem of how to interpret the information gathered. Since there is an absence of agreed-upon standards of evidence and inference in the field of psychoanalysis, no interpreta-tion can be demonstrated with certainty. For all of these reasons, then, it would seem prudent to regard psychological explanations of presidential behavior as suggestive rather than definitive.

Of all the writings relating to personality and the presidency, none has commanded as much attention as James David Barber's classic work, *Presidential Character: Predicting Performance in the White House* (1972). Defining personality as consisting of three components (character, worldview, and political style), Barber analyzes the personalities of thirteen twentieth-century presidents. (This number has since grown to fifteen with the publication of the second and third editions of his book.) In contrast to previous works in this area, Barber's book moved beyond a case-study approach and attempted to classify presidential personalities into four types. And he argued that each type could be expected to behave in predictable ways once in office. He was, in short, providing us with a theory of presidential behavior. In a more recent and equally intriguing work (*The Pulse of Politics*, 1980), Barber offered us another theory—one that focuses upon how the public's psychology (i.e., its electoral moods) influences the presidential person-ality types who are likely to be elected.

Both of the following selections relate to Barber's work. In the first, Michael Nelson offers an assessment of the strengths and weaknesses of Barber's theories as they apply both to presidential personality and the public's psychology. In the second selection Barber himself takes on the critics, responding to charges that his work is biased, popularized, unempirical, and overly preoccupied with person-ality to the near exclusion of other behavior-influencing variables.

Notes

1. See, for example, the following books:

David Abrahamsen, *Nixon vs. Nixon* (Farrar, Straus and Giroux, 1977).

James David Barber, *The Presidential Character: Predicting Performance in the White House*, 3rd ed. (Prentice Hall, 1985).

Fawn Brodie, *Richard Nixon: The Shaping of His Career* (W. W. Norton, 1981).

Eli Chesen, *President Nixon's Psychiatric Profile* (Peter Wyden, Publisher, 1973).

Lloyd DeMause and Henry Ebel, eds., *Jimmy Carter and American Fantasy: Psychohistorical Explorations* (Psychohistory Press, 1977).

Gary Fink, *Prelude to the Presidency: The Political Character and Legislative Leadership Style of Jimmy Carter* (Greenwood Press, 1980).

Betty Glad, *Jimmy Carter in Search of the Great White House* (W. W. Norton, 1980).

Doris Kearns, *Lyndon Johnson and the American Dream* (Harper and Row, 1976).

Bruce Mazlish, *In Search of Richard Nixon: A Psychohistorical Inquiry* (Penguin Books, 1972).

Bruce Mazlish and Edwin Diamond, *Jimmy Carter: A Character Portrait* (Simon and Schuster, 1979).

Gail Sheehy, *Character: America's Search for Leadership* (William Morrow, 1988).

2.1

Michael Nelson

James David Barber and the Psychological Presidency

Michael Nelson is associate professor of political science at Vanderbilt University and the author of The Presidency and the Political System. *Here he explores and assesses James David Barber's influential and widely debated theory of presidential character* (Presidential Character). *He also critiques Barber's theory of how the public's psychology—its electoral moods—has an impact on the presidential character types likely to be elected* (The Pulse of Politics).

The United States elects its president every four years which makes it unique among democratic nations. *Time* magazine runs a story about James David Barber every presidential election year, which makes him *unique* among political scientists.

Barber was 42 years old and chairman of the political science department at Duke University when the first *Time* article appeared in 1972. It was about a book he had just published through Prentice-Hall called *The Presidential Character.* The book argued that presidents could be divided into four psychological types, which Barber called "active-positive," "active-negative," "passive-postive," and "passive-negative." What's more, according to Barber via *Time*, with "a hard look at men before they reach the White House" voters could tell in advance what candidates would be like if elected: healthy "ambitious out of exuberance" like the active-positives; or pathologically "ambitious out of anxiety," "compliant and other-directed," or "dutiful and self-denying" like the three other, lesser types, respectively. In the 1972 election, Barber told *Time*, the choice was between an active-positive, George McGovern, and a psychologically defective active-negative, Richard Nixon.

Nixon won the election, but Barber's early insights into Nixon's personality won him and his theory certain notoriety, especially in the wake of Watergate. So prominent had Barber become by 1976, in fact, that Hugh Sidey used his entire *Time* "Presidency" column for October 4 just to tell readers that Barber was refusing to "type" candidates Gerald Ford and Jimmy Carter this time around. "Barber is deep into an academic study of this election and its participants, and he is pledged to restraint until it is over," Sidey reported solemnly. (Actually, Barber had told interviewers from *U.S. News and World Report* more than a year before

From *The Virginia Quarterly* (Autumn 1980). Reprinted by permission.

that he considered Ford an active-positive. Carter, who read Barber's book twice when it came out, was left to tell *The Washington Post* that active-positive is "what I would like to be. That's what I hope I prove to be." And so Carter would, wrote Barber in a special postelection column—for *Time*.

The 1980 election campaign has witnessed the appearance of another Barber book, *The Pulse of Politics*, and in honor of the occasion, two *Time* articles. This is all to the good, because the first, a Sidey column in March, offered more gush than information. ("The first words encountered in the new book by Duke's Professor James David Barber are stunning: 'A revolution in presidential politics is under-way. . . .' Barber has made political history before.") It wasn't until May 19 that a "Nation" section article revealed anything at all of what the new book was about, namely, Barber's cycle theory of 20th-century presidential elections. The theory holds, readers learned, that steady four-year "beats" in the public mood, or "pulse," have caused a recurring alternation among elections of what Barber calls "conflict," "conscience," and "conciliation" ever since 1900. *Time* went on to stress, though not explain, Barber's view of the importance of the mass media both as a reinforcer of this cycle and a potential mechanism for helping to break us out of it.

The kind of fame that *Time's* infatuation with Barber has brought him comes rarely to scholars, more rarely still to political scientists. For Barber, it has come at some cost. Though his ideas now have a currency they otherwise might not have, the versions of those ideas that have circulated most widely are so cursory as to make them seem superficial or even foolish—instantly appealing to the naive, instantly odious to the thoughtful. Partly because of this, Barber's reputation in the intellectual community as *un homme sérieux* has suffered. In the backrooms and corridors of scholarly gatherings, one hears "popularizer," the ultimate academic epithet, muttered along with his name.

This situation is in need of remedy. Barber's theories may be seriously flawed, but they are serious theories. For all their limitations—some of them self-confessed—they offer one of the more significant contributions a scholar can make: an unfamiliar but useful way of looking at a familiar thing that we no longer see very clearly. In Barber's case, the familiar thing is the American presidency, and the unfamiliar way of looking at it is through lenses of psychology.

II

A sophisticated psychological perspective on the presidency was long overdue when Barber began offering one in the late 1960s. Political scholars long had taken as axiomatic that the American presidency, because executive power is vested in one person and only vaguely defined in its limits, is an institution shaped largely by the personalities of individual presidents. But rarely had the literature of personality *theory*, even in its more familiar forms, been brought to bear. As Erwin Hargrove reflected in post-Vietnam, mid-Watergate 1974, this failure was the source of some startling deficiencies in our understanding of the office. "We had assumed," he wrote in *The Power of the Modern Presidency*, "that ideological purpose was sufficient to purify the drive for power, but we forgot the importance of character." Richard Neustadt's influential *Presidential Power*, published in 1960, was typical in this regard; it simply took for granted that "a President's success in maximizing power for himself serves objectives far beyond his own . . . [W]hat is good for the country is good for the President, and *vice versa*."

Scholars also had recognized for some time that the attitudes Americans hold toward the presidency are psychologically as well as politically rooted. Studies of schoolchildren had found that they first come to political awareness by learning of, and feeling fondly toward, the president. There was also a sense that popular nationalistic emotions that in constitutional monarchies are directed toward the king are deflected in American society onto the presidency. Again, however, this awareness manifested itself more in casual observation (Dwight Eisenhower was a "father figure"; the "public mood" is fickle) than in systematic thought.

The presidencies of John Kennedy, Lyndon Johnson, and Nixon changed all that. Surveys taken shortly after the Kennedy assassination recorded the startling depth of the feelings that citizens have about the office. A large share of the population experienced symptoms classically associated with grief over the death of a loved one: they cried; were tired, dazed, nervous; had trouble eating and sleeping. A quick scan through history found similar public responses to the deaths of all sitting presidents, popular or not, by murder or natural causes. If Kennedy's death illustrated the deep psychological ties of the public to the presidency, the experiences of his successors showed even more clearly the importance of psychology in understanding the connection between president and presidency. Johnson, the peace candidate who rigidly pursued a self-defeating policy of war, and Nixon, who promised "lower voices" only angrily to turn political disagreements into personal crises, projected their personalities onto policy in ways that were both obvious and destructive. The events of this period brought students of the presidency up short. As they paused to consider the nature of what I will call the "psychological presidency," they found Barber standing at the ready with the foundation and first floor of a full-blown theory.

Barber's theory offers a model of the presidency as an institution shaped largely by the psychological mix between the personalities of individual presidents and the public's deep feelings about the office. Beyond that, it proposes methods of predicting what those personalities and feelings are likely to be in given instances. These considerations govern *The Presidential Character* and *The Pulse of Politics*, books that we shall examine in turn. The problem of what is to be done on the basis of all this knowledge—of how we can become masters of our own and of the presidency's psychological fates—also is treated in these books, but receives its fullest exposition in other works by Barber.

III

The primary danger of the Nixon administration will be that the President will grasp some line of policy or method of operation and pursue it in spite of its failure. . . . How will Nixon respond to challenges to the morality of his regime, to charges of scandal and/or corruption? First such charges strike a raw nerve, not only from the Checkers business, but also from deep within the personality in which the demands of the superego are so harsh and hard. . . . The first impulse will be to hush it up, to conceal it, bring down the blinds. If it breaks open and Nixon cannot avoid commenting on it, there is a real setup here for another crisis.

James David Barber is more than a little proud of that passage, primarily because he wrote it on Jan. 19, 1969, the eve of Richard Nixon's first inauguration.

It was among the first in a series of speeches, papers, and articles whose purpose was to explain his theory of presidential personality and how to predict it, always with his forecast for Nixon's future prominently, and thus riskily, displayed. The theory received its fullest statement in *The Presidential Character*.

"Character," in Barber's usage, is not quite a synonym for personality, but he clearly thinks it "the most important thing to know about a President or candidate." As he defines the term, "character is the way the President orients himself toward life—not for the moment, but enduringly." It is forged in child-hood, "grow[ing] out of the child's experiments in relating to parents, brothers and sisters, and peers at play and in school, as well as to his own body and the objects around it." Through these experiences, the child—and thus the man to be—arrives subconsciously at a deep and private determination of what he is fundamentally worth. Some emerge from all this with high self-esteem, the vital ingredient for psychological health and political productiveness; the rest face the further problem of searching out an external, and no more than partially compensating, substitute. Depending on the source and nature of their limited self-esteem, Barber suggests, they will concentrate their search in one of three areas: the affection from others that compliant and agreeable behavior brings; the sense of usefulness that comes from performing a widely respected duty; or the deference attendant with dominance and control over people. Because politics is a vocation rich in opportunities to find all three of these things—affection from cheering crowds and backslapping colleagues, usefulness from public service in a civic cause, dominance through official power—it is not surprising that some less than secure people find a political career rather attractive.

This makes for a problem, Barber argues: if public officials, especially presi-dents, use their office to compensate for private doubts and demons, it follows that they will not always use it for public purposes. Affection-seekers will be so concerned with preserving the good will of those around them that they rarely will challenge the status quo or otherwise rock the boat. The duty-doers will be similarly inert, though in their case, it will be the feeling that to be "useful" they must be diligent guardians of time-honored practices and procedures that will account for this. The danger posed by the power-driven, of course, is the greatest. They will seek their psychological compensation not in inaction, but action. Since such action will be motivated by the desire to maintain or extend their personal sense of domination and control through public channels, it is almost bound to take destructive form: rigid defensiveness, aggression against opponents, or the like. Only those with high self-esteem are secure enough to lead as democratic political leaders must lead, with persuasion and flexibility as well as action and initiative. And Barber recognizes that even they sometimes will fail us, psycho-logical health being a necessary but not a sufficient condition for successful political leadership.

All this—the theoretical element in Barber's character analysis—is fairly straight-forward and plausible. Moving to the predictive realm is more problematic. How in the heat and haste of a presidential campaign, with candidates notably unwilling to bare their souls publicly for psychoanalytic inspection, are we to find out what they are really like?

Easy enough, argues Barber: to answer the difficult question of what motivates a political man, just answer the simpler ones in its stead: Is he "active" or "passive"? ("How much energy does the man invest in his Presidency?"); and is he "positive" or "negative"? ("Relatively speaking, does he seem to experience his political life as happy or sad, enjoyable or discouraging, positive or negative in its main effect?") According to Barber, the four possible combinations of answers to these questions turn out to be almost synonymous with the four psychological strategies people use to enhance self-esteem. The "active-positive" is the healthy one in the group. His high sense of self-worth enables him to work hard at politics, have fun at what he does, and thus be fairly good at it. Among 20th-century presidents, Barber places Franklin Roosevelt, Harry Truman, Kennedy, Ford, and Carter in this group. The "passive-positive" (William Howard Taft, Warren Harding) is the affection-seeker; though not especially hard-working in office, he enjoys it. The "passive-negative" neither works nor plays. As with Calvin Coolidge and Eisenhower, it is duty, not pleasure or zeal, that gets him into politics. Finally, there is the power-seeking "active-negative," who compulsively throws himself into his presidential chores even though the effort does not satisfy him. In Barber's view, active-negative Presidents Woodrow Wilson, Herbert Hoover, Johnson, and Nixon all shared one important personality-rooted presidential quality: they persisted in disastrous courses of action (Wilson's League of Nations battle, Hoover's depression policy, Johnson's Vietnam, Nixon's Watergate) because to have conceded that they were wrong would have been to cede their sense of control, something their psychological constitutions could not allow.

The Presidential Character caused quite a stir when it came out in 1972. Not surprisingly, it generated some vigorous criticism as well. Many argued that Barber's theory is too simple: his four types do not begin to cover the range of human complexity. At one level, this criticism is as trivial as it is true. In spelling out his theory, Barber states very clearly that "we are talking about tendencies, broad directions; no individual man exactly fits a category." His typology is offered as a method for sizing up potential presidents, not for diagnosing and treating them. Given the nature of election campaigning, a reasonably accurate shorthand device is about all we can hope for. The real question, then, is whether Barber's shorthand device is reasonably accurate.

Barber's intellectual defense of his typology's soundness, quoted here in full, is not altogether comforting:

> Why might we expect these two simple dimensions [active-passive, positive-negative] to outline the main character types? Because they stand for two central features of anyone's orientation toward life. In nearly every study of personality, some form of the active-passive contrast is critical; the general tendency to act or be acted upon is evident in such concepts as dominance-submission, extraversion-introversion, aggression-timidity, attack-defense, fight-flight, engagement-withdrawal, approach-avoidance. In everyday life we sense quickly the general energy output of the people we deal with. Similarly we catch on fairly quickly to the affect dimension—whether the person seems to be optimistic or pessimistic, hopeful or skeptical, happy or sad. The two baselines are clear and they are also independent of one another: all of us know people who are very active but seem discouraged, others who are quite passive but seem happy, and so forth. The activity baseline refers to what one does, the affect baseline to how one feels about what he does.
>
> Both are crude clues to character. They are leads into four basic character patterns long familiar in psychological research.

In the library copy of *The Presidential Character* from which I copied this passage, there is a handwritten note in the margin: "Footnote, man!" But there is no footnote to the psychological literature, here or anywhere else in the book. The casual reader might take this to mean that none is necessary, and he would be right if Barber's types really were "long familiar in psychological research" and "appeared in nearly every study of personality." But they aren't, and they don't; as Alexander George has pointed out, personality theory itself is a "quagmire" in which "the term 'character' in practice is applied loosely and means many different things." Barber's real defense of his theory—that it works; witness Nixon—is not to be dismissed, but one wishes he had explained better why he thinks it works.

Interestingly, other critics have taken Barber's typology to task for being not simple enough, at least not for the purpose of accurate preelection application. Where, exactly, is one to look to decide if down deep Candidate Schuengel is the energetic, buoyant fellow his image-makers say he is? Barber is quite right in warning analysts away from their usual hunting ground, the candidate's recent performances in other high offices. These "are all much more restrictive than the Presidency is, much more set by institutional requirements," and thus much less fertile cultures for psychopathologies to grow in. (This is Barber's only real mention of what well might be considered a third, coequal component of the psychological presidency: the rarefied, court-like atmosphere—so well described in George Reedy's *The Twilight of the Presidency*—that surrounds presidents and which allows those whose psychological constitutions so move them to seal themselves off from harsh political realities.) But Barber's alternative—a study of the candidate's "first independent political success," or "fips," in which he found his personal formula for success in politics—is not all that helpful either. How, for example, is one to tell which "fips" was first? In Barber's appropriately broad definition of "political," Johnson's first success was not his election to Congress, but his work as a student assistant to his college president. Hoover's was his incumbency as student body treasurer at Stanford. Sorting through someone's life with the thoroughness necessary to arrive at such a determination may or may not be an essential task. But clearly it is not a straightforward one.

These theoretical and practical criticisms are important ones, and they do not exhaust the list. (Observer bias, for example. Since Barber provides no clear checklist of criteria by which one is to type candidates, subjectivity is absolutely inherent.) But they should not blind us to Barber's major contributions in *The Presidential Character*: a concentration on the importance of presidential personality in explaining presidential behavior; a sensitivity to its nature as a variable (power does not always corrupt; nor does the office always make the man); and a boldness in approaching the problems voters face in predicting what candidates will be like if elected.

IV

The other side of the psychological presidency—the public's side—is Barber's concern in *The Pulse of Politics*, which was published by W. W. Norton midway through this year's primary season. The book focuses on elections, those occasions when because citizens are filling the presidential office, they presumably feel (presidential deaths aside) their emotional attachments to it most deeply. Again, Barber presents us with a typology; the public's election moods come in three varieties: "conflict," "conscience," and "conciliation," and this time the types appear in recurring order as well, over 12-year cycles. Again, the question he raises—what is the nature of "the swirl of emotions" with which Americans surround the presidency?—is important and original.

But again, too, the reasoning that underlies Barber's answer is as puzzling as it is provocative. Although his theory applies only to American presidential elections in this century, he seems to feel that the psychological "pulse" of conflict, conscience, and conciliation has beaten deeply, if softly, in all humankind for all time. Barber finds it in the "old sagas" of early man, and in "the psychological paradigm that dominates our age's thinking: the ego, instrument for coping with the struggles of the external world [conflict]; the superego, warning against harmful violations [conscience]; the id, longing after the thrill and ease of sexual satisfaction [conciliation]." He finds it firmly reinforced in American history: conflict in our emphasis on the war story ("In isolated America, the warmakers repeatedly confronted the special problem of arousing the martial spirit against distant enemies. . . . Thus our history vibrates with *talk* about war"); conscience in America's sense of itself as an instrument of divine providence ("our conscience has never been satisfied by government as a mere practical arrangement"); conciliation in our efforts to live with each other in a heterogeneous "nation of nationalities." In the 20th century, Barber argues, these themes became the controlling force in the political psychology of the American electorate, so controlling that every election since the conflict of 1900 has fit its place within the cycle (conscience in 1904, conciliation in 1908, conflict again in 1912, and so on). What caused the pulse to start beating this strongly, he feels, was the rise of the national mass media.

The modern newspaper came first, just before the turn of the century. "In a remarkable historical conjunction," writes Barber, "the sudden surge into mass popularity of the American daily newspaper coincided with the Spanish-American War." Since war stories sold papers, daily journalists wrote about "politics as war," or conflict, too. In the early 1900s, national mass circulation magazines arrived on the scene, taking their cues from the Progressive reformers who dominated that period. "The 'muckrakers'—actually positive thinkers out to build America, not destroy reputations" wrote of "politics as a moral enterprise," an enterprise of conscience. Then came the broadcast media, radio in the 1920s and television in the 1950s. What set them apart was their commercial need to reach not just a wide audience, but the widest possible audience. "Broadcasting aimed to please, wrapping politics in fun and games . . . conveying with unmatched reach and power its core message of conciliation." As for the cyclic pulse, the recurring appearance of these public moods in the same precise order, Barber suggests that there the dynamic is internal: each type of public mood generates the next. After a conflict election ("a battle for power . . . a rousing call to arms"), "reaction sets in. Uplift is called for—the cleansing of the temple of democracy"— in short, conscience. But "the troubles do not go away," and four years later "the public yearns for solace," conciliation. "Give that four years to settle in and the time for a fight will come around again," and so on.

In *The Pulse of Politics*, unlike *The Presidential Character*, the difficulties arise not in the predictive gloss (a calendar will do; if it's 1980, this must be a conciliating election), but in the theory itself. If anything, an even more secure intellectual foundation is needed here than with the character theory, for this time there is an assertion not only of types, but of an order of occurrence among them as well. Once again, however, there are no footnotes; if Barber is grounding his theory in external sources, it is impossible to tell—and hard to imagine—what they are. Nor does the theory stand up sturdily under its own weight: if, for example, radio and television are agents of conciliation, why did we not have fewer conciliating elections before they became our dominant political media and more since? Perhaps that is why some of the retrospective predictions Barber's theory leads to are as questionable as they are easy to make: Coolidge-Davis in 1924 a conflict election?; Eisenhower-Stevenson in 1952 conscience?; Nixon-Humphrey-Wallace in 1968 conciliating?

The most interesting criticism pertinent to Barber's pulse theory, however, was made eight years before it appeared by a political scientist who, also concerned with the public's presidential psychology, wrote of it in terms of a "climate of expectations" that "shifts and changes. Wars, depressions, and other national events contribute to that change, but there is also a rough cycle, from an emphasis on action (which begins to look too 'political') to an emphasis on legitimacy (the moral uplift of which creates its own strains) to an emphasis on reassurance and rest (which comes to seem like drift) and back to action again. One need not be astrological about it." (A year earlier this scholar had written that although "the mystic could see the séries . . . marching in fateful repetition beginning in 1900 . . . the pattern is too astrological to be convincing.") Careful readers will recognize the identity between the cycles of action-legitimacy-reassurance and conflict-conscience-conciliation. Clever ones will realize that the passage above was written by James David Barber in *The Presidential Character*.

V

There is, in fact, a good deal about the public's political psychology sprinkled here and there in *The Presidential Character*, and the more of it one discovers, the curiouser and curiouser things get. Most significant is the brief concluding chapter on "Presidential Character and the Moods of the Eighth Decade" (reprinted unchanged in the 1977 Second Edition), which contains Barber's bold suggestion of a close fit between the two sides of his model. For each type of public psychological climate, Barber posits, there is a "resonant" type of presidential personality. This seems a central point in his theory of the presidency: "Much of what [a president] is remembered for," he argues, "will depend on the fit between the dominant forces in his character and the dominant feelings in his constituency." Further, "the dangers of discord in that resonance are great."

What is the precise nature of this fit? When the public cry is for action (conflict), "[i]t comes through loudest to the active-negative type, whose inner struggle between aggression and control resonates with the popular plea for toughness . . . [The active-negative's] temptation to stand and fight receives wide support from the culture." In the public's reassurance (conciliation) mood, "they want a friend," a passive-positive. As for the "appeal for a moral cleansing of the Presidency," or legitimacy (conscience), the mood "resonates with the passive-negative character in its emphasis on *not doing* certain things." This leaves the active-positive, Barber's president for all seasons. Blessed with a "character firmly rooted in self-recognition and self-love, [t]he active-positive can not only *perform* lovingly or aggressively or with detachment, he can *feel* those ways."

What Barber first offered in *The Presidential Character*, then, was the foundation of a model of the psychological presidency that was not only two-sided, but integrated as well; one in which the "tuning, the resonance—or lack of it" between the public's "climate of expectations" and the president's personality "sets in motion the dynamic of his Presidency." He concentrated on the personality half of his model in *The Presidential Character*, then firmed up (after "de-astrologizing" it) and filled in the other half—the public's—in *The Pulse of Politics*. And here is where things get so curious. Most authors, when they complete a multivolume opus, trumpet that fact. Barber does not. In fact, one finds in *The Pulse of Politics* no mention at all of presidential character, if public climates of expectations, or of "the resonance—or lack of it" between them.

At first blush, this seems doubly strange, because there is a strong surface fit between the separate halves of Barber's model. In the 18 elections that have been held since Taft's in 1908 (Barber did not type 20th-century presidents farther back than Taft), presidential character and public mood resonated 12 times. The six exceptions—active-negative Wilson's election in the conscience year of 1916, passive-negative Coolidge's in conflictual 1924, active-negative Hoover's and passive-negative Eisenhower's in the conciliating elections of 1928 and 1956, active-negative Johnson's in conscience-oriented 1964, and active-negative Nixon's in conciliating 1968—perhaps could be explained in terms of successful campaign image-management by the winners, an argument that also would support Barber's general point about the power of the media in presidential politics. In that case, a test of Barber's model would be: did these "inappropriate" presidents come to grief when the public found out what they really were like after the election? In every instance but Eisenhower's and Coolidge's, the answer would have been yes.

But on closer inspection it also turns out that in every instance but these two, the presidents who came to grief were active-negatives, whom Barber tells us will do so for reasons that have nothing to do with the public mood. As for the overall 12 for 18 success rate for Barber's model, it includes seven elections won by active-positives, whom he says resonate with every public mood. A good hand in straight poker is not necessarily a good hand in wild-card; Barber's success rate in the elections not won by active-positives is only five of 11. In the case of conscience elections, only once did a representative of the resonant type—passive-negative—win, while purportedly less suitable active-negatives won three times. A final problem is born of Barber's assertion, made in the face of his prediction that Ronald Reagan would be a passive-positive president, that in the post-New Deal era of big government at home and active government abroad, the demands of the presidency—and of seeking it in the modern campaign mode—effectively will screen out passive types as would-be presidents. (In the period from 1929 to the present, the only passive president has been Eisenhower, and Barber admits that "his case is a mixed one.") Since two of his three moods—conscience and conciliation—are said to resonate with passive presidents, their elimination from contention rather trivializes the question of fit as Barber has posed it.

VI

I leave it to Barber to explain his failure to claim credit for what he has done, namely, offered and elaborated a suggestive and relatively complete model of the psychological presidency. Perhaps he feared that the lack of fit between his mood and personality types—the public and presidential components—would have distracted critics from his larger points.

In any event, the theoretical and predictive elements of Barber's theory of the presidency are sufficiently provocative to consider carefully his prescriptions for change. Barber's primary goal for the psychological presidency, it should be noted, is that it be "de-psychopathologized." He wants to keep active-negatives out and put healthy active-positives in. He wants the public to become the master of its own political fate, breaking out of its electoral mood cycle, which is essentially a cycle of psychological dependency. With presidency and public freed of their inner chains, Barber feels, they will be able to join to forge a "creative politics" or "politics of persuasion," as he has variously dubbed it. It is not clear just what this kind of politics would be, but apparently it would involve a great deal more open and honest sensitivity on the part of both presidents and citizens to the ideas of the other.

It will not surprise readers to learn that, by and large, Barber dismisses constitutional reform as a method for achieving his goals: if the presidency is as shaped by psychological forces as he says it is, then institutional tinkering will be, almost by definition, beside the point. Change, to be effective, will have to come in the thoughts and feelings of people: in the information they get about politics, the way they think about it, and the way they feel about what they think. Because of this, Barber believes, the central agent of change will have to be the most pervasive, media journalism; its central channel, the coverage of presidential elections.

It is here, in his prescriptive writings, that Barber is on most solid ground, here that his answers are as good as his questions. Unlike many media critics, he does not assume imperiously that the sole purpose of newspapers, magazines, and television is to elevate the masses. Barber recognizes that the media are made up of commercial enterprises that also have to sell papers and attract viewers. He recognizes, too, that the basic format of news coverage is the story, not the scholarly treatise. His singular contribution is his argument that the media can improve the way it does all of these things at the same time, that better election stories will attract bigger audiences in more enlightening ways.

The first key to better stories, Barber argues, is greater attention to the character of the candidates. Election coverage that ignores the motivations and developmental histories of its protagonists is as lifeless as dramas or novels that did so would be. It also is uninformative—elections are, after all, choices among people, and as Barber has shown, the kinds of people candidates are has a lot to do with the kinds of presidents they would be. Good journalism, Barber argues in a 1978 Prentice-Hall book called *Race for the Presidency*, would "focus on the person as embodying his historical development, playing out a character born and bred in another place, connecting an old identity with a new persona—the stuff of intriguing drama from Joseph in Egypt on down. That can be done explicitly in biographical stories." Barber is commendably diffident here—he does not expect reporters to master and apply his own character typology. But he does want them to research the candidates' lives for recurring patterns of behavior, particularly the rigidity that is characteristic of his active-negatives. (Of all behavior patterns, he feels rigidity "is probably the easiest one to spot and the most dangerous one to elect.") With public interest ever high in "people" stories and psychology, Barber probably is right in thinking that this kind of reporting not only would inform readers, but engage their interest as well.

This goal—engaging readers' interest—is Barber's second key to better journalism. He finds reporters and editors notably, sometimes belligerently, ignorant of their audiences. "I really don't know and I'm not interested," quotes Richard Sallant of CBS News. "Our job is to give people not what they want, but what we decide they ought to have." Barber suggests that what often is lost in such a stance is an awareness of what voters need, namely, information that will help them decide whom to vote for. He cites a study of network evening news coverage of the 1972 election campaign which found that almost as much time was devoted to the polls, strategies, rallies, and other "horse-race" elements of the election as to the candidate's personal qualifications and issue stands combined. As Barber notes, "The viewer tuning in for facts to guide his choice would, therefore, have to pick his political nuggets from a great gravel pile of political irrelevancy." He adds that "Television news which moved beyond telling citizens what momentary collective preferences are as the next primary approaches, to telling them what they need to know—precisely on the issue of presidential choosing—might yet enlist intellectual apparatus." Critics who doubt the public's interest in long, fleshed-out stories about what candidates think, what they are like, and what great problems they would face as president would do well to check the ratings of CBS's "60 Minutes."

Barber's strong belief, then, is that an electorate whose latent but powerful interest in politics is engaged by the media will become an informed electorate, and that this will effect its liberation from the pathological aspects of the psychological presidency. On the one hand, as citizens learn more of what they need to learn about the character of presidential candidates, they will be less likely to elect defective ones. On the other hand, this process of political learning also will equip them better to act "rationally" in politics, freed from their cycle of emotional dependency on the presidency. So sensible a statement of the problem is this, and so attractive a vision of its solution, that one can forgive Barber for cluttering it up with types and terminologies.

James David Barber

The Presidential Character

James David Barber is professor of political science at Duke University. In the most recent edition of his much discussed book, The Presidential Character, *Barber answers those critics who charge that his analysis is biased, popularized, lacking in empirical rigor, and overly preoccupied with personality as an explanation for presidential behavior.*

Answering the Critics

A critic, they say, is the fellow who goes out on the battlefield after the battle and shoots the wounded. *The Presidential Character* has not been without its critics, some of whom show so little interest in the problem the book addresses that it would take a whole course in American politics to straighten them out. Those who deny that who the President is can make a mighty difference in public policy, for example, ought to read other books before they take on this one. Those who think social science is poised at the brink of perfection—almost ready to explore and prescribe with scientific precision—surely should not take time from their own production of such works to study this one. Those whose taste is for political entertainment (wondering what the king is doing tonight) can find much zippier stories in the grocery store press. But not all the critics drop into these dustbins of inquiry. Responding to serious concerns about how to improve our chances for better Presidential choice can at least help clarify what I have meant to do in these pages, even if the achievement still falls short.

1. *Bias.* The easiest criticism is to assert that I have cooked my facts to suit my theory or my own political philosophy or partisan purpose. If examples are offered, the criticism can be dealt with and perhaps profited from: history corrects history. Lacking examples of supposed bias, my interest in the criticism flags. The saving fact is this: the information this book relies on is not my secret preserve. it is public knowledge. And it is, for Presidents, quite extensive. Progress in this field will happen, if at all, by *testing alternative theories against the facts.* The information is there waiting for the critic who wants to demonstrate that his theory fits the

From *The Presidential Character: Predicting Performance in the White House*, 3rd ed., by James David Barber. Englewood Cliffs: Prentice-Hall, 1985. Reprinted by permission of the author.

empirical reality better than mine does, that I have ignored or slighted or hyped data which support a more useful pattern of prediction.

2. *Personalism.* Does *The Presidential Character* put too much stress on the psychology of an individual? What about the institution of the Presidency? What about the situation a President is trying to deal with—does not that shape action importantly? What about the impact of events—unpredictable lightning bolts which transform the political landscape? Can you really boil it all down to the psyche of one middle-aged man?

Not all, I'd say, but a lot. Please notice that the book includes, for every President, an account of the power situation and the climate of expectations extant at the time. The world beyond the President's nose is not ignored. But the stress is on the person; in the study of the Presidency, that is realism. For in fact—however much we might wish it otherwise—the Presidency remains an extraordinarily personalized office. It has grown its own bureaucracy (the White House staff, the Executive Office of the Presidency), but the bureaucrats, like the press, concentrate enormous curiosity and the most arcane calculations on the Presidential state of mind. They understand that, insofar as the Presidency is concerned, situations and events take their political coloration and direction from the ways the President and the intimate aides he has selected interpret them. In short, personalism in the Presidency is an existential reality, not the product of some exotic psychological theory. The way to reform that, if it needs reform, is not to deny it, but to confront and correct it.

3. *Citizen shrinks?* A comic criticism is that the book is written in ordinary English and therefore cannot be serious social science. On the contrary, the discipline of writing for the public rather than for specialists only is more, not less, rigorous. Put into American, a significant proportion of social science reveals itself as fantastic or banal. Writing for the culture at large opens the theory and data to a much wider arena of competition, including, but reaching far beyond the obscure little circles in which technicians discuss the public business in a private language. Still, are citizens capable of making these difficult character judgments? Shouldn't the public debate stick to the issues rather than getting involved in personal psychology? I think the first answer is that the choice is a false one: the public not only can make character judgments, they *must* make them, and thus they *do* make them. A person must be picked for President, a person judged better for that job than alternative persons. From day one of the Presidency right down to the present day, public discussion has centered on the qualities of those particular human beings—including, but far from confined to, what they hoped to do if elected. The question is not whether citizens should get into the act of psyching out Presidents, but how they can do that better.

There is room for a great deal of improvement in public deliberation on the choice of a President. The key to that improvement is the progress of journalism, for the public at large is almost totally dependent on journalism to tell us what we need to know about potential Presidents. While they are still few and far between, certain highly professional journalists have taken to generating data on candidates' backgrounds, practices, and perceptions in interesting and informative style. Much of it comes too late: after the conventions, the candidate biographies appear. Deeper, longer stories may be postponed to inauguration day. But the experience of repeated Presidential failure has aroused public demand for, and thus the journalistic supply of, analyses of character, style, and worldview, along with all the horse-race hoopla, campaign travelogues, and utopian issue pieces. In another book, *The Pulse of Politics*, I explore how journalists could enhance, at one and the same time, their popular appeal and their contribution to public judgment on these matters. Nothing less than the reshaping of the democratic dialogue will address this fundamental problem, and the journalists who ask the questions and report the answers will shape that conversation for good or ill.

4. *Psychoanalytic mumbo jumbo?* Unless the historians have missed him completely, the United States does not seem to have had a psychotic President—that is, a President suffering from such terrible mental illness that he cast himself adrift from the real world. There ought to be a psychiatrist in the White House, as part of the President's medical team, in case that comes along, especially in this nuclear age in which even a temporary lapse into insanity could be fatal for us all. But that horror is likely to develop, if it ever does, after a President is ensconced in the Oval Office. In the selection phase, with its continuous public scrutiny, Presidential psychosis would stand out like a sore thumb and relegate the candidate quickly to the political outer darkness. It would take a psychotic genius to wend his way through the multifarious jumps and dives the system sets for him without revealing his broken personality.

This book addresses a different problem: short of psychoses, how can we identify patterns of likely Presidential performance before the election? Psychoanalysis, which is essentially a personal therapy, can help and harm that effort. The harm is the wildly speculative overinterpretation of blips of behavior indicative of deep-running currents of the unconscious. Freud's interest in errors as one clue (among many) to underlying personality patterns finds in the campaign gaffe story its mocking imitation. An isolated little verbal mistake is snatched from the flow of experience and turned into an icon of neurosis. It may take weeks for the candidate and his media managers to get it back into context, twisting and turning through various apologetic, explanatory, and expiational rituals. That is a silly business. Its predictive batting average is approximately zero. Anyone who thinks this is that kind of book ought to see his or her psychiatrist.

The helpful link between psychoanalytic literature and what goes on in these pages is a shared interest in pattern discernment. Year after year, patients have been bringing to the mind-doctors their individual terrors and worries. Each is unique, like a fingerprint. But like fingerprints, the "presenting symptoms" patients display are patterned. The same basic bundles of trouble show up again and again, enabling the psychiatrist to diagnose before he prescribes. Which therapy works best is far more controversial than which familiar pattern is present. Like many other observers, then, psychoanalytic ones aid in the work of President-picking by systematically telling what they see, in the light of what main similarities among cases their colleagues have noticed through the years.

5. *The Iron Box.* Before one takes comfort in the fact that his critics contradict one another, he should entertain the possibility that both sides are right. On the one hand, the book jams together such strange combinations as Wilson and Nixon, Taft and Reagan, Coolidge and Eisenhower, Ford and Roosevelt—obviously very different folks. On the other hand, it details the peculiarities of individual lives, thus obviously sacrificing pattern for the variety of cases. The problem with such criticisms is in the word "obviously." For what is similar and what different is only superficially obvious. Newton's various laws hold for big rocks and little rocks, round ones and square ones, blue ones and brown ones.

Presidents different in many ways may be similar in crucial ways. The similarities are very important, because it is only by the discernment of similarity that generalization and, consequently, prediction can be made. Science—including social science—progresses by the extension of webs of similarity. The real question is, how far can we go with how few character similarities? The answer is empirical, but we cannot get to the answer until the question is posed in meaningful—not obvious—terms.

To proceed to the next question, namely what more can we learn by reviewing the uniqueness of the case, in no way contradicts the first question. The one adds to the other. Placing an individual in a category is an act of abstraction, not an assertion of identity. The concrete, individual life history details fill in the broad-brush sketch. Indeed, in the very process of categorical placement, one brings up evidence pointing in other directions, so that, for example, one notes Kennedy's tendency to withdraw (passive-negative), Truman's compulsive tendencies (active-negative), and Roosevelt's bent for compliance (passive-positive), through on balance all three are active-positives. It is a matter of dominance, or regnancy of certain qualities over others, rather than "pure" types unsullied by variation. The advance over uniformity or randomness in such a scheme is what makes it worth the trouble.

6. *Fake active-positives?* Did I teach Jimmy Carter how to smile? Did Ronald Reagan ride his horse to make me think him active? Aside from fleeting mea-glomaniacal moments, I doubt it. Neither needed my book to motivate him to seem to be what our culture wants him to be: energetic and optimistic. Thus Eisenhower, even without the benefit of *The Presidential Character*, pasted his campaign smile over his bored brain and gave up his twice-a-week golf for the rigors of the campaign trail. Even Herbert Hoover was known to grin while campaigning. How then can we make reasonable assessments of and predictions about candidates who are acting in such uncharacteristic ways? Even the campaign biographies and, later, heavily partisan first-term accounts are notably distorted in their reporting. Therefore, are not the data themselves far too shaky to sustain the theory?

As for performance during the campaign, I agree. The *average* candidate for President is not a practiced professional actor: he will have a hard time keeping up a character-contradicting act over a period of months. But some can come close and a few, like Reagan, have the dramatic talent to play Henry V while feeling like Polonius, for weeks on end. Furthermore, the role of campaigner contrasts markedly with the role of President, so that reactions to the one may be significantly different from reactions to the other. The campaign worldview, for example, is hypothetical and subjunctive—what he would do—as distinct from the visions upon which a President has to act. The campaign tests style differently from the Presidential tests; Presidential negotiating skill, for instance, gets little examination in the rush of campaigning. Running for President is part of being President, typically, as a race for a second term looms ahead. But the regular Washington work is so different from campaigning in critical ways that it would be folly to read the campaign to find the President.

The corrective is to survey the candidate's *past:* how, over a long period of years, has he behaved and expressed himself on the key questions? That does mean reliance on biographies or journalism, with their partisan biases. But for the particular purpose of predicting performance in the White House, we are in the first place not particularly interested in the biographer's evaluations. What we are after are reports of experiences, not attributions of virtue or vice. Quite often even a quite biased account will furnish *information* of value and interest for testing categorical hypotheses. Of course, politicians and writers have been known to make up stories. There the best corrective is another biography or deep profile, preferably written from a different perspective, against which to check the facts. Not even that process eliminates error, as the revelations about Lyndon Johnson's history, recounted above, make clear. But by concentrating on the time before the Presidential bug bit the man and by drawing on as wide a variety of sources as practical, the researcher can usually move a quantum leap beyond the casual impressions of the campaign. There the truth will out. Jimmy Carter's mother taught him to smile. Ronald Reagan was riding horses back when he was still an FDR Democrat.

7. *The Mechanists.* A "model"—squares and circles connected by lines and arrows—is not to be found in *The Presidential Character.* Neither is a kind of chemistry manual where another researcher can pop together ingredients in given proportions and automatically produce a character analysis. There are still in social science some incredible optimists who really believe we are on the verge of breaking through into a wonderful land of mechanical research, in which highly significant findings are ground out of little whirring models set in motion by precise instructions. That has been about to happen for far too many years now. In fact, the results to date have been less than inspiring. In real politics, strictly structural-mechanical reforms have been noted for "unanticipated consequences." In political science, the mechanists' awesome techniques typically turn out eminently neglectible results. The attempt to squeeze the blood of culture and history out of the research enterprise has not, so far, done much to strengthen knowledge.

The findings in this book do not depend upon the author's authority or insight, if any, because the evidence and inference are right out there in the open for all to see and test as they see fit. But this work does depend on a degree of common sense. The "instruments" and "operations" involved are simple: you read biographies and take notes when you find material relevant (pro or con) to the various hypothesized key concepts, such as first independent political success. Not claiming to be Freud, my approach is like his, as expressed in the first sentence of *The Defense of Neuro-Psychoses:* "After a close study of several patients suffering from phobias and obsessions a tentative explanation of these symptoms forced itself upon me; and as it later enabled me successfully to divine the origin of similar pathological ideas in other cases, I consider it worthy of publication and of further tests." It is important to keep awake while reading, to notice all the appropriate incidents, to hold in mind the comparative context, to prefer the specific to the global statement, to move toward a judgment of the balance among competing interpretations—in other words, to use one's head and keep at it.

8. *Change in adulthood.* It seems unfair to the middle-aged to suggest that character, worldview, and style are pretty well set by the time young adulthood is over. Our culture has always valued change, has often confused it with progress. Ours is the land of beginning again. The dominant religion preaches the possibility of late-life salvation. In recent years, many have switched careers and spouses well after thirty, and many have shifted "life styles" as they move into the "golden years." New research has also charted interesting patterns of

development in adulthood that should contribute significantly to our understanding of political leadership.

My reading of the biographies and psychological studies still leaves me thinking that the weight of the evidence is for continuity over change. Every character elaborates itself throughout life, but after thirty or forty years character is rarely transformed. Styles and worldviews are more malleable, but there too the continuities are more impressive than the changes. In short, given the present state of knowledge of the subject, I would advise the citizen choosing a President not to count on major changes in basic personality, basic beliefs, or basic political skills as that creature of habit moves into the White House. The scientific question remains an empirical one: the mere assertion that change is possible is trivial. What is needed is research to test the significance and explanatory and predictive power of theories of midlife change applied to real life politicians.

9. *Downplaying worldview.* Worldview is not neglected in any case depicted in *The Presidential Character*. But it clearly gets short shrift compared with character and style. Again, this becomes an empirical question; we need studies of the hypothesis that the worldview of a President-to-be is a valuable (i.e., prediction-improving) clue to the performance of a President-as-is. My reading is that not even Herbert Hoover carried through consistently on his pre-Presidential beliefs and that not even Reagan, that supposedly ultimate ideologue, can be scored high on worldview carry through. But the material is there, waiting for the research which will demonstrate the power of belief as predictor.

It is natural for scholars, whose own world is a world of ideas, to make more of political belief systems than the facts warrant. In public opinion research, it came as shocking news when the early voting studies showed how little attention people paid to "ideology" in the Eisenhower years. We tend to forget that the dominant American political belief has been pragmatism, an anti-ideology, a philosophy of not putting too much weight on philosophy. Politicians in particular, perhaps even more than their counterparts in business, tend to run with their fingers in the air, testing the popular breeze to find the currently compelling concepts. Sorting back through Presidency after Presidency, one encounters instance after instance of principle adjustment, so that a behaviorally meaningful concept of worldview has to be pitched at a relatively high level of abstraction. Certainly "conservative" and "liberal" do not go far as explainers of what happens.

Perhaps one day we will get a President whose character and style lend great force to a mistaken worldview—say, an active-positive fascist rhetorician. Such a President could, I suppose, do considerable harm. But in the historical cases reviewed in this book, no active-positive character—of whatever worldview—did, or was likely to, let an ideological commitment carry him over the brink into political disaster. Given time to see harmful consequences actually developing into tragic ones, the active-positive turns aside from the path of rigidification. In economic policy, environmental matters, the maneuvering of alliances, and other familiar lines of policy, in which disaster can be avoided by learning, by the observation of the actual course of events, there should be time for a reasoning and life-loving leader to see, think, and dodge.

Given time . . .but there is one decision-area in which time is disappearing: nuclear attack, by accident or design. Our survival may depend on the emergence of a new dimension of political imagination, the capacity of leaders to project from the realities of the day into the probabilities of the future. This capacity acquires an urgent relevance in the picking of a President.

10. *Inside my head.* The funniest critics are those who focus on whether I got the book's basic typology. A very wide selection of original thinkers have been suggested, ranging from Karen Horney and Harold Lasswell to Eric Berne and Norman Vincent Peale. Surely I stole it somewhere, the thesis seems to be, and once we find out where, we will be in a position to assess its validity. At least one critic has suggested I got it from him, but then, alas, ruined it. These originologists suppose a predestined course once the intellectual ball starts rolling.

The truth is simpler. Having been committed to institutions of higher education since age sixteen, I had read a fair amount when I wrote my doctoral dissertation, pushing age thirty. At least some residue of that reading was in my mind as I tried to make sense of responses some state legislators had given to my inquiries, responses which seemed strangely inconsistent in that they showed virtually no relationship between measures of satisfaction and measures of activity. By a twist of the mental dial, I entertained the conjecture that the data might be right—and if so, how could that be? It could be if there were legislators who enjoyed passivity and others who were disappointed with activity. And so there were, in significant numbers and (when one went into their interviews) displaying common patterns of adaptation. The crucial step was the question, not the answer. And that was, of course, but the first step in a long process of detailed studying, checking and cross-checking, reading and elaborating and extending, which eventually gave shape to the present effort.

It is impossible for me to sort out which of my teachers in their classrooms and in their books may be guilty or innocent of what degree of influence. I take up the question last, among criticisms, as it is doubtless the silliest. Newton may or may not have been beaned by someone else's apple, but what is interesting is what, in a lifetime of labor, he made of the event.

It may be that someday down through the years the United States will develop a political system in which the Presidency is but one of several major forces. Certainly it seems likely that the Congress will eventually reconvert itself from a fragmented collection of little specialized hierarchies into a single deliberative body in which equal representatives debate and decide the major political questions of the day. It is at least possible that the steady preachment of one scholar after another urging the revitalization of political parties will take hold and come to pass. No other political mechanism ever invented has approximated the party's success in building a common front linking the leaders and the lead in a common purpose. It is even conceivable that the Supreme Court, and the whole legal structure it stands atop, will learn how to break through the toils of complexity that now threaten the very legitimacy of the idea of law itself and stand as the trusted ultimate guardians of American justice.

If any of that ever happens, I am willing to predict, a President will be in the middle of the fight. The era this side of the great horizon is and will be a Presidential era. It will be up to Presidents, more than any other force of government, to grapple with the terrors and the possibilities of a new age, a new world, a new generation of vicious and worthy Americans.

That age will throw at Presidents-to-be two overarching challenges. Will we find ways to harness the enormous new powers of technology and organization to the ancient task of building a humane and life-sustaining polity? Will we find ways, in time, to turn aside from the escalating probability that our world and all that is in it will pass into oblivion because humans could not control their explosives? Presidents who know how the world works and how Washington works in it, Presidents who have mastered the skills it takes to make the White House an efficient machine for social progress, Presidents who can call up from their own characters the steady, hopeful, insistent reason to shape a good life from a mixed society—such we yet may find before the great American adventure stops.

 Chapter Three

The President and the Public

Abraham Lincoln once observed that "In this and like communities, public sentiment is everything. With public sentiment nothing can fail, without it nothing can succeed."[1] Nearly forty-five years later this view was echoed by political scientist Woodrow Wilson just four years before he was elected to the presidency: "Let him [the president] once win the admiration and confidence of the country, and no other single force can withstand him, no combination of forces will easily overpower him."[2] While both men overstate the point, the fact remains that presidents who enjoy wide public support will find it a good deal easier to work their will. Most of what a president wants to accomplish, after all, requires the support of Congress in one way or another. Given the constitutional limitations on his office, as well as the absence of guaranteed support from members of his own party, presidents are compelled to enlist congressional support rather than command it. At the same time, however, Congress is also an elected body and as such cannot remain insensitive to the level of support which the president enjoys in the general population. Thus, to the extent that legislators perceive the president as popular, they will prove more receptive to his programs and more muted in their criticism.

If broad public support provides the president with important leverage over other decision-makers, it is equally clear to some scholars that sustaining such support has become increasingly difficult for our recent presidents. The following two selections speak to this difficulty. In the first, Thomas Cronin suggests that a modern president is destined to lose his popularity because the public entertains unrealistic and frequently conflicting expectations of what it wants from him. Other scholars, meanwhile, argue that political and institutional changes have increasingly placed the president in a "no win" situation with the public, thereby inhibiting his ability to sustain public support. In the second selection, Richard Rose examines this contention and rejects it.

Notes

1. Cited in Jack Valenti, *A Very Human President* (W. W. Norton, 1975), p. 261.
2. Woodrow Wilson, *Constitutional Government in the United States* (Columbia University Press, 1908), p. 79.

Thomas C. Cronin

The Paradoxes of the Presidency

Thomas Cronin, a former White House fellow, currently teaches political science at Colorado College. In this article he contends that the public holds conflicting, even contradictory, expectations about what it wants from a president. Cronin explores some of these contradictory expectations and their implications for presidential performance and the public's evaluation of presidential behavior.

Why is the presidency such a bewildering office? Why do presidents so often look like losers? Why is the general public so disapproving of recent presidential performances, and so predictably less supportive the longer a president stays in office?

The search for explanations leads in several directions. Vietnam and the Watergate scandals must be considered. Then too, the personalities of Lyndon Johnson and Richard Nixon doubtless are factors that soured many people on this office. Observers also claim that the institution is structurally defective; that it encourages isolation, palace guards, "groupthink" and arrogance.

Yet something else seems at work. Our expectations and demands are frequently so paradoxical as to invite two-faced behavior by our presidents. We seem to want so much so fast that a president, whose powers are often simply not as great as many of us believe, gets condemned as ineffectual. Or a president will overreach or resort to unfair play while trying to live up to our demands. Either way, he seems to become locked into a rather high number of no-win situations.

The Constitution is of little help in explaining any of this. Our Founding Fathers purposely were vague and left the presidency defined imprecisely. They knew well that the presidency would have to provide the capability for swift and competent executive action, yet they went to considerable length to avoid enumerating specific powers and duties, so as to calm the then ever-present popular fear of monarchy.

Plainly, the informal and symbolic powers of the presidency today account for as much as the formal ones. Too, presidential powers expand and contract in response to varying situational and personality changes. Thus the powers of the presidency are interpreted in ways so markedly different as to seem to describe different offices. In some ways the presidency today is an open mandate for nearly

From *Public Opinion*, volume 5, number 6, (December/January, 1983). Reprinted with the permission of the American Enterprise Institute for Public Policy Research.

anything its occupant chooses to do with it. In other ways, however, our beliefs and hopes about the presidency very much shape the character and quality of the presidential performances we get.

The modern (post-Roosevelt II) presidency is riddled through with various expectations that are decidedly paradoxical. Presidents and presidential candidates must constantly balance themselves between conflicting demands. An inspection of what it is that we expect of presidents and would-be presidents suggests that very often we simultaneously expect contradictory kinds of performances, contradictory kinds of personalities. It is not unreasonable to conclude that these paradoxes may sometimes make for schizophrenic presidential performances.

We may not be able to resolve the inherent contradictions and dilemmas these paradoxes point up. Still, a more rigorous understanding of these conflicts and no-win or near no-win situations should encourage more sensitivity to the limits of what a president can achieve. Exaggerated or hopelessly contradictory public expectations doubtless encourage a president to attempt more than he can accomplish and to overpromise and overextend himself.

Perhaps, too, an assessment of *the paradoxed presidency* may impel us anew to revise some of our unrealistic expectations of the institution of the presidency and encourage in turn the nurturing of alternative sources or centers for national leadership.

A more realistic appreciation of presidential paradoxes might help presidents concentrate on the practicable among their priorities. A more sophisticated and tolerant consideration of the modern presidency and its paradoxes might relieve the load so that a president can better lead and administer in those critical realms in which the nation has little choice but to turn to him. Like it or not, the vitality of our democracy still depends in large measure on the sensitive interaction of presidential leadership and an understanding public willing to listen and willing to support when a president can persuade. Carefully planned innovation is nearly impossible without the kind of leadership a competent and fairminded president can provide.

Each of the paradoxes is based on apparent logical contradictions. Each has important implications for presidential performance and public evaluation of presidential behavior. A better understanding may lead to the removal, reconciliation, or more enlightened tolerance of the initial contradictions to which they give rise.

1. The Gentle and Decent/but Forceful and Decisive President

Opinion polls time and again indicate that people want a just, decent, humane "man of good faith" in the White House. Honesty and trustworthiness repeatedly top the list of qualities the public values most highly in a president these days. However, the public just as strongly demands the qualities of toughness, decisiveness, even a touch of ruthlessness.

Adlai Stevenson, George McGovern and Gerald Ford were all criticized for being "too nice," "too decent." (The *Mayaguez* incident was one of Ford's only aberrations—and predictably he was applauded for being "very presidential" that month.) Morris Udall, who was widely viewed as a decidedly decent candidate in the 1976 race for the Democratic nomination, had to advertise himself as a man of strength. Being a "Mr. Nice Guy" is too easily equated with being too soft. The public dislikes the idea of a weak, spineless or sentimental person in the White House.

LBJ's sometimes schizophrenic behavior is illustrative. He could sign a vital civil rights bill and a few hours later oversee bombing the hell out of Hanoi. Perhaps, too, this paradox may explain the unusual extraordinary public fondness for President Eisenhower. For he was at one and the same time blessed with a benign smile and a reserved, calming disposition. Yet he also was the disciplined, strong, no-nonsense, five-star general. Perhaps his ultimate resource as president was this reconciliation of decency and decisiveness, likeability alongside demonstrated valor.

Jimmy Carter appears to appreciate one of the significant byproducts of this paradox. He has noted that the American male is handicapped in his expressions of religious faith by those requisite masculine qualities—overt strength, toughness and firmness.

Carter's personal reconciliation of this paradox is noteworthy: "But a truer demonstration of strength would be concern, compassion, love, devotion, sensitivity, humility—exactly the things Christ talked about—and I believe that if we can demonstrate this kind of personal awareness of our own faith we can provide that core of strength and commitment and underlying character that our nation searches for."

Thus this paradox highlights one of the distinctive frustrations for presidents and would-be presidents. We demand the *sinister* as well as the *sincere*, President *Mean* and President *Nice*; tough and hard enough to stand up to a Khruschev or to press the nuclear button, compassionate enough to care for the ill-fed, ill-clad, ill-housed. The public in this case seems to want a soft-hearted son of a bitch. It's a hard role to cast and a harder role to perform for eight years.

2. The Open and Sharing/but Courageous and Independent Presidency

We unquestionably cherish our three-branched system with its checks and balances and its theories of dispersed and separated powers. We want our presidents not only to be sincere but to share their powers with their cabinet, the Congress and other "responsible" national leaders. In theory, we oppose the concentration of power, we dislike secrecy and we resent depending on any one person to provide for all our leadership. In more recent years (the 1970's in particular) there have been repeated calls for a more open, accountable and deroyalized presidency.

The other side of the coin, however, rejects the call for deroyalization. It rejects as well the idea that openness is the solution; indeed it suggests instead that the great presidents have been the strong presidents, who stretched their legal authority, who occasionally relied on the convenience of secrecy and who dominated the other branches of government. This point of view argues that the country in fact often yearns for a messiah, that the human heart ceaselessly reinvents royalty and that Roosevelts and Camelots, participatory democracy notwithstanding, are vital to the success of America.

Some people feel we are getting to the point where all of us would like to see a deroyalized, demythologized presidency. Others claim we need myth, we need symbol. As one person put it: "I don't think we could live without the myth of a glorified presidency, even if we wanted to. We just aren't that rational. Happily, we're too human for that. We will either live by the myth that has served us fairly well for almost two hundred years, or we will probably find a much worse one."

The clamor for a truly open or collegial presidency was opposed on other grounds by the late Harold Laski when he concluded that Americans in practice want to rally round a president who can demonstrate his independence and vigor:

> A president who is believed not to make up his own mind rapidly loses the power to maintain the hold. The need to dramatize his position by insistence upon his undoubted supremacy is inherent in the office as history has shaped it. A masterful man in the White House will, under all circumstances, be more to the liking of the multitude than one who is thought to be swayed by his colleagues.

Thus it is that we want our president not only to be both a lion and a fox, but more than a lion, more than a fox. We want simultaneously a secular leader and a civil religious mentor; we praise our three-branched system but we place capacious hopes upon and thus elevate the presidential branch. Only the president can give us heroic leadership. Only a president can dramatize and symbolize our highest expectations of ourselves as a chosen people with a unique mission. If it seems a little ironic for a semi-sovereign people (who have so recently celebrated the bicentennial of the power-to-the-governed experiment) to delegate so much hierarchical and semi-autocratic power to their president, this is nonetheless precisely what we continually do.

We want an open presidency and we oppose the concentration of vast power in any one position. Still, we want forceful, courageous displays of leadership from our presidents. Anything less than that is condemned as aimlessness or loss of nerve. Further, we praise those who leave the presidency stronger than it was when they entered the institution.

3. The Programmatic/but Pragmatic Leader

We want both a *programmatic* and a *pragmatic* person in the White House. We want a *moral* leader, yet the job forces the president to become a *constant compromiser.*

On the one hand, Franklin Roosevelt proclaimed that the presidency is preeminently a place for moral leadership. On the other hand, Governor Jerry Brown aptly notes that "a little vagueness goes a long way in this business."

A president who becomes too committed risks being called rigid; a president who becomes too pragmatic risks becoming called wishy-washy. The secret, of course, is to stay the course by stressing character, competence, rectitude and experience, and by avoiding strong stands that offend important segments in the population.

Jimmy Carter was especially criticized by the press and others for avoiding commitments and stressing his "flexibility" on the issues. This prompted a major discussion of what became called the "fuzziness issue." Jokes spread the complaint. ("When you eat peanut butter all your life, your tongue sticks to the roof of your mouth, and you have to talk out of both sides.") Still, his "maybe I will and maybe I won't" strategy (as well as his talking softly about the issues while carrying a big smile) proved very effective in overcoming critics and opponents who early on claimed he didn't have a chance.

What strikes one person as fuzziness or even duplicity appeals to another person as remarkable political skill, the very capacity for compromise and negotiation that is required if a president is to maneuver through the political minefields that come with the job.

Most candidates view a campaign as a fight to win office, not an opportunity for adult education. Barry Goldwater in 1964 may have run with the slogan "We offer a *choice*, not an echo," but many Republican party regulars who, more pragmatically, aspired to win the election, preferred "a *chance*, not a *choice*." Once in office, presidents often operate the same way; the electoral connection looms large as an issue-avoiding, controversy-ducking political incentive.

4. An Innovative and Inventive/Yet Majoritarian and Responsive Presidency

One of the most compelling paradoxes at the very heart of our democratic system arises from the fact that we expect our presidents to provide bold, innovative leadership and yet respond faithfully to public opinion majorities.

Walter Lippmann warned against letting public opinion become the chief guide to leadership in America, but he just as forcefully warned democratic leaders: Don't be right too soon, for public opinion will lacerate you! So most presidents fear being in advance of their times. They must *lead us*, but also *listen to us*.

We want our presidents to offer leadership, to be architects of the future, providers of visions, plans and goals. At the same time we want them to stay in close touch with the sentiments of the people. To *talk* about high ideals, New Deals, Big Deals and the like is one thing. But the public resists being *led* too far in any one direction.

Most of our presidents have been conservatives or at best "pragmatic liberals." They have seldom ventured much beyond the crowd. John Kennedy, the author of the much acclaimed *Profiles in Courage*, was often criticized for presenting far more profile than courage; if political risks could be avoided, he shrewdly avoided them. Kennedy was fond of pointing out that he had barely won election in 1960 and that great innovations should not be forced upon a leader with such a slender mandate. Ironically, Kennedy is credited with encouraging widespread public participation in politics. But Kennedy more often than not reminded Americans that caution was needed, that the important issues are complicated and technical, and best left to the administrative and political experts.

Presidents can get caught whether they are coming or going. The public wants them to be both *leaders* of the country and *representatives* of the people. We want them to be decisive and rely mainly on their own judgment, yet we want them to be very responsive to public opinion, especially to the "common sense" of our own opinions. It was perhaps with this in mind that an English essayist once defined the ideal democratic leader as "an uncommon man of common opinions."

5. Taking the Presidency Out of Politics

The public yearns for a statesman in the White House, for a George Washington or a second "era of good feelings," anything that might prevent partisanship or politics-as-usual in the White House. In fact, however, the job demands a president to be a gifted political broker, ever-attentive to changing political moods and coalitions.

Franklin Roosevelt illustrates well this paradox. Appearing so remarkably nonpartisan while addressing the nation, he was in practice one of the craftiest political coalition builders to occupy the White House. He mastered the art of politics—the art of making the difficult and desirable possible.

A president is expected to be above politics in some respects and highly political in others. A president is never supposed to act with his eye on the next election; he's not supposed to favor any particular group or party. Nor is he supposed to wheel and deal or twist too many arms. That's politics and that's bad! No, a president, or so most people are inclined to believe, is supposed to be "president of all the people." On the other hand, he is asked to be the head of his party, to help friendly members of Congress get elected or reelected, to deal firmly with party barons and congressional political brokers. Too, he must build political coalitions around what he feels needs to be done.

To take the president out of politics is to assume, incorrectly, that a president will be so generally right and the general public so generally wrong that a president must be protected from the push and shove of political pressures. But what president has always been right? Over the years, public opinion has been usually as sober a guide as anyone else on the political waterfront. Anyway, having a president constrained and informed by public opinion is what a democracy is all about.

In his reelection campaign of 1972, Richard Nixon in vain sought to reveal himself outwardly as too busy to be a politician; he wanted the American people to believe he was too preoccupied with the Vietnam War to have any personal concern about his election. In one sense, Mr. Nixon may have destroyed this paradox for at least a while. Haven't the American people learned that we *cannot* have a president *above* politics?

If past is prologue, presidents in the future will go to considerable lengths to portray themselves as unconcerned with their own political future. They will do so in large part because the public applauds the divorce between presidency and politics. People naively think that we can somehow turn the job of president into that of a managerial or strictly executive post. Not so. The presidency is a highly political office, and it cannot be otherwise. Moreover, its political character is for the most part desirable. A president separated from or somehow above politics might easily become a president who doesn't listen to the people, doesn't respond to majority sentiment or pay attention to views that may be diverse, intense and at variance with his own. A president immunized from politics would be a president who would too easily become isolated from the processes of government and too removed from the thoughts and aspirations of his people.

In all probability this paradox will be an enduring one. The standard diagnosis of what's gone wrong in an administration will be that the presidency has become too politicized. But it will be futile to try to take the president out of politics. A more helpful approach is to realize that certain presidents try too hard to hold themselves above politics—or at least to give that appearance—rather than engaging in it deeply, openly and creatively enough. A president in a democracy has to act politically in regard to controversial issues if we are to have any semblance of government by the consent of the governed.

6. The Common Man/Who Gives an Uncommon Performance

We like to think that America is the land where the common sense of the common man reigns. We prize the common touch, the "man of the people." Yet few of us will settle for anything but an uncommon performance from our presidents.

This paradox is splendidly summed up by some findings of a survey conducted by Field Research Corp., the California public opinion organization. Field asked a cross section of Californians in 1975 to describe in their own words the qualities a presidential candidate should or should not have. Honesty and trustworthiness topped the list. But one of his more intriguing findings was that "while most (72 percent) prefer someone with plain and simple tastes, there is also a strong preference (66 percent) for someone who can give exciting speeches and inspire the public."

It has been said that the American people crave to be governed by men who are both Everyman and yet better than Everyman. The Lincoln and Kennedy presidencies are illustrative. We might cherish the myth that anyone can grow up to be president, that there are no barriers, no elite qualifications. But the nation doesn't want a person who is too ordinary. Would-be presidents have to prove their special qualifications—their excellence, their stamina, their capacity for uncommon leadership.

The Harry Truman reputation, at least as it flourishes now, demonstrates the apparent reconciliation of this paradox. Fellow-commoner Truman rose to the demands of the job and became a gifted decision-maker, or so his supporters would have us believe.

Candidate Carter in 1976 nicely fit this paradox as well. Local, down-home, farm boy next door, makes good! The image of peanut farmer turned gifted governor and talented campaigner contributed greatly to Carter's success as a national candidate, and he used it with consummate skill.

A president or would-be president must be bright, but not too bright; warm and accessible, but not too folksy; down to earth, but not pedestrian. Adlai Stevenson spoke too eloquently, and President Ford's talks dulled our senses with the banal. Both suffered because of this paradox. The Catch-22 here, of course, is that the very fact of an uncommon performance puts distance between a president and the truly common man. We persist, however, in wanting both at the same time.

7. The Inspirational/But Don't-Promise-More-Than-You-Can-Deliver Leader

We ask our presidents to raise hopes, to educate us, to inspire. But too much inspiration will invariably lead to disillusion and cynicism.

We enjoy the upbeat rhetoric and promises of a brighter tomorrow. We genuinely want to hear about New Nationalism, New Deals, New Frontiers, Great

Societies, and New American Revolutions; we want our fears to be assuaged during "fireside chats" or "a conversation with the president"; to be told that "we are a great people," that the "only fear we have to fear is fear itself," and that a recession has "bottomed out." So much do we want the drive of a lifting dream, to use Mr. Nixon's corny phrase, that the American people are easily duped by presidential promises.

Do presidents overpromise because they are congenital optimists or because they are pushed into it by the demanding public? Surely it is an admixture of the two. But whatever the source, few presidents in recent times were able to keep their promises and fulfill their intentions. Poverty was not ended, a Great Society was not realized. Vietnam dragged on and on. Watergate outraged a public that had been promised an open presidency. Energy independence remains an illusion just as crime in the streets continues to rise.

A president who does not raise hopes is criticized as letting events shape his presidency, rather than making things happen. A president who eschewed inspiration of any kind would be rejected as un-American. For as a poet once wrote, "America is promises." For people everywhere cherishing the dream of individual liberty and self-fulfillment, America has been the land of promises, of possibilities, of dreams. No president can stand in the way of this truth, no matter how much the current dissatisfaction about the size of big government in Washington, and its incapacity to deliver the services it promises.

William Allen White, the conservative columnist, went to the heart of this paradox when he wrote of Herbert Hoover. President Hoover, he noted, is a great executive, a splendid desk man. "But he cannot dramatize his leadership. A democracy cannot follow a leader unless he is dramatized."

8. The National Unifier/National Divider

One of the most difficult to alleviate paradoxes arises from our longing simultaneously for a president who will pull us together again and yet be a forceful priority setter, budget manager and executive leader. The two tasks are near opposites.

We remain one of the few nations in the world that calls upon our chief executive to also serve as our symbolic, ceremonial head of state. Elsewhere these tasks are spread around. In some nations there is a monarch *and* a prime minister; in other nations there are three visible national leaders—the head of state, a premier, and a powerful party head.

In the absence of an alternative, we demand that our presidents and our presidency act as a unifying force in our lives. Perhaps it all began with George Washington, who so artfully performed this function. At least for a while, he truly was above politics and an ideal symbol for our new nation. He was a healer, a unifier and an extraordinary man for all seasons. Today we ask no less of our presidents than that they should do as Washington did.

However, we have designed a presidential job description that compels our contemporary presidents to act as national dividers. They necessarily divide when they act as the leader of their political party; when they set priorities that advantage certain goals and groups at the expense of others; when they forge and lead political coalitions; when they move out ahead of public opinion and assume the role of national educator; when they choose one set of advisers over another. A president, if he is to be a creative executive, cannot help but offend certain interests. When Franklin Roosevelt was running for a second term some garment workers unfolded a great sign that said, "We love him for the enemies he has made." Such is the fate of a president on an everyday basis; if he chooses to use power he usually will lose the good will of those who preferred inaction over action. The opposite is of course true if he chooses not to act.

Look at it from another angle. The nation is torn between the view that a president should primarily preside over the nation and merely serve as a referee among the various powerful interests that actually control who gets what, when and how, and the view which holds that a president should gain control of governmental processes and powers so as to use them for the purpose of furthering public, as opposed to private, interests.

Harry Truman said it all very simply. He once said there are 14 or 15 million Americans who have the resources to have representatives in Washington to protect their interests, and that the interests of the 160 million or so others are the responsibility of the president.

Put another way, the presidency is sometimes seen as the great defender of the people, the ombudsman or advocate-general of "public interests." Yet it is sometimes also (and sometimes at the same time) viewed as the enemy—hostile to the people, isolated from them, wary of them, antagonistic.

This debate notwithstanding, however, Americans prize the presidency as a grand American invention. As a nation we do not want to change it. Proposals to weaken it are dismissed. Proposals to reform or restructure it are paid little respect. If we sour on a president, the conventional solution has been to find and elect someone better.

9. The Longer He Is There/the Less We Like Him

Every four years we pick a president and for the next four years we pick on him, at him, and sometimes pick him entirely apart. There is no adequate pre-presidential job experience, so much of the first term is an on-the-job learning experience. But we resent this. It is too important a position for on-the-job learning, or at least that's how most of us feel.

Too, we expect presidents to grow in office and to become better acclimated to the office. But the longer they are in office, the more they find themselves with more crises and less public support. There is an apocryphal presidential lament which goes as follows: "Every time I seem to grow into the job, it gets bigger."

Simply stated, the more we know of a president, or the more we observe his presidency, the less we approve of him. Familiarity breeds discontent. Research on public support of presidents indicates that presidential approval peaks soon after a president takes office, and then slides downward at a declining rate over time until it reaches a point in the latter half of the four-year term, when it bottoms out. Thereafter it rises a bit, but never attains its original levels. Why this pattern of declining support afflicts presidents is a subject of debate among social scientists. Unrealistic early expectations are, of course, a major factor. These unrealistic expectations ensure a period of disenchantment.

Peace and prosperity, of course, can help stem the unpleasant tide of ingratitude, and the Eisenhower popularity remained reasonably high in large part because of his (or the nation's) achievements in these areas. For most presidents, however, their eventual downsliding popularity is due perhaps as much to the public's inflated expectations of the presidency as to a president's actions. It is often as if their downslide in popularity would occur no matter what the president did. If this seems unfair, even cruel, this is nonetheless what happens to those lucky enough to win election to the highest office in the land.

And all this occurs despite our conventional wisdom that the *office makes the man*, "that the presidency with its built-in educational processes, its spacious view of the world, its command of talent, and above all its self-conscious historic role, does work its way on the man in the Oval Office," as James MacGregor Burns put it. If we concede that the office in part does make the man, we must admit also that time in office often unmakes the man.

10. What it Takes to Become President/May Not Be What Is Needed to Govern the Nation

To win a presidential election it takes ambition, ambiguity, luck, and masterful public relations strategies. To govern the nation requires all of these, but far more as well. It may well be that too much ambition, too much ambiguity and too heavy a reliance on phony public relations tricks actually undermine the integrity and legitimacy of the presidency.

Columnist David Broder offers an apt example: "People who win primaries may become good presidents—but 'it ain't necessarily so.' Organizing well is important in governing just as it is in winning primaries. But the Nixon years should teach us that good advance men do not necessarily make trustworthy White House aides. Establishing a government is a little more complicated than having the motorcade run on time."

Likewise, ambition (in very heavy doses) is essential for a presidential candidate, but too much hunger for the office or for "success-at-any-price" is a danger to be avoided. He must be bold and energetic, but carried too far this can make him cold and frenetic. To win the presidency requires a single-mindedness of purpose, and yet we want our presidents to be well-rounded, to have a sense of humor, to be able to take a joke, to have hobbies and interests outside the realm of politics—in short, to have a sense of proportion.

Another aspect of this paradox can be seen in the way candidates take ambiguous positions on issues in order to increase their appeal to the large bulk of centrist and independent voters. Not only does such equivocation discourage rational choices by the voters, but it also may alienate people who later learn, after the candidate has won, that his views and policies are otherwise. LBJ's "We will not send American boys to fight the war that Asian boys should be fighting," and Richard Nixon's "open presidency" pledges come readily to mind. Their pre-presidential centrist stands were later violated or ignored.

Political scientist Samuel Huntington calls attention to yet another way this paradox works. To be a winning candidate, he notes, the would-be president must put together an *electoral coalition* involving a majority of voters appropriately distributed across the country. To do this he must appeal to all regions and interest groups and cultivate the appearance of honesty, sincerity and experience. But once elected, the electoral coalition has served its purpose and a *governing coalition* is the order of the day. This all may sound rather elitist, but presidential advisor Huntington insists that this is what has to be:

> The day after his election the size of his majority is almost—if not entirely—irrelevant to his ability to govern the country. What counts then is his ability to mobilize support from the leaders of the key institutions in society and government. He has to constitute a broad governing coalition of strategically located supporters who can furnish him with the information, talent, expertise, manpower, publicity, arguments, and political support which he needs to develop a program, to embody it in legislation, and to see it effectively implemented. This coalition must include key people in Congress, the executive branch, and the private-sector "Establishment." The governing coalition need have little relation to the electoral coalition. The fact that the president as a candidate put together a successful electoral coalition does not insure that he will have a viable governing coalition.

Presidential candidate Adlai Stevenson had another way of saying it in 1956. He said that he had "learned that the hardest thing about any political campaign is how to win without proving that you are unworthy of winning." The process of becoming president is an extraordinarily taxing one that defies description. It involves, among other things, an unending salesmanship job on television.

Candidates plainly depend upon television to transform candidacy into incumbency. Research findings point out that candidates spend well over half their funds on broadcasting. Moreover, this is how the people "learn" about the candidates. Approximately two-thirds of the public report that television is the best way for them to follow candidates and about half of the American public acknowledge they got their best understanding of the candidates and issues from television coverage.

Thus, television is the key. But an aspirant has to travel to every state and hundreds of cities for at least a four-year period to capture the exposure and the local headlines before earning the visibility and stature of "serious candidate." For the most part, it becomes a grueling ordeal, as well as a major learning experience.

What it takes to *become* president may differ from what it takes *to be* president. It takes a near-megalomaniac who is also glib, dynamic, charming on television and relatively hazy on the issues. Yet we want our presidents to be well-rounded, not overly ambitious, careful in their reasoning and clear and specific in their communications. It may well be that our existing primary and convention system adds up to an effective testing or obstacle course for would-be presidents. Certainly they have to travel to all sections of the country, meet the people, deal with interest group elites and learn about the bracing issues of the day. But with the Johnson and Nixon experiences in our not-too-distant past, we have reason to reappraise whether our system of producing presidents is adequately reconciled with what is required to produce a president who is competent, fair-minded, and emotionally healthy.

Perhaps the ultimate paradox of the modern presidency is that it is always too powerful and yet it is always too inadequate. Always too powerful, because it is contrary to our ideals of a government by the people and because it must now possess the capacity to wage nuclear war (a capacity that unfortunately doesn't permit much in the way of checks and balances and deliberative, participatory government). Always too inadequate, because it seldom achieves our highest hopes for it, not to mention its own stated intentions.

The dilemma for the attentive public is that curbing the powers of a president who abuses the public trust will usually undermine the capacity of a fair-minded president to serve the public interest. In the 187 years since Washington took office, we have multiplied the requirements for presidential leadership and we have made it increasingly more difficult to lead. Certainly this is not the time for mindless retribution against the already fragile institution of the presidency.

Neither presidents nor the public should be relieved of their responsibilities of trying to fashion a more effective and fair-minded leadership system simply because these paradoxes are widely agreed upon. Nor is it enough to throw up our hands and say: "Well, no one makes a person run for that crazy job in the first place." These paradoxes are enduring ones. We shall have to select as our presidents persons who understand these contrary demands and who have a gift for the improvisation that these paradoxes demand. It is important for us to ask our chief public servants occasionally to forgo enhancing their own short-term political fortunes for a greater good of simplifying the paradoxes of the presidency.

While the presidency will doubtless remain one of our nation's best vehicles for creative policy change, it will also continue to be an embattled office, fraught with the cumulative weight of these paradoxes. We need urgently to probe the origins and assess the consequences of these paradoxes and to learn how presidents and public can better coexist with them. For it is apparent that these paradoxes serve to isolate and disconnect a president from the public. Like it or not, the growing importance of the presidency and our growing dependence on presidents seem to ensure that presidents will be less popular and increasingly the scapegoat when anything goes wrong.

Let us ask our presidents to give us their best, but let us not ask them to deliver more than the presidency—or any single institution—has to give.

3.2

Charles W. Ostrom and Dennis M. Simon

Managing Popular Support: The Presidential Dilemma

Charles W. Ostrom is professor of political science at Michigan State University, and Dennis M. Simon is assistant professor of political science at Southern Methodist University. In this essay they argue that, as compared to earlier presidents, recent presidents have had a difficult time maintaining their popularity, while at the same time, due to changing political conditions, public support has never been more essential to presidents. They consider what conditions and events are most decisive in influencing presidential popularity, and they examine the viability of various strategies that a president might adopt in order to maintain or enhance his standing with the public.

In recent years there has arisen a substantial new literature on the American presidency. This research includes empirical analyses of popular support for presidents (e.g., Hibbs, 1982a, 1982b; MacKuen, 1983), program initiation in the executive branch (e.g., Light, 1982), and the determinants of the president's legislative success (e.g., Edwards, 1980). Additionally, increasing attention has been directed to questions of how presidents can cope with the constraints imposed on the office. The results are several works which examine presidential leadership of public opinion (e.g., Edwards, 1983), approaches to bureaucratic control (e.g., Nathan, 1983), and strategies for handling the seemingly contradictory roles of the office (e.g., Greenstein, 1982). Finally, the new literature also consists of evaluative and normative analyses of the problems and failures experienced by modern or post-war presidents (e.g., Cronin, 1980; Hodgson, 1980).

This study has three objectives. The first is to present a coherent scheme for studying the relationships among presidential decision making, public support for the president, and the character of policy outcomes. Second, our discussion is designed to develop the proposition that there is a dynamic, reciprocal relationship between presidential decision making and public support for the president. Such a relationship implies that public support is both a result and a determinant of the president's choices. Our third objective is to examine the consequences of this reciprocal relationship. The discussion will suggest that this relationship influences both the character of public policy and the ability of the president to survive politically. As a result, the analysis also provides some initial evidence for evaluating claims regarding the inevitable plight and failures of modern presidents.

The Growing Prominence of Public Support

The relationship between public support and the power of the president is both substantial and intriguing. In *Presidential Power*, a widely acclaimed analysis published in 1960, Richard Neustadt observed that the power of a president is largely determined by his ability to persuade. This power, it was argued, cannot be equated with the image of unlimited authority conveyed in textbook descriptions of the office. It is not constant during the tenure of a single president or for different presidents. Rather, the power to persuade depends upon the president's ability to acquire and exploit three resources: constitutional and statutory prerogatives, a favorable reputation among Washington decision makers, and public support.

Although public support was only one of three, approximately co-equal determinants of presidential power in Neustadt's original characterization, the political landscape has changed in the years since Neustadt's study was originally published. Since that time the prominence of public support has been enhanced for several reasons. First of all, the president's prerogatives—the authority to act unilaterally—have been narrowed by a reassertive Congress (e.g., Sundquist, 1981). Second, the value of the political party, both as an organization useful to the president and as the tie that binds decision makers to presidential goals, has declined, further depleting the president's resources. Finally, because the public has grown increasingly distrustful of government and politicians, political experience has become more of a liability than an asset in electoral campaigns. As the election of both Jimmy Carter and Ronald Reagan suggest, the image of an outsider to Washington and the rhetoric of anti-government appear to be the more electorally-profitable strategies. Yet, such strategies also make it more difficult to cultivate a favorable reputation among those in Washington who will ultimately be the targets of the president's persuasive efforts. In sum, presidents now enter office with fewer prerogatives, derive less value from the political party, and are confronted by an increasingly skeptical Washington establishment. As a consequence, the president is forced to rely on popular support and this, in turn, has enhanced its prominence as a determinant of presidential power.

The growing relationship between presidential power and public opinion is not solely due to the structural changes in American government since the original publication of Neustadt's work. The behavior of modern presidents is now subjected to closer scrutiny as well. It is continuously monitored, analyzed, and broadcast to a public that has come to rely on television as *the* major source of information about politics and government. In effect, the president serves as the focal point of television news coverage. While television transmits information, polling organizations measure public reaction to this information, particularly via the presidential approval question. The approval or performance rating of the president has itself become a regular feature in newspaper headlines and network news broadcasts.[1] Together, television and public opinion polling have narrowed the gulf between the president and the public.

The Value of Popular Support

Although it is clear that the president's public standing has grown more newsworthy during the past thirty years, the significance of these performance evaluations remains subject to debate. For example, in his analysis of the modern presidency, Pious (1979) argues that factors such as the president's public standing exert, at best, a marginal impact on presidential power. Further, there are those who regard such performance evaluations with outright skepticism. Thus, Roll and Cantril (1972) have argued that "popularity ratings represent little more than an artifact of the polling technique created in response to journalistic interest, and they certainly are not meaningful for guidance at the presidential level." Essentially, such observations assert that aside from the journalistic curiosity that the polls stimulate, public evaluations of presidential performance have little political consequence. This implies that the potential significance of public support is tied to its value as a determinant of political outcomes and behaviors. If public support is unimportant in explaining outcomes, then, as Roll and Cantril suggest, presidents could be advised to ignore the polls and scholars encouraged to direct their attention elsewhere. However, such is not the case.

A variety of empirical research shows that public support exerts an impact on the following outcomes: (1) congressional elections (e.g., Tufte, 1978); (2) presidential elections (e.g., Boyd, 1972); (3) roll call support among members of Congress (e.g., Edwards, 1980); (4) presidential victories on congressional roll calls (e.g., Simon, 1981); (5) citizen assessments of congressional performance (e.g., Davidson, Kovenock, and O'Leary, 1966); (6) citizen confidence in the institution of the presidency (e.g., Dennis, 1975); and (7) citizen trust in government (e.g., Miller, Brudney, and Joftis, 1975). Although assessments of a president's performance are not the sole determinants of such attitudes or behaviors, it is clear that evaluations of the president's performance are instrumental to successful presidential decision making. This suggests that the pattern of public support over time will exercise a noteworthy influence on the fortunes of an administration.

Trends in Popular Support

The enhanced status of presidential popularity has been marked by a strong downward trend in monthly support.[2] Table 1 shows that there are substantial differences in the mean level of public support for each president from 1953–1980. Whereas both Eisenhower and Kennedy enjoyed popularity levels in excess of 65%, subsequent presidents have not fared as well. In fact, when one looks at the overall picture, there is a marked downward trend in average approval from term to term during the 1953–1980 period. Table 1 also suggests that there have been two major eras in public support for the president. From 1953 to 1963 the average level of popular support was in excess of 65% and the standard deviation was very small. In fact during this eleven year period, a president's popularity dipped below 50% only once. From 1964 to 1980 the picture is much different. The average level of public support is barely 50%. Thus, subsequent presidents have inherited the problems of their predecessors and faced the new problems that developed with a reduced amount of their most apparent resource—public support.

Table 1

TERM-BY-TERM APPROVAL

Presidential Term	Mean APP	Std. Dev. APP	High	Low
Eisenhower	65.2%	7.0	79%	49%
Kennedy	70.3%	7.2	83%	57%
Johnson	55.6%	13.4	80%	35%
Nixon	50.8%	12.1	68%	24%
Ford	47.5%	6.5	71%	37%
Carter	46.3%	12.4	75%	21%
1953–1963	66.5%	7.4	83%	49%
1964–1980	50.7%	12.4	80%	21%
1953–1980	56.3%	12.7	83%	21%

Not only has the average level of public support for the president deteriorated over time, but low levels of support appear to imprison the president. To identify low levels of support, we have divided the president's approval ratings into three popularity zones.[3] Table 2 provides a comparison of month to month changes during the 1953-1980 period. An examination of the diagonal entries suggests that there is a great deal of stability. When a president is in Zone 1 at time t, the probability of remaining there at time t + 1 is .92; for Zone 2, this probability is .72; and for Zone 3, this probability is .89. Of particular interest is the fact that, once in Zone 2, the president has an equal, though small, probability of moving to either Zone 1 or Zone 3. However, once a president enters Zone 3 there is very little chance of getting out. Thus, not only is there a trend in popular support, but once a president's popularity enters a lower zone, there is a very small probability of moving back into the higher zone. This presidential track record clearly support Greenstein's (1982) observation that "the American Presidency has become conspicuously problematic, devouring its incumbents with appalling regularity." Given these trends and the accompanying conclusion that American presidents are being devoured, it is important to determine whether (1) the decline in support is inevitable and (2) whether, once in popularity Zone 3, the president is trapped.

Table 2

MONTH-TO-MONTH CHANGES IN POPULARITY ZONES

		Time T + 1		
		Zone 1	Zone 2	Zone 3
Time T	Zone 1	181 (.92)	15 (.08)	0 (.00)
	Zone 2	10 (.14)	52 (.72)	10 (.14)
	Zone 3	1 (.02)	6 (.09)	55 (.89)

Note: Row percentages in parentheses

The Determinants of Popular Support

To address the issues of inevitability and impossibility, it is necessary to answer three questions: (1) what *standards* are employed to evaluate presidential perform- ance; (2) what is the relative importance of these standards; and (3) what specific outcomes and conditions are associated with these standards.

Although the recent literature that offers comprehensive explanations of popu- lar support (e.g., Kernell, 1978; Hibbes, 1982a, 1982b; MacKuen, 1983) has ad- dressed many of these questions, the reliability and validity of the answers must be questioned because the literature has had a difficult time with the Eisenhower administration. Either the models cannot explain his consistently high levels of popularity (e.g., Kernell, 1978) or his tenure in office has been omitted from the analysis (e.g., Hibbs, 1982a, 1982b; MacKuen, 1983). The strategy of omission presents a number of problems for the conventional wisdom. First, Eisenhower was the last president to serve two complete terms and emerge with his public standing intact; in short, he was the quintessential popularity manager. Second, he faced a war, a scandal, and a significant economic downturn without suffering the staggering declines in popularity that have beset subsequent presidents. Just as surely as we must account for the future, we must be able to account for the past.

The first question focuses on the standards or dimensions of presidential evaluation. Two basic types of standards are discussed in the literature. First, there is general agreement that the public holds the president responsible for maintaining a reasonable quality of life (Kernell, 1978; Hibbs, 1982a, 1982b). Any deterioration is viewed as the result of presidential incompetence. The president, from this point of view, must strive to maintain peace, prosperity, and domestic tranquility. Second, both MacKuen (1983) and Brody (1983) suggest that there is an emotional and dramatic component to presidential evaluations. From this per- spective, the president must act in a dramatic fashion to arouse the public and thereby retain their esteem. This implies that the public judges the president "by his ability to evoke the proper symbolic responses when he acts." Because the dramatic feature of "events on the public stage have a substantial impact on popularity" (MacKuen, 1983), each president must engage in "high politics" and cultivate the image of an astute manager of crises and events.

Our second question pertains to the relative importance of the evaluative standards over time. The key issue is whether the public evaluates each president according to the same standards. The overwhelming consensus is that to some extent they do. The research provides an answer in the sense that the models use the same sets of factors to account for the rise and fall in presidential approval. However, existing models also include term-specific factors to account for "con- stant" differences between administrations. For some reason, there is a different equilibrium level for each president. In addition, some empirical work has estimated different coefficients for each president (e.g., Kernell, 1978; MacKuen, 1983).

One possible explanation for the term-to-term differences may be the result of changes in the structure of public priorities over time. To explore this possibility, we have relied on the responses to the following Gallup question: "What do you think is the most important problem facing the country today?" On 79 occasions between 1953 and 1980, this item was administered to national samples. These responses can be employed to measure the relative salience or importance that the public attaches to quality of life concerns such as war, general foreign affairs, social unrest, economic malaise, and other domestic problems. To accomplish this task, we have grouped all responses to the most important problem question into four general categories. ECOMOST, FORMOST, SOCMOST, and VIETMOST represent the proportions of the public who identified the economy, foreign affairs, social unrest, and the Vietnam War as the most important problem in a given poll.

Table 3

MOST IMPORTANT PROBLEM BY POPULARITY ZONE			
Problem	Zone 1	Zone 2	Zone 3
ECOMOST	20%	42%	45%
FORMOST	39%	10%	5%
SOCMOST	16%	19%	14%
VIETMOST	7%	18%	14%

Table 3 presents the average value of each of these proportions for each popularity zone. Perhaps the most interesting finding is that the president is most likely to be in Zone 1 when foreign policy is the most important problem. Our foreign policy category is defined to include those problems in which the themes of preserving the peace and harmonious international relations are dominant. The most frequently cited examples are the threat of war or nuclear war, relations with the Soviet Union and China, resisting communist expansion as well as more specific concerns relating to Berlin and Cuba. The association of foreign policy and Zone 1 stems from the consensual nature of these issues. That is, they resemble valence issues (Stokes, 1966; Page, 1978) in the sense that underlying preferences are nonideological and focus upon conditions that are positively valued by the public. Most importantly, because the idea of an external threat is voiced, a we/they point of view prevails and reinforces the consensus. When such issues of dissensus as the economy, social unrest, and war are dominant, a president will not remain in Zone 1. Insofar as these issues are concerned, there is very little difference between Zones 2 and 3. Thus the increased importance of the issues of dissensus coupled with the attendant outcomes has led to an acceleration of the decline. To some extent, the relative salience of the problems in the most important category are responsible for the downward trend. These results and examples lead to the general conclusion that the impact of any outcome on popular support is *jointly dependent* upon the *quality* of an outcome and the *perceived salience* of the performance dimension to which the outcome pertains.

The third question focuses upon the specific determinants of popular support. Despite much disagreement about measurement and the precise specification of the approval equation, the research is in general agreement on two points. First, the public standing of the president is experiential and not determined by some mechanistic set of predispositions (e.g., time into the term). Second, there is a growing consensus that the following factors will exert an impact on public support: the economy (unemployment and inflation), war (casualties, troops deployed), scandal (severity and duration), and presidential events (international crises, diplomatic initiatives, and domestic disruptions).

Table 4 presents a comparison of the key determinants of public support and the three presidential popularity zones. These data clearly show each zone is associated with a different configuration of outcomes. On one hand, Zone 1 is marked by moderate levels of unemployment and relatively low levels of inflation, troops in Vietnam, servicemen killed in Vietnam, and scandal-months. On the other hand, Zone 3 is marked by relatively low levels of unemployment and relatively high levels of inflation, killed in Vietnam, and scandal-months. Thus, rather distinct quality of life profiles accompany the movement from Zone 1 to Zone 3. An examination of the set of presidential rally-type events reveals that there is only a moderate relationship between the frequency of the events and the popularity zones.[4]

Table 4

AVERAGE MONTHLY VALUES OF EXPLANATORY VARIABLES BY POPULARITY ZONE

Variable	Zone 1	Zone 2	Zone 3
Economic			
Unemployment	5.1%	5.8%	4.7%
Inflation	2.5%	5.3%	8.2%
Vietnam War			
US Troops	57	149	129
US Killed	75	182	260
Scandal-Months*	.05	.15	.26
Rally Events (per month)			
Foreign	.13	.11	.15
Domestic	.06	.07	.11
Overall	.19	.18	.26

*Scandals include: Sherman Adams (2/58–12/58), Walter Jenkins (10/64), Watergate (3/73–8/74), Bert Lance (7/77–1/78), Peter Bourne (8/78), Billy Carter (7/80).

The results presented in Tables 3 and 4 suggest that the decline in the time path of public support both between and within presidential terms is *not* governed by some repeatable and unalterable dynamic. Instead, it has an experiential base. The president is evaluated on the basis of the quality of life and events during his term in office. This implies that, in principle, presidents can formulate successful strategies for avoiding or escaping from Zone 3.

Presidential Decision Making

For the president seeking to avoid a decline or to move out of Zone 3, there are essentially three available courses of action. First, he can try to alter the standards used to judge his performance. This approach is likely to be difficult because bases of evaluation have remained fairly constant throughout the past thirty years. An examination of Gallup's compilation of the most important problem reveals that the issues of peace, prosperity, and domestic tranquility have dominated the public's agenda for each of the past thirty years. Indeed, as we have argued elsewhere (Ostrom and Simon, 1983a), the three major problems constitute a set of fundamental demands upon which presidential performance is to be judged. Therefore, as a management strategy this approach is not likely to be successful.

Second, the results in Table 3 have important implications for managing popular support: a president can try to change the salience of the evaluative dimensions. This is potentially effective because the relationship between public support and a given performance dimension is relative; for example, the impact of the economy on public support will depend not only on the quality of economic outcomes but also upon the perceived importance of competing problems such as international or domestic instability (Ostrom and Simon, 1983a). The fact that public concern focused on consensual issues throughout the 1950s explains why the recession of 1958 cost Eisenhower significantly fewer approval points than the penalty imposed on Nixon during the early 1970s when public priorities were more concentrated on the economy. Similarly, the value of the relatively prosperous economy of 1965-67 to Johnson was negated as public attention increasingly focused on the Vietnam War. Perhaps the most overt use of this strategy occurred when Nixon directed the public's concern away from the Vietnam War to social problems. Although he was not totally successful, the war exacted a smaller toll on Nixon's public standing and allowed him to escape the fate experienced by Johnson (Ostrom and Simon, 1983a). Even though altering the salience of performance criteria is possible, it involves diverting the public's attention to some other problem that is more pressing. Unless the new problem is consensual in nature or can be solved in short order, the shift in salience is likely to be unsuccessful in raising popular support.

The final, and most accessible, strategy option available to the president is to take actions that will bring about an acceptable quality of life or focus attention on the political stage. There are two considerations that will have an impact on the president's choice of strategy in this context. First, he will be concerned with the *probability of success*. Given the persistence of the problems associated with the quality of life concerns, it seems clear that innovative, comprehensive, and coordinated action will be required. According to Pious (1979), for example, innovation may assume one of two forms. It may substantially expand the scope of government authority, creating new agencies, missions, and operating procedures. Innovation may also operate in the opposite direction by retracting government authority through retrenchment and program dissolution. Both forms of innovation share the commonality of significantly altering the status quo. A comprehensive policy is oriented toward the long run, addresses all dimensions of a problem, and employs a variety of techniques in an effort to achieve an enduring solution. Finally, a coordinated policy is one that overcomes the jurisdictional rivalries inherent in the congressional committee system and the administrative conflicts in the executive branch. The problem of achieving an innovative, comprehensive, and coordinated policy depends upon a president's ability to influence other relevant actors. As such, success is not guaranteed.

The probability of success associated with acting on the political stage is substantially greater. All a president needs to do is to find an appropriate stage; he can amplify a crisis, give a speech, or go on a trip. The probability of success is enhanced because the president is able to act unilaterally. In this way, a president, through his command role, can take actions that have no direct consequences for the public and be evaluated positively. All that is required is an independent presidential action and the publicity that it generates. As such, success is highly likely.

The second consideration is the *nature of the benefits* to be derived from a given strategy. If a president is able to bring about the intended changes in the quality of life, the benefits are likely to be substantial. If an improved quality of life persists, the political benefits will also endure. This positive impact will be enhanced over time because of the retrospective evaluations of the president's performance (e.g., Hibbs, 1982b; Ostrom and Simon, 1982a). A president's popular support is affected by both the current and past conditions.

Actions on the stage of high politics, however, are likely to generate immediate though transitory benefits. Because such behavior has a consistent, albeit short-lived, impact on presidential popularity, it becomes a quick fix for a president looking to enhance his standing with the public.

Therefore, attempts to manage public support can take one of two forms: improve the quality of life or engage in some form of political drama. The probability of success and the benefits vary considerably. The presidential decision calculus involves choosing between two strategies. One strategy, directly attacking the quality of life problem, has a lower probability of success and a higher potential pay-off. The other strategy, acting on the political stage, has a higher probability of success and a lower potential pay-off. It would appear that, from an expected value point of view, the benefits that follow from a quality of life strategy will offset the lower probability of success and make it the obvious presidential choice. However, this characterization of a presidential management calculus overlooks one very important factor—the importance of public support.

As Neustadt (1960) notes, any chance of bringing about desired outcomes lies in maintaining a high level of public support.

> A President's prestige . . . may not decide the outcome in a given case but can affect the likelihoods in every case and therefore is strategically important to his power. If he cares about his prospects for effectiveness in government, he need be no less mindful of the one than the other.

Declining approval, therefore, translates into a declining probability of success for subsequent presidential decisions and actions. As such, the public standing of the president will exert an impact on which policy choices are made. This, in turn, implies that presidential support and presidential policy making will be *reciprocally* related. On one hand, presidential policy making will influence public support to the extent that the choices of the president (a) influence the outcomes for which the president is held responsible or (b) are dramatic enough to trigger the rally effect. On the other hand, because public support determines the president's ability to influence other actors and thus the probability that a given initiative will be successful, public support will determine both the range and feasibility of the choices available to the president. All in all, this reciprocal relationship creates a decidedly political context for presidential government.

We have shown (Ostrom and Simon, 1983b) that this reciprocal relationship can generate a vicious circle that undermines successful policy making. For example, the relative influence of Congress and the president on the content of public policy will vary as approval moves from Zone 1 to Zone 3. It is likely, therefore, that policy making will grow more incremental and uncoordinated as approval declines. This, in turn, reduces the prospect that durable solutions for existing problems will be constructed and implemented. Consequently, popular support will continue to decline. This vicious circle not only undermines the effectiveness of the president as a policy maker but also threatens his ability to survive politically.

This reciprocal relationship and the vicious circle that it produces are at least partially responsible for the observation in recent scholarship on the presidency that the office has been in a period of crisis since the late 1960s. It is a crisis whose consequences include uncoordinated policy making, institutional deadlock, non-decisions, and increasing reliance on dramatic political events (e.g., Hodgson, 1980; Light, 1982). It is not coincidental that recognition of these problems by presidential scholars and the development of vicious circles in public support have arisen at roughly the same time.

Conclusion

To avoid such vicious circles, a president can choose between two basic strategy-types: long-term (improve quality of life) or short-term (engage in high politics). Since the public imposes a specific form of accountability on the president—it hinges on results—a long-term approach, which may provide the cure, is likely to be preferred. However, because a long-term approach can generate the vicious circles, a short-term approach, which provides an immediate increase in popular support, may be utilized once approval begins to decline.

A president faces a dilemma concerning his choice of a long-term or short-term approach. The policy consequences of choosing one strategy over the other are enormous. What we have referred to as the long-term approach is likely to direct the president's actions and energies toward the solution of the principal problems of the day, whereas the short-term approach emphasizes resource maintenance as an end in itself. However, as approval declines, any policies or programs directed at quality of life concerns are not likely to yield comprehensive and innovative solutions to problems but instead are likely to be incremental modifications of existing programs or piecemeal attempts to solve broad-based problems. This, in turn, enhances the attractivenss of the short-term approach. However, because its impact is short-lived, a president must continue to operate on the stage of high politics or he must focus on enduring solutions to social problems.

To understand the current plight of presidential government, it is important to recognize the underlying structure of the president's resource dilemma. The long-term strategy of trying to improve quality of life outcomes has a very high potential pay-off and a low probability of success. In addition, it takes time for the innovations to provide an improvement in the quality of life. As time passes, a president's approval will decline because not only are current outcomes unacceptable but the public also exacts a price for the past (e.g., Hibbs, 1982b). The short-term strategy of engaging in political drama has a high probability of success and a transitory political pay-off. By itself it can do little but provide bumps and wiggles on the downward course of approval. Because the president is held accountable for outcomes, the resource reservoir will become increasingly shallow if the fundamental problems are not solved. To be sure, political drama can be used to provide occasional bursts of support. However, such actions are credible only if used infrequently and to create a *window of opportunity* for the passage of policies designed to have a long-term impact. Therein lies the dilemma. There are times when a president must adopt a pure short-term or resource enhancement strategy to get out of Zone 3. At other times explicit consideration must be given to the use of a mixed strategy. Unless a president is able to develop a coherent mix of long- and short-term strategies, he is sure to meet with electoral retribution and become another in the line of one-term presidents.

The prospects for solving the current crisis are not encouraging. What is required is a comprehensive strategy for avoiding the problems associated with Zone 3. There are several premises upon which such a strategy must be constructed. First, the continuous scrutiny and evaluation of presidential performance is an integral part of modern presidential government. Second, public support is a key presidential resource. Its impact is felt throughout the term. Third, the protection of this resource must be recognized as a critical *instrumental goal* in the president's strategic calculations; because of its impact, concern with public support must be continuous. Fourth, public support is based upon experience; it depends upon a set of outcomes and actions for which the president is held responsible. Although difficult, it is possible for a president to avoid the vicious circle; he will remain in Zone 1 or 2 only if he is able to fashion his choices in a manner that influences the standards upon which he is judged, the relative salience of these performance dimensions, and the outcomes connected to those standards.

Notes

1. For example, during Reagan's first 28 months in office, his general job performance has been evaluated 44 times by Gallup, 24 times by Harris, and 12 times by CBS/*New York Times* (*Public Opinion*, April/May, 1983).

2. The source of the public opinion data employed in this analysis is the Gallup poll. See Ostrom and Simon (1983a) for a discussion of how the monthly measure of popular support was constructed.

3. In defining these three zones, the 50% approval level is emphasized because it represents the point at which the president either gains or loses majority support in the public. Thus, we have stipulated that the president is in Zone 1 whenever his popularity is over 55%, in Zone 2 whenever his popularity is between 45% and 55%, and in Zone 3 whenever his popularity is below 45%. Although arbitrary, these categories do provide a meaningful categorization of the president's power situation. A president whose popularity is greater than 55% is clearly a majority president. Similarly, an approval level below 45% is symptomatic of a minority president. Finally, a president whose popularity hovers around 50% is on the verge of becoming a minority president. Furthermore, it is an open question as to whether his support will decline to even lower levels.

4. In this exercise, we have relied upon the events listed in Table 1 of MacKuen (1983). Although the selection of these events and the assessment of their impact on public support remains a subject of debate (see, for example, Edwards, 1983), MacKuen's list is the most comprehensive published to date. We next examined this list and selected those events that directly involved the president. That is, we identified those events that would not have occurred without an intentional action on the part of the president. To this list we have added similar events for the Eisenhower and Kennedy years. Finally, we have included four additional events that were inexplicably out of the MacKuen collection (1974 trip to USSR, 1975 trip to China, Sadat/Begin signing peace agreement, and the 1980 proposal to reinstitute draft registration). This augmented set of events was then partitioned into foreign and domestic subsets.

References

Boyd, Richard. 1972. "Popular Control of Public Policy," *The American Political Science Review* (June): 429-449.

Brody, Richard A. 1983. "That Special Moment: The Public Response to International Crises," paper presented for delivery at the annual meeting of the Western Political Science Association, Seattle.

Cronin, Thomas E. 1980. *The State of the Presidency,* 2nd edition (Boston: Little, Brown).

Davidson, Roger H., David M. Kovenock, and Michael K. O'Leary. 1966. *Congress in Crisis* (Belmont, CA: Wadsworth).

Dennis, Jack. 1975. "Dimensions of Public Support for the Presidency," paper prepared for delivery at the annual meeting of the Midwest Political Science Association, Chicago.

Edwards, George C., III. 1980. *Presidential Influence in Congress* (San Francisco: Freeman).

Edwards, George C., III. 1983. *The Public Presidency* (New York: St. Martin's).

Fiorina, Morris P. 1977. *Congress: Keystone of the Washington Establishment* (New Haven: Yale).

Greenstein, Fred I. 1982. *The Hidden Hand Presidency* (New York: Basic Books).

Hibbs, Douglas A., Jr. 1982a. "On the Demand for Economic Outcomes," *Journal of Politics* (May): 426-462.

Hibbs, Douglas A., Jr. 1982b. "The Dynamics of Political Support for American Presidents among Occupational and Partisan Groups," *The American Journal of Political Science* (May): 312-323.

Hodgson, Godfrey. 1980. *All Things to All Men* (New York: Simon and Schuster).

Kernell, Samuel. 1978. "Explaining Presidential Popularity," *The American Political Science Review* (June): 506-522.

Light, Paul C. 1972. *The President's Agenda* (Baltimore: Johns Hopkins).

MacKuen, Michael. 1983. "Political Drama, Economic Conditions, and the Dynamics of Presidential Popularity," *The American Journal of Political Science* (May): 165-192.

Miller, Arthur H., Jeffrey Brudney, and Peter Joftis. 1975. "Presidential Crises and Political Support," paper prepared for delivery at the annual meeting of the Midwest Political Science Association, Chicago.

Nathan, Richard P. 1983. *The Administrative Presidency* (New York: Wiley).

Neustadt, Richard. 1960. *Presidential Power* (New York: Wiley).

Ostrom, Charles W., Jr., and Brian L. Job. 1982. "The President and the Political Use of Force," paper prepared for delivery at the annual meeting of the American Political Science Association, Denver.

Ostrom, Charles W., and Dennis M. Simon. 1983a. "Promise and Performance: A Dynamic Model of Presidential Popularity," unpublished ms.

Ostrom, Charles W., and Dennis M. Simon. 1983b. "Managing Popular Support: The Presidential Dilemma," paper prepared for delivery at the annual meeting of the American Political Science Association, Chicago.

Page, Benjamin I. 1978. *Choices and Echoes in Presidential Elections* (Chicago: University of Chicago Press).

Pious, Richard. 1979. *The American Presidency* (New York: Basic Books).

Rohde, David W., and Dennis M. Simon. 1983. "Presidential Vetoes and the Congressional Response," paper prepared for delivery at the annual meeting of the American Political Science Association, Chicago.

Simon, Dennis M. 1981. *Presidential Management of Public Support,* unpublished Ph.D. dissertation, Michigan State University.

Stokes, David E. 1966. "Spatial Models of Party Competitions" in Angus Campbell, et al, *Elections and the Political Order* (New York: Wiley).

Sundquist, James L. 1981. *The Decline and Resurgence of Congress* (Washington, DC: Brookings).

Tufte, Edward. 1978. *Political Control of the Economy* (Princeton: Princeton University Press).

 Chapter Four

The President and Congress

Much of what a president wants to accomplish must be done in partnership with the legislative branch. Establishing and maintaining this partnership is, as all our presidents have discovered, no easy task. Indeed, the constitutional structure fashioned by our Founding Fathers virtually guaranteed that it would be otherwise. Each branch is organically distinct from the other; each is chosen by and responsive to different constituencies; and each possesses power that can be used to frustrate the will of the other. There have, of course, been occasions in this century when the relationship between the president and Congress evinced a high degree of cooperation—the early years of the Wilson, Franklin Roosevelt and Johnson presidencies—but these are the exceptions to the more normal pattern of struggle.

As James Sundquist points out in the first selection, scholars have long viewed political parties as an indispensable device for muting this struggle. And indeed, for the greater part of our history control of both branches by one party was the rule rather than the exception. In the last thirty-six years, however, our elections most of the time have given us divided government, thereby heightening the conflict between the legislative and executive branches. Arguing that this state of affairs has imperiled the government's ability to address domestic and foreign policy issues in a timely and coherent manner, he considers what steps might be taken to correct the problem.

Sundquist is not alone in voicing concerns about divided government. On the contrary, in 1987 the Committee on the Constitutional System, composed of eminent scholars (including Sundquist) and practitioners of politics, called for major changes that would significantly curb the separation of powers principle in our Constitution.[1] In the second selection, James Q. Wilson questions the wisdom of such proposals. Not only does he reject the contention that unresolved domestic and foreign policy problems are primarily attributable to separation of powers, but he further maintains that the rationale for this principle is as compelling today as it was two hundred years ago.

Notes

1. See Committee on the Constitutional System, *A Bicentennial Analysis of the American Political Structure* (Committee on the Constitutional System, 1987).

James L. Sundquist

Needed: A Political Theory for the New Era of Coalition Government in the United States

James L. Sundquist is senior fellow emeritus at the Brookings Institution and author of a half dozen books on American politics and government. Constitutional Reform and Effective Government *(1987) is his latest. Noting that parties have long been viewed as an indispensable mechanism for unifying the separated branches of the federal government, thereby providing coherence to the policymaking process, Sundquist argues that the prevalence of divided government in the last thirty-six years has imperiled the nation's ability to address critical domestic and foreign policy issues. In light of this development, he considers what corrective measures might be taken.*

On 8 November 1988, when the American voters decreed that Republican George Bush would succeed Ronald Reagan in the White House but the opposition Democratic Party would control both houses of the Congress, it was the sixth time in the last nine presidential elections that the electorate chose to split the government between the parties. As in 1988, so in the earlier elections of 1956, 1968, 1972, 1980, and 1984, the people placed their faith in Republican presidential leadership but voted to retain Democratic majorities in the House of Representatives and in the first three of those elections (as well as in 1988), Democratic majorities in the Senate also.

This is something new in American politics. When Dwight D. Eisenhower took his second oath of office in 1957, he was the first chief executive in seventy-two years—since Grover Cleveland in 1885—to confront on Inauguration Day a Congress of which even one house was controlled by the opposition party. Sometimes the opposition would win majorities in the House or the Senate, or both, at the midterm election, but even such occasions were relatively rare. In the fifty-eight years from 1897 through 1954, the country experienced divided government during only eight years—all in the last half of a presidential term—or 14 percent of the time. Yet in the thirty-six years from 1955 through 1990, the government will have been divided between the parties for twenty-four years—exactly two-thirds of that period.

A generation ago, then, the country passed from a long era of party government, when either the Republican or the Democratic Party controlled both the

Reprinted with permission from *Political Science Quarterly* 103 (Winter 1988-89).

presidency and the Congress almost all of the time, to an era when the government was divided between the parties most of the time. Under these circumstances, the United States has its own unique version of coalition government—not a coalition voluntarily entered into by the parties but one forced upon them by the accidents of the electoral process.

It is the argument of this article that the advent of the new era has rendered obsolete much of the theory developed by political scientists, from the day of Woodrow Wilson to the 1950s, to explain how the United States government can and should work. That theory identified the political party as the indispensable instrument that brought cohesion and unity, and hence effectiveness, to the government as a whole by linking the executive and legislative branches in a bond of common interest. And, as a corollary, the party made it possible for the president to succeed in his indispensable role as leader and energizer of the governmental process; it accomplished that end because the congressional majorities, while they would not accept the president's leadership by virtue of his constitutional position as chief executive—institutional rivalry would bar that—would accept it in his alternate capacity as head of the political party to which the majorities adhered.

The generations of political scientists who expounded this theory paid little attention to how the government would and should function when the president and the Senate and House majorities were not all of the same party. They could in good conscience disregard that question because intervals of divided government in their experience had been infrequent and short-lived. Whenever the midterm election brought a division of the government, anyone concerned about that could take a deep breath and wait confidently for the next presidential election to put the system back into its proper alignment. As late as 1952 it had always done so in the memory of everybody writing on the subject. But since 1956, that has no longer been a certainty. It has not even been the probability. And that represents a momentous change in the American governmental system, for institutional processes and relationships are profoundly altered when the unifying bond of party disappears.

This article briefly reviews the antiparty doctrine that the Framers wrote into the Constitution but promptly abandoned. Then it presents the theory of party government and presidential leadership as it was explicated by authoritative and influential political scientists in the era that ended in the mid-1950s, and finally discusses the implications of the obsolescence of that theory since the transformation of the governmental system during the past three decades.

The Antiparty Theory and Its Abandonment

Party government was, of course, not the intent of the Framers who met in Philadelphia in 1787. Quite the opposite. Their views—which are well known and need not be set forth at length here—were, in a word, antiparty. The word "party" appears only rarely in James Madison's account of the proceedings of the 1787 convention. The preferred terms were "faction" and "cabal," and they were used only for purposes of condemnation. No more powerful diatribe against political parties has ever been penned than *The Federalist*, particularly Madison's No. 10, in which he denounced "the violence of faction" as "this dangerous vice" that introduces "the instability, injustice, and confusion" that have "been the mortal diseases under which popular governments have everywhere perished." If a majority party can win the whole of governmental power ·Madison reasoned, what is to prevent it from oppressing the minority? As Madison saw it, the natural party division would be between "those who hold and those who are without property," between "those who are creditors, and those who are debtors." He feared that a majority party made up of the propertyless would exhibit "a rage for paper money, for an abolition of debts, for an equal division of property."

In *The Federalist*, particularly in No. 10 but also in Nos. 47, 48 and 62, Madison saw the whole constitutional design as a defense against the danger that any "interested and overbearing majority" or "sinister combinations" could gain control of the entire government. Raising decisions to the national level would place them in the hands of men who had risen above the factionalism of the states, and factions would be more difficult to organize on a national scale. The separation of powers among the branches—and within the legislature between two bodies—would further guard against the threat that majority rule might lead to "tyranny" and "oppression." And so would the method devised for selecting the president. Rejecting the two obvious ways of making that choice—either election by the people directly or election by the Congress—the Framers conceived that peculiar institution, the electoral college, as a nonpartisan, antiparty apparatus, a kind of search committee, not unlike those that corporations and universities and city councils set up nowadays to select a new executive. The college would be made up of men mostly unknown to each other, who would not meet as a body, who would not even be in communication across state lines. As Madison put it at the Convention, "there would be little opportunity for cabal, or corruption.[1]

George Washington, who presided over both the convention and the newly-formed government, tried to lead in the nonpartisan manner that the Constitution contemplated. But before the end of his first term, he witnessed the rise of factionalism not only in the Congress but also within his own cabinet. Washington expressed his dismay in his celebrated farewell address in which—echoing *Federalist* No. 10—he warned his countrymen "in the most solemn manner against the baneful effects of the spirit of party generally." That spirit, the "worst enemy" of democratic governments everywhere, said Washington, serves to "distract the public councils . . . enfeeble the public administration . . . agitates the community with ill founded jealousies and false alarms . . . foments occasional riots and insurrection . . . opens the door to foreign influence and corruption," can lead to "frightful despotism," and all the rest.[2] And Washington's successor, John Adams, concurred in his inaugural address that the "spirit of party" is one of the "natural enemies" of the Constitution.[3]

But by the end of his term, the spirit of party was flourishing. In the election of 1800, a fledgling two-party system—reflecting to a degree the cleavages between the propertied and the landless, between creditors and debtors, which Madison had identified as fundamental—was in operation, with two slates of candidates running nationally. The electoral college was hardly formed when it ceased to be the intended body of nonpartisan statesmen with complete discretion and independent judgment and became what it has since remained—a body of faceless partisans that merely registers the choice of the voters between or among national party candidates. "The election of a President of the United States is no longer that process which the Constitution contemplated," one of the Framers, Rufus King, told the Senate in 1816.[4] In his retirement years, James Madison himself acknowledged that parties are "a natural offspring of Freedom."[5] By that time of course, Madison had been elected and reelected president as a party nominee.

The Theory of Party Government and Presidential Leadership

Madison did not expound a new theory to supplant the one that he had been so instrumental in embedding in the Constitution. But without benefit of much explicit doctrine, the nation's political leaders developed in practice the system of party government—as distinct from nonpartisan government—that settled into place in the Jacksonian era and prevailed throughout the next century and a quarter. In each presidential election two national parties sought exactly what the Madisonian theory written into the Constitution was supposed to forestall: the capture of all three of the policy-making elements of the government—the presidency, Senate and House—by the same faction or party, so that the party could carry out its program.

No major party has ever said, "We want only the presidency," or only the Senate or the House. They have always said, "give us *total* responsibility." Since early in the nineteenth century, they have presented their programs formally in official party platforms. Asking for total power in the two elected branches, they have been eager to accept the total responsibility and accountability that would accompany it.

That was the theory of party government; and not only the politicians, but the people accepted it. The parties lined up naturally on opposite sides of whatever were the great issues of the day—creating a national bank, opening the West with turnpikes and railroads and canals financed by the national government, prohibiting slavery in the western territories, raising or lowering tariffs, mobilizing the national government to help the victims of the Great Depression, and so on. The people listened to the arguments of the two parties and made their choices. And when they did, the party they elected had a full opportunity to carry out its mandate, because when the voters chose a president each four years they normally entrusted control of the Congress to the president's party, thus making it fully responsible. From Andrew Jackson's time until the second election of Dwight Eisenhower in 1956, only four presidents—Zachary Taylor elected in 1848, Rutherford B. Hayes in 1876, James A. Garfield in 1880, and Grover Cleveland in 1884—had to confront immediately upon inauguration either a House of Representatives or a Senate organized by the opposition. In the nineteenth century these results may have been largely an artifact of the election process itself. The parties printed separate ballots listing their slates, and the voter selected the ballot of the party he preferred, marked it, and dropped it in the box. Yet after the government-printed, secret ballot came into universal use early in this century, straight-ticket voting and the resultant single-party control of the government continued to prevail. The voters gave the Republican Party responsibility for the entire government in the 1900s, again in the 1920s, and finally in 1952; and they chose the Democratic Party in the 1910s, 1930s, and 1940s. No president in the first half of this century ever had to suffer divided government upon taking office, and few had the problem even after the normal setback to the president's party in the midterm election.

As soon as political science emerged as a scholarly discipline, its adherents began to pronounce and elaborate the theoretical foundation of the system of party government that was in being. Parties were not only natural, since people were bound to organize to advance their differing notions as to the goals and programs of government, but the scholars concluded that they were useful and necessary too. Among their uses was the one that is the concern of this paper: their utility in unifying a government of dispersed powers and thereby making it effective.

In his review of the literature on political parties in the late nineteenth century, Austin Ranney found that Woodrow Wilson "was perhaps the first American scholar in his period to attack the principle and deplore the effects of separation of powers, and to consider methods for by-passing it."[6] The primary method was to accept the political party as the unifier of the separate powers. "The organization of parties," write Wilson, "is, in a sense, indistinguishable from the legislature and executive themselves. The several active parts of the government are closely united in organization for a common purpose, because they are under a common direction and themselves constitute the machinery of party control."[7] And they had to be united because, wrote Wilson, "our government is a living, organic thing, and must . . . work out a close synthesis of active parts which can exist only when leadership is lodged in some one man or group of men. You cannot compound a successful government out of antagonisms."[8]

Ranney traces the evolution of these concepts through other members of what he calls the "party-government school": A. Lawrence Lowell, who believed that the "almost unworkable" American governmental system "requires the services of the parties if it is to work at all" and Henry Jones Ford and Frank J. Goodnow, who agreed in their analysis of "the fallacious principle and harmful effects of the separation of powers" and joined "in arguing that parties are the only agency available in America for inducing some kind of coordination and harmony between the legislative and executive branches."[9]

At the time these men were writing early in the twentieth century, party organizations had reached the nadir of corruption and bossism. Reformers sought to weaken them—and succeeded—through the introduction of direct primaries, nonpartisan local elections, and other innovative measures. Yet the doctrine that political parties were indispensable at the national level lived on in political science literature and by the 1940s had clearly become the dominant theory. "[F]or the government to function," wrote V. O. Key, Jr., in the first edition of his influential textbook on political parties, "the obstructions of the governmental structure must be overcome, and it is the party, through extra-constitutional expedients, that accomplishes this end."[10] James MacGregor Burns took up the theme in his *Congress on Trial*: "If there is no way to harmonize the separated organs of government, sustained and effective action may be impossible. It is that vital function of integration that the majority party should fulfill. Operating through both branches of Congress and through the committees as well, having as its chief the occupant of the White House . . . the majority party should be the perfect instrument for carrying out a popular mandate."[11]

By the time the Committee on Political parties of the American Political Science Association made its landmark report in 1950, it could simply assert, without feeling obliged to argue the case, that political parties are "indispensable instruments of government," necessary "to furnish a general kind of direction over the government as a whole" and for "integration of all of the far-flung activities of modern government." It then offered a series of reforms that would make the parties better organized, more tightly disciplined, and hence "more responsible."[12]

The report stirred up a storm of criticism in political science journals and textbooks that continued into the next decade and even longer, culminating in the recantation and devastating critique by one of its members, Evron M. Kirkpatrick. He found the report guilty of "lack of clarification, justification, or analysis of the norms," of "both normative slovenliness and empirical inaccuracy."[13] But his and the earlier criticisms were directed not at the concept of the party government as such but at the realism and the desirability of the committee's proposed reforms, which sought to enable parties to impose a greater measure of discipline on their elected officials in the government. The debate was joined on whether party government should and could be made *more* responsible, not whether it should exist at all. Nobody argued that the parties as they existed in 1950 were too tightly disciplined, and that the need was that they be made *less* responsible. Nobody argued that the ideal system was the one that was to be ushered in a few years later: coalition government in which *no* party is or can be held responsible.[14]

Indeed, the concepts expressed by Wilson and his colleagues at the turn of the century and by Key and Burns in the 1940s maintained their hold long after the era of party government had, scarcely noticed, come to its end.[15] These are excerpts from authoritative textbooks:

Howard Penniman, 1952—But far more important is their [the parties'] services in neutralizing the effect of the check-and-balance system. . . . [S]ince the constitution provides no means of combining the dispersed and disconnected organs of government, the parties, in seeking to control them all and bind them to a common purpose, discharge an essential func- tion. . . . A party, once put in command of the various agencies of the government, will make them respond to a common impulse and work in harmony. Such power carries with it responsibility; and the voters can in some measure enforce that responsibility by transferring power to the rival party.[16]

Clinton Rossiter, 1960—It has not been an easy constitution with which to make policy quickly and to govern efficiently, which is exactly the kind of constitution the framers intended it to be. The gaps that separate the executive from the legislature . . . have often been as discouraging to men of good will as to men of corrupt intent. . . . For this reason we need more, and more easily traveled, bridges across the gaps, and our major parties provide two that we could hardly afford to be without.[17]

Frank J. Sorauf, 1968— . . . the American parties contribute to the function- ing of the American political system by providing a unifying focus in a system of dispersed political authority. . . . To the fragmentation of the nation and the fifty states multiplied by the three-fold separation of powers in each, the two great national political parties bring a unifying force . . . which helps to hold the disparate fragments together.[18]

David B. Truman, 1971—It is as appropriate to observe today as it was at the turn of the century . . . when Henry Jones Ford was producing his studies of American politics, that the national political party is the "sole efficient means" of producing "union between the executive and legislative branches of the government."[19]

Gerald Pomper, 1980—The Constitution has served us well, but only because we have not adhered to its provisions rigorously. . . . Amendment of the Constitution, in practice rather than in law, has enabled the parties to bridge its gaps through such integrative institutions as the national nominating conventions, the joint meetings of the president and congressional party leadership, the House and Senate party caucuses. . . .[20]

Milton C. Cummings, Jr. and David Wise, 1985—Because political parties are involved in the governmental process, they serve to link different parts of the government: the president communicates with party leaders in Congress; the two houses of Congress communicate in part through party leaders. . . . In sum, political parties perform vital functions in the American political system. They . . . [as one function] link various branches and levels of government.[21]

Like the Committee on Political Parties, the later writers who saw political parties as the unifying instrument in the governmental system generally agreed that they often failed to perform that function satisfactorily. Decentralized and federal in their organization, without authoritative central institutions, and made up of diverse ideological and cultural elements, the parties lacked discipline. Yet even without the reforms recommended by the committee, the political party was seen as nonetheless succeeding to some degree in bridging the gaps between the separated branches of the government.

Thus, Rossiter credits "the simple fact" that the president and roughly half of the Congress "are all brothers in the same political lodge" helping to close and bridge the "gaps" between the branches. The parties, he wrote, continue "to keep all our independent centers of power in touch with one another."[22] And Sorauf, while noting that party cohesion in the Congress and in state legislation is "irregular, sporadic, and imperfect" on substantive issues, "in the aggregate an important measure of party discipline does exist." He continues:

Neither the American parties nor the voters can meet the demands which the classic model of party responsibility imposes on them. But binding the various sectors of the party together—despite all that divides them—is an inarticulate ideology, a commitment to a set of issue positions which sets the activists, candidates, and voters of one party apart from those of the other. In a loose, often distressingly imprecise sense, the two parties are distinct groups of "like-minded" men. Out of that tentative and limited agreement on issues comes enough cohesion to produce a modest, if variable, degree of responsibility. The American approximation of party government does indeed fall far short of the model of party responsibility and the hopes of the reformers, but the role of the political party in organizing government and the debate on public issues cannot be ignored.[23]

And how is that degree of party discipline and responsibility achieved? In the national government, political scientists proclaim with virtual unanimity that it is through presidential leadership. When the party serves its unifying function, it is because the members of the president's party in the Congress recognize the president as not merely the head of the executive branch but as the leader of the band of "brothers in the same political lodge." In enacting as well as in administering the laws, the government cannot move dynamically and prudently without a recognized and accepted prime mover, a leader. And that leader is logically and necessarily the man chosen by the whole national party to carry its standard, and who has done so successfully in the most recent presidential election. Besides, the president has the resources of the entire executive branch to help him to develop coordinated programs. "The President proposes and the Congress disposes" long ago became the catch phrase to describe the legislative process.

Austin Ranney notes that, of the "various devices by which American presidents and other politicians have tried to join together, for purposes of getting the government to work, what the Constitution so successfully put asunder," most "fall under the general heading of 'presidential leadership of Congress.' " He summarizes:

> The ideas underlying all of them are that America, like every other country, must sometimes take swift, coherent, and purposeful action . . . that Congress . . . cannot by itself initiate such action; the president . . . is the only official who can take the lead; and that the basic problem of American government is finding and perfecting institutions that will enable the president to lead Congress with maximum effectiveness.[24]

Political scientists played no small role in creating those devices of presidential leadership. They refined and embellished, if they did not originate, the concepts of the executive budget that were enacted in the Budget and Accounting Act of 1921. They dominated the task forces of the President's Committee on Administrative Management, whose report in 1937 laid the basis for expanding the executive office of the president and giving the chief executive the mechanisms for serving effectively as the general manager of the government. And they heartily acclaimed the assertion by the president of leadership in the legislative process. The identification of the president as chief legislator has been traced back to Howard Lee McBain's *The Living Constitution*, published in 1927. By the 1940s, no textbook on American government failed to highlight the president's legislative role, usually in a section carrying the phrase "chief legislator" in the title.

"The president is usually considered both chief administrator and chief legislator," write Pendleton Herring in 1940. "The public expects the president to lead Congress; Congress is unable to produce coherence of direction to rival his." And "to meet the demands of the hour," Herring continued, "Presidential leadership is the answer."[25]

These sentiments were echoed and reechoed in the political science literature of the next several decades, as these samples illustrate:

> *V. O. Key, Jr., 1942*—The only common point about which leadership and direction of the party may be established for the conduct of the Government is the Presidency. It is the President who determines the major issues on which Congress acts; and it is the President who attempts, with or without success, to bring the party members in the House and Senate to the support of his policy.[26]

Charles S. Hyneman, 1950—It is imperative, as I see it, that the President take a lead in suggesting and formulating proposals which, when found acceptable by a majority in each house of Congress, will provide the legislative base for these programs of government. . . . There is every reason to believe that we will get effective legislative solutions for our toughest problems only if the President supplies vigorous leadership in legislation.[27]

Clinton Rossiter, 1956— . . . we may therefore consider [the President] to be the Chief Legislator. . . . [w]e may . . . consider him as *leader of Congress*. . . . [t]he complexity of the problems it is asked to solve . . . has made external leadership a requisite of effective operation.

The President alone is in a political, constitutional, and practical position to provide such leadership, and he is therefore expected, within the limits of propriety . . . to guide Congress in much of its lawmaking activity. Indeed, since Congress is no longer minded or organized to guide itself, the refusal or inability of the President to serve as leader results in weak and disorganized government.[28]

Richard E. Neustadt, 1960—an expert search for presidential influence contributes to the energy of government and to the viability of public policy. . . . In a relative but real sense one can say of a President what Eisenhower's first Secretary of Defense once said of General Motors: what is good for the country is good for the President and *vice versa*.[29]

Robert K. Carr, Marver H. Bernstein, and Walter F. Murphy, 1963—A modern democracy must try to devise and carry into effect positive policies for the solution of its social problems. It is an inescapable fact of American politics that the President alone can supply the kind of intelligent and aggressive leadership that is essential if this is to be done in the United States. . . . The nature of the times in which we live makes it absolutely essential for the President to lead Congress.[30]

Charles E. Lindblom, 1968—Because leadership in Congress is fragmented through the committee system and because congressmen know that someone or some small group has to take responsibility for organizing a legislative program, congressmen have informally conferred on the President both the authority and the positive responsibility, to the near exclusion of any similar role for themselves, to propose major legislation. Clearly, presidential authority for legislative leadership is now well established.[31]

In his analysis of what he termed "the textbook presidency" of the 1950s and 1960s, Thomas E. Cronin found that the texts "[w]ith rare exceptions . . . not only devised and approved but openly celebrated an expansive theory of presidential power." Among the more vivid of the many quotations he assembled were those terming the presidency "the great engine of democracy," "the American people's one authentic trumpet," "the central instrument of democracy," and "a kind of magnificent lion who can roam widely and do great deeds. . . ." Cronin wrote at a time of reaction against the "imperial presidency" revealed by Vietnam and

Watergate, and his purpose was to define a more realistic and accountable presidency. Yet he himself stopped well short of rejecting the doctrine of presidential leadership that had evolved in the earlier decades: "The promise of the American presidency may have been oversold, overstated, and stretched beyond reality, but denying the importance and the need for effective presidential leadership would be to overstate the case, as well as misleading."[32]

Somewhat startling in retrospect is the absence in all pre-1970s literature of any noticeable fear that presidential leadership might be transmuted into presidential imperialism and party cohesion into party docility and congressional subservience. A century and a half of experience had evidently convinced political scientists that the "frightful despotism" foreseen by Washington and the political "oppression" that haunted Madison were figments of an eighteenth-century imagination fevered by the struggle against George III. The preeminent instance in all that time of usurpation of power by a president—that of Abraham Lincoln at the outset of the Civil War—had turned out, after all, to be a necessary assertion of leadership in the noblest of causes. So too, it seemed, were the unilateral interventions of Franklin Roosevelt on the side of the Allies in the months before Pearl Harbor. In 1947, Louis Brownlow, of Roosevelt's Committee on Administrative Management, could exult that "during the whole history of the thirty-two presidents, not one has been recreant to his high trust—not one has used his power to aggrandize himself at the expense of our settled institutions."[33] The Committee on Political Parties even turned the argument around; it had the foresight to acknowledge the possibility of presidential excess but contended that disciplined parties would restrain an ambitious president by forcing major decisions into the context of a party's collective leadership. Neustadt's dictum that what is good for the president is good for the country would prevail until Vietnam and Watergate—and later Irangate—aroused scholars to an awareness that presidential power might be abused. Yet even after Vietnam and Watergate, Cronin appeared to speak for most political scientists in holding that "the importance and the need for presidential leadership" had not been invalidated by events. In the year of the Nixon resignation, a textbook writer could still reiterate the established doctrine:

> . . . the President has become the primary source of initiative in the American political system. Domestic programs will lack consistent direction if he does not supply it. . . . His need for a steady sense of direction is even greater where international and military affairs are concerned, because these decisions are generally made in the innermost circle . . . and he is *the* indispensable member of any innovating groups.[34]

By the 1960s, political science had developed a dominating theory as to how the American constitutional system should—and at its best, did—work. The political party was the institution that unified the separated branches of the government and brought coherence to the policymaking process. And because the president was the leader of his party, he was the chief policy maker of the entire government, presiding directly over the executive branch and indirectly working through and with his party's congressional leadership over the legislative branch as well.

The Old Theory in a New Era

This established theory presupposed one essential condition: there would in fact be a majority party in control of both branches of government. Rereading the literature of the midcentury, one is struck with how easily this condition was taken for granted. The writers could well do so, for in the twentieth century until 1955, the government had been divided between the parties only for four periods of two years each, and in each case in the last half of a presidential term—those of Taft, Wilson, Hoover, and Truman. A scholar who happened to be writing during or immediately after one of these intervals (or who was commenting on state governmental systems) might observe in parenthetical style that divided government could sometimes obscure responsibility, impede leadership, and thus thwart the fulfillment of the party government ideal. But the aberration was passed over quickly, without interrupting the flow of the basic argument. In the normal state of affairs, one party would have control of the policy-making branches of government; the other would be in opposition.

Thus, in the passage quoted earlier from the 1942 book by V. O. Key, Jr., such phrases as "the party in power," "the President's majority in Congress," and "when it [the party] takes control of the Government" appear repeatedly. In the 1952 edition of the same book, Key inserted a paragraph on how the Republican majorities in the Congress behaved in the 1947–1948 period of divided government. But the earlier phrases—"the party in control of the government," "the party in power," "the President and his congressional majority"—survived in their original unqualified form.[35] Hyneman, in his 1950 book, distinguished between "the party that has control of the government" and "the party out of power" and declared: "it is in the nature of things that [the president] will call upon the Congress that goes into power with him to lay a base in law and appropriations for the program that he has sponsored." Hyneman recognized the possibility of divided government, but saw it as the outcome only of midterm elections and accordingly found the remedy in a revision of terms of office so that presidential and congressional elections will coincide.[36] The report of the Committee on Political Parties confined its recognition of divided government to one subordinate clause of eight words; elsewhere it referred with casual ease to "the party in power," "the majority party," or "the dominant party," and to "the opposition party" or "minority party."[37] In contrast, Sorauf, writing in 1968, put considerable emphasis on divided government as an impediment to effective party government. Referring particularly to state governments, he termed the division of government between parties as "by far the most important institutional barrier to the coordination of legislative and executive decisionmaking under the aegis of a unifying political party. . . ."[38]

Divided government invalidates the entire theory of party government and presidential leadership, both elements of it. Divided government requires that the United States "construct a successful government out of antagonisms," which Wilson warned could not be done, and renders impossible the "close synthesis of active parts" that he found necessary. How can a party cast its web over the dispersed organs of government to bring a semblance of unity, in Key's phrase, if it controls but one of the branches? How can the majority party fulfill Burns's "vital function of integration," or rally the government's elements behind Penniman's "common purpose," or provide Rossiter's "bridges across the gaps," or

Sorauf's "unifying force" if there is no majority party? How can the president lead the Congress if either or both houses are controlled by the party that fought to defeat him in the last election and has vowed to vanquish him, or his successor as his party's candidate, in the next one? But if the president cannot lead, Rossiter has told us, "weak and disorganized government" must follow. Our "toughest problems," Hyneman has admonished, will in that circumstance remain unsolved.[39]

The question at once arises: In our twenty-two years thus far of forced coalition government, have those gloomy forecasts been fulfilled? Eleven Congresses during the administrations of four presidents would appear to have given ample time for putting the established theory to the test. Unfortunately, however, the test results are bound to be uncertain and would still be so if another two score years of experience were added. There will not be agreement on whether, and to what extent, and during what periods the government has in fact been "weak and disorganized," or even on whether those characteristics are wholly undesirable. "That government is best which governs least" is still an aphorism of wide appeal, and the weaker and more disorganized the government the less governance it can inflict. Moreover, to rest a theoretical proposition on concrete examples from history is to invite debate on the merits of each example and to call forth counterexamples. And when the instances are so recent that they involve current personalities or groups—Democrats and Republicans, conservatives and liberals—the debate is distorted by the emotional attachments of the debaters. Moreover, almost any failure or success can be ruled out of consideration as attributable to accidents of personality or to circumstances beyond the control of the institutions however organized. So, in the absence of proven and acceptable methodology for evaluating the performance and success of governments, any judgment about institutional structures will necessarily embody the biases and the values of whomever is the judge. But if that is the best that can be done, so be it. If there is any worth at all to the contention that a government cannot function without the unifying web of party, as Key held, the judgment must be made on whatever is the soundest basis that can be contrived.

My own conclusion is that the predictions of the sages of the earlier generation have been borne out in this modern era of divided or coalition government. True, in the administrations of the four Republican presidents who had to make their peace with House Democratic majorities—and usually Democratic Senate majorities as well—there were significant accomplishments. President Dwight D. Eisenhower achieved a successful bipartisan foreign policy, and President Ronald Reagan managed to carry enough Democrats with him to enact for better or worse the essentials of his economic program in 1981. In subsequent Reagan years, the Congress and the administration collaborated across party lines to enact measures to bring illegal immigration under control, rescue social security, and reform the tax code. But Eisenhower and the Democratic Congress were stalemated on domestic measures throughout his six years of coalition government; the Nixon-Ford period was one of almost unbroken conflict and deadlock on both domestic and foreign issues; and the last seven years of Reagan found the government immobilized on some of the central issues of the day, unwilling to follow the leadership of the President or anyone else and deferring those issues in hope that somehow the 1988 election would resolve matters and render the government functional again.

By common consent, the most conspicuous among the urgent but unresolved problems has been, of course, the federal budget deficit, which has been running at between $150 billion and $200 billion a year since the great tax cut of 1981 took effect. The national debt now stands at well over $2 trillion, more than doubled in seven years of divided government. The United States has suffered the shock of falling from the status of a great creditor nation to the world's largest debtor nation, living on borrowing from abroad. The huge trade deficit, the shortfall in investment, and high interest rates are all blamed on the inability of the government to get the budget deficit under control. For all these reasons, virtually all of the country's responsible leaders—the president, the congressional leaders, and members of both parties in both houses—have for nearly over half a dozen years been proclaiming loudly and in unison that the nation simply cannot go on this way. The experts from outside—in the academic world, the Federal Reserve System, on Wall Street, in foreign countries—likewise agree that these deficits are economically perilous, whether or not they can be termed morally outrageous as well.

But during all that time that the country has seen a virtual consensus on the urgency of this problem, its governmental institutions have floundered in trying to cope with it. President Reagan sent the Congress his program, but the Congress flatly rejected it. The legislators in their turn floated suggestions, but the President killed them by promising a veto if they were passed. The congressional leaders and others pleaded for a summit meeting between the executive and legislative branches to hammer out a common policy. Finally, in November 1986, the meeting took place. But it is a measure of the national predicament that it took a half-trillion-dollar collapse in the stock market—a five-hundred-billion-dollar panic— before the two branches of the U.S. government would even sit down together. It was easier for Mikhail Gorbachev to get a summit meeting with the President of the United States than it was for the Speaker of the United States House of Representatives. And even the domestic summit that was finally held essentially papered over the problem rather than solved it.

Or we can draw examples of the failure of coalition government from international affairs. The country lost a war for the first time in history—in Vietnam— after another period of floundering in search of a policy, with the president pulling in one direction and the Congress in another. And the situation in Nicaragua was throughout the Reagan years almost a replica of Vietnam. The government could adopt no clear and effective policy at all; it could neither take measures strong enough to force the Sandinista government out of power, as the President and his administration wished to do, nor accept that government and make peace with it, as many in the Senate and the House would like. Then there is the Iran-contra debacle. President Reagan in his own summation of that episode spoke of the "failure" of his policy, of "a policy that went astray," of "the damage that's been done," and he blamed it all on mistrust between the executive and legislative branches.[40]

But, some will argue, even if these or other instances can indeed be considered governmental failures attributable to mistrust between the unwilling partners of a forced coalition, the performance of recent unified government has been no better. The Kennedy and Carter years cannot claim overwhelming success, they will maintain, and while Lyndon Johnson proved to be a spectacular presidential leader of the Congress in the enactment of his Great Society measures in 1964 and

1965, he also led the country into the quagmire of Vietnam that in turn launched a devastating spiral of inflation. That is the difficulty of arguing from cases, as I suggested earlier.

Nor is it any more profitable to look abroad for answers to the effectiveness of unified compared to coalition government. It is easy to demonstrate that Britain's unified governments have not always been successful, and that in continental countries coalition governments (which, it is important to note, are quite different from ours) have not always failed. For better or worse, the discussion of the relative merits of unified over divided government has to be pursued in abstract terms, as it was for the most part in the political science literature cited earlier.

The essence of the theoretical argument in favor of the unified government has been and is: For coherent and timely policies to be adopted and carried out—in short, for government to work effectively, as the established theory held—the president, the Senate, and the House must come into agreement. When the same party controls all three of these power centers, the incentive to reach such agreement is powerful despite the inevitable institutional rivalries and jealousies. The party *does* serve as the bridge or the web, in the metaphors of political science. But in divided government, it is not merely the separated institutions of government that must overcome their built-in rivalries but the opposing parties themselves. And that is bound to be a difficult, arduous process, characterized by conflict, delay, and indecision, and leading frequently to deadlock, inadequate and ineffective policies, or no policies at all.

Competition is the very essence of democratic politics. It gives democracy its meaning, and its vitality. The parties are the instruments of that competition. They are and should be organized for combat, not for collaboration and compromise. They live to win elections in order to advance their philosophies and programs. Therefore, each party strives and must strive to defeat the opposing party. But in a divided government, this healthy competition is translated into an unhealthy, debilitating conflict between the institutions of government themselves. Then, the president and Congress are motivated to try to discredit and defeat each other. Yet these are the institutions that, for anything constructive to happen, simply have to get together.

The average citizen reacts by simply condemning all politicians as a class. "Why don't those people in Washington stop playing politics and just get together and do what's right?" But that is not in the nature of things. Political parties, as the textbooks have always told us, are organized because people have genuine, deep disagreements about the goals and the programs of their societies. If a coalition government is to work, the leaders of committed groups have to be willing to submerge or abandon the very philosophies that caused them to organize their parties in the first place. They have to set aside the principles that are their reason for seeking governmental power. And they will do that only under compulsion of clear and grave necessity—usually, in other words, after deadlock has deteriorated into crisis.

In the American form of coalition government, if the president sends a proposal to Capitol Hill or takes a foreign policy stand, the opposition-controlled House or houses of Congress—unless they are overwhelmed by the president's popularity and standing in the country—simply *must* reject it. Otherwise they are saying the president is a wise and prudent leader. That would only strengthen him and his party for the next election, and how can the men and women of the congressional majority do that, when their whole object is to defeat him when that time arrives? By the same token, if the opposition party in control of Congress initiates a measure, the president has to veto it—or he is saying of his opponents that they are sound and statesmanlike, and so is building them up for the next election.

So when President Reagan sent his budgets to the Congress, the Democrats who controlled both houses had to pronounce them "dead on arrival," as they did. And when they came up with their alternatives, the President had to condemn them and hurl them back. Eventually, when the stream of recrimination and vetoes ran dry each year, some kind of budget was necessarily adopted; but it did not reflect the views of either party, and in terms of the consensus objective of deficit reduction it was a pale and ineffective compromise. Neither party would take responsibility, neither could be held accountable, each could point the finger at the other when the things went wrong.

In such circumstances, the people in their one solemn, sovereign act of voting cannot render a clear verdict and thus set the course of government. Elections lose their purpose and their meaning. The President, all through 1988, was saying, "Don't blame me for the budget deficit. It's those Democrats in Congress." And the Democrats were replying, "Don't blame us. Blame that man in the White House for not giving us the proper leadership." In November, the voters were not able to hold anybody clearly responsible, because, in fact nobody had been.

Our struggles with coalition government have demonstrated also the truth of the established wisdom concerning presidential leadership: in the American system there is simply no substitute for it. The Congress has 535 voting members, organized in two houses and in innumerable committees and subcommittees; every member is in principle the equal of every other member, and nobody can give directions to anybody else and make them stick. Such a body is simply not well designed for making coherent, decisive, coordinated policy. As the old theory told us, the system works best when the president proposes and the Congress disposes, when the president sets the agenda and leads, as everyone expects him to.

But how can leaders lead if followers don't follow? In divided government, presidential leadership becomes all but impossible. The president is not the leader of the congressional majority. He is precisely the opposite—the leader of their opposition, the man they are most dedicated to discredit and defeat. With great fanfare and immense hope, the people elect a president each four years. But then, most of the time these days, they give him a Congress a majority of whose members tried their best to beat him in the last election and will do so again in the next. To lead in those circumstances would be beyond the capability of any mortal. No one should blame presidents when they fail in a time of coalition government. It is the system that is at fault.

Nobody planned it this way. The country in no way made a conscious decision thirty years ago to abandon the responsible-party system that had served it well for almost the whole life of the nation. It was simply an accident of the electoral system. Almost unique in the world, the United States has an electoral process that permits people to split their tickets—to vote one way for president and the other way for Congress, if they so choose. And that is what enough of them have done to produce a divided outcome most of the time of late.

Re-reconciling Theory and Practice

Today there is a disjunction between theory and practice, between the long-accepted and not-yet-abandoned ideas about how the government of the United States should work and the way in which it is now compelled to try to work. How can theory and practice once again be synchronized?

First, can the practice be altered to fit the therapy? In other words, is there any way to restore party government as the normal, rather than abnormal, state of affairs? Theoretically, there is. But only by altering the electoral system that lets ticket-splitting determine the composition of the government. That would mean fundamental change in the Constitution, and it only takes a split second of reflection to convince anyone that politically and practically it cannot be done. It would take the utter collapse of government to make such change possible.

The constitutional amendment might take any of several forms, the simplest of which would be a revision of the ballot to make ticket-splitting impossible in national elections. That would in effect return the country to the nineteenth-century mode, when straight-ticket ballots were printed and handed out by the parties—except that the ballots would now be government-printed and the secrecy of the vote protected. The voters would select one from among two or more party slates or "team tickets" that included each party's candidates for president, vice president, Senate, and House. This is not a totally outlandish idea, because voters now choose between team tickets for president and vice president. If that principle were extended to Senate and House candidates as well, it would be almost a certainty that every incoming president would have a Congress of his own party to work with and to lead. A subtle variant of this scheme would be to require a party's candidates for Congress to be its candidates for the electoral college also, so that a voter could cast a ballot for president only by casting it for the congressional candidate as the elector. A different approach would be to create bonus seats in the House and Senate, to be awarded to the president's party in sufficient number to give it control of the Congress.

But any of those ideas would be anathema to the members of Congress, who under normal constitutional amendment procedures would have to initiate the change. Because the amendment process requires extraordinary majorities—two-thirds of the House and Senate and three-fourths of the state legislatures—it demands in effect bipartisan agreement. Therefore, both parties would have to see benefit in the change. But since redistribution of power is a zero-sum game that creates both winners and losers, one party is bound to lose. In the current case it would be the Democrats, for any of these proposals would have given the Republicans control of the Congress during much or all of the time that they have held the presidency. The Democrats in the Congress would never take a second look at any team ticket scheme that would make them stand or fall with a George McGovern or a Walter Mondale, and that would convert their majorities into minorities every time their candidate for president was beaten. And the Republicans would not perceive the advantage for their party, however obvious that advantage may have been throughout the past twenty years. Faced with a team ticket proposal, they would remember how many seats they would have lost with Barry Goldwater back in 1964 and play it safe.

If practice cannot be changed to fit the established theory of party government, then what are the prospects for the development of new theory? If coalition government is what the United States must live with most of the time, can political leadership and political science produce an alternative theory that tells us how that kind of government can be made to work?

On this question, today's political scientists, who would appear to have the primary obligation to make suggestions, fall into three groups. The first consists of those who are happy with the way the government works now. They simply reject the party-government and presidential-leadership theories of the preceding generation. They find divided government acceptable enough, and maybe even better than party government, for it more certainly safeguards individual liberties and assures that rash and impulsive actions can be forestalled—in domestic affairs, at least. This is the position of traditional conservatives who still echo the fears of government that dominated the eighteenth century, and is a wholly arguable and defensive position. But ironically, these conservatives are joined now by their exact opposites—the typical liberal Democrats, whose gut reaction is, "Thank God for divided government under President Reagan. It saved us from Judge Robert Bork, and war in Nicaragua, and all kinds of other follies." These liberals were *for* party government and presidential leadership when their man—FDR or John Kennedy or another Democrat—was in the White House, but they were against it when the President was Ronald Reagan.

The second group is made up of the intellectual heirs of the dominant school of the midcentury, still true believers in party government and presidential leadership. It includes such survivors of that school as James MacGregor Burns, who was a leader in the formation of two current reform organizations, the Committee on the Constitutional System and the Committee for Party Renewal, both of which attempt to bridge the separate worlds of academic science and practical politics. The Democrats in this group had to swallow hard in the Reagan era, but forced their reason to overcome their emotions so that they could say, "We're willing to let the Republicans have their day—even under Reagan—because they will be held accountable, they will discredit themselves, and then we will have our day." The Democrats are now joined, too, by some of their exact opposites—the new breed of conservative activists who have found that divided government can frustrate them too, when the public mood swings their way. Those in this group in both parties believe that in the long run a government that is able to act, even if it makes mistakes, is less dangerous than one that is rendered impotent by deadlock and division. A government with the capability to act will also have the capability to correct its errors (or its successor can) but there is no recourse when a government is inert, lethargic, paralyzed. Accordingly, scholars in this group believe that reform measures are in order, but they are apt to put the question aside because of the hopelessness of advocating changes in the Constitution.

The third bloc of political scientists and apparently the largest, even among specialists in American national government, is made up of those who have not found it necessary to take a stand at all. This group can be charged with evading what is surely one of the most crucial intellectual questions facing students of American government—one that the previous generation of political scientists explicitly asked and answered.

There are many reasons that scholars of government might prefer to evade the question. One was mentioned earlier—methodology. How is the general performance of a government to be evaluated, anyway? How can the effects of divided government be separated from the effects of all the other factors that influence outcomes—the temperaments and capabilities of individual leaders, the economic and social circumstances of a given time, and the actions of the other peoples and nations that share the globe—so that one can render a quasi-scientific judgment as to whether unified or divided government is the superior model for America? These are daunting questions, but no one needs precise quantitative answers. Informed judgments are needed based on the best methods of analysis that are available, as rough as those may be.

Some of the other reasons for evading the issue are less respectable. It is not satisfactory to argue that an intellectual effort is unnecessary because the new era will shortly end and the country will return to party government of its own accord. A third of a century has already elapsed since 1955, and the tendency of the voters to elect Republican presidents and Democratic Senates most of the time, and Democratic Houses all of the time, appears to be as firmly fixed as anything in national politics, reinforced rather than weakened from election to election. Those who would rely on this argument should provide a convincing explanation for predicting an automatic restoration of the previous order.

Nor is it satisfactory to contend, as many do, that a basic principle of democracy forbids questioning the desirability of coalition government: that of majority rule. A majority of the people evidently want divided government, runs this argument, and therefore they are entitled to have it, whether it is good for them or not. After all, the people rule. But this argument assumes that divided government is the people's intent, more or less conscious, rather than the essentially chance outcome of the electoral system that was not designed by those who use it. Clearly the latter is the case: divided government is a historical and procedural accident. The era of coalition government was not ushered in three decades ago by the sudden appearance of an overwhelming popular demand for that form of government as such. In 1956, the first presidential election year of the new era, a majority of voters liked Eisenhower and a majority wanted to retain their incumbent Democratic congressmen; but those were not the same majorities. In that year and in every one of the divided-government elections since, a large majority of the voters in fact voted a straight ballot, either Republican or Democratic, for national offices. It was the ticket-splitting *minority*, often a small minority, that gave the country its divided government. There is no evidence from electoral behavior that the public at large has deliberately rejected the long-accepted doctrine of party government; reliable public opinion polling data on the abstract question do not exist.

In short, fence straddling on this issue is not intellectually defensible. Either the dominant pre-1954 view of the desirability of party government and presidential leadership as the model and the ideal was right or it was wrong. That two systems so diametrically opposite as party government and coalition could serve the country equally well is a virtual mathematical impossibility, and that they could come close to equality is highly improbable. One or the other necessarily has to be the superior model for America, and political scientists have a responsibility to determine which it is and inform the country of their judgment.

Not that the discipline would ever speak with a single voice, of course, or even reach the level of agreement that prevailed in the 1940s and 1950s. But political scientists have the responsibility to grapple with the question individually, and by pooling their wisdom and debating opposing views to see whether a broad area of agreement might emerge.

Those who think that the model of party government and presidential leadership was wrong, and who would advance the post-1955 structure of coalition government as the new ideal, have an obligation to provide a new body of theory that will tell us what is the substitute for presidential leadership and congressional followership, how the partners in the American coalition government should relate to one another for that type of government to function well, and how those relationships can be brought about. What is the role of parties in such a system, and will strengthening them simply intensify the confrontation between the branches and render deadlocks more implacable? Should the agitation within the discipline for stronger parties be reversed and should weaker parties be made the goal? How would the weakening of congressional parties affect the efficiency of the Congress and its status vis-à-vis the presidency? Does the answer—or part of it, at least—lie in bipartisan mechanisms such as the one that resolved the social security issue and the National Economic Commission that was created in 1988 to grapple with the budget deficit? Can these be multiplied and regularized to anticipate and forestall crises rather than simply cope with them when they reach the desperation stage? If we are to accept coalition government as ideal, or even as satisfactory, we need a body of theory as fully developed as the one it superseded, followed by institutional innovation based on the new theory. No such body of theory has even begun to emerge.

By the same token, those who still cherish the idea of party government have an obligation of equal gravity. They must come to grips with the question of how our election system, or the composition and powers of the branches of government, should be altered to restore unified government as the normal state of affairs. And if that means—as it surely does—that the Constitution itself should be changed, how can that be brought about? That question obviously is not one for the fainthearted. But for any serious student of American government to contend that all of the issues raised by coalition government can simply be set aside, because whatever is is best, is not an answer. The times demand a more responsible political science than that.*

*An earlier version of this article was presented as a paper to the 1988 annual meeting of the American Political Science Association, Washington, D.C., 3 September 1988.

Notes

1. Max Farrands, ed., *The Records of the Federal Convention of 1787*, rev. ed., 4 vols. (New Haven, Conn.: Yale University Press, 1966), 2, 29, proceedings of July 17, notes of James Madison.

2. James D. Richardson, ed., *A Compilation of the Messages and Papers of the Presidents* (New York: Bureau of National Literature, 1897), vol. I, 210–11.

3. Ibid., 221.

4. *Annals of Congress*, 14 Cong. 1 sess., 216, reprinted in Farrand, *Records*, III, 422. King was a delegate from Massachusetts to the Constitutional Convention, but moved to New York during the following year.

5. Note to his speech at the 1787 Convention on the right of suffrage, apparently written about 1821, when he was preparing his record of Convention proceedings for publication. Ibid., 452.

6. Austin Ranney, *The Doctrine of Responsible Party Government* (Champaign: University of Illinois Press, 1954), 36, fn. 39.

7. Woodrow Wilson, *Constitutional Government in the United States* (New York: Columbia University Press, 1911), 211–12, quoted by Ranney, *Doctrine*, 36.

8. Ibid., 60, quoted by Ranney, *Doctrine*, 35.

9. Ranney, *Doctrine*. The quotations are from Ranney's summations of their views, 62 and 97. Ranney also devotes chapters to two writers who distrusted parties as the "enemy of democracy"—M. I. Ostrogorski and Herbert Croly.

10. V. O. Key, Jr., *Politics, Parties, and Pressure Groups* (New York: Crowell, 1942), 495. By the third edition, published in 1952, Key had rephrased the sentence in the more eloquent form in which it remained in subsequent editions: "Yet, for government to function, the obstructions of the constitutional mechanism must be overcome, and it is the party that casts a web, at times weak, at times strong, over the dispersed organs of government and gives them a semblance of unity," 693.

11. James MacGregor Burns, *Congress on Trial* (New York: Harper and Bros., 1949, republished by Gordian Press, 1966), 45.

12. Committee on Political Parties, *Toward a More Responsive Two-Party System*, supplement to the *American Political Science Review* 44 (September 1950), also published by Rinehart & Co., 1950. Quotation from Rinehart ed., 15, 16.

13. Evron M. Kirkpatrick, "Toward a More Responsible Two-Party System: Political Science, Policy Science, or Pseudo-Science," *American Political Science Review* 65 (December 1971): 965–90.

14. Thus a theme of one of the earliest critical responses to the Report was that the Committee "underestimated present party responsibility," that parties do in fact present clear alternatives to the voter, and that "most of the majority program is carried into effect." Julius Turner, "Responsible Parties: A Dissent from the Floor," *American Political Science Review* 45 (March 1951): 143–52.

15. The remarkable failure of political scientists to recognize the significance of the transition from the era of party government to a new era of coalition government is evident, for example, in a book entitled *The New American Political System*, Anthony King, ed., (Washington, D.C.: American Enterprise Institute, 1978), which in ten chapters by eminent writers does not even mention divided government as an element of the new system.

16. Howard Penniman, *American Parties and Elections*, 5th ed. (New York: Appleton-Century-Crofts, 1952), 164–65. (Penniman was a member of the Committee on Political Parties.)

17. Clinton Rossiter, *Parties and Politics in America* (Ithaca, New York: Cornell University Press, 1960), 62–63.

18. Frank J. Sorauf, *Party Politics in America* (Boston: Little, Brown, 1968), 18.

19. David B. Truman, *The Governmental Process*, 2d ed. (New York: Alfred A. Knopf, 1971), 531–32.

20. Gerald Pomper, "The Contribution of Political Parties to American Democracy" in Pomper, ed., *Party Renewal in America: Theory and Practice* (New York: Praeger, 1980), 7.

21. Milton C. Cummings and David Wise, *Democracy Under Pressure: An Introduction to the American Political System*, 5th ed. (San Diego: Harcourt Brace Jovanovich, 1985), 248.

22. Rossiter, *Parties and Politics*, 63.

23. Sorauf, *Party Politics*, 14, 393–94.

24. Ranney, "The President and His Party" in Anthony King, ed., *Both Ends of the Avenue* (Washington, D.C.: American Enterprise Institute, 1983), 131–32.

25. Pendleton Herring, *Presidential Leadership* (New York: Farrar and Rinehart, 1940), 12, 145–46.

26. Key, *Politics, Parties*, 504–05.

27. Charles S. Hyneman, *Bureaucracy in a Democracy* (New York: Harper and Bros., 1950), 565.

28. Rossiter, *The American Presidency* (New York: Harcourt, Brace 1956), 14, 46.

29. Richard E. Neustadt, *Presidential Power* (New York: John Wiley and Sons, 1960), 183–85.

30. Robert K. Carr, Marver H. Bernstein, and Walter F. Murphy, *American Democracy in Theory and Practice*, 4th ed. (New York: Holt, Rinehart and Winston, 1963), 372, 374.

31. Charles E. Lindblom, *The Policy-making Process* (New Haven, Conn.: Yale University Press, 1968), 72.

32. Thomas E. Cronin, *The State of the Presidency* (Boston: Little, Brown, 1975), 25–29.

33. Louis Brownlow, *The President and the Presidency* (Chicago: Public Administration Service, 1949), a compilation of lectures given in 1947.

34. Dorothy Buckton James, *The Contemporary President*, 2d ed. (Indianapolis: Pegasus, 1974), 307–08.

35. Key, *Politics, Parties*, 3d ed., 702–03, 692, 711.

36. Hyneman, *Bureaucracy*, 566, 573.

37. Committee on Political Parties, *Toward a More Responsible Two-Party System*, 8, 1, 18, 34, 35, 41, 51.

38. Sorauf, *Party Politics*, 361.

39. Fortunately for believers in party government, the problem of intra-party cohesion and discipline that so preoccupied the writers of the midcentury has to a large extent been solved by the events. The realignment of the party system since they wrote has produced Democratic and Republican parties that are more homogeneous than at any time within the memory of anyone now living; the minority wings that were once strong enough to disrupt the internal unity of both parties have withered. First to fade were the liberal Republicans, who until a couple of decades ago were potent enough to seriously contest for the presidential nomination; they are now ineffectual remnants that did not even put forward a candidate in 1988. Their mirror-image counterparts, the conservative Democrats, have been vanishing as well, although more slowly. Since the New Deal era, their wing of the party has been virtually confined to the South, and for thirty years its base there has been steadily eroding as conservatives find their political home in the burgeoning Republican Party. New Democratic senators from the South are no longer the Byrds, Robertsons, Eastlands, Russells, Thurmonds, and Hollands, who automatically voted with the Republicans on major issues and made life miserable for Democratic presidents, Senate majority leaders, and House speakers; for the most part they are people who fit quite comfortably into the moderate-to-liberal national party, such as Terry Sanford, Bob Graham, and Wyche Fowler. (Strom Thurmond himself became a Republican long ago, and the son of Democratic Senator A. Willis Robertson made his race for the presidency in the Republican, not the Democratic, caucuses and primaries.) The same transformation has taken place in the House.

So the Republicans have become a solidly right-of-center party, very much in Ronald Reagan's image. If Republicans ever were to capture the Congress, they would have a little trouble attaining the unity necessary for true party government. And the Democrats, if and when they elect a president, will demonstrate a cohesion that will astound those who recall the schismatic party of thirty or even twenty years ago. Moreover, the reforms of congressional organizations and procedures, which have strengthened the position of party leaders, party policy committees, and party caucuses, make it far more likely now that the cohesive Democratic majorities in the Congress would be able to overcome any obstruction that the truncated conservative wing might still attempt.

40. Address to the nation, 12 August 1987, as reported in *New York Times*, 13 August 1987.

4.2

James Q. Wilson

Does the Separation of Powers Still Work?

James Q. Wilson is the Collins Professor of Management and Political Science at the University of California, Los Angeles. He was previously the Shattuck Professor of Government at Harvard University. He is the author or coauthor of ten books on politics and on crime-related topics. Unpersuaded by those who claim that the separation of powers has become a serious hindrance to effective government, Wilson contends that the reasons for preserving this constitutional principle are as compelling today as they were over two hundred years ago.

If one is asked to explain why the American government acts as it does with respect to almost any policy issue, the chances are probably eight in ten that the right answer is the separation of powers. The existence of three separate institutions with independent constitutional standing and, in two cases, distinct electoral constituencies is what distinguishes American government from parliamentary democracies. The separation of powers is the source of the enormous influence that Congress exercises over both the broad outlines and minute details of public policy, an influence that has led Daniel Patrick Moynihan to remark that the United States is the only major government with a legislative branch and that leads many European observers to doubt that this country is really governed at all. The separation of powers is also at the root of the courts' authority to declare presidential and congressional acts unconstitutional and thus is a major cause of one kind of judicial activism.

If one is asked what is wrong with American government, the odds are great—maybe not eight in ten, but better than one in two—that the reply will refer to some aspect of our politics that can be explained by the separation of powers: "The president cannot negotiate for the United States on delicate foreign policy matters." "Congress meddles in the work of bureaucratic agencies." "There are too many government leaks to the press." "The Pentagon is not under strong, unified management." "There are too many patronage (i.e., political) appointees in government agencies." "There are too few policy-oriented (i.e., political) appointees in government agencies."

If one makes a list of the most frequently proposed alterations in our constitutional arrangements, the odds are high that these proposals will call for a

From *The Public Interest* 86 (Winter 1987). Reprinted with permission.

reduction in the separation of powers: "Let the president put some members of Congress in his cabinet." "Have the president and members of Congress who are from the president's party run as a team." "Allow the president to dissolve Congress." "Allow Congress to call for a special presidential election." "Curb the power of judicial review."

If one listens to the reflections of presidents and their aides, no matter whether they are liberals or conservatives, the most common complaint is that the president does not have enough power. Roosevelt, Truman, Eisenhower, Kennedy, Nixon, Carter, Reagan: All have remarked on how little the president can do compared to what the public expects him to do. Roosevelt, Truman, and Nixon appointed commissions (the President's Commission on Administrative Management [PCAM], the Hoover Commission, and the Ash Commission) to advise them on how best to extend their control over the bureaucracy; Nixon (like many presidents before him) tried to impound funds that Congress had ordered him to spend; Carter made a largely futile effort to weaken congressional control over the bureaucracy; Ford and Reagan have argued the War Powers Act, which requires congressional participation in presidential decisions to commit armed forces, is unconstitutional. And on and on.

It is as if almost everybody were expressing devotion to the Constitution in general but not to the central principle on which it rests. Does anybody like the separation of powers? Can anything good be said for it?

The Separation of Powers in the Courts

There is one group devoted to the principle: the Supreme Court. It may be activist in interpreting the Bill of Rights, but on the separation of powers it has adopted the most literal readings of the Constitution. In 1926, it held that Congress cannot deny to the president the right to remove an executive official he has appointed[1] (nine years later the Court modified that ruling to allow congressional restrictions on presidential appointments to independent regulatory commissions).[2] In 1975, it held that President Nixon could not impound (i.e., fail to spend) funds appropriated by Congress.[3] The following year it decided that Congress could not appoint members of the Federal Election Commission.[4] In 1983, it overturned the legislative veto, a procedure whereby Congress had granted discretionary authority to the president or subordinate officials subject to the right of Congress to block a proposed exercise of that authority by adopting a resolution.[5] Three years later it struck down a part of the Gramm-Rudman deficit reduction act because the across-the-board spending reductions mandated by the act were, under certain circumstances, to be executed by the Comptroller General. It seems that, because the Comptroller General can be removed by Congress, he is subservient to Congress and so cannot exercise "executive powers."[6]

From time to time, the Court recognizes that the Founders never intended to create a government based on a strict separation of powers but rather one based, in the words of Richard E. Neustadt, on separate institutions sharing powers. But whenever the Court finds a statement specifying how those powers are to be shared, it tends to give to those words the most narrow construction. For example, its objection to the legislative veto was that such congressional resolutions have the force of law even though they are not signed by the president (never mind that the president may have signed a law creating the system of legislative vetoes); a law, to be a law, "shall be presented to the President of the United States" for his signature or veto as required by the language of Article I. And in the Gramm-Rudman case, the Court was unimpressed by the fact that the Comptroller General, since the creation of the post in 1921, has been a largely nonpartisan and neutral officer who serves a fifteen-year term and who can only be removed for cause and with the assent of both the president and Congress.

It is hard to find an area of constitutional law in which the Court has been as nonactivist as with respect to the separation of powers. The uncharitable may argue that the Court's faithfulness to text on this issue is necessary to empower it to be activist on other issues, for without strict adherence to the doctrine of separated powers the Court itself might not be able to assert the authority, nowhere mentioned in the Constitution, to declare acts of Congress unconstitutional. Perhaps; certainly *Marbury v. Madison* (1803), the first case to announce the Court's power to invalidate acts of Congress, was also the first case to argue that Congress had violated the separation of powers (by attempting to enlarge the original jurisdiction of the Court).

Whatever the Court's motives, its words echo hollowly in the halls of contemporary political debate. Scarcely any other voice is raised in praise of the separation of powers, except in the most abstract sense. Separated powers are a fine idea, it would seem, except when they prevent me from having my way.

Of course, it was precisely to prevent officials from having their way that powers were separated in the first place. As Chief Justice Burger said in the Court's opinion in the Gramm-Rudman case, the institutions of government were deliberately arranged to create a system that "produces conflicts, confusion, and discordance." Few presidents probably cared for that arrangement very much, but their complaints were of little moment during the century and a half or so when the national government played a minor role in public affairs (except in wartime, and then the Court, with only a few exceptions, allowed the president quite sweeping powers free of any but the most essential congressional checks). Once the national government began—or tried to begin—to play a large role, presidents, and people who looked to the president for action, visibly and audibly chafed under their constitutional restraints.

The Case Against the Separation of Powers

There have always been two distinct, though often intertwined, strands in the case against the separation of powers. One is the liberal case: The federal government should play a large and active role in human affairs by supplying services, reducing economic inequality, and catering to the demands of those who find themselves at a disadvantage in the marketplace. During most of this century, presidents have been more sensitive to the urban and industrial constituencies who make these demands than has Congress. Therefore, the powers of the president should be enlarged and those of Congress (or those parts of Congress that are "obstructionist") should be reduced. From this perspective, it made sense to weaken the authority of congressional committees, or at least the committees headed by powerful conservatives (such as the House Rules Committee under the leadership of the legendary Judge Howard Smith of Virginia). It also made sense to call, as did James MacGregor Burns and E. E. Schattschneider, for strong political parties headed by the president, or presidential candidates, that would be able to command the loyalty of party members in Congress to the president's program and supplant the loyalty those members gave to committee chairmen. When Burns wrote of the "deadlock of democracy," he was writing of the political barriers to the enactment of a liberal agenda.

The other case is the rationalist one. Whether policies are liberal or conservative, they should be made decisively, efficiently, and on the basis of comprehensive principles. The public interest was not well served by simply adding up individual preferences into a "patchwork" or "crazy quilt" of inconsistent programs administered in "wasteful" ways by "duplicative" agencies. The public interest was better served by having a unitary view of what was good for the nation "as a whole." Only a single official could design and propose an internally consistent set of policies based on some overriding principle. In our system that person is the president. Therefore, the president should have more power. In this view, it made sense to give the president firmer control over the bureaucracy, equip him with sufficient staff to develop programs and oversee their administration, empower him to recognize government agencies, and strengthen his hand in dealing with Congress. In theory, a rationalized national government could serve either liberal ends (by enacting broad welfare and regulatory programs) or conservative ones (by cutting waste, reducing spending, and simplifying or minimizing regulation). The rationalist view especially emphasized the foreign policy role of the president. With Tocqueville, it noted that diplomacy is especially difficult in a democracy owing to the need for secrecy, speed, and unity of action, all hampered by the fact that the president must share power with Congress.

The existence of two arguments against checks and balances helps explain why a liberal, Harry Truman, could appoint a conservative, Herbert Hoover, to recommend ways of improving government; why presidents of all stripes have been able to make plausible cases in favor of enhancing their powers; and why movements for constitutional "reform" are able to recruit conservative business-men as well as liberal academics into their ranks.

These reform movements, though they have helped change aspects of the presidency, have not had a fundamental impact on the separation of powers. To the extent of the separation of powers has been altered, it has been the result of events more than plans, events that helped liberals more than rationalists.

Liberals achieved the enactment of a large part of their agenda as a consequence of two windows of opportunity that opened thirty years apart. The Great Depression enabled an overwhelming Democratic majority in Congress, aided (after 1935) by a slim but solid majority on the Supreme Court, to lay the foundations for the modern welfare state. In 1965, a landslide electoral victory by Lyndon Johnson and the arrival of a liberal majority in both houses of Congress set the stage for a vast expansion of the welfare state and the enactment of dozens of consumer- and environmental-protection laws.

Rationalists made some gains in wartime, when the president gained enhanced authority over the government and the economy, but most of these gains faded with the return to peace. Otherwise, rationalists have had to plug away at small, painfully won changes—the passage of the Budget and Accounting Act in 1921 (that created the Bureau of the Budget and the General Accounting Office), the acquisition by the president in 1935 of the power to reorganize by executive order (subject to a legislative veto), the expansion of the White House office pursuant to the recommendations of the PCAM, the passage of the Legislative Reorganization Act of 1946 that reduced the number of standing committees of Congress and laid the groundwork for the growth in congressional staff, and the creation in 1978 of the Senior Executive Service (SES) to permit more flexible use of high-level bureaucrats. Some of these changes, especially the creation of the Bureau of the Budget and the attendant growth of presidential control over the budget and the legislative agenda, were of great moment, but many proved to be short-lived or chimerical gains. The power to reorganize expired, and now that the legislative veto has been deemed unconstitutional, it probably cannot be revived. The White House staff has grown so much that it has become a bureaucratic problem in its own right. The reduction in the number of congressional committees was quickly followed by the growth in the number of subcommittees, leaving authority in Congress at least as decentralized as it had once been. The Senior Executive Service has been a disappointment: Not many top-level bureaucrats moved from one agency to another, rarely was a SES member fired, and the availability of cash bonuses did not seem to enhance performance.

Moreover, the very success of the liberals in supplying the agenda for and expanding the role of the federal government was achieved at the cost of major setbacks for the rationalist cause. The government became big before the president became institutionally (as opposed to personally) powerful. What Roosevelt and Johnson created, their successors could not easily manage. Moreover, the liberal gains in the late 1960s and early 1970s were accompanied by a radical decentralization of Congress. Liberal majorities in the House and Senate confronted the conservatives holding power as chairmen of certain key committees, such as the House Rules Committee and the House Ways and Means Committee. To move their agenda onto the floor where its passage was assured, liberals had to unseat committee chairmen they regarded as obstructionist, enhance the power of individual members at the expense of committee chairmen, modify the rules to make it harder to bottle up legislation in committee, and (in the Senate) alter, slightly, the cloture rule to reduce the threat of a filibuster. The effect of these changes, chiefly wrought by the House Democratic caucus, was to increase the power of individual congressmen and reduce the power of congressional leaders.

Politically, if not constitutionally, powers became more rather than less separated. The president now was held responsible for every imaginable domestic and foreign problem, but his capacity to make a systematic response to these problems was reduced by two changes: The growth in the size of the government had contributed to the growth in the number and variety of interest groups that sought to block presidential initiatives, and the decentralization of Congress reduced the president's ability to negotiate with a handful of congressional leaders who could help build legislative majorities.

Critics of the separation of powers could have made one of two responses to this state of affairs. The rationalist might have argued for a reduction in the size and scope of the federal government on the grounds that our policy commitments now exceeded our capacity to manage them. Or the rationalist could have reaffirmed his alliance with the liberals by arguing for more profound and sweeping changes—necessarily involving constitutional revision—in order to reduce the separation of powers sufficiently to permit the president to direct affairs in the new order By and large, rationalists have chosen the second course, and so we have such groups as the Committee on the Constitutional System (CCS), led by Lloyd Cutler, C. Douglas Dillon, and Senator Nancy Landon Kassebaum. Thirty or forty years ago, I surmise, such a group would have been arguing for a stronger Bureau of the Budget, a bigger White House staff, a more effective civil service system, fewer congressional committees, and (perhaps) stronger political parties. Most of those things happened, but now they seem inadequate to the task of directing a vast federal government. And so the call has gone out for constitutional reform.

To the CCS and its supporters, the need for fundamental change is almost self-evident. perhaps that is why so little of their writing is devoted to making the case for change. The most important essay, Lloyd Cutler's "To Form a Government," [7] is almost the only systematic effort to explain why we need to modify the separation of powers. Given their premises, of course, the need for change *is* virtually self-evident. To them, the public interest is a discoverable set of principles and goals from which right actions can be inferred. The means to achieve these ends must be comprehensively and efficiently related to those ends. This is more easily done by one mind than by 535, by an official responsible to a national electorate than by one beholden to many small electorates, and by a person able to carry out his policies subject to the check of electoral defeat than by one who cannot carry out any policies at all without first overcoming countless checks by subcommittees, committees, interest groups, and houses of Congress. The rationalist position, like rationality itself, seems to require little defense.

The intent of the Framers

But of course the Framers of the Constitution were not trying to create a government that would discern national goals and serve them efficiently and with dispatch; they were trying to create a limited government that would serve only those goals that could survive a process of consultation and bargaining designed to prevent the mischief of factions and the tyranny of passionate majorities or ambitious politicians. The CCS and its allies understand this but argue that conditions have changed since 1787: Public affairs today are more complex, interdependent, and fraught with peril than they were in the nineteenth century, and so we must modify our governing arrangements in order to meet these new challenges.

It is not difficult, of course, to produce a litany of difficulties facing the nation: a large budget and trade deficit, the threat of nuclear war, a complex array of international commitments, an economy painfully adjusting to new kinds of international competition, the cancer of crime and drug abuse, and so on. But it is not clear that these "new realities" are fundamentally different from the kinds of problems faced by Washington's first administration and it is certainly far from clear that they constitute a case for constitutional change.

The first administrations had to salvage a disrupted economy, pay off or otherwise settle a crushing war debt funded by worthless paper, worry about the presence of hostile British forces in Canada and a British navy at sea, cope with French control of the Mississippi River valley and Spanish control of Florida, put down a rebellion of Pennsylvania farmers protesting the tax on whiskey, reconcile the deep ideological divisions stirred up by the French Revolution, make legitimate the government in the eyes of skeptical Anti-Federalists and Jeffersonian Democrats, do battle with Indians waging war on the periphery of the new republic, and settle the hotly contested Jefferson-Adams presidential race by going to thirty-six ballots in the House of Representatives. Hardly simple times; hardly an easy test for the new constitutional order. It survived.

Today, the case for constitutional change is being made to a nation prosperous and at peace whose political institutions enjoy unquestioned legitimacy. Decision making is as contentious and protracted now as it was two hundred years ago, but under circumstances that are far more conducive to success and popular support than once was the case. In 1986, one can only be amused to reread the 1974 essay by Charles Hardin on why our government was then in crisis and why only major "constitutional surgery" could correct it. Watergate, the supposedly "imperial presidency," and popular distrust of government were the crisis; the cure required these changes: electing the president and Congress for coterminous four-year terms, abolishing the office of vice president, allowing Congress to remove a president by a vote of no confidence, giving the president an automatic majority in the House of Representatives, and so on. Of course, the "crisis" ended without any of these "cures." Watergate was handled by the normal constitutional procedures—congressional investigations, criminal trials, and the prospect of impeachment—and the presidency and the president are once again in high repute.

Real and Imagined Problems

But generalities cannot settle the matter. Let us look at the specific ways in which the constitutional system is allegedly defective: the deficit, economic policy, and foreign affairs.

1) *The deficit.* C. Douglas Dillon has argued for a parliamentary democracy because, unlike our system, it would more effectively address the problem of the deficit. There are two things wrong with his argument. The first is that there is no evidence at all that the deficit is a consequence of the separation of powers. At the President's request, taxes were cut. At the President's request, defense spending was increased. At the President's request, the Social Security system was preserved intact, with minor adjustments in tax and benefit levels. At the President's request, budgets were submitted that were not in balance. There are important differences between what the President has requested and Congress has approved with respect to many spending bills, but all of these differences, if resolved in the president's favor, would not produce a balanced budget. The deficit would be somewhat less, but not substantially so, if all presidential requests were automatically enacted by a subservient Congress. If Mr. Dillon is worried about the deficit, he need not vote for constitutional reform; he need only have voted against Mr. Reagan.

The second difficulty with the Dillon argument is immediately apparent when we examine the budgets of parliamentary democracies. There are important conceptual problems in comparing deficits across nations—consider, for example, the problem of comparing governments that do and do not own major industries, or that of comparing deficits between high- and low-inflation countries. Taking into account all these problems, Vito Tanzi of the International Monetary Fund, using data from the Organization for Economic Cooperation and Development (OECD), produces estimates for the 1984 deficit, measured in percentage of gross national product, that are arranged from high to low in Table I:

Table I.

DEFICIT COMPARISON ACROSS NATIONS FOR 1984[a]	
Country	Percentage of GNP
Italy	12.4
Ireland	12.3
Belgium	10.3
Greece	9.8
Denmark	6.0
Netherlands	5.9
Spain	5.7
Canada	5.3
Sweden	3.5
UNITED STATES	3.1
United Kingdom	2.8
Japan	2.3
Germany	1.4
Norway	− 2.4

[a] *Source:* Vito Tanzi, "The Deficit Experience in Industrial Countries," in Phillip Cagan, ed., *The Economy in Deficit* (Washington, D.C.: American Enterprise Institute, 1985), pp. 94–95.

Every nation on this list with a fiscal deficit except ours has a parliamentary democracy; that is to say, it is not governed in accordance with the separation of powers. Japan, Germany, and Norway have deficits smaller than ours; Italy, Ireland, Belgium, Greece, Denmark, the Netherlands, Spain, and Canada have much larger ones; France, Sweden, and the United Kingdom are about on a par with us. The safest conclusion that can be drawn from this list is that form of government has no effect on the size of the deficit.

A bolder inference, for which a case might be made, is that parliamentary regimes, by concentrating power in the hands of the executive, facilitate the adoption of new spending measures designed to satisfy the constituencies that brought the prime minister and his party into power. David Cameron has shown, for example, that government spending as a percentage of the gross domestic product and the rate of increase in that spending over the last twenty years or so has been higher in Belgium, France, Italy, the Netherlands, Norway, Sweden, and West Germany than in the United States. Only in Spain and Japan did the government spend less, and the rate of increase in spending in these countries was faster than it was in this country.[8] Moreover, much (but not all) of the difference between high- and low-spending nations is associated with leftist party control of the government. In any nation, liberals can win elections; in the United States, it is harder for them (or for conservatives) thereby to win control of the government. Parliamentary democracies may have the ability to make the "hard choices" the rationalists want, but it is far from clear they have any desire to do so. What is clear is that it is easier for them to make the easy choices.

2) *Economic policy.* We are constantly reminded that we live in an interdependent world undergoing rapid technological and economic change. Those who remind us of this situation claim that the United States does not respond to that change very well. We save and invest too little. We import too much. We allow jobs to be destroyed by Asian competitors. We fail to rebuild our smokestack industries. We regulate in cumbersome ways. We have too many small farmers. Our legal system imposes costly delays.

The implication of these criticisms is that there is a correct economic policy that a bold president would implement. (Among my students at UCLA, there is a widespread belief that a sufficiently bold president would turn out to be either Lee Iaccoca or Peter Ueberroth.) If the right president can be found, then he should be given the freedom to design and carry out his economic policy. If he fails, the voters will punish him at the next election; if he succeeds, the voters will reward him (unless, of course, constitutional reformers have succeeded in limiting him to a single six-year term).

In support of the virtues of greater decisiveness and comprehensiveness in economic policymaking, one can point to the fact that many other industrial nations have been more successful than the United States in taxing consumption (for example, the value added tax) and rewarding investment (for example, by not taxing capital gains). There is also evidence from several studies of other countries that their system of environmental regulation is less adversarial and less legalistic but just as effective as that in the United States.[9]

These are weighty arguments, but it is not clear they weigh in favor of movement toward a parliamentary regime. First, it is not obvious what economic policy is correct. Of course, advocates of a rationalist governing system will respond that, though no one knows for certain what policies will work, at least a strong, executive-centered system will permit us to try a given policy. Their view is that a yes-or-no referendum by the public is a better check on economic policymaking than a detailed scrutiny and amendment by Congress. I am not convinced. We may make new economic policy in half-hearted steps or tolerate inconsistent economic programs, but we thereby hedge our bets and avoid the extreme swings in policy that are characteristic of some other regimes. Britain nationalized, denationalized, renationalized, and then denationalized again several of its basic industries. France appears on the verge of doing the same.

Second, it is increasingly implausible to use "deadlock" as a word to describe economic policymaking in America. After many decades of increased regulation of prices and conditions of entry in such industries as domestic banking, aviation, securities trading, and telecommunications, a more or less measured and careful process of deregulation began that, though far from constituting a revolution, has revealed this nation's capacity for learning and self-correction. After decades during which Democrats demanded steeply progressive tax rates and Republicans went along in return for extensive deductions, the president and Congress renegotiated the terms of that old compact in favor of a system with less steep rates and fewer loopholes.

Third, the adversarial and legalistic nature of economic regulation here, while indisputable, reflects many factors in addition to the separation of powers. No doubt the separation of powers intensifies the adversarial nature of our regulatory system by empowering congressional critics of current regulatory law and enabling the courts to play a large role in reviewing and reversing regulatory decisions. But we live in an adversarial culture, the product of centuries devoted to defining politics as a struggle over rights. We are deeply imbued with a populist suspicion of the sort of behind-the-scenes negotiations that characterize regulatory policymaking in England and Sweden. The centralized nature of political and economic life abroad facilitates the settlement of issues by negotiations among peak associations, whereas here the decentralized political order and the more competitive economic one make it impossible to commit either the government or economic actors to the syndicalist pattern of decision making so often seen in Europe.

3) *Foreign policy.* Lloyd Cutler makes much of President Carter's inability to get the Senate to ratify the SALT II treaty in 1979. A president able to "form a government" would have been able to commit this country to such a treaty. Cutler points out that no prime minister is faced with the need to obtain senatorial ratification of treaties.

True enough. But one moment: The Senate rarely fails to ratify a treaty. It has approved something approaching a thousand treaties and turned down about twenty and just five in this century, of which only the Treaty of Versailles, establishing the League of Nations, was an important defeat. Of course, it can talk a treaty to death, as it almost did with SALT II (the *coup de grace* was not Senate but Soviet behavior—the USSR invaded Afghanistan before the treaty could come to a vote). But in general the Senate tends to go along.

The crucial question should not be whether the president should have more power over the Senate but whether the treaties that failed ratification were in the public interest. Just before describing Carter's problems with SALT II, Cutler speaks of the need for "making those decisions we all know must be made." Was SALT II such a decision? If so, Cutler leaves the argument unstated. Strong arguments can be and were made against it. Many thoughtful people believed that it was a bad treaty. The notion that ratification should be made easier so that the real check on the success of the president's policy is public reaction at the next election is chimerical: People rarely, if ever, vote for or against presidents because of the treaties they have signed, for the obvious reason that, barring some dramatic incident, the people have no way of knowing whether the treaty was a good or bad idea.

Foreign policy is more than treaties, of course. It is not hard to think of circumstances in which one would want the president to have a freer hand. It is not hard to think of ways of giving him a freer hand. If constitutional reformers are so keen on supplying a freer hand, it is curious that they spend so much time discussing quasi-parliamentary procedures and so little time discussing the virtues of repealing the War Powers Act, modifying congressional supervision of the Central Intelligence Agency, and eliminating the legislative veto over arms sales, none of which requires a constitutional amendment. One wonders whether the rationalists are really rationalists and not actually liberals in rationalist clothing, eager to have a president powerful enough to sign arms-control and nuclear-test-ban agreements but not strong enough to commit troops to Grenada or Lebanon or provide aid to anti-Marxist rebels in central America or Angola.

Still, a strong case can be made that in negotiating with foreign powers, the president of the United States is in an awkward position, not simply or even mainly because he must get the Senate to ratify his treaties, but because he must publicly negotiate simultaneously with both Congress (and congressionally am-plified domestic pressures) and the foreign power. When President Nixon was negotiating with the North Vietnamese to end the war in Southeast Asia, he had to make concessions to both Congress and the enemy, reducing any incentive the enemy had to make concessions in return. As President Reagan negotiates with the Soviet Union over arms control, it would be difficult for him to make credible and useful offers to constrain deployment of antisatellite weapons or the "Star Wars" defense system if Congress, in advance of the negotiations, places, on its own initiative, constraints on these weapons. It is hard to play poker if someone on your side frequently proclaims that you will give away certain chips regardless of what your opponent may do.

But it is unlikely that any of the most frequently discussed constitutional changes would materially improve the president's bargaining position. Putting members of Congress in the cabinet, letting the president serve a six-year term, or having the president and House members run as a team would leave the president and Congress in essentially the same relationship they are now: rivals for control over the direction of foreign policy.

The Unwritten Constitution

There are two fundamental arguments for a constitutional system of separate institutions sharing powers: It helps preserve liberty and it slows the pace of political change. Those arguments are as valid today as they were in 1787. Individual liberties are more secure when the actions of one part of the national government can be checked by, or appealed to, another. Political change is slower, and so the growth of new programs and public spending is slower, when any new proposal must survive the political obstacle course of bureaus, subcommittees, committees, and Houses of Congress.

Rationalists may view the delays, confusion, and inconsistencies produced by this system as costly, as of course they are. But they should not assume that if the costs were reduced or eliminated by reducing or eliminating the separation of powers, the advantages of this system would remain. Even Lloyd Cutler recog-nizes that a congressional system has some advantages over a parliamentary one; for one thing, the former permits investigations of executive misconduct that the latter does not. Watergate comes quickly to mind, but there are many other examples—Teapot Dome, defense procurement scandals, civil rights abuses, and organized crime. On a smaller scale, one cannot complain to one's congressman about an injustice and have much hope of redress if the power of Congress has been reduced.

Liberal proponents of reducing the separation of powers know full well that it impedes political change and that, I believe, is the major reason they favor such a reduction. At one time they might have worried that an executive-dominated system would threaten liberty, but they have become accustomed (and with good reason) to looking to the courts for the protection of personal liberty, and so this worry no longer seems as serious. That it is a larger state they wish and not simply a more efficient one is evident from the fact that, whereas they have often been eager to curb the independence of Congress, they have never (since 1935) been eager to curb the independence of the courts. yet judicial independence is probably as much a source of delays, confusion, and uncertainty as is congressional independence (consider how court review affects the operation of public schools, the management of prisons, or the settlement of personal injury claims). If over the last half century the courts had been under the control of conservative rather than liberal activists (or even under the control of conservatives, period), I imagine that liberal enthusiasm for constitutional reforms would not stop at the courthouse door.

Defending the principle of separation of powers is not the same as defending the practices that have developed around these constitutional principles. Don K. Price, like me, argues against constitutional change but argues in favor of changes in the "unwritten constitution," those customs and arrangements that allow a government of separate institutions to work at all.[10]

The most important provision of the unwritten constitution is the internal organization and procedures of Congress. The Constitution requires that the House and the Senate as a whole enact legislation, but it is silent on how many additional "enactments" must occur within the House and the Senate. At one time, there were virtually no congressional committees and no chairmen, at another time there were many powerful chairmen; at one time members of the House had great autonomy, at another time they yielded immense authority to the Speaker; at one time the House Rules Committee dominated the legislative process, at another time it played a smaller role; at one time seniority alone determined who should be chairman, at another time the party caucus influenced the choice of chairmen.

Leadership in the States

The variety of unwritten constitutions that can exist within a system of separate institutions is revealed by the experience of American state legislatures. No one can understand the politics of California by reading its constitution, because nowhere does it mention the extraordinary power exercised by the speaker of the assembly. Willie Brown is not elected speaker by the voters of the state, yet next to Governor George Deukemjian he is the most powerful official in that state. People accustomed to think of a lieutenant governor as a political nobody would not be prepared for the extraordinary power enjoyed by the lieutenant governor of Texas, who not only presides over the state senate but chooses the members and chairmen of its committees. If you went to Mississippi to do business with the state, you might think it important to meet the governor, but most people there will tell you that it is more important to meet with the speaker of the House. Like his counterparts in California and several other states, Speaker C. B. "Buddie" Newman of Mississippi can control the composition and leadership of key committees and determine the fate of much legislation.

The Congress of the United States, by contrast, is extremely decentralized and individualized. Speaker Sam Rayburn during the 1950s was not nearly as powerful as Speaker Thomas Reed in the 1890s, but he was far more powerful than Speaker Tip O'Neill in the 1980s. Congress, especially the House, has chosen to have weak leadership; in principle it could choose to have strong leadership. The methods are neither obscure nor unconstitutional: vest in the speaker or the majority leader the power to select and remove committee chairmen; change campaign finance laws so that the House and Senate campaign committees could raise and spend large sums of money on behalf of individual candidates and place control of these entities firmly in the hands of the speaker or majority leader; reduce the ability of individual members to create their own political action committees or to receive funds directly from the political action committees of others; and strengthen the power of the speaker or the majority leader to choose which committees shall consider bills and which bills will come to the floor for a vote. All of these things are done in state governments operating under essentially the same separation-of-powers principles as shape the national government.

It is not entirely clear why state legislatures (including such progressive ones as those in California, Massachusetts, and New York) should have resisted the tides of individualization and decentralization that have engulfed Congress. But two things are clear: First, the weakening of congressional leadership has been accomplished chiefly at the initiative of liberals who regarded strong leaders and chairmen as a barrier to liberal policies. Second, that weakening has reduced, or at least vastly complicated, the ability of the president to negotiate effectively with Congress. If one wishes to preserve the system of checks and balances but facilitate the process of bargaining and reciprocity essential to its operation, it makes more sense to enable the president to negotiate with four or five congressional leaders who can make commitments than to require him (or his legislative affairs staff) to negotiate with scores or even hundreds of individual members, none of whom can commit anyone but himself.

I am not optimistic that Congress will restore strong leadership. As I have written elsewhere,[11] there are very few examples in American history of people who possess certain powers voting to give them up or of people deciding they favored less democracy rather than more. And even if congressional leadership is strengthened, the president will certainly not be able to dominate the leaders who emerge. But it is in this area of the unwritten constitution that remedies for the defects of the separation of powers must be found. There are no constitutional remedies short of the abolition of the principle itself, and that is a price that two hundred years of successful constitutional government should have taught us is too high to pay.

Notes

1. Myers v. United States, 272 U.S. 52 (1926).
2. Humphrey's Executor v. United States, 295 U.S. 602 (1935).
3. Train v. City of New York, 420 U.S. 35 (1975).
4. Buckley v. Valeo, 424 U.S. 1 (1976).
5. Immigration and naturalization Service v. Chadha, 103 S. Ct. 2764 (1983).
6. Bowsher v. Synar, 106 S. Ct. 3181 (1986).
7. Lloyd N. Cutler, "To Form a Government," *Foreign Affairs*, Fall 1980, pp. 126–143.
8. David R. Cameron, "Does Government Cause Inflation? Taxes, Spending, and Deficits," in Leon N. Lindberg and Charles S. Maier, eds., *The Politics of Inflation and Economic Stagflation* (Washington, D.C.: Brookings Institution, 1985), pp. 230–232.
9. David Vogel, *National Styles of Regulation* (Ithaca, N.Y.: Cornell University Press, 1986); Steven J. Kelman, *Regulating America, Regulating Sweden* (Cambridge, Mass.: MIT Press, 1981).

10. Don K. Price, *America's Unwritten Constitution* (Baton Rouge, La.: Louisiana State University Press, 1983).

11. James Q. Wilson, "Political Parties and the Separation of Powers," in Robert A. Goldwin and Art Kaufman, eds., *Separation of Powers—Does It Still Work?* (Washington, D. C.: American Enterprise Institute, 1986, pp. 18–37.

 Chapter Five

The President
and the Bureaucracy

The president sits atop the largest and most complex entity in the federal government. Currently, the executive branch consists of fourteen departments and fifty-six independent agencies, commissions, and corporations all employing some 2.9 million civilian employees, eighty-eight percent of whom are scattered throughout the fifty states and around the world.

Despite the fact the president heads the executive branch, few twentieth-century presidents have felt they were masters of their own house. Indeed, were one to interview a president on the frustrations of the office, it would not be long at all before he mentioned the problems he encounters in securing the support and cooperation of this vast bureaucratic establishment. An outburst from Harry Truman best exemplifies this frustration: "I thought I was president, but when it comes to these bureaucracies, I can't make them do a damn thing." Of course, the president *is* able to exercise a measure of control over the bureaucracy through his power of appointment, his power to reorganize the executive branch, and his use of various coordinating procedures. These powers are not absolute, however. Some are subject to constitutional, statutory, and political limitations. Moreover, none of these powers is exercised in a vacuum, for the bureaucracy has power resources of its own, such as expertise, permanence, and carefully nurtured alliances in and outside government. Finally, it should be noted that even if presidents were not encumbered by the realities identified here, effective control over the bureaucracy would be less than complete if only because of its size and complexity.

In campaigning for the presidency, Ronald Reagan repeatedly inveighed against the size and intrusiveness of the federal government. This attitude, combined with a belief that career bureaucrats were unsympathetic to his conservative agenda, fueled his administration's comprehensive effort to gain control over the bureaucracy. The strategies used for this purpose, as well as their ultimate impact, are detailed by Peter Benda and Charles Levine in the first article of this chapter. In the second, Bert Rockman focuses more generally on the relationship between presidents and the bureaucracy. Noting that a mismatch of incentives makes inevitable a certain degree of tension between the president and career bureaucrats, he explains why the strain has become more severe in the last twenty years. Rockman believes that this development is not in the long-term interest of the president, and he outlines a presidential management strategy designed to enlist greater cooperation from the permanent government.

Peter M. Benda and Charles H. Levine

Reagan and the Bureaucracy: The Bequest, the Promise, and the Legacy

Peter M. Benda is assistant professor in the Department of Political Science at Swarthmore College. Charles H. Levine, now deceased, was Distinguished Professor of Government and Public Administration at American University in Washington, D.C. Here they chronicle and evaluate the Reagan administration's unparalleled attempt to gain greater control over the bureaucracy via centralization, devolution, privatization, administrative modernization, and cost control.

When Ronald Reagan took office on 20 January 1981, he was taking control of a damaged institution. The Presidency had been rocked by the Watergate scandal, the Iran hostage crisis, and a decade of economic "stagflation." The Carter administration had left office discredited—unable in the minds of the electorate to manage the nation's affairs in matters big or small. Some of President Carter's difficulties were directly traceable to the widespread perception that he had failed to deliver on one of his major promises in the campaign of 1976, that is, to make the government and its principal agent, the bureaucracy, more "manageable."

The 1980 Reagan campaign made similar promises. To avoid the problems that had undermined the Carter Presidency, the Reagan White House formulated a plan that was at once more limited and yet considerably more ambitious than its predecessor. In fact, from the outset, the Reagan administration pursued a campaign to maximize presidential control over the federal bureaucracy that was more *self-conscious* in design and execution, and more *comprehensive* in scope, than that of any other administration of the modern era.

Near the end of President Reagan's second term, the neat logic tying together the administration's policy goals, administrative strategies, and overall institutional objectives for a strong Presidency no longer seems to retain its original coherence. Although some policy goals have been achieved in whole or in part and some management strategies have worked as planned, the administration's hope for a strong Presidency based on tight control over an effective and efficient bureaucracy has only partially materialized.

In searching for an explanation as to why the Reagan administration's management strategy has only partly succeeded, one is drawn to contradictions inherent

Peter M. Benda and Charles H. Levine, "Reagan and The Bureaucracy: The Bequest, The Promise and The Legacy." *The Reagan Legacy*, ed. by Charles O. Jones (Chatham, NJ.: Chatham House, 1988), pp. 102-142. Reprinted by permission.

in the logic of the original plan and to counterproductive administrative tactics that came to light as the plan unfolded over the President's two terms in office. Historians are likely to point to the Iran-*contra* scandal in late 1984 as the signal turning point of the Reagan Presidency. But smaller and less noticed administrative breakdowns and developments have contributed to the mixed record of success.

To understand why and how these problems arose, it is necessary to understand that the Reagan administration's objectives for managing the executive branch have remained consistent over the years, but its tactics have changed, especially in the President's second term. Thus, while the White House continues to espouse three central goals for the administrative arm of government—the political control and coordination of policy formulation *and* implementation; "debureaucratization" through devolution and privatization; and administrative cost cutting through systems modernization, productivity improvement, and the tight control of personnel costs—it has several times changed directions in attempting to achieve them.

This chapter reviews these developments in order to assess their effects on the Reagan administration's ability to achieve its goals as well as their longer-term implications for the relationship between the Presidency and the bureaucracy. We address five important and related questions:

1. What did Reagan inherit from Carter?
2. What control and coordination devices did Reagan add?
3. What "debureaucratization" (i.e. devolution and privatization) strategies were found workable?
4. What management initiatives served to modernize government, enhance productivity, and cut administrative costs?
5. What short- and long-term effects did these initiatives have on the institutional capacity of the federal government and its workforce?

What Carter Left to Reagan

The Reagan administration received three legacies from the Carter experience: (1) some lessons about what *not* to do; (2) some lessons about what *to* do; and (3) some mechanisms for better controlling the executive branch. In the first category, Reagan administration strategists concluded that President Reagan should not be drawn into the political quagmire that surrounds large-scale executive branch reorganization efforts. Unlike Carter, who entered the reorganization process with only vague notions of "streamlining" the executive branch, President Reagan had a vision for changing government that minimized the value of redesigning the formal administrative structure of the executive branch. Moreover, Carter's attempt to rationalize the budget process taught Reagan strategists that attempting to reform budgeting through changes in the format and processes of budgeting would yield more paper than product. The control and reduction of government spending would eventually have to be accomplished through political control of the appropriations process, not changes in budgetary techniques. Finally, Carter's experience with deregulation underscored the importance of having a unified team to implement reform.

On the positive side, Carter's experience taught Reagan that special councils like the President's Management Improvement Council could spotlight ideas for the modernization and improvement of administrative processes. Carter's effort to attack instances of fraud, waste, and abuse in the bureaucracy by using inspectors general also proved to be a popular idea that Reagan would later expand upon. Finally, Carter's civil service reform, in addition to reforming the federal personnel system's institutional structure, also introduced the notion of "pay for performance" to parts of the federal workforce—an idea that would be encompassed in a major pay-reform package proposed by the Reagan administration in 1986.

The third cluster of bequests that Carter left Reagan concerned the machinery for managing the federal government. Most of these tools, like the creation of the inspectors general, regulatory review, and civil service reform, enhanced the ability of the President to gain greater control over the bureaucracy. Thus, although the Carter administration never fully succeeded in making the bureaucracy "manageable," it did contribute significantly in providing ideas and structures that strengthened President Reagan's hand in 1981.

The Reagan Managerial Strategy

Questions about the administrative legacies of the Reagan era are important because the effort to reshape the organization and administrative apparatus used to carry out government's role has been an intregal component of the so-called Reagan revolution. Such questions are not easily answered because in its approach to management the Reagan administration has pursued a threefold strategy of centralization, devolution and privatization, and administrative modernization and cost control, whose long-term implications are difficult to gauge.

Part of the difficulty in assessing the Reagan administration's approach to executive branch management lies in the fact that the various elements of its managerial strategy did not emerge fully blown when President Reagan assumed office in 1981, but came to light only gradually or in phases. Thus, the administration's agenda for management improvement and reform, which initially betrayed a strong centralizing impulse, was later offset by an increased emphasis on decentralization and devolution—shifting in accordance with a changed political environment. But while combining tactics of centralization and decentralization in one overall management strategy may be ultimately compatible, the attempt to move in both directions at once can give rise to distinctive problems, tensions, and mixed results.

Centralizing Control

Personnel Selection

The Reagan administration assumed office with a keen awareness of the need to ensure that the politics that won President Reagan the 1980 election would not be forgotten in managing the government. In particular, Reagan and his key advisors recognized that making effective use of the President's appointment power would be an essential ingredient in translating Reagan's electoral mandate into a successful managerial strategy.

In fact, efforts to recruit a loyal team of supporters began as early as April 1980 when long-term Reagan adviser Edwin Meese III asked Pendleton James, a former White House official, to set up a personnel operation. Using five criteria as their guide—compatibility with the President's philosophy, integrity, toughness, competence, and being a team player—James and his staff set about the daunting task of identifying candidates for 3000-plus "political" appointments Reagan would be authorized to fill on entering office. Following the election, these efforts were intensified. With James at the helm, the Reagan administration "undertook transition personnel selection with more forethought, with a larger commitment of resources, and with more attention than any administration ever." The high priority President-elect Reagan and his key advisors attached to the careful screening of potential appointees was born of one overriding concern. Essentially, they sought to avoid repeating what all concerned regarded as a crucial mistake committed by incoming Presidents Nixon and Carter. Each of these Presidents had initially allowed department heads considerable leeway in selecting their principal subordinates and assembling their own management teams—a decision both came to regret. President Reagan and his aides were determined not to fall into this trap. Hence, even while the new President was publicly extolling the virtues of cabinet government, steps were being taken to ensure that ultimate control over subcabinet appointments—indeed, over *all* lower-level political appointments—would remain firmly in the hands of the White House.

The task of ensuring tight control over appointments fell principally to the White House Office of Presidential Personnel (OPP) under the leadership of Pendleton James. Generally regarded as something of a "stepchild" in the ranks of White House offices, the OPP emerged from the shadows during the early stages of the Reagan Presidency to become a key force in mobilizing the support that would be necessary to carry out the Reagan agenda. James himself was accorded the rank of assistant to the President and given an office in the West Wing of the White House. With a staff of over a hundred, the OPP not only assumed principal responsibility for recruiting and selecting appointees for all cabinet-level and agency-head positions but carefully screened candidates for vacancies at the assistant, deputy, and undersecretary levels, as well as directorships of major agency subunits. Indeed, the OPP was "directly involved in recruiting and approving persons for all political positions at levels below the cabinet right down to private secretaries." Even with a large staff and the help of a new computerized tracking system, the OPP could not have handled a personnel operation of this magnitude without some imput from the departments and agencies concerned, nor did it always have the clout to dictate appointments at the subcabinet level. There can be no question, however, that the OPP played an instrumental role in the entire recruitment and selection effort. It successfully discharged its responsibility to ensure careful White House scrutiny of and control over a vast array of personnel decisions, thereby laying the groundwork for the implementation of the Reagan managerial strategy. As James put it, "We handled all the appointments: boards, commissions, Schedule Cs, ambassadorships. . . . [I]f you are going to run the government, you've got to control the people that come into it."

Cabinet Councils

By refusing to delegate the appointment authority to members of the cabinet, and by insisting on demonstrated ideological compatibility with the personal loyalty to the President as necessary conditions for employment, the Reagan White House clearly sought to offset the likelihood that the administration's appointees would end up becoming more responsive to their own bureaucracies, interest groups, or Congress than to the Reagan agenda. Needless to say, the Reagan approach was not immune to criticism. Some observers argued that the administration leaned too far in the direction of White House control, that undue emphasis was placed on ideological purity at the expense of other considerations (especially prior government experience and/or managerial competence), and that the comparatively slow pace at which lower-level appointments were made "did little to facilitate the transition in the administration of the executive branch." Several of the administration's early major appointments, notably of Anne Gorsuch Burford and James Watt, to head the Environmental Protection Agency (EPA) and the Department of the Interior, proved politically costly. In addition, the number of administration appointees who have faced or may yet face prosecution for alleged transgression of federal conflict-of-interest and related statutes clearly has been a major source of embarrassment.

These criticisms notwithstanding, the administration clearly succeeded in bringing about a unprecedented depth of loyalty and activism among its appointees through the careful and systematic use of the appointment power. As Elizabeth Sanders recently observed, the result of the high priority the President and his aides assigned to White House control of personnel is that "Reagan has achieved a degree of loyalty and coherence in the bureaucracy that other Presidents have longed for. . . .His practices (in this respect) differ from those of his predecessors in their effectiveness, not their intent." The use of appointment power may have contributed importantly to the triumph of Reagan management," but it was far from the only factor. Nor was it the only device utilized by the administration in its effort to ensure bureaucratic "responsiveness" to the Reagan agenda. Despite the care taken in appointing the cabinet and filling key executive posts, the President and his key aides remained extremely wary of the possibility that these officials might "marry the natives" (i.e., end up functioning as departmental advocates to the White House rather than as a team of White House emissaries to the departments).

To prevent this scenario from coming to pass, the Reagan White House was convinced that additional steps were needed to keep those in cabinet and subcabinet positions at a safe distance from the career civil servants who comprise the "permanent government." This promised to become more difficult with the passage of time, once the departments and agencies were operating at full strength and the "cycle of accommodation" between political appointees and the career civil service had set in. The President and his aides had to devise a way to counteract the potential threat such an "accommodation" might pose to vigorous and unified pursuit of the Reagan agenda—without, however, allowing relations between the White House and the departments to degenerate into a we/they confrontation.

It would seem to present no small challenge to devise a scheme that would serve these potentially conflicting objectives. Within months after the administration came to office, however, the groundwork had been laid for a set of institutional arrangements that proved (for a time at least) remarkably well adapted to this purpose. At the heart of this set of arrangements was a system of "cabinet councils," established in February 1981 at the recommendation of Presidential Counselor Edwin Meese III. Originally, there were five councils—the Cabinet Councils on Economic Affairs (CCEA), Commerce and Trade (CCCT), Human Resources (CCHR), Natural Resources and Energy (CCNRE), and Food and Agriculture (CCFA)—"consisting of from six to ten cabinet Secretaries and the heads of EOP cabinet-level offices as principal members, including a departmental secretary as chairman *pro tempore*." Two additional cabinet councils, one Legal Policy (CCLP), the other on Management and Administration (CCMA), were established in January and September 1982.

In general terms, cabinet councils operated at the second or third tier in the Reagan White House policy apparatus. Their primary function was to serve as focal points to pull together executive branch and White House resources and facilitate coordinated action on a number of important but decidedly second-level policy issues that affected the interests of more than one department or agency (ranging from coal exports [CCCT] and dairy price supports [CCFA] to outer continental shelf leases [CCNRE] and family planning regulations [CCHR]). Some of the councils (notably the CCEA) were quite active, and each played a useful role in providing a forum, under the overall supervision of the White House Office of Policy Development (OPD), for cabinet deliberation on issues of common concern. Despite their affiliation with the OPD, however, these councils dealt with what one commentator has characterized as "a host of matters that scarcely fit the term *policy development*; they (were) more concerned with facilitating implementation of agendas." In the end, Hugh Helco has suggested, the cabinet councils served to underscore the primacy of a few key actors in domestic policy affairs by "forcing departmental policy development into a system of strategic decision making closely held at the White House."

That the cabinet council system was designed to keep political executives focused on the Reagan agenda while insulating them from the permanent departmental bureaucracies is apparent in the "rules of the game" on which the system's operation was predicted. The primary rule, as James P. Pfiffner has observed, was that "issues were not to be brought up to the President on a bilateral basis, but that all issues (were) to be 'roundtabled' by discussing them at a cabinet meeting." Obviously, the requirement that all issues be "roundtabled" made it that much harder for individual cabinet secretaries to act as effective advocates or brokers for particular policy proposals impressed on them by the career bureaucracy. Any such proposal would have to survive "the scrutiny and criticism of cabinet peers and White House staff members" before making its way higher up the chain of command.

Of course, an individual cabinet secretary might still try to end-run the councils and lobby the President on his or her own, but White House staffers were continually on guard against this possibility, and Reagan himself appears to have been generally unreceptive to special appeals of this kind.

While the cabinet council system therefore seems to have fulfilled White House hopes and expectations during Reagan's first term, the President's second term brought with it major changes of both personnel and structure. In April 1985, the seven separate councils were eliminated, their functions absorbed into two new major policy councils: the Domestic Policy Council, chaired by Attorney General-designate Edwin Meese III, and the Economic Policy Council, headed by the new secretary of the treasury, James Baker. Although President Reagan claimed that this reorganization of the Executive Office policy apparatus reflected his continuing commitment to cabinet government, the action "was interpreted generally as a further centralizing of power in the White House." In fact, the changes made during the early stages of Reagan's second term seem to have had even more of a centralizing effect than some of their proponents had intended. As Pfiffner points out, although "dual roles of Meese and Baker had the potential to give them major influence across the full range of domestic policy development, . . .[new chief of staff, Donald] Regan's domination of the White House policy apparatus and personnel did not allow that to happen." The principals began to "go their own way," largely ignoring the cabinet council system in pursuit of policy objectives of particular concern to them. In general, White House decision making during the early phases of Reagan's second term appears to have been characterized by the kind of lack of communication and mutual distrust that came to light during and after the Iran-*contra* revelations, not to be remedied—and only partially at that—until Howard Baker replaced Regan as the President's chief of staff.

The Office of Management and Budget

As the first-term cabinet council experiment suggests, certain Reagan administration institutional innovations undertaken with a view to strengthening presidential authority over the "permanent bureaucracy" may be said to have gone the way of history. No account of developments in this area could be complete, however, that failed to take cognizance of the role of the Office of Management and Budget (OMB). And here the Reagan administration has left a mark that seems likely to endure. Although the authority of what used to be known as the Bureau of the Budget (BOB) over agency affairs has been expanding fairly steadily since it was made part of the new Executive Office of the President in 1939—its original role in supervising preparation of the executive budget having been augmented over time by the power to (among other things) clear agency legislative proposals and establish agency personnel ceilings—the Reagan years have witnessed a notable acceleration in this trend. Indeed, for better or ill (and opinions vary widely on this score), the OMB seems destined to emerge from the Reagan years as a more formidable instrument of presidential control than ever before.

Budgetary Control. Much of the OMB's prominence in the Reagan years can be attributed to David Stockman, Reagan's OMB director from 1981 to 1985. A former representative from Michigan, Stockman brought to his post an intimate familiarity with the often arcane dynamics of the congressional budget process and soon developed a deserved reputation for brilliance for his detailed grasp of domestic programs and expenditures. Convinced no less than the President himself that those expenditures had to be sharply reduced, Stockman took a number of quick and decisive steps with the assistance of White House officials and his OMB staff to restore the budget as an instrument of presidential policy.

"Whether or not as a designed administrative strategy," Frederick C. Mosher has observed, "OMB made administrative decisions on agency policies and programs during the spring of 1981 with little reference to the departments and agencies concerned." The success of what Stockman would later refer to as a "divide-and-conquer" strategy—OMB and the White House imposing program and spending cuts on the President's new cabinet secretaries—was the first step in the stunning 1981 "Reagan budget juggernaunt." Subsequently, through the novel use of the congressional reconciliation process, the administration succeeded in pushing through the Congress over 100 pages of changes (affecting more than 250 programs) in authorizations and appropriations in the budget for fiscal year 1982.

The "budget juggernaut" was an event of considerable significance. Among other things, it served as another object lesson for the new members of Reagan's cabinet, underscoring in no uncertain terms that whatever the nature of the President's commitment to "cabinet government," authority over departmental budgets, like authority over personnel, would not be delegated. More important, it brought about unprecedented across-the-board cuts in domestic programs and expenditures, thereby contributing significantly to the goal of reducing the federal government's role in the nation's economic and social life that President Reagan had proclaimed as central to his administration's agenda.

One should not lose sight, however, of the longer-term costs of the strategy OMB's Stockman and the White House used to achieve these results. In the first place, many members of Congress regarded the Reagan/Stockman actions in 1981 as overstepping the conventional boundaries of the executive role in the budget process. They appreciated the perversity of the fact that the Budget and Impoundment Control Act of 1974, which was designated to enhance congressional control over the budget and limit that of the President, had been manipulated to achieve the opposite effect. At the least, reconciliation would henceforth no longer be acceptable as a major device for shaping presidential policy. Second, the quality of figures, assumptions, and projections on which the administration relied in 1981 left much to be desired, and the executive budget lost a good deal of credibility as a "responsible" document. Thereafter, many in Congress were simply not prepared to give the administration's (or OMB's) calculations the benefit of the doubt. For this and other reasons, every budget Reagan submitted after 1981 was promptly pronounced "dead on arrival" and almost completely ignored on Capitol Hill.

Regulatory Review. While OMB Director Stockman's high-profile effort to "sell" the first Reagan budget and legislative economic package catapulted OMB onto the front pages of the newspapers on 1981, the agency was far from quiescent on other fronts. Within a month after the President assumed office, the administration had taken a number of important steps in an effort to bring executive agency regulatory activity more directly under presidential supervision and control than ever before, and it had become unmistakably clear that it intended OMB to play a major role in the effort.

The promulgation on 17 February 1981 of Executive Order 12291 on "Federal Regulation," which lay the groundwork for OMB's assumption of that role, represented far more than the mere continuation of a trend. To be sure, White House-level oversight mechanisms established with a view to ensuring some measure of presidential input into and control over agency regulatory decision making had become ever more elaborate in character (and ever more comprehensive in scope) since the Nixon administration initiated the process with the introduction of its "Quality of Life" in 1971. But Executive Order 12291, whose chief requirement was that all "major" agency regulatory proposals survive cost-benefit analysis, represented a departure in kind from what had come before, and it was to be followed by a second directive, Executive Order 12498 of January 1985, which further consolidated presidential control over the regulatory process. Seidman and Gilmour have captured the essence of the transformation wrought by the "Reagan revolution" in regulatory review very well:

> One result of the Nixon, Ford, and Carter measures was to broaden somewhat the President's authority over (executive agency) regulations, but it is evident that the central objective was to stem the mounting flood of regulations and to reduce the burden on the private sector. *No one had yet perceived that review of regulations would take its place with budgetary review as one of the principal management tools available to the President.*

What steps brought this transformation about? In this as in other spheres, the Reagan administration moved very quickly to effect major changes in inherited institutional arrangements. The promise to eliminate burdensome and unnecessary regulations had figured as a prominent theme in Ronald Reagan's campaign, and the new President took prompt steps to begin to redeem that pledge. Two days after he assumed office, the White House announced the creation of a Task Force on Regulatory Relief, chaired by Vice-President George Bush, to review "major regulatory proposals by executive agencies" and to help formulate regulatory policy. The creation of the task force provided an early and clear signal of the Reagan administration's intention to establish a more centralized, top-down system for control of agency regulatory activity.

The Task Force on Regulatory Relief (which was disbanded in August 1983) made its most important contribution to the Reagan regulatory program by playing a lead role in the development of Executive Order 12291. This presidential directive, whose stated purpose was "to reduce the burdens of existing and future regulations, increase agency accountability for regulatory actions, (and) provide for presidential oversight of the regulatory process," effected a number of significant changes in the procedural and substantive requirements laid down in Carter's Executive Order 12044. In essence, the new order (1) directed that, "to the extent permitted by law," all "major" rules issued by executive branch agencies survive cost-benefit analysis; and (2) authorized the director of OMB, who has charged with reviewing agency Regulatory Impact Analyses (RIAs) detailing the costs and benefits of all such rules, to delay their implementation in proposed or final form.

Considerable controversy has surrounded several of Executive Order 12291's specific provisions, particularly its cost-benefit analysis requirements, and the manner in which they have been applied. Two other preliminary points about the order's implementation warrant special emphasis, for each contributed significantly to the larger dispute engendered by the launching of the Reagan regulatory review program.

First, was the administration's decision to lodge day-to-day responsibility for ensuring agency compliance with the requirements of Executive Order 12291 in the newly established Office of Information and Regulatory Affairs (OIRA) within OMB. This office had been created by the Paperwork Reduction Act of 1980, which was enacted in the waning days of the Carter Presidency. The act was passed by

Congress only after steps had been taken to allay concerns about the possibility that it might be used to increase OMB's authority over the substantive policies and programs of the departments and agencies. In its report accompanying the bill, the Senate Governmental Affairs Committee noted that provisions had been added to guard against this possibility, and emphasized, with respect to OIRA, that it did "not intend that regulatory reform issues which go beyond the scope of information management and burden be assigned to the office."

The move to use OIRA as a comprehensive clearinghouse for regulations was almost immediately challenged on the grounds that the President had exceeded his constitutional authority in promulgating Executive Order 12291. On balance, however, this objection probably took a "back seat" to another concern that appears to have loomed larger in the eyes of OMB's critics both in and out of Congress, which had to do with the large element of *secrecy* that characterized OIRA's role in the review process. This is the second important preliminary point to bear in mind in seeking to understand the controversy surrounding the Reagan regulatory review program.

The regulatory clearance process under Executive Order 12291 necessitates frequent contact between officials in OMB and the executive branch agencies whose rules are submitted to OIRA for review. Despite the fact that the Executive Order authorized the OMB director to delay publication of "major" rules until he (or the OIRA staff) was satisfied that its cost-benefit requirements had been met, the Reagan administration, at least initially, *made no provision whatsoever to enable "outsiders" to become apprised of what transpired during the course of OMB-agency negotiations over a particular rule*, that is, to discover whether or how OMB's intercession may have shaped the outcome of the rulemaking process. Moreover, while the prospect of secret communication between White House officials and agency regulation writers was disturbing enough in its own right, critics argued that the problem was compounded by the administration's failure to impose any limitations on the freedom of task force members or OIRA staff to meet "off the record" with outside private parties who might have a stake in the outcome of the review process. In effect, the administration thereby afforded regulated firms who felt that agency officials had not taken their concerns sufficiently into account an additional opportunity to make their influence felt "through the back door."

The lack of procedural safeguards in the Reagan regulatory review program also fueled controversy about the cost-benefit analytic requirements of Executive Order 12291 and how these provisions might be (or were being) applied in practice. Critics pointed to OMB's requirement that a very high 10 percent "discount rate" be used in attempting to put a price value on the future benefits of regulation as one piece of evidence that cost-benefit analysis was not being used as a neutral decision-making tool, but instead represented a "thinly disguised justification for deregulating business and industry." The secrecy of the entire review process only served to reinforce that perception.

Neither the sometimes vociferous congressional criticism of its regulatory review program nor the occasional reprimands OMB received from reviewing courts deterred the Reagan administration from aggressively implementing Executive Order 12291. By the end of Reagan's first term, it became apparent that although the vast majority of rules submitted to OIRA were "nonmajor" and cleared without much delay or controversy, the total number of rules sent to OMB for clearance had declined appreciably, indicating that the administration's efforts to reduce the overall volume of federal regulation were paying off. The period between 1981 and 1984 also witnessed a steady decline in the percentage of total rules found consistent with the Executive Order and without need for changes (from 87.3 percent in 1981 to 78.0 percent in 1984), while the percentage of those found consistent after "minor" changes increased considerably (from 4.9 percent in 1981 to 15.2 percent in 1984). In short, while there was a perceptible "slowdown" in overall regulatory activity during Reagan's first term—a fact reflected in the sharp decline in the total number of rulemaking documents published in the *Federal Register*—OMB's influence over agency regulatory decision making expanded steadily over the four year.

Shortly after the 1984 election, the Reagan administration took another major step forward in its effort to centralize control over executive agency regulatory activity by promulgating Executive Order 12498, which requires each agency to develop an annual "regulatory program" to be submitted to OIRA specifying "all significant regulatory actions . . .planned or underway, including . . .the development of documents that may influence, anticipate, or could lead to the commencement of rulemaking proceedings." In a very real sense, Executive Order 12498 may be regarded as the culmination of the Reagan administration's efforts to bring the "permanent bureaucracy" firmly under direct presidential supervision and control. For each item on the annual submissions required under that order, the burden is on the agency to "explain how they are consistent with the administration's regulatory principles." If OMB decides that a proposed "prerulemaking action" (including, for example, the decision to create a task force to investigate the seriousness of certain health or safety risks) is inconsistent with the administration's regulatory principles, the agency is precluded from taking that action. And if during the year the agency decides to undertake an activity that was not originally part of the approved program, it must first seek OMB's approval. Indeed, under Executive Order 12498, *all* agency regulatory action is *automatically* stayed until OMB certifies that the action is "consistent . . .with the administration's policies and priorities."

While the promulgation of Executive Order 12498 promised to place OMB even more firmly in command of the regulatory process, congressional opposition to the administration's regulatory program intensified during the President's second term. This was particularly true in the House, where, in 1986, a number of representatives led by John Dingell (D-Michigan), chairman of that chamber's Energy an Commerce Committee, prevailed on their colleagues to eliminate fiscal 1987 funding for OIRA. Although the Senate ultimately refused to go along, some concessions were wrung from the administration and OMB along the way. For example, OMB responded to congressional criticism of OIRA's "closed" review process by agreeing to adopt new procedures designed to increase public disclosure of the office's review of agency regulations under Executive Order 12291 and of agency regulatory programs under 12498.

Some senators hailed this last decision to "open up" the review process, but critics countered that the new disclosure procedures did not go far enough and would do little to stymie OMB's growing authority over regulatory decision making. And in fact, despite mounting criticism in and out of Congress, OIRA during the second term became more aggressive in reviewing agency regulations. The number of total rules found "consistent without change" under Executive Order 12291 declined an additional 9.7 percent between 1984 and 1986, while the number of those found "consistent with change" was up an additional 7.8 percent (from 15.2 percent to 22.9 percent) during the same time.

Reagan's successor may not share his particular priorities in regulatory policy, but it seems unlikely that the next President will elect to dismantle the very effective regulatory and paperwork-clearance mechanisms the Reagan administration has put in place. The establishment of these mechanisms was central to the process whereby the administration succeeded in fashioning "the most powerful budget bureau since the office was created in 1921."

"Debureaucratization": Devolution and Privatization

The most direct way to diminish the federal government's role in economic and social affairs in simply to reduce the range of activities in which it is involved. The Reagan administration clearly appreciated this fact and sought to eliminate many federal domestic programs outright. This effort may be regarded as one element of a broader campaign to "debureaucratize" the federal executive establishment—that is, to place greater reliance on third parties, such as state and local governments, private firms, and nonprofit organizations to perform functions or provide services previously entrusted to the national government.

The process of consciously transferring federal responsibilities to the states and localities is referred to as *devolution*, while *privatization* refers to attempts to transfer governmental responsibilities to the private sector. The discussion that follows examines the Reagan administration's initiatives in each sphere.

Devolution

In his first inaugural address, President Reagan proclaimed that a central objective of his administration would be "to demand recognition of the distinction between the powers granted to the federal government and those reserved to the states or to the people." This statement signaled an attempt to chart a new course in intergovernmental affairs. Rather than seek to strengthen and improve the management of existing intergovernmental programs, as most earlier reformers had done, the Reagan administration set out to work a fundamental redistribution of responsibilities between the local, state, and federal governments.

In the administration's view, such a redistribution of responsibilities was necessary to redress imbalances in the federal system resulting largely from the increased reliance during the 1960s and 1970s on federal grants-in-aid to state and local governments as a preferred means for carrying out domestic programs.

The Reagan administration believed that this attempt to expand the scope of the national government's involvement in social and economic policy represented a serious "overreaching" of federal authority, both in the sense that it infringed on functions properly reserved to the states or localities and in the sense that many domestic programs could be run more effectively at the state or local level. It was also concerned that grants-in-aid programs had rendered the states and localities overly dependent on federal resources and unduly constrained by a host of federal requirements, and that outlays for federal aid as a whole, which nearly doubled in the 1960s and continued to expand rapidly in the 1970s, reaching an all-time high (17 percent of all federal spending) in 1978, were taking too big a "bite" out of the budget.

The Reagan intergovernmental agenda thus called for reductions in or the termination of federal aid programs wherever possible. This was to be accompanied by efforts to relax or eliminate national rules and standards that constrained the flexibility of state and local officials in using federal monies they *did* receive. Important steps toward achieving these objectives were taken with the passage of the 1981 Omnibus Reconciliation Act. This legislation achieved the first absolute reduction in federal aid outlays in several decades (from $94.8 billion in FY 1981 to $88.2 billion in FY 1982). Some sixty grant programs were simply eliminated, while funding levels for others were dramatically reduced. At the same time, seventy-seven "categorical" grant programs were consolidated into nine broader, more flexible "block" grants—the largest such conversion in history.

These early Reagan intergovernmental initiatives provoked a good deal of controversy. Although the administration sought to justify a large-scale reduction in federal assistance in part on the grounds that this "rollback would encourage state and local governments to expand the scope of their activities, skeptics argued that Reagan was "not seeking to shift government responsibilities anywhere as much as he (was) seeking to abolish or reduce interventions he (did) not like." And while grant consolidation "has long been advocated as a good technique for streamlining both federal and recipient management, the fact that many of Reagan's block-grant proposals were linked to substantial funding reductions elicited considerable protest from the recipients (i.e., state and local officials) as well as from members of Congress, many of whom traditionally have been wary of block grants, primarily out of concern that state and local officials cannot be trusted to channel funds to those regions and people most in need. Thus, while the administration was able to achieve "some remarkable legislative successes in grant consolidation and domestic expenditure reductions" in 1981, it created a climate of suspicion that placed its subsequent intergovernmental reform proposals, most notably its ambitious 1982 "Federalism Initiative," in serious jeopardy.

The Federalism Initiative, which President Reagan unveiled in his 1982 State of the Union address, was the most serious attempt the administration made to "devolve" domestic program responsibilities back to the states and to clarify the allocation of functions between the state and federal governments. The initiative had two major components: a "swap" (or tradeoff) component affecting the nation's three largest means-tested transfer programs, and a "turnback" component affecting approximately forty-five categorical grant programs. The "swap" component called for the federal government to assume full responsibility for Medicaid, which provides medical care for the poor and is the largest of the income transfer programs. In exchange, the states would assume complete responsibility for the AFDC (Aid to Families with Dependent Children) and food stamp programs. The "turnback" component proposed a phased withdrawal of the federal government from programs in education, community development, transportation, and social services. A Federalism Trust Fund of $28 billion would be used to fund the turnback programs during a four-year transition period, after which both the fund and special federal taxes supporting it would begin to phase out, "leaving it to the states to determine whether or not to replace lost revenues and services." Although negotiations between top administration and state and local government representatives on the details of the Federalism Initiative were conducted throughout 1982, it is very unlikely that whatever package they might have come up with would have received a serious hearing in Congress, which was distinctly unreceptive to the scheme. As David R. Beam has noted, the timing of the initiative's introduction did not help the administration's cause; "The turnback and tradeoff initiates aroused hostility, in part, because they were advanced along with proposals to reduce aid and outlays in a period of economic distress. The impression was created that *federalism* was nothing more than a code word for stringent expenditure cuts." In any event, no agreement was reached and no legislation was ever forwarded to Congress. Nor did the administration fare much better in 1983 when it unsuccessfully proposed a revised version of the initiative (concentrating on consoldation of a number of existing grant programs into four "megablock" grants).

In the aftermath of these experiences the Reagan administration seemed to have lost much of its enthusiasm for far-reaching proposals to "debureaucratize" the federal government through the formal devolution of functions back to the states. While it continued indirectly to attempt to transfer much of the burden for domestic programs to the states and localities, for the most part the Reagan intergovernmental agenda in the President's second term shifted toward narrower and more "conventional" reform measures, such as streamlining administrative requirements for grants-in-aid (through revisions of OMB Circular A-102) and reducing federal regulatory and paperwork burdens on state and local governments.

Privatization

While "debureaucratization" through devolution received relatively less emphasis after 1983 or so, the administration appears to have been responsive to conservatives who urged that "shifting government functions to the private sector" should be the "central theme" of its second-term efforts to cut the budget and reduce the size and influence of the federal executive establishment. Indeed, although "privatization" had been an important part of the Reagan agenda from the outset, it was accorded an even higher priority in the President's second term.

Privatization can take two basic forms: (1) when the government simply decides to withdraw from certain activities by transferring or selling assets or programs entirely to the private sector; (2) when government places greater reliance on the private sector to *produce* services that it decides to *provide*.

Perhaps the most important means by which the administration has sought to advance the cause of privatization has been to insist on greater use by federal agencies of "contracting out," that is, to rely on private firms retained under contract to deliver the goods or services for which agencies have been assigned responsibility. In August 1983, OMB revised its contracting-out directive (Circular A-76), simplifying public versus private cost comparisons in a way calculated to enhance private-sector involvement. This revision of Circular A-76 drew sharp criticism (especially from federal employee union representatives) on the grounds that its relatively lax standards would permit the transfer of responsibility for public functions that were too important to be entrusted to third parties and that such a policy threatened seriously to undermine the long-term, "in-house" capacity of the federal government. For its part, OMB "argued that it was good policy to make government employees 'compete for business' with the private sector, and estimated that the government spent at least $20 billion a year in activities that could appropriately by performed by private business." The administration has actively promoted other activities under the broad rubic of privatization. It has, for example, urged increased application of user fees, whereby users of government facilities or beneficiaries of government services are assessed a charge sufficient to cover all or part of the cost of their maintenance or provision. It has also advocated greater use of vouchers with a view to enabling individuals to purchase a particular service, at government expense or with government support, from either public or private sources.

The Privatization movement gained additional momentum in President Reagan's second term, as reflected in the establishment in September 1987 of the President's Commission on Privatization. This twelve-member body issued a report supporting earlier administration proposals to sever the federal government's financial ties to AMTRAK and to sell two Naval Petroleum Reserves (NPRs) as well as five power marketing administrations (PMAs). In addition, the privatization commission urged that serious consideration be given to turning various delivery services now controlled by the U.S. Postal Service, as well as some federal prisons, over to private contractors. It also advocated increased use of vouchers for federally subsidized housing, medical care, and schooling.

In general, the Reagan administration's privatization efforts have met with mixed results. Congress did agree to the administration's proposal to sell off CONRAIL and to the sale of some federal loans, but on the whole has been reluctant to endorse the administration's push (and that of conservative "think tanks") for more and more privatization of governmental functions.

In the Reagan administration, the impetus toward privatization was as much directed toward cost savings as toward philosophical goals. The fact that its various privatization initiatives have appeared to many to represent little more than ad hoc attempts to reduce the budget has left the administration vulnerable to the charge that it has not given sufficient attention to developing sound principles to govern the allocation of functions between the public and private sectors. Nonetheless, it would be a serious mistake to dismiss the emphasis on privatization as nothing more than an ideological "reflex." On the contrary, this promises to represent one of the Reagan administration's more important legacies.

Management Reform: Modernizing and Economizing

Although reducing the range of activities in which the federal government was involved was a major aim of the Reagan managerial strategy, the administration was also (and perhaps equally) concerned with ensuring that the functions that remained with the federal government would be operated in the most cost efficient and effective manner possible. This was reflected in the administration's management improvement and reform initiatives, whose story breaks down into two periods, first- and second-term initiatives. The hallmarks of the first period were the establishment in September 1982 of the Cabinet Council on Management and Administration (CCMA) and the formal inauguration of the President's

Management Improvement Program—"Reform '88." The midway point in the second term, early 1987, marked the beginning of the Reagan administration's final management improvement push.

First-Term Initiatives

There were ten initial Reform '88 objectives, aimed mostly at reducing costs and enhancing revenue collection. The ten goals were to (1) upgrade federal cash management systems; (2) increase collection of debts owed the government; (3) encourage the sale of surplus government property; (4) foster efficient and effective management and eliminate fraud and abuse through strengthening internal accounting and administrative controls; (5) identify unliquidated obligations on agency books; (6) recover funds owned agencies as a result of audits; (7) reduce nondefense workyears by 75,000 full-time equivalents from 1982 to 1984; (8) limit wasteful spending on government periodicals, pamphlets, and audiovisual products; (9) achieve significant savings through systematic reform of procurement practices (e.g., amending and making greater use of A-76 contracting-out review procedures); and (10) reduce government paperwork and thereby limit costs to individuals, private organizations, and state and local governments.

While the projects of Reform '88 quickly became a centerpiece of the Reagan administration's intention to make the federal government more efficient, cost effective, and "businesslike," responsibility for forging and directing management reform efforts during the Reagan years was by no means the exclusive province of OMB. Many significant management initiatives were promoted or coordinated by two special presidential councils established during Reagan's first term. The first was the President's Council on Integrity and Efficiency which was discussed earlier. The mandate given the second council, the President's Council on Management Improvement (PCMI), established in May 1984 and consisting mostly of departmental assistant secretaries for administration, was considerably more comprehensive. The PCMI was charged to oversee and coordinate ongoing management improvement projects to formulate additional long-range plans to promote improved management systems.

The establishment of the PCIE in Reagan's first term provided an indication of the administration's willingness to entrust important management initiatives to groups formally operating outside OMB. This practice became clearer after September 1982 when the administration announced the creation of the Cabinet Council on Management and Administration (CCMA) under the leadership of Edwin Meese III. This was an especially noteworthy development because it provided, for the first time, an official unit in the White House responsible for the overall coordination and direction of management reform efforts, including those undertaken by OMB.

Although the establishment of the CCMA was an important event, the most visible management improvement initiative of Reagan's first term had its origins elsewhere. This was the President's Private Sector Survey on Cost Control (PPSSCC), better known as the Grace Commission after its chairman, J. Peter Grace. The Grace Commission was composed of task forces headed by 161 top private-sector executives. In a 47-volume report to the President issued in January, 1984, the commission recommended programs and management changes in 36 areas of the federal government; 2478 recommendations were made that promised savings of $424 billion over a three-year period after implementation. Dispute over the accuracy of the Grace Commission's figures and the feasitility of many of its recommendations continued unabated well into Reagan's second term.

By the end of Reagan's first term, there were indications that the administration's approach to management improvement was beginning to change. Part of the reason for this change can be traced to ever expanding criticisms coming from Congress and other sources outside the executive branch. Another part may be traced to a recognition within the administration that centralization may have gone too far.

Although the administration, commenting on its first-term management initiatives, proclaimed that it had embarked on a broad program "to ensure a continued, organized emphasis on management improvement" and that Reform '88 and other measures had resulted in "substantial progress," not all observers agreed with this rosy assessment. Comptroller General Bowsher, head of the U.S. General Accounting Office (GAO), for example, suggested that the administration's record revealed the limits of highly centralized approach to management improvement, that is, one of which principal reliance is placed on central agencies (OMB, OPM, and GSA) rather than operating agencies. In its 1983 report *Revitalizing Federal Management*, the National Academy of Public Administration (NAPA) expressed a similar view, asserting that the accretion of control systems had produced a situation in which procedure overwhelmed substance. Administrative systems and increasingly centralized and detailed administrative procedures had produced a "managerial overburden" that had become a barrier to the responsiveness and cost effectiveness of government. NAPA recommended an enhancement of federal managers' roles and appropriate flexibility and discretion to allow them to provide leadership for their administrative units.

Although these criticisms and recommendations were clearly at odds with the centralizing thrust of its first-term management improvements efforts, there was evidence even prior to the start of President Reagan's second term to suggest that the administration was beginning to take them to heart. This was reflected, for example, in the establishment in May 1984 of the PCMI, which symbolized the administration's willingness to take steps to "shift the center of concentration and effort for management reforms" into the hands of a few senior agency managers and supervisors, as NAPA had urged in its 1983 report.

Second-Term Initiatives

The creation of the PCMI proved to be a precursor of a subtle shift in management emphasis. In 1986 the administration announced that continued attention would be devoted to furthering earlier initiatives like fraud prevention, payment integrity, improved cash and loan portfolio management, procurement reform, and reduction in regulatory and paperwork burden. However, new initiatives would be undertaken to improve the productivity of federal programs and the development of shared administrative support services among federal agencies with field organizations scattered around the country. This last initiative was explicitly assigned to the PCMI for development and coordination.

The final stage of the Reagan administration's management improvement efforts began in early 1987 with a reorientation of the "M side" of OMB.

Recognizing that only two years remained in the President's second term, the new associate director for management, Jerry Riso, began to narrow the agency's management focus down to two priorities: (1) upgrading the financial management capacity of the departments and agencies; and (2) productivity improvements. These two developments, along with Reform '88 initiatives in areas like credit and loan management that were still under way, constitute the "final push" of the Reagan administration to modernize and economize federal management systems. The idea behind these projects was to provide enough program activity so that their momentum would carry them to completion in the next administration.

In summary, perhaps the Reagan administration's most lasting contribution to the organization and operation of the federal government will be the result of its efforts to modernize the "nuts and bolts" of management. Operating through several vehicles, the administration has focused efforts to improve how the federal government handles cash management, debt collection, real property, procurement, computer planning, travel, and other administrative overhead expenses. Although some people have charged that these efforts do not amount to management improvement in the broad sense and in reality are little more than "penny pinching" to respond to huge budget deficits, from a historical perspective one must conclude that the Reagan administration has initiated valuable, badly needed reforms in areas overlooked by previous administrations.

Reagan and the Federal Workforce

The final and probably most problematic legacy of the Reagan years has been to bring to a head some long-standing problems confronting the civil service system. Over the course of the Reagan Presidency concern has grown about a perceived erosion in the quality, morale, and effectiveness of the federal workforce. While most discussions of the civil service and its problems focus on the Senior Executive Service (SES) and equivalent levels, fragmentary and impressionist evidence suggests that the problem goes deeper and spreads wider into the professional, technical, scientific, and administrative corps that make up the bulk of the career service.

Some of the causes for the problems surrounding the civil service can be directly attributed to the Reagan administration's efforts to reshape the size and scope of the administrative state. President Reagan has often stated his preference for less costly government, more privatization of government functions, more use of contracting out, and more tightly controlled and cost-effective operation of those functions left with government employees. This adds up to a personnel policy of a smaller, less expensive, and less autonomous workforce.

Needless to say, the Reagan agenda for the federal workforce was hardly welcomed by federal workers. But its negative implications were compounded by statements and actions of the Reagan administration's original appointee as director of the Office of Personnel Management, Donald J. Devine, who took a decidedly negative view of what he considered to be the excessive pay, benefits, and prerogatives of federal employees. During his four-year term, Devine reorganized the agency and shaped its policy priorities in ways that many critics thought "politicized" OPM and damaged the civil service. Rather than serve as an aggressive proponent of a high-quality workforce and modern human resource management, as its supporters had hoped, OPM under Devine was viewed by many as a principal agent of the Reagan administration's "war on the bureaucracy." To buttress this perception, Devine's critics pointed to his tendency to engage in "bureaucrat bashing" and his advocacy of a rigid separation between political and career appointees in the policy process (i.e., political appointees should make policy decisions that career employees will carry out without question). While the criticism of the Merit Systems Protection Board (MSPB) and its independent Office of Special Counsel was less severe, it too was criticized for failing to provide adequate protection for "whistleblowers" or to protect federal employees from merit-system abuses.

Much of the early anger of federal employees toward the Reagan administration's personnel policy focused on its efforts to change the shape and cost the federal workforce. Immediately after taking office, President Reagan not only instituted a government-wide hiring freeze but also announced his intention to reduce federal civilian employment in nondefense agencies by nearly 100,000 people. The Carter administration had scheduled personnel cuts in its 1981 and 1982 budget protections, but Reagan promised deeper and more focused cuts in domestic agencies. Part of this strategy was in response to what Reagan regarded as dangerous reductions in defense spending. From 1970 to 1980, civilian employment in the Department of Defense (DOD) had fallen from 56 percent of total civilian employment to 41 percent. While never specifiying the exact number of civilian employees to be added to DOD, Reagan proposed to increase DOD spending from 23 percent to 38 percent of the federal budget, thereby implying a significant increase in the size of DOD's civilian workforce.

The shifts in policy and budget priorities between 1981 and 1984 forced or encouraged many employees in targeted agencies to leave government service. To accommodate such shifts, several domestic agencies were forced to engage in "reduction in force" (RIF) procedures that caused more than 12,000 federal employees to lose their jobs in 1981 and 1982, several thousand others to be "bumped" down to lower-level jobs, and thousands more to leave the government voluntarily. Especially hard hit were the Departments of the Interior, Health and Human Services, Commerce, Agriculture, and Education, and some smaller agencies like the Community Services Administration and the General Services Administration (GSA).

The hiring freeze, budget cuts, and RIFs reduced the number of nonpostal domestic agency employees by 133,000 from 1981 to 1986. However, increases in the DOD, the Internal Revenue Service (IRS), the State Department, Justice, and the Veterans Administration have more than made up for the reductions. In fact, with the increase in the Postal Service of 121,000 employees during the first five years of the Reagan administration, the overall civilian workforce actually increased by nearly 5 percent, to over 3 million.

The Reagan administration's attempt to reduce the cost of the bureaucracy by changing the distribution of civilian employees from domestic agencies to DOD was complemented by efforts to reform federal pay, retirement, and other benefits. While a number of proposals produced little in the way of legislation or concrete action, the administration did proceed on three fronts to constrain personnel-related costs. These efforts included (1) consistently resisting recommendations to raise pay for all ranks of the civil service as well as top political appointees, members of Congress, and the judiciary; (2) introducing changes in federal employee health insurance policy that reduced the government's future contributions to health insurance by several million dollars; and (3) introducing changes in the retirement system that allowed federal employees of trade off assured benefits for "portability" (i.e., the option to leave federal service with retirement benefits intact).

While constraining the costs of pay and benefits for federal employees and reshuffling the civilian workforce between domestic and defense agencies can be recognized as a coherent policy, two other Reagan personnel policies involving political appointees and the contracting out of government operations to the private sector can be understood as part of a broader strategy to control the bureaucracy and cut its size.

In its use of political appointees the Reagan administration extended a process of increasing the number of such appointees at all levels of the bureaucracy that has escalated during the Carter administration. While the increases under Reagan were not large (and were offset by decreases in the number of political appointees in the SES), the Reagan administration targeted more of its nearly 3000 political appointees for line management positions than had its predecessor. According to Patricia Ingraham, "One outcome of these increased numbers and SES flexibility (was) the creation of new management lines and systems . . . (allowing) top level political executives to bypass career managers and to rely instead upon lower level political appointees, (thereby reducing) the role and influence of career managers." The practice of bypassing top career managers for day-to-day policy advice has been called "jigsaw puzzle management." (This describes a method of using career civil servants to carry out programs while keeping them in the dark as to the overall strategy being pursued.) Although heralded by some conservatives as the best way to manage the career workforce, this management style has been widely criticized by career executives and other observers of federal program management. In 1985, 70 percent of respondents to a survey of federal career executives said that they believed the Reagan administration had failed to create conditions favorable to good management; 51 percent saw "the career/political working relationship as a deterrent to effective management." As noted earlier, one of the principal steps taken by the administration to encourage more "privatization" was its 1983 revision of OMB Circular A-76 on contracting out. Naturally, this move was greeted with anger and frustration by federal workers whose jobs might be affected by their unions.

Throughout the Reagan years, federal unions often charged the adminstration with being "antilabor/antiunion" and with refusing to negotiate constructively with them over work rules, employee rights, and the scope of collective bargaining. In addition to opposing contracting out and privatization more generally, the unions unsuccessfully opposed the Reagan administration's introduction of drug testing in the workplace. In 1987, in the face of a presidential veto, the unions sponsored a major revision in the fifty-year-old Hatch Act, which limits the participation of federal employees in political activities. This occurred after the leaders of three large federal unions were suspended from their mostly symbolic federal jobs for endorsing candidates in the 1984 election.

Impacts of the Reagan Administration's Personnel Policies

The Reagan administration's treatment of the federal workforce has caused several serious problems in the recruitment and retention of a high-quality workforce. At the entry level, budget cutbacks at OPM have had the direct effect of discouraging new recruits because they led to the closing of some job information centers and a stoppage in the distribution of publications intended to help potential employees find their way through the federal hiring maze. Among senior career employees, the growing "pay gap" between the public sector and the private sector and the management styles of political appointees, have taken their toll on morale and the decision to stay in or leave the federal service. A 1986 survey of all career executives who left the SES in fiscal year 1985 identified the short terms of political appointees and their lack of qualification for their jobs as important reasons for the dissatisfaction and departure of career employees.

The size and seriousness of the present pattern of retirements is captured by table 4.1, which presents SES retirements through fiscal year 1986. The table shows that retirement rates were initially high from 1979 to 1981, then leveled off, and peaked again in 1985. Some observers have voiced a concern that a serious "brain drain" will occur if present patterns continue.

Table 4.I

DEPARTURES FROM THE SENIOR EXECUTIVE SERVICE ON AN ANNUAL BASIS, 1979–86

Year	Positions Allocated	Positions Vacated during the Year	Percentage of Allocated Positions
1979	8413	390[a]	4.6
1980	8602	1185	13.8
1981	8235	1307	15.9
1982	8211	717	8.7
1983	8041	678	8.4
1984	8064	684	8.5
1985	8044	906	11.3
1986	7758	792	10.2

Sources: Letter from James E. Colvard, deputy director, Office of Personnel Management, to Joseph E. Ross, director of Congressional Research Service, II December 1986; final 1986 data supplied by OPM's Office of Executive Personnel. Reliable data on annual departures from executive ranks, prior to the creation of the SES, are not available, according to the OPM.

[a] 13 July 1979 to 31 December 1979.

Evaluation of the Reagan Managerial Strategy and Legacy

Just as the Carter administration's legacy can be sorted into three categories— what to do, what to avoid, and ideas and institutional mechanisms left behind—so, too, one can undertake to assess the Reagan legacy. The most pronounced feature of the early years of the Reagan Presidency was the strong and concerted effort to secure top-down presidential control over the whole of the federal executive establishment. As we have seen, the central elements of this strategy were (1) extensive use of the appointment power to "infiltrate" the bureaucracy with appointees loyal to the President; (2) use of the cabinet council system and other interagency mechanisms to keep political appointees focused on the Reagan agenda; (3) strengthening of OMB budgetary, regulatory, and paperwork clearance powers as instruments of presidential control; and (4) continued articulation of the broad principles of "conservative" approaches to the organization and the management of the federal government and its workforce.

The centralizing and cost-control impulses reflected in early Reagan management improvement initiatives (e.g., the establishment of the President's Council on Integrity and Efficiency and the launching of Reform '88) were instrumental in shaping the administration's entire approach to executive branch management. The emphasis on top-down control to enhance "efficiency" and "accountability" has been an important element in the administration's campaign to make the federal government more efficient and "businesslike" all along, and remains an "article of faith" among top echelons of the Reagan administration. It is important to point out, however, that Congress often has been a willing partner in these reform efforts. The legislature's receptivity to control-oriented management reforms had already been demonstrated during the Carter years, when Congress enacted such key bills as the Inspectors General Act of 1978 and the Paperwork Reduction Act of 1980. The rapid spate of additional management reform legislation passed during Reagan's first term—including the Prompt Payment Act of 1982, the Debt Collection Act of 1982, and the Single Audit Act of 1983, as well as the Federal Manager's Financial Integrity Act of 1982 and the Deficit Reduction Act of 1984—amply attests to the fact that Congress shared the administration's conviction that strong central controls were necessary to ensure that federal management systems would be kept modern and up-to-date.

Finally, it should be acknowledged that the Reagan administration's focused efforts to modernize the "nuts and bolts" of management and thereby reduce the overhead administrative expenses of government add up to some valuable changes in the way the federal government conducts its operations. The administration's successes in these low-visibility but costly management areas are likely to encourage future administrations to carry on the modernization effort as new ideas and opportunities develop.

Notwithstanding these accomplishments, which may turn out to be the Reagan administration's most lasting contribution to the organization and operation of government, it is important to recognize some of the liabilities associated with the administration's approach. In the first place, the accountability and cost-control orientation of efforts like Reform '88 reinforced an approach to management improvement that some argue is not conducive to constructive management reform. Second, the top-down aproach that characterized that effort seems to have exacerbated a tendency that, in the opinion of many informed observers, has proven to be one of the main obstacles to managerial effectiveness in government, namely, the tendency for federal management to get caught up "in excessive centralization and inflexible, negative controls." This is not to say that some valuable lessons about presidential direction of the executive branch have not been learned. For example, Laurence E. Lynn, in assessing the centralization strategy, warns critics that "failure to understand the Reagan experiement in public management will mean that a valuable lesson for future administrations—

administrations that may have more positive views of government—will be missed. That lesson is that loyal and competent supporters in key executive branch positions can be a potent tool of administrative leadership." In Lynn's view, the importance of combining a reasonably coherent philosophy of government with (1) the institutional apparatus of OMB to give it operational meaning; (2) the appointment of appropriately skilled cabinet and subcabinet officials who share the President's vision; and (3) the subsequent delegation of authority over execution to these appointees, subject to oversight by the executive office, cannot be underestimated.

The partial "turnaround" in the Reagan managerial strategy in the President's second term, which emphasized more delegation of authority, can be attributed to two factors. First is the widespread recognition that the administration had in fact succeeded in securing firm top-down control through the use of the first two tactics Lynn described. But second, the administration began to realize that once control was well established, it could begin to "deregulate" federal management in accordance with concepts and techniques borrowed from the private sector—an emphasis that would comport very nicely both with its desire to make government more "businesslike" and with its concern to deregulate the American economy as a whole. Similarly, the tactics of devolution and privatization can also be understood as serving the Reagan administration's broader political purpose of decentralizing government responsibility.

But this strategy can give rise to serious questions about policy coordination and accountability. The Reagan administration's efforts to redeem a vision of a limited government that divests itself of functions by transferring them to the private sector, which will then drive the economy forward, has sometimes created blurred lines of control—the opposite effect of what the entire centralizing thrust presumably was designed or intended to achieve. Thus, while the administration has provided what amounts to a catalogue of management tactics ranging from user fees to shared support services, only in very few cases has it succeeded in combining them into complete systems. Meanwhile, federal managers have been left to thrash about in an environment made more complex by the very strategies the administration thought would simplify government.

The two great disasters of the Reagan years, the *Challenger* tragedy and the Iran-*contra* scandal, provide a clue to the management problem. In both cases, the government became engaged in webs of decision making and action that relied heavily on the judgment of private firms and individuals. These networks were so tangled that clear lines of accountability disappeared, and distinctions between private action and public responsibility became all but meaningless to the participants. When the political dust had settled, no one was sure who was to blame.

Debate over the complexity of modern government calls into question the institutional capacity of the Presidency to cope with it. To what extent has the Reagan administration enhanced or depleted this capacity? On the positive side, Reagan reduced some of the complexity of governing by picking a few central objectives to guide his administration's efforts and showed future Presidents how they might use flexible instruments like cabinet councils and the Office of Presidential Personnel (OPP) to keep their programs on track. Reagan also strengthened a few key administrative mechanisms, such as regulatory review, that may prove valuable to future administrations with decidedly different policy goals. On the negative side, some critics have argued that Reagan has damaged, perhaps irreparably, two vitally important institutions that will be needed to address future problems effectively: OMB, and the senior ranks of the career civil service. In the case of OMB, the Reagan years witnessed a marked increase in the numbers of influence of political appointees at the expanse of the career staff. In the view of some long-term observers of the agency, this has seriously compromised OMB's reputation for political neutrality and its institutional capacity. Lost in the process is the agency's ability to speak with authority on a broad range of policy, budget, and management issues. Similarly, by more carefully screening, placing, and directing political appointees in the upper levels of executive branch agencies and in some places encourageing (or at least tolerating) contentious relations between its appointees and career officials, the administration has succeeded in driving many of the latter into retirement. This development may deprive the next administration, and perhaps future administrations as well, of a very valuable resource and make the task of governing all the more difficult.

Indeed, in retrospect, one cannot help but wonder whether the Reagan administration's approach to seizing control of the bureaucracy by pushing aside senior career managers was necessary. Although Reagan, like Carter and several Presidents before him, harbored a deep distrust of the loyalty and responsiveness of the career civil service, there is little or no evidence to support his apparent conviction that they were impediments in the way of accomplishing his agenda. More generally, we would argue that a principal failing of the Reagan administration lay in its apparent inability or unwillingness to set aside its own management strategy to take a serious look at the problem of the long-term erosion of the capacity of the federal workforce—a dubious legacy that the next administration will surely have to face.

This question becomes all the more important when viewed in conjunction with what we would suggest is the Reagan administration's most positive legacy, namely, to reshape the dialogue about the proper scope of government; the appropriate machinery of government; and the respective roles of the public, private, and nonprofit sector workforces in the service delivery process. Even though the administration has failed fully to persuade Congress or the public that its answers to these questions are the right ones, it has nonetheless succeeded in legitimizing debate over these fundamental issues in a way that assures they will remain on the public agenda for many years.

Bert A. Rockman

The President and the Permanent Government—
"Hitting the Ground Standing"

Bert Rockman is professor of political science at the University of Pittsburgh. He is the author of The Leadership Question *and coauthor of* Bureaucrats and Politicians in Western Democracies. *Noting that a mismatch of incentives makes some degree of tension between the president and career bureaucrats inevitable, Rockman maintains that the relationship has become more strained under recent presidents. Believing that such antagonism is not in a president's long term interest, he suggests how presidents can engage the bureaucracy more effectively.*

Presidents and the Career Executive—
A Disengaged Relationship

American presidents are almost never directly engaged with their senior career officials. The relationship of presidents to the permanent government is a remote one at best. Except for an occasional ceremony, for example, civil servants do not keep company with American presidents, nor are they even greatly involved directly with their cabinet secretaries. Certainly senior civil servants are not a presence in the fashion that is the case in most European countries or Japan. From time to time, of course, exceptionally agile career officials from the foreign service or the civil service make their way into high and visibly influential posts. Frank Carlucci, who has served in important posts across four presidential administrations—Republican and Democrat—is an example of this rare breed of highly influential and visible career official. In the American system, unlike others however, the price of engagement is usually the loss of one's civil service tenure.

To presidents, the permanent government is something that is out there. It is a distant and remote *them*—almost an alien creature. The White House tends to be suspicious of the *them* out there. Consequently, the White House usually seeks to reduce the role of senior career officials in policy making on the premise that there already is a surplus of advice and advisers. Who needs more? As I shall note a bit later, this skeptical perspective lends itself toward limiting the civil servant's role to a strictly managerial one.

Presidents also want to have as much flexibility as possible to manage programs they believe are central to their interests in ways that they also believe are compatible with their interests.[1] Presidents, however are rarely experienced in management. They are most likely to act as chiefs, not chief executives.[2] Manipulating symbols, not managing details, is the forte of most aspirants to, and successful incumbents of, the White House. To the extent that presidents are likely to be involved in managing, it is organizing their entourage in the White House with which they will be most concerned. Any president's sense of "the government" inevitably is a constricted one. It consists largely of that small handful of people with whom the President has direct relations.

From Distance to Distaste

Despite the seeming distance of the rest of government, at some point in the 1970s bureaucratic distance somehow became equated with bureaucratic resistance. Because the Federal government grew so rapidly in terms of programs and especially expenditures from the mid 1960s to the latter part of the 1970s,[3] the federal bureaucracy became a favorite subject for abusive political rhetoric—more favored as a target by the Republican Right than the Democratic Left, to be sure, but not immunized from criticism by either wing. As a general attack on the growth and perceived intrusiveness of the Federal government, the Republican Right frequently portrayed the bureaucracy as symptomatic of a malignant growth of government that sapped initiative and productivity, eroding both the private sector and the discipline provided by markets. Bureaucracies and career bureaucrats, consequently, were viewed as either self-interested in their programs and their budgetary expansion or ideologically committed to them.[4]

At the same time, the Democratic Left increasingly grew critical of the career bureaucracy, suspecting it of being more interested in its perks than its programs and more apt to respond routinely than innovatively. From both Left and Right, then, the bureaucracy was viewed as a deadweight on change, in desperate need of being transformed. Because bureaucracies are stable elements resistant to short term change, a path of lesser resistance, that of shifting responsibility increasingly to politically appointed decision makers came to be emphasized with increasing vigor. Whether these accusations about the career bureaucracy are true is of lesser significance than the fact that the career bureaucracy had become a source of contention at a time when political positions had themselves become increasingly contentious.

In such a climate, this anti-bureaucratic sentiment has been reflected by presidents, especially the most recent presidencies of Reagan and Carter. Each demeaned the established government in rhetoric, and each made appointments of some noncareer personnel who were notably antipathetic to the career bureaucracy. It was earlier, however, during the Nixon administration that resentment against the career bureaucracy became evident. This resentment stemmed from Nixon's view of the career bureaucracy as politically biased against the policies of his administration.[5]

Pluralism Among Career Executives

The career bureaucracy is not a monolith. While it is natural for career officials to be committed to the activities they are engaged in, government itself is almost never traveling along a clear trajectory. Its career officials, as a collective entity, tend to be committed to the various multiple and sometimes contradictory objectives that the government, overall, is committed to.[6] For the most part, officials in spending agencies generally prefer more to less; those at the Office of Management and Budget (OMB), on the other hand, prefer less to more.

Martin Anderson, in his memoirs of the Reagan Presidency, notes, in this regard, that the drastic budget cuts proposed early in the Reagan administration relied extensively upon a strategy of coopting OMB early into the process of budget analysis. This meant relying heavily on the career professionals at OMB. Anderson asserts that, "In effect, that first year we acted as if the OMB professionals were part of the White House staff and treated them that way."[7]

Note that bureaucrats in the spending agencies are treated rather differently. Shortly before the passage quoted above, for example, Anderson notes that in prior administrations "it did not take long . . . for the cabinet officers to be seduced by the professional bureaucrats and the natural constituencies of their departments."[8] In other words, bureaucrats' interests and the logic of their roles are frequently conflictual and competitive. The implication is that a wise president will invest substantially in officials whose roles favorably dispose them to support of presidential goals—whatever these may be.

Interdependence Between the Chief Executive and the Federal Executive

Certainly, who sits in the oval office—what that president's priorities are and how clearly they are articulated, what his staff and appointments are like, what his style of policy management is, and even (perhaps most important) what his rhetoric is about—affects the senior civil service. Although many senior civil servants, at any point in time, are engaged in matters that are far from the president's priorities, they are hardly immune from either the style or goals of the political leadership.

When the style is one of command and the goals are radical departures from the status quo, relations between senior careerists and the presidential administration will be delicate at best, and hostile at worst.

Equally, however, presidents are affected by the willingness and ability of career executives to adapt to new directions, their capability for derailing or seeing through presidential initiatives, and their motivation (or lack thereof) for helping their appointed superordinates and keeping them out of trouble. This is indeed a strange relationship, if relationship is even the right word. Though presidents and senior civil servants rarely see one another, each is dependent upon the other. Presidents are reluctant to admit that, of course, in large part because they are incapable of seeing what experienced civil servants can do *for* them rather than *to* them.

Factors Governing the Political-Administration Nexus

Regardless of the exact nature of the relationship between any given president and the career bureaucracy, the relationship is governed perhaps most powerfully by broader factors. One of these factors is the theory that legitimates the career bureaucracy. The largely analytic distinction between administration and politics is, among the industrial democracies, most firmly planted in the United States, whatever the actual state of affairs. This distinction implies that senior career officials are to be public managers, possessing limited discretion. What they decidedly are not to be are molders of policy. In the Federal Republic of Germany, by contrast, senior bureaucrats are not only expected to be molders of policy, they are legally required to be involved. In general, in other industrialized democracies, the politics management distinction is less evidently in vogue as an operating theory of the political leadership.

A second factor has to do with the institutional nature of the American political system and its division of political authority. This division, operationally, means that there are multiple and sometimes conflicting authorities (and thus ambiguous directions). When there is conflict, bureaucrats will be suspect in someone's eyes because two conflicting directions cannot be simultaneously obeyed. The system of divided authority, however, also means that senior career officials in the U.S. often can have better access *outward* toward the Congress than *upward* through their departments.[9] The distance between senior career officials and department secretaries is very large; between senior career officials and the White House, it is cavernous.

A third factor has to do with rhetorical context. Big government is a negative symbol in the United States. Rhetorically, therefore, the career bureaucracy is an inviting target for ridicule or worse.

Beyond these broader factors are also ones that reflect the existing atmosphere—salary compression, limited opportunities for promotion, and losses of influence. These conditions have soured senior career officials to some degree. Many of them have been in senior positions only during a period in which the bureaucracy and bureaucrats have been subject to conditions of strong budgetary constraint, limited discretion, and low morale. Whether there is a crisis of the senior civil service or not cannot easily be answered, but is a problem that the next president will need to address if, in the longer term, the proficiency and quality of the public service are to be preserved or enhanced. The difficulty, though, is that, for reasons to be discussed below, presidents have no obvious short-term incentives to try to remedy the underlying malaise of the senior civil service.

Presidential Interests and Civil Service Interests— A Mismatch of Incentives

Presidents and senior civil servants begin their distant relationship with very different incentives. For presidents, their aim is to make change or at least to make it appear as though they are making change. Campaign slogans are filled with the language of change, particularly, but not exclusively, in the candidacies of the opposition party.

Civil servants, on the other hand, have invested in the past and have little incentive to change, which is not exactly the same thing as saying that they will not change. Naturally, then, these two distant participants in the executive branch—the President and the senior career bureaucrats—have a certain mismatch of incentives. This natural awkwardness has been fueled especially in recent years by the anti-government, anti-Washington rhetoric of the past decade and a half. Many civil servants have tended to see presidents, their White House entourages, and some of their appointments in the departments as inexperienced and unwilling to listen to advice regarding alternative pathways to their objectives. For their part, presidents believe the career bureaucracy is obdurately opposed to new directions.

Both perspectives—that of the president and that held by the career officials— have some truth attached to them. Presidents have a short time to make their mark; bureaucrats have a longer perspective. Presidents trust *their* people—those who form their entourage. To the extent, however, that career bureaucrats become identified with a given administration's policies or personalities, they will lose their ability to be viewed as effective servants of any other administration's policies. From the bureaucrat's perspective, the problem is summed up in the picturesque analogy drawn by a senior career official in the Interior Department:

> If I'm a politician and you're a bureaucrat, I'm gonna stand over there and I'm gonna wave at you and I'm gonna say, 'come on over here in the burro pen,' and I'm gonna get you as far in that burro pit as I can get you. But you better not get there. If you do, you're gonna be in trouble. . . . The more I think about that, that is a tremendous philosophical statement . . . because I know that the administration is gonna try to pull you to their way of thinking as far as they can, and the next administration when there's a turnover is gonna do it the other way. I think it's our job to keep the objective . . . without getting into the burro pit.[10]

The fundamental problem for presidential management is to find an acceptable balance between what it is that a president needs to know and what it is that he wants to do.[11] When presidents hold intense and passionate convictions, they may be less likely to tolerate "wimpish" bureaucrats who fail to share their own, or perhaps even any, convictions.[12] If leaders know what they want to do, it also may be that they think they have correspondingly less need to know about alternatives or feasibilities. As a species, politicians are inclined to do, not to doubt.

In the long run, of course, if government is to achieve intelligent direction, the prudence and conservatism of civil servants and the more radical instinct of politicians are complementary. But this desirable long term equilibrium is not likely to be seen in the short term, and it should be remembered that presidents generally have a strong short-run interest in pushing their own objectives. Equally, career executives tend to have an interest in the protection of their own projects and programs. When these are threatened, there are potential allies to be summoned. As noted already, of course, any president's policy agenda will displease some civil servants more than it will displease others. Defense department, law enforcement, and OMB bureaucrats generally have fared better during the Reagan years than have other sectors of the bureaucracy. Technical or management specialists, arguably, may be faring better than program generalists. This probably is inevitable.

The matter of mismatched incentives, however, remains as a general problem. One way of dealing with that, of course, is for a president to encourage turnover in the senior civil service by making the job less attractive—in other words, continuing present tendencies. Evidence has surfaced in Great Britain of vastly increased turnover in the civil service during the nine years of Margaret Thatcher's prime ministership.[13] Although interpreting turnover rates is more ambiguous in the United States, there is strong evidence of a transformation in the ideology of American senior career officials over the course of a decade and a half in the direction of greater receptivity to the agendas of Republican presidents.[14]

In the long run, however, the effects of accelerated turnover and diminished attractiveness of career positions are bound to be negative. A less attractive career will likely reduce the yield of highly qualified candidates, and those most likely to leave are apt to be among the most talented. That, in short, is the omnipresent danger in a strategy of devaluing the career service.

Ironically, it may be that both Mrs. Thatcher in Britain and Mr. Reagan in America have sought not to politicize the civil service but to depoliticize it by sharpening the distinction between politics and administration. In this formulation, politicians make policy, and civil servants are supposed to manage it efficiently.[15] But, at least within the United States, less and less room is available for managerial judgment as increased control over the management of details is being centered within OMB. OMB's initiatives, however, often have been rejected by equally precise countermanding instructions from Congress. This growing tendency for micro-management has come to limit the ability of civil servants in the departments to make judgments. Hence, it also has increased the frustrations and reduced the attractiveness of the job.

Without a massive and unforeseeable institutional change in the relationship between senior career officials and presidents (resulting in more extensive career penetration of political decision-making bodies such as exists in Europe), senior career officials will be mostly out of sight and out of mind for presidents. The career service will be a distant *them*. The ability of senior career executives to have their experience felt in higher decision-making councils of government will depend upon the quality of presidential appointees in the departments and their relationships to the White House. High quality appointees can help steer the presidential agenda while mediating the perspectives of the political leadership to the civil servants and vice versa. But high quality, experienced, and judicious political executives are hard to find, sometimes difficult to appoint (because ideologues see them as 'sell-outs'), and extremely problematic to retain.

Finding Common Ground

In spite of the short term mismatch of career service incentives and presidential interest, the country needs to have the leadership that presidents can provide and the dedication and detailed knowledge that career officials can bring to government. The difficulty lies in synergizing these traits. Careerists have the knowledge to steer political leaders away from trouble if they are trusted to do so. To do that, civil servants cannot simply be managers in the most technical sense, but, instead, also must be sensitive to the politics of governing. For political leaders, however, one aspect of their leadership is generating motivation. Presidents, of course, are more naturally attuned to motivating their political followers than the bureaucracy—and spurring one often runs counter to stimulating the other. In this regard, if the machinery of government is to function effectively, it is necessary for presidents to motivate career officials and to prevent a longer term degradation of the public service. The actual operations will be in the hands of appointed intermediaries but that, as has been noted, requires careful selection of the appointees.

From the newly-elected president's perspective, it is important to realize that the role of the civil service and the machinery of government (other than the arrangement of personalities on the White House staff and in some of the cabinet departments) is on the farthest back of all the back burners. Such issues have no direct popular political impact. Party constituencies have an interest largely in patronage or furthering ideological goals, and, increasing, the latter. Thus, of all the things a president-elect is likely to consider during the period of transition, this is clearly among the very least unless, of course, it is seen as intrinsically important to the accomplishment of the presidential agenda.

There is good reason to believe that these issues were more central to the Reagan team before entering the White House than to just about any other presidency for several reasons. The first is that the Reagan team wanted to disconnect sharply from past policies in certain areas. Secondly, to do this, the Reagan team needed to find a set of appointees who were firmly committed to this disconnection. Thirdly, the Reagan team needed to placate, as the Carter team before it had, certain voluble party constituencies of a highly anti-establishment bent. Appointing individuals who represented these constituencies to positions within the bureaucracy was perceived as a necessary and perhaps also desirable strategy. Fourth, the Reagan team, for either budgetary or symbolic political reasons (or both), wanted to cut the size of the administrative corps, thus, instituting fairly significant reductions-in-force (RIFs). Fifth, in areas of special interest to the politics and policies of the Reagan Presidency, it was important to have in place senior career officials who could accommodate well to the policy changes that a Reagan Presidency would push. Consequently, the Reagan team paid unusual attention to the bureaucracy, although not in a form that senior bureaucrats necessarily found desirable. By virtue of their efforts (and undoubtedly other powerful factors in the environment), the Reagan Administration ultimately found itself working with a senior bureaucracy less instinctively hostile to its general policy objectives than, for example, had been the situation faced by Richard Nixon by the time he turned his attention to the bureaucracy late in his administration.

How presidents ultimately connect to the permanent government depends immensely on their own personal styles, their experiences, and their agendas. A so-called *conviction* politician such as Reagan need not act as though there is a permanent government at all. Those of a more consensus-building style (or with views still in the process of formulation) may be more inclined toward making use of a broad set of advisory channels. The advice of civil servants, in this context, almost never is direct. Rather, it is funneled through departmental agents who may bring these views (though never advertised as such) to the White House.

A President Bush or Dukakis would be temperamentally very different than President Reagan and neither would be engaged in a powerful effort to disconnect from the past. A President Bush would be a President with extensive experience in working with senior career officials—foreign service operatives in his diplomatic posts in China and the U.N., and senior career officials at the C.I.A. Moreover, he also had been a member of the House of Representatives with some feel for the relationships that bureaucrats and appointees must maintain with congressional committees and subcommittees. For his part, a President Dukakis clearly exhibits some of the tendencies that civil servants have; for example, an appreciation of the fact that details make a difference.

None of this, of course, need predict anything—and it well may not. But if it does, it probably means that the style of governance brought to the White House is likely to be more compatible with the perspectives of career officials than those that most recently have been on exhibition. It is most unlikely that 'revolutions' will emanate from a Bush or Dukakis White House. That prospect offers real opportunity for either a Bush or Dukakis Administration to seek to revitalize the career service. Unlike the Reagan administration's emphasis on "hitting the ground running," a Bush or Dukakis presidency, less filled with a sense of certainty about its agenda, is more likely to "hit the ground standing". That offers an early change for stability and competent management.

Although there is common ground to be reached between the White House and the permanent government, the issue, being one of low salience, faces two obstacles. Thus, the memo writer who handles this aspect of the presidential transition will first face the problem of getting the president-elect's attention, and secondly, convincing him that the problem of the career service should be responded to. Such a memo-writer will no doubt need a deft hand, but a rough draft of that memo might have features in common with the one below.

A Memorandum to the President-Elect

TO: The President-Elect
FROM: Transition Team on the Career Bureaucracy
RE: Relations with the Permanent Government

In the next two months you will need to address a number of issues and problems, the effective handling of which will be crucial to the success of your presidency. Most of them will seem more immediately pressing than that which is the subject of this report—how to deal with the career government. Obviously, substantive policy areas of central importance no doubt will occupy much of your time—the budget, revenue options, the trade deficit, health care financing, U.S.-Soviet relations, the Middle East, etc. Formulating policy strategies and initiatives certainly are of foremost importance. Understandably, so also are strategies needed to deal with our political constituencies, the media, and, especially, with Congress.

Beyond these, however, is an issue of considerable, if not always self-evident, importance. That is, how can we strengthen our ability to manage competently our programs and policies and avert, to the extent possible, avoidable mistakes? These issues are not front end ones. They do not appear pressing for now. But a failure to effectively engage the apparatus of government will produce problems later. It is necessary, therefore, to develop an effective management strategy.

Critical to achieving such a strategy is the organization of workable relations between our political appointees and the senior career officials. This a delicate relationship because while we need good working relationships to get things done and to avert mistakes, we also want to make sure that our appointees stay on the administration's track and avoid being merely spokespersons for the existing department view. John Ehrlichman referred to this during the Nixon administration as the problem of "marrying the natives." As we will note later, it is important to get political executives who are in tune with our goals, yet experienced in public management. No administration has been blessed in recent times with an abundance of such people. It also will be important to develop regular small group structures, such as the Reagan Cabinet Councils, so that cabinet members and their subordinates regularly work together with cross-cutting issues.

There are no simple formulas for ensuring that those to whom we delegate, in fact, work on our behalf. There have been a variety of presidential models ranging from Eisenhower's so-called board of directors style to Johnson's frenetic entrepreneurial style. All have strengths and weaknesses and, in turn, are dependent upon presidential temperament and agenda. On the whole, however, it seems less and less possible for presidents to draw everything toward themselves. If appointees are not given authority, it will be increasingly difficult to get high quality personnel. At the same time, mechanisms for coordination and integration are vitally important. These must be run from the White House but in a manner that draws in rather than removes cabinet members and their deputies from the action.

Let us return to the problem of the career service, however. We need to have their experience working for us, not against us. Clearly, we will need self-discipline which also means a larger definition of responsiveness than John Ehrlichman's postulate, "When we say 'jump,' they should ask 'how high?' "

What steps might be taken?

Boost the Profession of Government

For the reasons alluded to earlier, low morale within the career executive is a growing problem. Relatively low pay, a compressed pay scale, diminished status, scapegoating (Reagan in Moscow blames oppression in the Soviet Union on *their* bureaucracy!), and loss of influence are taking their toll, and there is real worry that the future quality of the career executive will be eroded.

Unfortunately, the present budget crisis and Gramm-Rudman provide little leeway to tackle the problem of material incentives. For the foreseeable future, reducing budgetary deficits will have to take priority over spending claims, especially ones as unpopular as pay increases for bureaucrats. Only the minimum can be done here, and that no doubt means a loss of some individuals on the General Schedule (GS) salary scale. Having recently accepted salary increases for the federal judiciary and federal executives (greatest among cabinet secretaries and subcabinet appointees), Congress will be reluctant to soon approve such increases again.[16] In view of these generalized constraints, we will not be able to do much except to offer our sympathy. (Alas, we cannot do this too publicly since the public has a notable shortage of sympathy for tenured executives who may be making $65,000 or $70,000.) The true comparison, of course, is with what these individuals could be making (though without the grant of tenure) in the private market. But that comparison will not carry much weight. Although some modest experiments regarding salary incentives can be implemented, these are unlikely to affect the system as a whole.

Given that we will not be able to alleviate problems of salary in the foreseeable future, are there other means of compensation for preventing erosion of civil service quality?

Fortunately, some simple and even symbolic steps may be possible. What are these?

Beginning with Kennedy (with an exception during the brief Ford Presidency), every president has spoken ill of the government and, by implication, of those who have chosen government as a profession. Distrust of the senior executive has been especially rampant during the latter stages of the Nixon administration and the earlier stages of the Reagan administration. Carter's anti-government rhetoric was more diffuse, but certainly not flattering to the civil service.

The anti-government tone of the 1970s and early 1980s may now be spent. Some of the social and economic regulatory excesses of the 1960s and 1970s have been harnessed and, if anything, there could be some support for reestablishing modest government intervention. In any event, there seems little short-term political profit to be gained by any further bureau-bashing and a great deal of cost.

Taking the opportunity to say some good things about the dedication and competence of civil servants and foreign service officers ought to be considered on appropriate occasions. This can be taken as a signal of trust and confidence in the career service—evidence of an outlook that they count and that their work is appreciated even when it cannot be matched by financial compensation. In general, when confidence is offered by political leadership, it is likely to motivate the career officials to do a better job in furthering the goals of the administration and in protecting against political vulnerabilities.

In its earlier stages the Reagan administration adopted a command style toward the career service which, in general, paralleled the last part of the Nixon Presidency. This clearly produced resentments, sometimes produced illegal behavior, and certainly generated strong reaction from political opponents and powerful restrictions when the opponents were able to gain the upper hand. During the early Nixon administration and throughout the Carter administration, the mode of treatment was one less obsessed with control and more characterized by indifference. One engages the bureaucracy but not in constructive ways; the other largely ignores the permanent government. It is possible that a view of government as a partnership between our ideals and goals and the experience, savvy, and expertise of civil servants might actually work best? Under the circumstances of a moderate presidency, that could be an operative formula.

Leadership Counts, So Make Good Appointments

The point of interface in the administration between career officials mostly will be at the assistant secretary or deputy assistant secretary level in the departments. This means that whoever the assistant secretaries are, especially, will be important. Care should be taken to ensure that the assistant secretaries are not only in tune with administration objectives but that they also are temperamentally inclined to work with others around them and to be accessible to careerists. Prior experience in the federal government is no guarantee as to how individuals will work out, but it is likely to incline them to some understanding of the role that civil servants have to play. It is important for individuals to have management skills and interpersonal skills in addition to the particular political or policy expertise they bring to their jobs.

As a general matter, effective department secretaries bring with them a high quality team of subcabinet appointees. And effective subcabinet appointees learn to get along with their senior career officials, or to work the system until they do get career people they feel comfortable with. The implication is that department secretaries should be politically experienced and judicious of temperament. (An example of this in the Reagan administration had been the appointment of Bill Brock to replace Ray Donovan as Secretary of Labor.) Department secretaries need to be able to provide policy leadership yet also appreciate the importance of management.

Vetting through a White House personnel office, of course, will (and should) continue to be an important function. (The Reagan White House elevated personnel vetting to a high art form.) But the Reagan White House provided very narrow criteria for vetting. One of the Reagan appointees, however, conceptualized the selection criteria properly:

> I think fundamentally we do a whole lot more to further the Reagan administration agenda by being careful than not. There certainly is a way to be responsive in terms of strategic thinking and that's the way I think we are responsive as opposed to the kind of nickel and dime stuff that [happens], and I don't think it's our obligation to hire every . . . party activist that comes down the pike just because they're party activists. [I mean] I'm glad that they got in and fought the good fight but I'm not sure that that means that they become the next assistant secretary for whatever.[17]

Increase the Responsibility of the Civil Service

Ultimately, it certainly will not hurt to consider the possibility that over time some consideration should be given to increasing the number of assistant secretary and deputy assistant secretary posts that might go to career officials (who could then be moved out of those posts but not out of the career service with changes in presidential administrations). Over the long run, this well could strengthen the capabilities of the civil service without weakening the capabilities of an administration's political leadership.

The search for politically appointed executives from the outside is never an easy one. A further balancing between "in and outer" entrants into the executive and career service personnel could reduce some of the pressures of executive search, and might well prove to be acceptable across the parties. Any reduction in executive positions upon which the Senate must pass could be seen, however, by the Congress as a potential infringement on the rights of confirmation.

The idea here might be to set up something equivalent to a Royal Commission to syndicate across the parties, the Congress, the Executive, and outside experts on public administration the responsibility for long term planning toward the future of the senior career service. With proper care, there is no way this can be a loser. Taking the initiative in combination with other measures should be viewed by the permanent government as a confidence-building step meant to strengthen its status. If it fails, then it is not the fault of the Bush/Dukakis administration but is attributable to the inability to develop a consensus around these issues system-wide.

Consult with Congress

As part of a larger strategy, advance consultation with Congress is advisable. That will not by itself guarantee success. Much depends upon the political character of the present Congress and the extent to which your election is viewed as decisive or, alternatively, as marked with ambiguity. Attempts to dominate Congress by breaking through subgovernments and so forth through exclusively administrative means, though, are likely to prove counterproductive over the course of your administration.

One of the reasons past administrations often have been suspicious about senior civil servants is that the White House perceives the careerists to be doing an "end-run" around administrative channels to the Congress. There is no doubt that there is an active relationship between senior career program managers and congressional staffers. Constitutionally, that is inevitable because, regardless of what we might like the situation to be, Congress shares authority over the bureaucracy with the Chief Executive. Confrontation between the White House and Congress will probably promote end-running behavior when interpretations of the law conflict. In this regard, it is probably likely to prove counterproductive to change statutory intent through administrative means and to set off confrontation with Congress. As part of a general strategy with Congress, it would be wise to avoid unnecessary friction because over the long haul there is no clear evidence that the executive can dominate the Congress simply through fiat.

We should avoid placing civil servants in the exceedingly difficult position of being caught between two implacable bosses (the White House and Congress), each requiring their allegiance but not getting that fully requited. The best way we can do that is by avoiding precipitous and unilateral action toward Congress and by working to get acceptable changes. Obviously, an election outcome in which the members of our party think that they might owe us something is the best situation from which to bargain.

In any event, the simple facts are that we cannot do better in negotiation with Congress than our political situation permits. Enticing as it is in the short run, however, we can make matters substantially worse by seeking (as the Nixon and Reagan administrations sometimes did) to govern exclusively through executive means.

Let us turn briefly to a few final points.

Think Through What Your Goals Imply

The clearer the signals received by career officials, the more likely they are to be able to respond to them or at least establish a frame of reference to deal with issues of implementation. In this respect, President Reagan's goals were remarkably transparent. He came to public life as an advocate. His philosophy was straightforward and in its structure very basic. This compensated a lot for his own passive management style. One did not need to ask often where he was going. That was a known.

But Mr. Reagan is a rare specimen of the presidential species in that regard. No matter how long a presidential candidate has been in the public eye, his image is not likely to be as sharp or as predictable as Mr. Reagan's has been. Neither Lyndon Johnson nor Richard Nixon, who certainly were around a long time, were very predictable in their policy goals. The same probably is true for a Bush/Dukakis presidency.

It is important to think through what your goals are. Inevitably these will go through mutation. But it is important to think about them in an integrated way; that is, what do they imply for each other? This provides a way to sort out priorities and clarify objectives. Others in Washington (as well as in the country) will be dependent upon the signals you send about your priorities. (That was a key part of Mr. Reagan's success.) The price of not thinking in this way can be seen in the Carter Presidency. The result was an overloaded agenda and a great deal of confusion about what the president actually wanted. If appointees are to help the White House, they need to know what objectives they are to be serving. And the President needs to know what the implications of his objectives are if the goals are to be effectively and realistically monitored. In essence, effective delegation occurs when goals are clear and priorities are well developed. Signals that are mostly ambiguous, by default, grant large amounts of uncharted discretion to the administrative agencies. That will beget an inordinate amount of inter-agency squabbling.

Coordination Must Accompany Delegation

In most respects, the White House cannot run the government directly. But mechanisms for coordination and integration are essential. At the very least, there is a need for central clearance. Working groups of administration officials need to be regularized. In general, it would not be a bad idea to bring career officials into these meetings as well. The Reagan cabinet councils seemed to operate more effectively than similar mechanisms had in the past. They provided a basis for inter-agency policy operations. For them to run smoothly, however, policy guidance from the White House is essential.

Deploy Existing Levers When Necessary

The Civil Service Reform Act of 1978 gives a presidential administration more leverage over the deployment of personnel than previously had been the case. The Reagan administration used provisions of the Senior Executive Service component of the act to good effect in advancing its goals in the departments. Among its provisions, a 10% non-career within any given department is permitted. The Reagan administration, naturally enough, tended to top-load departments with political appointees in those situations where they wanted to achieve a great deal of change and were skeptical that such would be carried out by the career officials.

These provisions should be used but must be used from time to time. Moreover, this degree of flexibility is common in continental systems. Top civil servants in West Germany, for example, who are identified with the previous government are retired from their posts *but not from the civil service*. Nevertheless, there is no *a priori* need to shuffle people around, nor is there even an inherent need to bump up against the limits of non-career deployment, at least if over the long term we wish to leave a legacy of a strengthened, more esteemed, and excellent civil service.

In Sum

The strategy offered here for dealing with the permanent government is softball rather than hardball. Playing softball has better long range prospects than playing hardball—an analogy that should be carefully considered in this context. So instead of hitting the ground running with much frenzy, there is a need to softly hit the ground standing and to consider how to engage the resources of the career bureaucracy to further administration goals. This is especially relevant to a moderate presidency that is less dogmatically anti-government than its predecessor.

There is no doubt that hitting the ground running provides some instant gratification and certainly comports well with cynical attitudes in Washington. The expectation that the bureaucracy belongs to a presidential administration is dangerous stuff because it will allow the erosion of experience, quality, and institutionalization in our government when those traits appear to be more necessary than ever. If it is simply a case of *ours* being replaced by *theirs* when administrations change, no President will be able to have confidence in the competence of the executive branch. There is no doubt that a strategy of hitting the ground running can produce instances of stretching or even violating existing laws or, at least, of making bad judgments. The career service is there to help place bounds on that. Its expertise and experience can prove invaluable, and because senior bureaucrats are sensitive to the way of Washington, they can help assure that we also stay out of trouble. That seems to be part of any definition of good politics.

Notes

1. See Terry M. Moe, "The Politicized Presidency", in John E. Chubb and Paul E. Peterson (eds.), *The New Direction in American Politics* (Washington: The Brookings Institution, 1985), pp. 235–272.

2. For this formulation, see Richard Rose, The President: A Chief but Not an Executive", *Presidential Studies Quarterly* 7 (Winter 1977): 5–20.

3. For some data on this, see Bert A. Rockman, *The Leadership Question: The Presidency and the American System* (New York: Praeger, 1984), p. 23.

4. Among others in this regard, see William A. Niskanen, Jr., *Bureaucracy and Representative Government* (Chicago: Aldine-Atherton, 1971); Richard P. Nathan, *The Administrative Presidency* (New York: John Wiley, 1983); Richard M. Nixon, *RN: The Memoirs of Richard Nixon* (New York:

Grosset & Dunlap, 1978); Martin Anderson, *Revolution* (San Diego: Harcourt Brace Jovanovich, 1988); and Stuart M. Butler, Michael Sanera, and W. Bruce Weinrod (eds.), *Mandate for Leadership II—Continuing the Conservative Revolution* (Washington: The Heritage Foundation, 1984).

5. Nixon, *RN* p. 768, *passim*.

6. See Richard Rose, *Managing Presidential Objectives* (New York: The Free Press, 1976).

7. Anderson, *Revolution* p. 248.

8. Anderson, p. 246.

9. See Joel D. Aberbach, Robert D. Putnam, and Bert A. Rockman, *Bureaucrats and Politicians in Western Democracies* (Cambridge, Mass.: Harvard University Press, 1981), pp. 228–237, and Joel D. Aberbach and Bert A. Rockman, *The Administrative State in Industrialized Democracies* (Washington: American Political Science Association, 1985).

10. Interview #005.

11. Bert A. Rockman, "The Style and the Organization of the Reagan Presidency", in Charles O. Jones (ed.), *The Reagan Legacy* (Chatham, NJ: Chatham House Publishers, 1988), pp. 3–29.

12. This portrait seems to fit the British prime minister Mrs. Thatcher more definitively than the American president, Mr. Reagan. But it certainly does fit some of those around Mr. Reagan and some of his appointees in the departments. See Anthony King, "Margaret Thatcher: The Style of a Prime Minister", in Anthony King (ed.), *The British Prime Minister*, revised second edition (Durham, NC: Duke University Press, 1985), pp. 96–140.

13. See Richard Rose, "Loyalty, Voice or Exit? Margaret Thatcher's Challenge to the Civil Service", in T. Ellwein, J. J. Hesse, Renate Mayntz, and F. W. Scharpf (eds.), *Yearbook on Government and Public Administration* (Boulder, CO: Westview Press and Baden-Baden, West Germany: Nomos Verlag, forthcoming).

14. See Joel D. Aberbach and Bert A. Rockman, "Ideological Change in the American Administrative Elite." Paper prepared for presentation at The Workshop on Patterns of Elite Transformation in Western Democracies at the ECPR Joint Session, Rimini, Italy, April 5–10, 1988.

15. For discussions of this formulation, see Richard A. Chapman, "The Changing Administrative Culture in the British Civil Service", in Colin Campbell, S. J., and B. Guy Peters (eds.), *Organizing Governance: Governing Organizations* (Pittsburgh: University of Pittsburgh Press, 1988), pp. 167–182; Joel D. Aberbach and Bert A. Rockman, "Political and Bureaucratic Roles in Public Service Reorganization", in Campbell and Peters, pp. 79–98; and Rose, "Loyalty, Voice or Exit?"

16. For a very useful discussion of problems of civil service compensation, see Charles H. Levine, "Human Resource Erosion and the Uncertain Future of the U.S. Civil Service: From Policy Gridlock to Structural Fragmentation", *Governance 1* (April 1988), pp. 115–143.

17. Interview #142.

Chapter Six

The President and the Media

While some presidents have had more cordial relations with the media than others, the relationship between the two institutions nevertheless remains an adversarial one. This is so because their interests are fundamentally in conflict. Given the absolute necessity of cultivating public support, a president will understandably attempt to project the most favorable image possible of himself and his administration. Thus, every effort will be made to maximize the good news and minimize, or even suppress, the bad. The interests of the media are quite different. Their primary obligation is to inform the public and to do so as quickly as possible. Thus, they will report on the president's failures as well as his successes. They will tell us where he has been inconsistent as well as consistent; when he has been less than candid as well as when he has boldly stated the facts. As months turn into years, the relationship between these two institutions typically becomes increasingly strained, with the media accusing a president of attempting to manage the news and a president just as vigorously charging the media with biased and unfair treatment. Only on the advice of Alexander Hamilton, for example, did George Washington delete from his Farewell Address a stinging indictment of the press charging that their publications "teemed with all the invective that disappointment, ignorance of the facts, and malicious falsehood could invent to misrepresent my politics and affections; to wound my reputation and feelings; and to weaken, if not entirely destroy the confidence you have pleased to repose in me."[1] While the press of the twentieth century has become considerably more responsible than that of Washington's day, presidential criticism has been no less biting. Thus, Woodrow Wilson observed that "Their lying is shameless and colossal."[2] Lyndon Johnson charged that "They warp everything I do, they lie about me and what I do, they don't know the meaning of truth. They are liars and cheats."[3] Richard Nixon made the point even more succinctly in a warning to a White House aide, "Remember—the press is the enemy."[4]

In the aftermath of Vietnam and Watergate—two events that reflected poorly on the presidents associated with them—some contend that the president/media relationship has grown particularly severe, with the media's perspective toward government having changed from a healthy skepticism to a not-so-healthy cynicism. This view is reflected in the first selection by Robert Entman. He contends that the media have complicated the task of presidential leadership by equating press interest with the public interest; dissolving the distinction between private and public leadership; focusing excessive attention on disputes within the executive branch; and imposing conflicting behavioral expectations on the president. In light of these complicating factors, he suggests various strategies a president should pursue in dealing with the media. Michael Grossman and Martha Kumar, on the other hand, reach conclusions that differ from the perceptions of presidents and others who see the media as overly negative in their coverage of the presidency. Based upon the examination of *Time* magazine and the *New York Times* over a twenty-five-year period (1953–1978), and *CBS* for a ten-year period (1968–1978), they find a consistent pattern of favorable coverage of presidents, with only some falloff in the post-Vietnam and Watergate period.

Notes

1. Cited in William Small, *Political Power and the Press* (W. W. Norton, 1972), p. 58.
2. Cited in *Ibid.*, p. 56.
3. Cited in *Ibid.*, p. 109.
4. Cited in William Safire, *Before the Fall* (Doubleday, 1975), p. 342.

6.1

Robert M. Entman

The Imperial Media

Robert Entman is the co-author of Media Power Politics *and teaches in the Department of Communication Studies at Northwestern University. His view is that the media complicate the task of presidential leadership by equating press interest with the public interest; by dissolving the distinction between public and private leadership; by focusing excessive attention on disputes within the Executive branch; and by imposing contradictory expectations on the president.*

President Reagan was elected after a lengthy campaign which dominated the domestic news and stimulated widespread expectations that his presence in the White House would really mark a fresh start for the nation. The media will be quick to focus on how well his performance matches his promises. In recent years—particularly since the Vietnam War—presidents and the media have seemed to be adversaries. For presidents, the question has not been *whether* the media would obstruct their leadership, but *when* and *how.* And journalists have suspected presidents of manipulating them and even of lying in order to further political objectives. At best, relations have been cool; at worst, hostile.

The media clearly have a responsibility to report what they find and to criticize effectively the institutions of government. It is right for reporters to be alive to the hazards of manipulation. On the other hand, from the president's point of view, they should not be allowed to reduce his capacity for firm leadership.

This chapter will outline some of the ways in which the media can and do obstruct the president. They include confusing the president's responsiveness to their demands with sensitivity to the public interest; inhibiting private negotiation between the president and other national leaders, particularly those in Congress; complicating executive management by magnifying conflict within the cabinet; and imposing conflicting standards of behavior which mean that, whatever he does, he cannot escape unfavorable judgment.

But the president is far from helpless. If he understands the limitations of his office, he can circumvent some of these problems and turn others into opportunities. He can use his "honeymoon"—the first few months in office—to reduce the unrealistic expectations which soon lead to frustration. He can negotiate with Congress in private. He can staff and manage his press office with discretion and care. And he and his staff can use the media selectively and with precision.

Presidents Can Manipulate But Not Dictate the News

The president's resources for managing media relations are well known (see Paletz and Entman 1981, pp. 57–59; Crouse 1973, pp. 227–56; Grossman and Rourke 1976, pp. 455–70). They include monopolizing and selectively releasing information; controlling the forum and timing of contact with the press; secrecy (Grossman and Rourke 1976, p. 459); cooptation of reporters and editors through personal friendship; televised news conferences orchestrated to convey favorable impressions (Paletz and Entman 1981, pp. 60–61); and applying licit and illicit pressure through government agencies such as the Federal Communications Commission. In general, these resources give the president an unmatched capacity to get the news he wants into the press. But keeping news out is another matter. Politicians and others with power—as well as journalists themselves—contribute significantly to the composite depiction of a chief executive.

Media Practices Thrust the President Into the News

Presidential management of the media is often compatible with journalists' needs. In choosing and defining political news stories, journalists look for a powerful cast of characters, for conflict or controversy between its members, and for potential personal impact on audiences. The prevailing definition of news allows a president to make news virtually whenever he wants to do so. Over the past two decades attention to the president has increased; 25 percent of all domestic national news now concerns presidents or presidential candidates.[1]

Among the processes that journalists use to construct political news stories are: *personalization*, the neglect of historical or structural explanations by concentrating on individuals whose deliberate choices cause events; *source standardization*, the use of the same group of informants on the beat; *dramatization*, the depiction of interactions of news personalities so as to generate audience interest, pity, fear, catharsis, where possible; and *surrogate representation*, the enforcement of government responsiveness to the public by pressing politicians to explain candidly their actions, motivations, and plans. Because these practices are almost universal, different media (and even the same ones) tend to repeat similar stories, themes, questions, and answers. These practices often help presidents. Personalization, for example, permits them to claim credit for just about anything the government does well; the duplication of content enables them to reach the entire electorate with the same basic message (cf. Paletz and Entman 1981, pp. 16–22; Kumar and Grossman 1980, pp. 5–7, 10–11).

The Tone of the News—Set by Journalist Incentives and Elite Opinions

Hindered by the president's control over much newsworthy information and constrained by conventional definitions of news, reporters and their editors nonetheless have considerable autonomy, especially in seeking out news that can be narrated as drama unfolding. In stories like these, their interests and his often diverge. Drama lies in stories of presidential involvement in domestic conflict and in history-making ventures, usually overseas. Drama is magnified when the outcomes are either highly uncertain or likely to mark a major change from previous patterns, or both. Reporters and editors face personal incentives—having little to do with ideological bias—to emphasize any drama they can find. Good for journalists' prestige but often bad for that of the president, dramatic stories which center on domestic conflict tend to convey the impression that the chief executive is incompetent, rigid, or cynical.

Aside from the president and his administration, the normal sources of national political news are Washington elites. When these congressmen, bureaucrats, and other powerful individuals generally agree with the president, journalists have few sources for concocting dramatic narratives. Such reporters emerge mainly when some elites decide to publicize their criticisms of the president.

Clashes among Washington newsmakers over presidential policy and purpose stimulate news. The more conflict, the more the media will fill with criticisms of the president. These undermine the president's preferred image as a competent consensus-builder. They publicize alternative views of policy problems and suggest solutions the president opposes. The conflict feeds on itself; the more discord, the more dramatic the story possibilities. Coverage which is damaging to the president further emboldens his opponents, as shown by the presidencies of Lyndon Johnson, Richard Nixon, and Jimmy Carter (Paletz and Entman 1981, pp. 65-78, on Nixon and Carter).

The contest between press and president is normally played out somewhere between the basking of the early John Kennedy and the thrashing of Richard Nixon. Within these bounds a president's skill at media relations can make news a little brighter. Maladroit media management does the reverse. But more important for the tone of the coverage may be the level of elite support the president enjoys and the treatment that news organizations and employees, acting out of their own habits and interests, afford presidential activities.

Four Media Impacts on Presidential Leadership

Journalists have taken a more aggressively critical stance toward the presidency since the perceived betrayals of Vietnam and Watergate. One facet of the practice of surrogate representation, the critical perspective assumes purely political motives behind presidential ideas and actions and then tries to confirm that theory by doggedly pursuing presidents and their aides until they admit its accuracy. Confined largely to the major national media, the technique seeks to enforce a moral and responsive *process* of presidential leadership. It casts a president less as a leader with special legitimacy than as a politician—one with a special calling and high responsibility, but a politician nonetheless.

The country has benefited from this approach, to a point. But the advantage of process-oriented reporting recedes if it prevents presidents from reaching their policy objectives; democracy requires effective policy as well as pristine process. This section explores four potentially damaging consequences of the media's skeptical mood.

Confusing Press Interests With the Public Interest

The press tends to judge a president's responsiveness to the public on the basis of his cooperativeness with reporters. They demand that he reveal and fully explain all his major decisions. This expectation is as unrealistic as it is self-serving. Unrealistic, because all presidents will—and to some degree should—make decisions they neither disclose in detail nor justify to the press. Self-serving, because the emphasis on full disclosure seems to be rooted more in the media's production practices than in a well-grounded theory of journalism's proper political role.

Open White House news sources make for cheaper production—fewer reporters and less hard work are required to ferret out information. James Deakin of the *St. Louis Post-Dispatch* (quoted in Purvis 1976, p. 49) defines the mission of White House news hunters: "We are . . . making a consistent attempt underneath all the bombast and fury of the press conference and the briefing, to find out why the president did what he did in the past."

The other major goal of the White House news corps is to find out what the president plans to do in the future. Yet a politician cannot explain past actions or future plans without trying to fit news reports to his political needs, to the expectations of his elite audiences. So the president and his staff are among the less-helpful sources on the president's plans. Better answers could be found by digging about Washington, probing the innards of the bureaucracy, plowing through congressional hearings and reports. To ask a president or press secretary why the president did something offers the appearance of critical reporting without its reality.

Consider televised press conferences. In most of them we learn mainly how the president parries, rephrases, and ignores tough queries. A president who has significant information to release will rarely do so involuntarily in response to a reporter's question; he will choose his own time and place. The event becomes a ritual of predictable thrust and parry. Reporters give a show of undaunted inquisitiveness; presidents, of ersatz candor.

Why a president does something should be less newsworthy than *what* he does. The "why" we largely know in advance; partly to help the country, partly to advance his policy goals, partly to protect his political future; post-Watergate reporters highlight only the latter. Citizens and voters need also (perhaps mainly) to know the "what"—what effects presidential policies will have on inflation and economic growth, on their children's education and health, and on national security (cf. Barber 1979, p. 21). But again, providing such information would require a more diligent, tedious brand of reporting along with a diminution of the drive to unmask the selfish political goals behind every presidential action.

Present practices often compel the president and his staff to reveal information they do not want to divulge. While on occasion this is beneficial to the public, press officers sometimes answer prematurely, incorrectly, or unwisely. They are upbraided if they backpedal, abandon, or repudiate the earlier position and excoriated if they refuse to respond at all. Yet this "news" may be hollow. Ron Nessen has described an egregious example. As the Vietnam War drew to its sorry finale in 1975, White House reporters continually hectored him with questions about when the United States would evacuate Saigon (Purvis 1976, pp. 45–46). But the Ford administration could hardly have revealed the answer—even if it knew—without jeopardizing the safety of those still in Saigon. More important, even if the answer had been forced out of the White House, knowing it would not have strengthened the citizen's voice in government in any meaningful way.

Dissolving the Distinction Between
Public Office and Private Leadership

Leadership has both public and private dimensions. One of a president's major tasks is to inspire the public. But publicity alone does not propel policies through the bureaucracy and Congress and into action. Leadership also entails private communication—in person, over the telephone, by letter—with power brokers and decision-makers. Presidents and their staff deploy technical arguments, emotional appeals, veiled threats, deft flattery, adroit bluffs, tantalizing hints—the whole repertoire of persuasive tools—*in private*. Publicity vitiates these tools. Media coverage of the tactics, their rationales, and different actors' reactions adds an extra dimension of strategic complexity into a president's already Byzantine political calculus.

A president once could manipulate tacit knowledge or nagging suspicions to his advantage. A member of Congress might say to himself, "I know he's flattering me but I like it" or "He sounds as if he might really carry out his (wholly implicit) threat," and then conclude "I'd better go along." Now, quite frequently, the president's underlying strategy is publicized. The press tells those on the receiving end what the president is trying to do to them, how, and why.

Consider Jimmy Carter's early run-ins with House Speaker "Tip" O'Neill. Carter failed to appoint one of O'Neill's cronies to a top administrative post. The personal offense given and taken was detailed in the press, as was Carter's calculated attempt to regain O'Neill's affection. Similar developments occurred in Carter's relationship with AFL-CIO president George Meany. Granted the Georgian's apparent ineptitude in such matters, it is doubtful that wide media coverage of his strained relationships and awkward attempts at reconciliation efforts made things easier.

This phenomenon corrodes presidential leadership in a number of ways. First, it increases the tactical intelligence of those he is trying to persuade. Without publicity, a president's manipulative maneuvers might not be recognized as such by his less-insightful adversaries and allies; when his tricks are exposed and dissected in the news, even the most obtuse lobbyist or senator can fend better. Second, once a president's technique for handling a particular task of persuasion is publicized, other actors are forewarned and hence forearmed. Third, the publicity changes the decision calculations of those the president attempts to lead. Public knowledge that a president is trying to soothe or strong-arm an individual may compel the latter to spurn the president's offer; it ill-behooves most politicians to appear to respond to presidential pressure or flattery. Fourth, such publicity may embarrass a president, generating pressure to avoid perfectly legitimate tactics of political life and reducing his list of options. It may also make his own responses to the political acts of others more problematic; he of all politicians must avoid appearing too willing to compromise with interests which are merely powerful or cunning. Finally, these persuasive tactics are quintessentially those of party maintenance: to the list of formidable centrifugal forces operating on party organizations and politics must be added the journalistic foible of publicizing a president's private leadership activities.

Complicating Executive Management

Beyond the direct focus of the chief executive himself, the White House staff, cabinet officers, and departments sometimes tumble into the media net. They are all politicized, loyal to the president, and thus part of his story. The media's attraction to presidential subordinates can pose management problems because of three strong media impacts—on the agendas of executive officials and agencies, on the relationships between those individuals and offices and the president, and on the president's control over information.

First, public attention is drawn only sporadically to most federal offices. When the Federal Aviation Administration, the Environmental Protection Agency, or the White House Counsel's office make major news, it is generally because reporters scent controversy over, say, a plane crash, a hazardous waste spill, or an ethically questionable legal maneuver on behalf of the president. These offices are hyper-sensitive to such publicity because they make the papers relatively infrequently. One bad story comprises a substantial portion of an entire year's coverage. Those involved tend to believe that the stories harm the agency's public image and reduce its clout with the president and Congress, so they scurry frantically to redress publicized misfeasance, clearing their normal and long-range agendas to focus on the object of attention. Not surprisingly, the bureaus anticipate and fear negative media reactions. They may become overly cautious and rigid in applying their rules to stave off future onslaughts.

Second, publicizing personality feuds and policy debates within the administra-tion complicates the president's task of coordinating his top officials. Stories about whose influence is ascending, whose plummeting, who is at whose throat or in whose pocket, can only exacerbate jealousies and tensions. Recall Rogers and Kissinger, Vance and Brzezinski. Highly publicized internecine quarrels make the president look like a poor manager, even if they are not his fault. Such reportage discourages frank and open dialogue between a president's advisors as it poisons the relationships among them.

Third, news can turn reputation into reality: a press imputation of clout can actually bestow influence (see *Fortune* 1979, pp. 36–49). So, innocently enough, cabinet officers and White House staffers cultivate reporters. But then they may leak information that undermines a president's proposals or credibility. The media's craving for conflict within the administration provides a tempting oppor-tunity. The threat of disobedience gives the president an incentive to limit access to the most important information to a very small group of trusted personal aides. This practice in turn overloads him with decisions and with public expectations.

Reinforcing Double Binds

Americans expect a great deal of their president. Above all, they want leadership; survey respondents indicating the country needs strong leadership increased from 49 percent in 1976 to 63 percent in 1979 (Wayne 1980, pp. 5, 9). But citizens are ambivalent; they have traditionally disapproved of many of the traits exhibited by strong leaders. Post-Watergate journalists have made this element of tradition into a creed. By subjecting presidents to a daily buffeting of charges and counter-charges of failure to fulfill the contradictory high standards of presidential office, news reports reinforce a number of double binds that tie the hands of leadership. For news of presidential defaults is unavoidable and unremitting; by satisfying one standard, a president frequently violates another.

The Man on the White Horse versus the Man in the White House. A president usually begins his term after a long election campaign during which media practices have encouraged him to indulge in oversimplified attacks on opponents, to promise to solve policy problems while simultaneously remaining fuzzy and uncontroverisal, and to avoid too many expressions of doubt, hesitation, and realism about the intractability of problems. Dominating the domestic news of election years, the very magnitude of campaign coverage implies that the selection of a new president can really make a difference. After the election, the press brims over with paeans to the overworked transition staff as it culls applications for posts in the new administration and selects only the brightest and the best. The composite picture is of a fresh beginning glistening with promise.

Then reality moves into the White House. Contradictory promises that slipped by in the hurly-burly of the campaign lose their luster. News reports call attention to the incompatibilities among proposals. Attacks on predecessors and opponents return to haunt the new incumbent as he realizes the complexity of the problems he faces or acknowledges them for the first time. Fuzziness is no longer an option, for a president's legislative proposals have to be specific: they force him to take a stand. Contumely and controversy inevitably follow, and with them, negative reporting. Supporters who relied upon the fulfillment of campaign slogans and symbols, or who read into them a message of future commitment, become disillusioned. Opponents see their charges confirmed.

If a president does propose a bold initiative to fulfill a campaign pledge, he often faces energetic opposition. The media are drawn to policy shoot-outs. Their eagerness to focus on his critics may implicitly impel him to avoid proposing innovative policies. The cautious president takes refuge in incrementalism—only to be assaulted all too often by accusations of failure to provide the courageous, visionary leadership the country's predicaments demand.

The media do not cause the cycle of boom and bust in public expectations; but their campaign coverage encourages the boom, their Washington coverage, the letdown. The new president needs to recognize the change in the logic of media relations that occurs when the campaign becomes incumbency. President Carter never did.

Machiavelli versus St. Francis. Journalists require the president to observe the norms of two distinct levels of discourse. On the first, which might be called personal discourse, journalists demand the same kind of decency and candor that people depend on for rational communication in everyday life. On the second level, that of political discourse, journalists recognize the significance of language for controlling the behavior of others, that is, for leadership. Yet reporters cry "Foul!" when a president responds to them as they expect him to respond to all other political actors—with strategic artifice and a calculated choice of data and words.

Consider another example from James Deakin. He has expressed deep resentment at the Nixon administration's misleading statements during the India-Pakistan war of 1971, calling them "an affront to the intelligence of reasonable people" (Purvis 1976, p. 48). Judged by norms of personal discourse, the administration's words *were* deceitful and offensive. But on the political level it would have been an affront to intelligence for the administration to subvert its own delicate policy initiative by announcing its strategy openly. And journalists would have pounced on any such careless and unstrategic revelation, as they later did when a different administration's United Nations ambassador (Andrew Young) spoke too freely. This problem confronts presidents in domestic policymaking as well.

A profile in courage versus a finger to the wind. One journalistic standard calls for the president to do what is best for the country, not what is popular. In his view, he should not pander to public opinion; he should point the populace in the right direction; where it is unmovable, he should plow ahead and damn the political consequences. Yet a president who takes this tack often gets into trouble. Attacks on his stewardship proliferate as his reported isolation from public opinion grows. It is alleged that a president who neglects the evidence of surveys and other public expressions misuses his great office, misreads his traditions and purposes.

John F. Kennedy's book, *Profiles in Courage*, revealed the continuing American ambivalence on this issue. But none of Kennedy's profiles were subject to the continual and contrary public jostling of these two incompatible standards which suffuses recent media reporting.

Again it should be emphasized that the press alone does not create these three warring expectations. It does, however, repeatedly thrust them into public consciousness—and thus into the calculations of the elites—by its intimate and insistent coverage of the presidency. In that way press reports frequently diminish a president's potential to transcend the double binds that tradition imposes.

Leading Congress by Seeking Public Support: Onward or Downward?

Under the circumstances just depicted, presidential leadership has become increasingly problematic. More than ever, a president's ability to lead comes down to his capacity to persuade (Neustadt 1980; cf. Sperlich 1975, pp. 406–30). Supportive public opinion may be a significant component of a president's stock of persuasive resources. Yet the double binds reinforced by the media have magnified the difficulty of meeting the public's expectations and retaining its approval.

There is a growing body of research on presidential popularity based on the Gallup Poll question, "Do you approve or disapprove of the way [the incumbent] is handling his job as president?" But there is little understanding of its impact on presidential power or its roots in media coverage. What follows, then, is one observer's speculative version of the relationship between the press, public support, and presidential success in Congress.

Why the Congress Decides

A president is only one of the forces acting on a Congress member. The most recent comprehensive studies have found that the president has little direct and distinct impact on most roll call votes.[2] This should not be surprising: Congress members cultivate independent local power bases which minimize their dependency on the president (cf. Mayhew 1974). As Congress has enhanced its ability to initiate and analyze proposals in recent years, even the president's power to dominate the congressional agenda has suffered.

The key to presidential success is probably in convincing legislative leaders, committee heads, and interest groups to support the president's policies. These three, along with members' constituents and their own personal beliefs, determine most decisions. If a president's position coincides with the dominant slant of these forces, legislators will go along. If not, under conditions of weak party organization, presidents have relatively little to offer individual members to induce them to buck the tide.

Enter public support. A president who has high public approval can argue that voting with him against the wishes of interest group moguls or legislative leaders will win accolades for the solons back home. Such claims may sway some members.[3] Public support might also enhance a president's ability to obtain the cooperation of committee, party, and interest group chieftains.

If there are any advantages to individual members in voting with a president against the push of other Washington power brokers, however, they must disintegrate when the president is perceived as unpopular. Then, going along with the president exposes members and leaders to guilt by association, as some Democrats discovered in the 1980 election.

Media Impact: More Harm Than Good?

Congressmen, along with the rest of the citizenry, receive a major part of their information about presidential popularity through the media. It comes not only from direct reporting of the Gallup Poll results but from the tone and content of editorials, columns, and news stories. Although research evidence is scant, it appears that lower Gallup ratings may stimulate less-positive portrayals of the president. When presidents seem to be in declining favor, the practice of surrogate representation may lead reporters to probe more sharply. Low approval rating and negative media coverage feed each other, heightening the perception that the president is floundering, deepening the drumbeat of decline—dissolving one of his few persuasive resources, the notion that public opinion is on his side.

Some scholars have unearthed a relationship between media content and approval rating. They find that when news of presidents' actions is good or better than what came before, presidential popularity tends to increase (Brody and Page 1975, pp. 136–47; Haight and Brody 1977, pp. 41–59). But other research indicates that economic conditions, national calamities, and partisan feelings have the major impacts on the approval rating. Growth in real income and employment is especially helpful; decline, harmful (Hibbs et al. 1980, p. 29; cf. Kernell 1978, pp. 506–72). Prosperity may contribute more to a president's support than can media notices, however glowing. If so, and if the above analysis of Congress is accurate, it may be that negative coverage can sap the president's leadership strength more decisively than positive news can fortify it.

The argument would go as follows. The economic situation, and the presence or absence of such disastrous domestic or foreign entanglements as Vietnam or Watergate, establish a baseline of approval. If events go well and the economy perks along, elite support will tend to be high and press coverage will tend to be favorable without a great deal of presidential machination. Approval ratings will rise—or not deteriorate unduly. If the economy remains volatile, if the international situation continues to be tense, the news will obtrude in two ways. The press will cover the economic dilemmas or the unresolved world tensions; because of popular expectations of the presidency, this news implicitly indicts the incumbent. And the press will report the elite controversy that generally envelops such problems. Lower approval ratings follow and help to produce more unfavorable coverage. A downward spiral ensues, compounding the president's difficulty in garnering elite support for the solutions the public expects.

What Is to Be Done? Reduce and Shift Media Focus

Although this paper focuses on the negative impacts on leadership, all is not lost. Particularly if he enjoys an ideologically sympathetic majority in Congress, the president still possesses the potential to fashion favorable media images, to garner public and elite support, and to get things done. And the positive contributions of good media relations should not be gainsaid. But neither should this potential obscure the obvious and veiled costs of the media's unyielding concentration on the White House. On balance, a chief executive would probably profit from engineering a reduction in the media's inordinate obsession with him. Then he should work to reshape the character of the coverage remaining.

Reduce Reliance on Media Events

Do not make a fetish of getting on television. One of the noteworthy changes in reporting since Vietnam and Watergate is that journalists now depict politicians' overt attempts to create media events just so. With a president involved, the media do cover the events—the Rose Garden ceremony, Carter's putatively nonpolitical hegira through the hinterlands, the minor announcement cloaked as major pronouncement. But if, as they transmit the events, reporters convey the political strategy behind them, they vitiate both.

Presidents have helped erect barriers to their own leadership by overemphasizing media events, which frequently only reinforce the cynicism of journalists and citizens alike.

Use the honeymoon to dampen, not raise, expectations. All new presidents enjoy a glowing press. Washington waits, journalistic deference prevails, as the pomp of inauguration and drama of peaceful transfer of power unfold (Kumar and Grossman 1980, p. 12; cf. Morris 1975, pp. 49–52). Coming directly after the legitimizing hoopla of an election, this coverage tends to raise approval levels—and expectations—to their highest points, whence they can only tumble. Although media-induced exhilaration encourages otherwise, the honeymoon is precisely the best time for new administrations to inject caution and realism into public (and journalistic) consciousness. If offered only after the inevitable failures come, such caveats appear as apologia rather than as prudence.

Reduce Publicized Conflicts with Congress

Handle the media's tendency to amplify conflict with Congress by negotiating in private. A president should not automatically assume that taking to the airwaves to publicize his position against that of a recalcitrant Congress will help. There is no assurance that the public will be swayed by his speech (recall the failures of President Ford's WIN, Carter's energy talks; cf. Mueller 1973; Sigelman 1979, pp. 542–61) or that an independent Congress would necessarily respond even if the public were moved. Moreover, televised appearances can inject precisely the element of open discord that draws attention to a president's congressional adversaries, elevating them to page one (and Walter Cronkite) rather than page thirty-six (*sans* TV). When Congress attacks publicly, presidents should not automatically respond in kind. It is astonishing how quickly the media lose interest when there is only one voice clamoring instead of two—especially when that one is *not* the president's. Consider the nearly instant disappearance from page one of the Iranian hostages (post-rescue mission) and Billygate (post-press conference) when President Carter stopped his constant public commenting. The lack of publicity might allow other, more effective, means of persuasion to operate.

Encourage party revival. For too long presidents have neglected their party organizations to build up personal followings through the media. This may make sense in primary and even fall election campaigns, but once in office the party organization, especially in Congress, should be his most valuable friend. Indirectly pressuring congressional party leaders through the media's putatively favorable impact on public opinion is less likely to work than is patient cultivation of organizational bonds.

Attempt to Change News Practices

Reduce reporters' expectations. Tame White House-beat reporting by decreasing reporters' expectations of full access to officials, by directly asserting that the demands of leadership require a modicum of confidentiality. Take advantage of the country's growing preference for strong leadership to legitimize this approach. And repeat frequently that bargaining and mutual adjustment are the essence of democratic politics, not its antithesis.

Shift reporters' attention from politics and plans to facts and figures. While discouraging discussions of the president's political motivations and strategies, staffers should be open and accommodating with the technical policy analysis that undergirds decisions. This tactic should defuse complaints about total inaccessibility. It could reduce the total volume of reporting, since dry data are often defined as unnewsworthy. To the extent data are covered, Americans would obtain more of that elusive information about the "what" of presidential policy. Such information, better than the current skeptical but banal stress on the "why," would enforce democratic accountability by telling citizens more clearly just "what" government is doing to and for them.

Discourage personal mingling between press officers, other White House staff, and journalists. While something surely is gained by social interaction, and it probably cannot be reduced very much, the president should realize that the advantages of personal friendships dissolve when the news gets juicy—as Ron Zeigler, Ron Nessen, and Jody Powell found. Co-optation works both ways. Reporters may get more out of presidential staff (for instance, through "off-the-record" backgrounders that can be used to frame on-the-record questions, or through alcohol- or fatigue-induced slips) than vice versa.

Beware the pitfalls of cabinet government. In the current environment of intense media attention, cabinet government could saddle the president with more responsibility for media relations without enhanced power to control them. The media might hold presidents accountable both for the decisions cabinet departments make and for the bad news they generate. Nixon, Ford, and Carter all promised a larger role for cabinets, yet their moves in that direction were stymied in part by media pressures. For the buck not only stops at the Oval Office; it inexorably *goes* there, no matter where it originated. The president will be asked to explain and justify the newsworthy controversies a cabinet member arouses, as suggested by the storms over Earl Butz's bad jokes and Joseph Califano's anti-smoking campaign. More autonomy for cabinet officers may make sense, but it might be wise to limit their authority to less-newsworthy (which are not always less-important) matters.

Staff the Press Office and Use the Media with Selectivity and Precision

Employ a press staff that understands how the national media cover incumbent presidents. This means selecting journalists or others who know well the operations of the Washington press corps. Those whose experience is limited to running advertising campaigns or state and local press offices should generally be avoided.

Keep the press staff (except the secretary) in the dark about the politics of White House decision-making. If press offices are not privy to the president's political strategies and future plans but are well briefed on policy substance, they can honestly fend off reporters' gossipy "why" inquisitions and steer the focus to the "what."

For pushing policy proposals, the media are most helpful early or late in the decision cycle. In the beginning, before there are set views, presidential talks can weave a favorable aura around a proposal. Later, near decision time, undecided members of Congress can occasionally be swayed by the smell of media attention a president kindles. But note the boomerang threat: if voting with the president means voting against home-district sentiment, publicity and visibility may be the last thing potential allies need.

Use the different media for the purposes they can best accomplish. For example, television is best for ephemeral rousing of mass sentiment through symbolism. It is not the medium for rational persuasion. Jimmy Carter's energy and inflation speeches provide a paradigm to avoid. The *New York Times, Washington Post,* and *Wall Street Journal* are the papers of record for the powers that be. These are the best places for agenda setting and reasoning with elites. These papers also guide the news judgments of the networks. *Time* and *Newsweek* are ready by the better-educated and politically interested public. News magazines can shape the issues their audience ponders and some of the standards their readers use to evaluate presidents and policy.

Pumping up approval ratings through the media is feasible mainly in connection with foreign policy initiatives and crises. The approval question probably taps a combination of what the public thinks the main job of the president is and how well he is doing it. When a chief executive is immersed in a major diplomatic quest (Begin and Sadat at Camp David, Nixon in China) or a threat to national sovereignty (the *Mayaguez*, Iranian hostage seizure), elites generally support him and drama suffuses the story. The president receives reams of positive coverage that focus overwhelming public attention on one aspect of his job: handling the foreign affair. Approval ratings usually spurt upward. But elite support, media favor, and public approval may fade as second guesses supplant the cheers. More important, the approval increase is linked to the initiative or threat. As these become old news, perceptions of the president's "job" revert to other (usually domestic) matters on which he is less likely to enjoy an elite consensus and beneficent press. But this story contains a useful lesson: to the extent that he can, a president should encourage circumscribed perceptions of what his proper "job" should be. That way, when asked if they approve of the way the president is handling it, more people are likely to respond affirmatively.

All the above tactics could fizzle or backfire. As Watergate showed, the media have considerable autonomy; if antagonized, they can strike back in many ways. The president must mix new techniques with traditional ones. Others will appear in time. Their success would measurably enhance his leadership.

Notes

James David Barber and Francie Seymour offered helpful comments on an earlier draft of this paper. I am grateful to them.

1. The figures vary from year to year. See Gans 1979, pp. 9-10; see also Kumar and Grossman 1980, pp. 5-7, 10-11; and Balutis 1976, p. 511.

2. See the findings of Kingdon 1973, pp. 169-91, and Clausen 1973, pp. 192-212, who finds presidential impact only on issues of international involvement; cf. Davis 1979, pp. 465-79, Neustadt 1980, pp. 212-16.

3. For evidence of weak correlations between approval ratings and success, see Edwards 1976, pp. 101-13.

References

Barber, James David. 1979. "Not the *New York Times." Washington Monthly* 11 (September).

Brody, Richard, and Page, Benjamin I. 1975. "The Impact of Events on Presidential Popularity: The Johnson and Nixon Administrations." In *Perspectives on the Presidency,* ed. Aaron Wildavsky. Boston: Little, Brown.

Crouse, Timothy. 1973. *The Boys on the Bus.* New York: Random House.

Fortune. 1979. "Candid Reflections of a Businessman in Washington" (29 January).

Grossman, Michael B., and Rourke, Francis E. 1976. "The Media and the Presidency: An Exchange Analysis." *Political Science Quarterly* 91.

Haight, Timothy R., and Brody, Richard A. 1977. "The Mass Media and Presidential Popularity, Presidential Broadcasting and News in the Nixon Administration." *Communications Research* 4.

Hibbs, Douglas A., Jr.; Rivers, R. Douglas; Vasilatos, Nicholas. 1980. "On the Demand for Economic Outcomes: Macroeconomic Performance and Mass Political Support in the United States, Great Britain, and Germany." Paper delivered at the annual meeting of the American Political Science Association, Washington, D.C., 28–31 August.

Kennedy, John F. 1955 *Profiles in Courage.* New York: Harper & Row.

Kumar, Martha J., and Grossman, Michael B. (with Leslie Lichter-Mason), 1980. "Images of the White House in the Media." Paper delivered at the annual meeting of the American Political Science Association, Washington, D.C., 28–30 August.

Mayhew, David R. 1974. *Congress, the Electoral Connection.* New Haven, CT: Yale University Press.

Morris, Roger. 1975. "Carter's Cabinet: The Who's Who Treatment." *Columbia Journalism Review* 14 (Sept./Oct.).

Mueller, John E. 1973. *Wars, Presidents and Public Opinion.* New York: John Wiley.

Neustadt, Richard E. 1980. *Presidential Power: The Politics of Leadership from FDR to Carter.* New York: John Wiley.

Paletz, David L., and Entman, Robert M. 1981. *Media Power Politics.* New York: Free Press.

Purvis, Hoyt, ed. 1976. *The Presidency and the Press.* Austin, TX: Lyndon B. Johnson School of Public Affairs, University of Texas.

Sigelman, Lee. 1979. "Rallying to the President's Support: A Reappraisal of the Evidence." *Polity* 11.

Sperlich, Peter W. 1975. "Bargaining and Overload: An Essay on *Presidential Power.*" In *Perspectives on the Presidency,* ed. Aaron Wildavsky. Boston: Little, Brown.

Michael Grossman and Martha Kumar

Images of the White House in the Media

Michael Grossman and Martha Kumar are the authors of Portraying the President: The White House and the News Media. *Both are professors in the Political Science Department at Towson State University. Based upon an examination of* CBS, *the* New York Times, *and* Time *magazine over a twenty-five year period, they find a consistent pattern of favorable coverage of presidents, with some falloff during the Vietnam and Watergate periods.*

Presidents perceive themselves to be in an ongoing war with the news media, a war in which they believe they lose most important battles. Lyndon Johnson believed that this war began immediately after he took the oath of office. "This man [Dan Rather] and CBS [are] out to get us any way Bill Paley can," the President complained after less than six months in office.[1] Like his predecessors, Johnson felt that unfavorable coverage harmed his ability to act as the national steward. When a *New York Times* reporter wanted access to the White House staff for a story he was doing on some of its members, Johnson wrote to his special assistant, Marvin Watson, that he would prefer not to grant the request because "no good can come from it."[2]

The reality was different, as indicated by a survey of White House stories appearing at the time in the *New York Times* and *Time* magazine. During President Johnson's first year in office, when he was complaining of his treatment by the news media, the ratio of favorable over unfavorable articles concerning the White House in the *New York Times* was better than six to one. In *Time* ten favorable articles appeared for each that was unfavorable. Johnson was enjoying the same strongly favorable coverage that his predecessors had received during their first years in office but, like them, he reacted strongly to stories he thought to be negative.

A striking feature emerging from twenty-five years of *Time* and *New York Times* articles and ten years of CBS News broadcasts is the consistent pattern of favorable coverage of the President. The number of negative articles has grown, but the favorable still outnumber the unfavorable. Johnson's successors have not received the same level of favorable coverage that he did early in his term, but in the post-Vietnam and Watergate period, the balance of press coverage of the

From Grossman, Michael Baruch and Martha Joynt Kumar. *Portraying the President*, The Johns Hopkins University Press, Baltimore/London, 1981, pp. 174-193.

White House has been favorable. Yet Presidents Ford and Carter, like their predecessors, complained about media treatment of their administrations.

Presidents have tended to blame their inability to achieve desired policy outcomes on the press because of its role in publicizing their administrations' failures. Presidents, George Reedy observed, have political problems, not press problems, but White House fingers continue to point to the press as the creator of problems. Near the end of his life Lyndon Johnson lamented, "From my viewpoint how they twisted and imagined and built and magnified things that I didn't think were true at all. I never thought it was the President's credibility gap, I thought it was their credibility gap. But they owned the papers and networks; I didn't. And they come out every day. And they could talk about my credibility, but there wasn't much I could do about their credibility."[3]

The Content Analysis

The content analysis of the news sources presented here is based on a sample of White House stories appearing in the *New York Times* and *Time* magazine from Eisenhower's inauguration in 1953 through August, 1978. It also includes analyses of stories from the CBS Evening News during a ten-year period beginning on August 6, 1968, when film was first collected at the Television News Archives at Vanderbilt University. Three coders read and viewed White House stories that appeared at fifteen-day intervals for the entire period. They compiled 8,742 White House stories: 5,270 from the *New York Times*, 2,550 from *Time*, and 922 from CBS News.

This content analysis does not provide a definitive portrait of media coverage of the presidency, but it does produce a clear picture of how the President and the White House were treated by three influential news organizations over a significant period of time. Each of the three organizations attempted as thorough coverage as can be found within that particular medium. The *New York Times* is important as a subject of study because of its role in shaping the opinions of the political and journalistic elite. *Time*, the inventor of the newsweekly format, has the largest national circulation, in addition to the broadest readership among Washington influentials. Of the three networks, CBS has made its White House coverage a top priority item for its evening news program. At times CBS has assigned twice as many correspondents to the White House as the other networks.

An analysis of the stories produced by these three organizations confirms three central points about press coverage of the White House: the favorable tone of the stories; the recurring patterns of the coverage from administration to administration; and the similarities in what the three consider to be a White House story. The continued production by the news media of favorable stories about the President has been mentioned. The study also provides evidence demonstrating the continuing character of the relationship between the White House and the news media. Press coverage tends to follow established patterns. The variations in the tone of stories and the frequency of their appearance demonstrated trends that appeared within and among administrations. Although each president did not start with the same number of stories and the same percentage of stories rated favorable, in almost every case the beginning of a president's term represented a high point for both.

Content analysis demonstrates the degree to which a White House story is a presidential story and the ways in which the coverage of the White House by the different news sources is similar. The similarities in the stories of the three are, in fact, much more obvious than their differences. The prominence of policy stories and the attention paid to personal stories, as well as the tone of different subject categories, are all strikingly alike in the three sources of news.

By studying the frequency of White House stories, their location in their publications, and the development of White House stories on television evening news programs, one can understand the dimensions of the increase in White House press coverage. The increase in the number of reporters assigned to the White House has also increased the types of stories coming from there, but at the same time there has been a tendency for all three news sources to cover the same kind of stories and for these stories to have remarkably similar tones. The importance of the increase in coverage is heightened by the similar trends of coverage in the three. When the White House fails to get a story covered "its way," the chances are that it will fail to do so in all of the news sources, not just in one of them. The similarities in story treatment present the White House with an opportunity to reach a broad audience in the way it wants to be portrayed. There are also substantial risks of which White House officials must be mindful.

Coverage of the White House

When all White House stories in the *New York Times* and *Time* are considered for the twenty-five-year period, one is struck by how favorable they are. Each organization presented two favorable stories about the White House for each that was unfavorable. CBS News presented far fewer favorable and more negative stories than the *Times* and *Time*. Because the aggregate number of CBS News stories was tabulated from the ten-year period that includes six years of Vietnam and Watergate, the CBS figures are not comparable to figures for the two print sources, which were based on stories for twenty-five years. Comparison based on a year-by-year analysis shows CBS News following the same trends as the other two.

The positive tone of the stories appears in the same proportions over the twenty-five-year period in the *New York Times* and *Time*. Each story was read by two coders. The figures in table 2 represent, first, articles that both coders found to be favorable to the White House; second, stories one coder found to be positive and other neutral; third, stories that both coders found to be neutral; fourth, stories ranked by one as neutral and by the other as negative; and fifth, articles judged by both coders to be negative. In our discussion of story tone, we restrict ourselves to those categories on which both coders agree. Thus when we mention a favorable tone, we cite only the positive-positive category, and the same is true when we mention the neutral and negative categories.[4]

By looking at the statistics for each administration one can see the similar favorable ratios in all three sources of news. Figures 1 and 2 are graphs showing the favorable and unfavorable story trends of the three. (The stories from which the data for the tables and figures in this chapter are taken appeared between January 1953 and August 1978, in the case of *Time* and the *Times*; CBS News stories covered the period from August 1968 to August 1978.) The deviations of CBS News from the oth-

Table 2

TONE OF WHITE HOUSE STORIES IN *TIME*, THE *NEW YORK TIMES*, AND CBS NEWS
(Figures express a percentage of stories.)

	Time (N = 2,550)	*New York Times* (N = 5,270)	CBS News (N = 922)
Positive-positive	44.9	39.5	31.6
Positive-neutral	15.1	9.2	6.9
Neutral	11.8	24.1	22.9
Negative-neutral	8.2	4.7	6.0
Negative-negative	20.0	22.5	32.6

Figure 1. Favorable White House Stories

(Figures represent the percentage of stories coded as positive by both coders. Figures are the aggregate for each administration.)

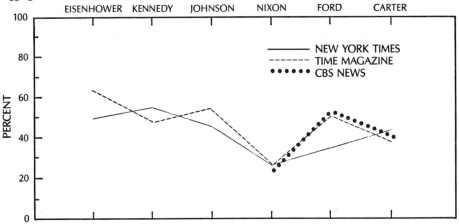

Figure 2. Unfavorable White House Stories

(Figures represent the percentage of stories coded as negative by both coders. Figures are the aggregate for each administration.)

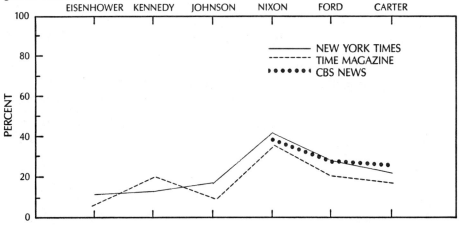

Table 3

TONE OF WHITE HOUSE PICTURES IN *TIME* AND THE *NEW YORK TIMES*,
AND FILMS ON CBS NEWS
(Figures express a percentage of pictures and films.)

	Time (N = 1,318)	New York *Times* (N = 792)	CBS News (N = 452)
Positive-positive	68.5	65.2	25.7
Positive-neutral	13.8	7.6	13.5
Neutral-neutral	15.0	24.5	52.4
Negative-neutral	0.7	0.8	4.4
Negative-negative	2.0	2.0	4.0

Table 4

SUBJECT CATEGORY OF POSITIVE STORIES AND PICTURES
(Figures express a percentage of all positive stories and pictures.)

	Stories		Pictures	
	Time (N = 87)	New York *Times* (N = 204)	*Time* (N = 102)	New York *Times* (N = 48)
President and Congress	17.5	25.8	55.1	44.1
President and administration	26.6	22.8	52.5	51.9
White House staff	38.7	42.1	69.4	51.4

er two during the period from 1968 to 1978 are not nearly as great as was indicated in table 2, which was based on aggregate figures. We did not prepare a graph to show trends in the neutral category because the figures show little fluctuation. The *Times* began the period with 21.4 percent of its stories having a neutral tone, and ended it with 23.2 percent; *Time* began and ended it with 12 percent neutral, and CBS News ended the period with 19.3 percent of its stories neutral, after a starting record of 31.2 percent. While the number of favorable stories gradually decreased as a percentage of the total number of stories, the number of negative stories increased over the twenty-five-year period.

Even more favorable are the pictures that accompany news stories. There were almost no negative pictures in either the *New York Times* or *Time*, and there were only a few negative films on the CBS News. In contrast to the two print sources, whose pictures were overwhelmingly favorable in tone, the majority of the CBS News film was relatively neutral (see table 3). Pictures often are favorable even when they accompany an unfavorable story. Articles about the relationships between the President and Congress and the President and his administration and among White House staff members were generally among the most negative types of stories that appeared in the *New York Times* and *Time* throughout the twenty-five-year period. As table 4 indicates, the stories in one subject area were favorable in less than 20 percent of the cases, and stories in no area were favorable in more than 42 percent of the cases. Yet of the pictures accompanying the stories, only in one area were the favorable pictures less than 50 percent of the total.

The number of articles about the White House rose markedly in both *Time* and the *New York Times* during the twenty-five-year period. On the other hand, CBS News remained fairly consistent in the attention it paid during the ten years included in this study. Because this twenty-five-year period included an assassination, a resignation, and an unelected president, it might be thought that these aggregate figures are not representative. But a comparison of the first years of each administration, a period that tends to be similar because news organizations report on the same kinds of stories, demonstrates the same trend. The figures also show that a large increase in stories occurred during different administrations for *Time* and the *Times*. The *New York Times* showed an appreciable increase in the Kennedy administration, whereas *Time* showed only a temporary gain then. An examination of tables 5 and 6 indicates that the sustained increase in coverage for *Time* occurred during the Nixon administration and continued for the first year and a half of Carter's term. The two print sources produced almost as many White House articles in the ten years from 1968 to 1978 as they had produced in the preceding fifteen. The average number of articles per issue of *Time* rose from 3.2 during the period from 1953 to 1968 to 5.1 in the last ten years studied. The *Times* reflected a similar increase. In the first period the *Times* averaged 7.6 stories; in the second, 10.2.

The White House stories in each issue or broadcast represented a major portion of the news space or time of each source of stories. The *New York Times*, with almost nine White House articles in each issue (including nearly two on every front page), pays close attention to the President's activities and actions. CBS News, with approximately twenty-three minutes to devote to news, devoted almost four stories each night to the White House, 23 percent of which appeared before the first commercial break, television news's equivalent of the front page. The President represents the single most important story that the network follows on a continuing basis. In its advertisements CBS News points to the thoroughness of its coverage. An ad that appeared in newspapers and magazines in 1979 pictured the three CBS White House correspondents standing with the White House in the background. The caption read: "The President doesn't make a move without them."

Patterns in White House Coverage

The continuing character of the coverage of the White House can be seen in two important fluctuations that appear in almost every administration: the number of stories and their tone. The largest number of stories and the largest number of favorable stories appear during the first year (see figure 3). Rarely does the tone rise after that first year.

There have been six administrations in the twenty-five-year span from 1953 to 1978. In all of them but two, those of Lyndon Johnson and Richard Nixon, there has been a consistent pattern in the number of White House stories appearing in all of the news sources studied. The pattern has been that the largest number of stories appear during the first year of the administration; the lowest number are found in the final year. In the Nixon administration the pattern was reversed. In

Table 5

WHITE HOUSE STORIES IN EACH ISSUE OR BROADCAST, BY ADMINISTRATION

	Time (N = 2,550)	New York Times (N = 5,270)	CBS News (N = 895)
Eisenhower	3.2	6.6	n.a.
Kennedy	3.8	9.1	n.a.
Johnson	2.8	8.3	n.a.
Nixon	5.1	11.1	4.2
Ford	4.5	8.8	3.8
Carter	5.9	9.3	3.7

Table 6

WHITE HOUSE STORIES IN EACH ISSUE OR BROADCAST, BY FIRST YEAR OF ADMINISTRATION

	Time	New York Times	CBS News
Eisenhower (1953)	3.8	7.6	n.a.
Kennedy (1961)	4.6	10.8	n.a.
Johnson (1964)*	2.7	8.7	n.a.
Nixon (1969)	3.5	9.7	3.6
Ford (1974–1975)*	5.0	9.6	4.3
Carter (1977)	6.3	9.6	3.8

*President Johnson's year runs from November 22, 1963, to November 21, 1964, and Gerald Ford's from August 9, 1974, to August 8, 1975.

Figure 3. Number of White House Stories

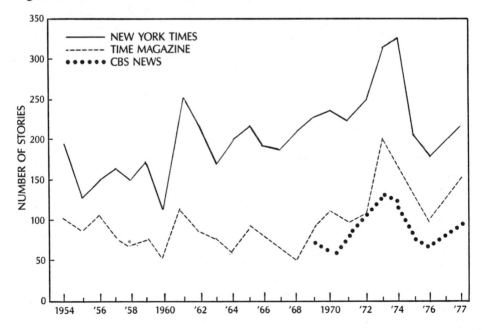

the *New York Times* and *Time*, 1969 was the year in which the Nixon administration had least coverage. Watergate shattered any normal patterns in press coverage in his administration with a tremendous increase in the number of stories in 1973 and 1974. The number decreased in 1975 and then returned to the configurations found earlier, with the high points at the start of an administration and the low points following.

The first year of an administration has received the largest number of stories not because of the high level of activity but because journalists believe that people are keenly interested in learning about the new arrivals. They want to know what the President is like and who his family members are. They want to know what he intends to do during his time in office, even if he is not prepared to bring forth solid proposals in his first month in office. After the media think the public's interest in who the people are in the administration has been satisfied, they turn toward articles on the President's actions. The number of stories declined in the second year, even though the administration might have been more active than it had been in its first year. If a president serves two terms, there probably would be a rise in coverage during his reelection campaign, as there was with President Eisenhower. Presidents tend to be more active and more visible during a campaign, and these activities give rise to an increased number of media contacts with him. The final year of an administration has represented a low point in the number of stories in all media for all presidents in the study expect President Nixon and President Johnson in the *New York Times*.

The first year of a president's term in office is also the time when the greatest percentage of favorable White House stories appear. The *New York Times* followed a pattern of having the highest percentage of favorable articles in the first year of an administration in all six administrations, while *Time* deviated from it in the Eisenhower and Kennedy administrations. CBS News followed the same pattern only in the Carter administration. The first year also has the lowest percentage of negative articles appearing in any year of the administrations. The end of the administration does not necessarily represent a low point in the percentage of favorable articles, as it does in the total number of articles written. Some administrations, such as those of Eisenhower and Ford, found that the articles written about them ended on a softer note than was employed at other points in their years in office. Figures 4 and 5 show the patterns of favorable and unfavorable articles in each year of the last six administrations.

While most administrations experience a pattern of decline in the favorable articles throughout their years in office, they have not all started at the same point. Presidents Eisenhower and Johnson started at a high percentage of favorable articles, with 58.6 percent and 63.4 percent respectively, in *Time*, but after the Johnson administration no president got over a 50 percent favorable rating the first year in *Time* and the *New York Times*.

The unfavorable articles follow a pattern fairly consistent with the favorable. In the administrations of Presidents Kennedy, Nixon, and Carter, the lowest percentage of negative articles appeared in the first year and the highest at the end of the administration in all of the news sources studied.

Just as there is an ebb and flow of articles through the years of an administration, there is one occurring within each year. A look at the monthly figures for the three news sources reveals that the *New York Times* shows a distinct pattern of heavier coverage during the first five months of the year, and *Time* and CBS News

Figure 4. Favorable White House Stories

(Figures represent the percentage of stories coded as positive by both coders.)

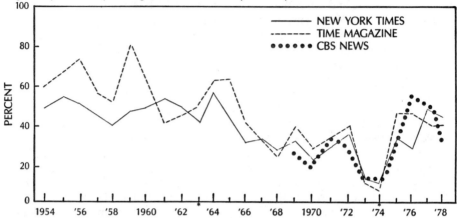

Figure 5. Unfavorable White House Stories

(Figures represent the percentage of stories coded as negative by both coders.)

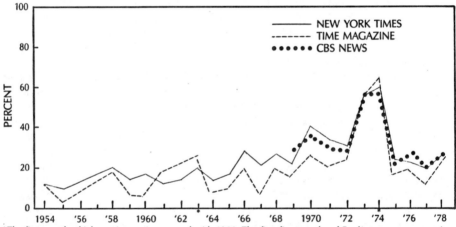

*The first month of Johnson's term is averaged with 1964. The first five months of Ford's term are averaged with 1975.

Table 7

AVERAGE NUMBER OF WHITE HOUSE STORIES IN EACH ISSUE OR BROADCAST, BY PARTS OF THE YEAR

	Time		New York Times		CBS News	
	Jan.–May	June–Dec.	Jan.–May	June–Dec.	Jan.–May	June–Dec.
Eisenhower	3.4	3.0	6.8	6.4	n.a.	n.a.
Kennedy	4.1	3.6	10.6	8.1	n.a.	n.a.
Johnson	3.2	2.4	9.3	7.6	n.a.	n.a.
Nixon	4.5	5.5	11.3	10.9	4.2	4.1
Ford	4.1	4.8	8.7	8.8	3.9	3.7
Carter	6.0	5.6	10.7	7.8	4.4	3.2
All admin-istrations	4.0	3.8	9.2	8.2	4.2	3.8

show a similar, though less clear, distribution. The *New York Times* has an average of 9.2 stories per issue on the White House during the first five months of the year, while for the remainder of the year the figure is 8.2 per issue. In most administrations the *New York Times* has considerably more articles in the first part of the year than in the second. The figures were fairly close for the year Nixon resigned, since one administration ended and the other, Ford's, began in August (see table 7).

The news media's coverage of the White House has been a response to the President's activities. The budget message, the State of the Union speech, a major legislative initiative, and an occasional foreign trip have occurred in the first part of the year; thus heavy media coverage reflects a full presidential schedule. During the summer and fall the stories tend to revolve around the President's vacation, a foreign policy speech, often at the opening session of the United Nations, and the preparation of the budget. The last seven months of the year have usually been slower than the first five.

When one looks over the full twenty-five-year period of *Time* and the *New York Times* in an effort to assess whether Vietnam and Watergate represented deviations, one can see in the period following the Nixon administration some of the earlier trends. More favorable articles reappeared, and although the percentages do not approach the high points of the Eisenhower and Kennedy administrations, neither do they maintain the lows found in the Vietnam and Watergate years. As the percentage of positive articles has decreased from the first period, the percentage of negative articles has increased (see tables 8 and 9). The percentage of neutral articles has remained fairly constant.

As the number of favorable articles changed over the period, so did the average number of White House stories during the years covered. The Vietnam and Watergate period represented the high point in White House coverage in addition to being the most negative period in recent years. The number of articles per issue or program was higher than the earlier period in all of the news publications, and higher than the later period in all but *Time* (see table 10). White House coverage has lost its relatively negative tone in the last four years, while at the same time there has been only a slight reduction in the attention paid to the White House.

The White House Story

The White House story is the President: who he is, what he does, and what his programs, actions, and goals are. White House media coverage reflects the public President. The President is the most important continuing story that the media deal with; he is of interest even when he is not active. Rarely does an issue of the *New York Times* or *Time* go to press or a CBS Evening News program appear without a White House story. In the sample of 656 issues of *Time*, 615 of the *New York Times*, and 236 programs of CBS, there were no White House articles in only 10 *Times* issues, 8 of the *New York Times*, and 8 CBS Evening News programs.

The White House story is a homogenized story. The three news sources show strikingly similar patterns in the types of stories they write and the subjects they cover as well as in the overall tone of their coverage. All three sources concentrate on news in their White House articles. There is some mixture, in varying degrees among the three, of editorials and opinion, analysis, and feature articles, but all focus their attention on news. Table 11 gives the breakdown of types of stories over

Table 8

	FAVORABLE WHITE HOUSE STORIES, BY TIME PERIOD					
	Time		New York Times		CBS News	
	Percentage	Number	Percentage	Number	Percentage	Number
1953–1965	58.9	655	50.0	1167	n.a.	n.a.
1966–1974	28.7	259	28.5	589	23.5	135
1974–1978	43.3	232	37.5	325	44.8	156

Table 9

	UNFAVORABLE WHITE HOUSE STORIES, BY TIME PERIOD					
	Time		New York Times		CBS News	
	Percentage	Number	Percentage	Number	Percentage	Number
1953–1965	10.9	121	11.0	257	n.a.	n.a.
1966–1974	31.6	285	35.2	727	38.2	219
1974–1978	19.4	104	23.4	203	23.6	82

Table 10

	AVERAGE NUMBER OF WHITE HOUSE STORIES IN EACH ISSUE OR BROADCAST, BY TIME PERIOD		
	Time	New York Times	CBS News
1953–1965	3.3	7.6	n.a.
1966–1974	4.2	10.0	4.0
1974–1978	5.1	9.0	3.8

Table 11

	TYPES OF WHITE HOUSE STORIES (Figures express number and a percentage of stories.)			
	Time (N = 2,550)	New York Times (N = 5,270)	CBS News (N = 922)	Total (N = 8,742)
News	2,052 80.5%	4,159 78.9%	836 90.7%	7,047 80.6%
Analysis	54 2.1%	138 2.6%	1 .1%	193 2.2%
Feature	341 13.4%	165 3.1%	16 1.7%	522 6.0%
Editorial	0	373 7.1%	69 7.5%	442 5.1%
Column	73 2.9%	257 4.9%	0	330 3.8%
Text	8 .3%	178 3.4%	0	186 2.1%
Time Essay	22 .9%	0	0	22 .2%

the twenty-five-year period for *Time* and the *New York Times* and the ten-year period for CBS News.

The similarities between the news sources are more prominent than their differences, with approximately 80 percent of their stories classified as news stories. The other 20 percent is where the variation lies between them. *Time* is a fairly uniform magazine; the tone of its articles varies little. It has no editorials although a *Time* "essay" appears periodically. Its column dealing with the White House is a signed article by their former White House correspondent and present bureau chief, Hugh Sidey. There is almost no presentation of either the text or content of speeches, news conferences, or other documents. *Time's* articles' function is to present interpretations. The major difference between *Time* and the other two news sources studied is the emphasis it places on feature articles. These are articles dealing with personalities, such as the President's family and perhaps some of his top staff members. The emphasis is on their personal tastes and activities, not their political actions.

The *New York Times* differs from both *Time* magazine and CBS News in the variety of coverage it presents. Both *Time* and the *New York Times* have been moving toward presenting news analysis in addition to their straight news stories, but the *New York Times* has broadened its coverage with columns and editorials. The *New York Times* regards itself as a newspaper of record, and because of that it will often include the text of speeches and documents, a news story describing them, and interpretation in the form of analysis, commentary, and editorials. The *Times* does not display the same interest in stories about people in the news as *Time*. CBS News has even less emphasis on personal stories than do the other two. Almost 91 percent of its stories are straight news, with editorials, particularly those of Eric Sevareid, being the only other prominent feature dealing with the White House.

In comparing *Time* and the *New York Times* according to the types of stories they print, a time breakdown for the periods 1953 to mid-1968 and mid-1968 to 1978 shows both publications moving toward increasing the variety in the types of news stories (see figure 6). In the last ten years there has been an increase in the number of news analysis stories. In a news analysis article the author presents an interpretation of the prospects of a presidential program by pulling together information and opinion from sources outside as well as inside the White House. *Time* now sometimes includes news analysis in its issues.

The breakdown of articles appearing in *Time* and the *New York Times* and on the CBS Evening News shows a similarity in definition of a White House story. Table 12 shows the distribution of stories by subject category. The same general categories of subjects were treated as important by the three news sources, although there was a difference in the amount of coverage they gave to each subject.[5] The category of program and policy stories was the largest during the last ten years. With one exception, the CBS News coverage of Watergate, all of the news sources had the following three subjects behind program and policy in significance: personal, activity, and Congress and administration stories. Program and policy is first because it represents the essence of what it is the President does.

The differences in emphasis given to White House subjects by the news sources depend in great measure upon the type of organization it is. *Time* is published weekly and therefore does not try to build a daily record of what the President does, as do the *New York Times* and, to a lesser extent, CBS News. The *New York*

Figure 6. White House Stories, by Type of Story and Two Time Periods

(Figures express a percentage of stories for *Time* and the *New York Times*.)

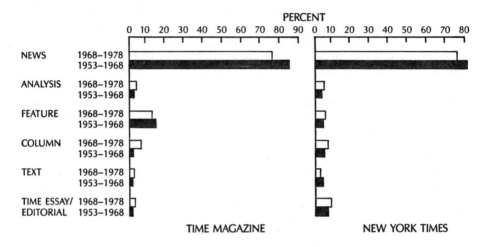

TIME MAGAZINE   NEW YORK TIMES

Table 12

SUBJECT CATEGORIES OF WHITE HOUSE STORIES, BY TWO TIME PERIODS
(Figures express a percentage of the total number of stories for each news source.)

	Time			*New York Times*			CBS News
	(N = 1,279)	(N = 1,269)	(N = 2,548)	(N = 2,824)	(N = 2,443)	(N = 5,268)	(N = 922)
	1953–68	1968–78	Total	1953–68	1968–78	Total	1968–78
Program and policy	30.1	30.6	30.4	24.8	24.7	24.7	32.3
Activity	24.4	15.9	20.2	35.7	24.4	30.5	18.4
Personal	23.7	17.0	20.4	13.7	10.5	12.2	9.9
Vice president	9.2	4.7	6.9	6.4	5.6	6.1	5.6
Congress and admin-istration	7.3	10.3	8.8	10.5	11.5	10.9	10.5
Election	2.5	6.0	4.2	5.2	8.4	6.7	8.1
Staff	1.6	5.8	3.6	2.2	3.4	2.7	1.8
President and press	1.2	2.4	1.8	1.5	1.4	1.4	1.1
Watergate	0	7.2	3.6	0	10.2	4.7	12.2

Times closely follows what a president does each day, the speeches he gives, the news conferences he holds, his business trips, ceremonies, and bill signings. *Time* gives an attention to personal stories that neither CBS News nor the *New York Times* gives. As a weekly magazine *Time* can given attention to the newsmakers as people, something that is harder to do in a daily newspaper or television program. The dailies must concentrate on what is going on that day and what will happen the next. CBS News, with severe time constraints, can do little else than cover the basics of what the President is doing and plans to do. CBS News, however, paid proportionately greater attention to Watergate than either the *New York Times* or *Time*. While not a visual story, it was one that interested its viewers, and CBS News probably gave it more attention than the other two networks.

A comparison of the *New York Times* and *Time* magazine over the full twenty-five-year period shows that the same four categories of subjects ranked highest during the whole time period with both publications. *Time* remained consistent in the ranking of the four during the whole time period, but the *New York Times* did change. All top four categories shifted between the two periods. The *New York Times* gave much less attention to activities of the President in the second period, but since the Watergate category does represent an activity (since it took up the President's and the staff's time), this shift may not be significant. Both the *New York Times* and *Time* reduced in relative terms the amount of attention they gave to personal stories about the President.

In each news source, the focus throughout the period of White House stories is the President. Staff stories have increased in both publications, particularly in *Time*, but stories about the vice president have declined over the period. The President, what he is doing and what he hopes to do, are their central concern; next by a wide margin are stories about those close to him and his relations with Congress and the bureaucracy.

The wide variation in the tone of articles and the similarities in the treatment of subjects by the three news sources can be seen in the bar graphs in figure 7. The

Figure 7. Positive White House Stories, by Subject Category

(Figures express a percentage of stories.)

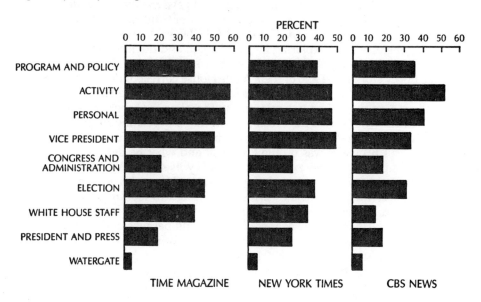

Table 13

PROGRAM AND POLICY STORIES
(Figures express the percentage of all program and policy stories represented by each category.)

	Time	New York Times	CBS News
General	11.3	1.8	.9
Foreign	8.5	12.3	17.4
Domestic	9.4	8.5	11.7
Budget	1.2	2.1	2.3
Total program and policy stories as a percentage of total stories	30.4	24.7	32.3

graphs show the nine subject categories and measure the degree to which each has been treated in a favorable tone.

The similarity of the tone of the different categories in all three news sources means that the White House can predict with some accuracy the response a particular action is going to generate in the media. Two categories, activity and personal, are clearly favorable. While the White House cannot prevent the publication of articles on certain subjects, such as the President's relationship with Congress and the bureaucracy, the predictability of media response to particular subjects does mean that the White House can wage an offensive on negative stories by getting out some favorable ones in areas over which they do have some control.

While the three news sources treat certain kinds of stories in a similar manner, there is a tendency of each to put its own spin on a story. The program and policy area illustrates some of the ways in which each treats the same subject. Table 13 shows the emphasis that each of the news sources gave to the four subjects within the general program and policy area. *Time* paid the greatest amount of attention to general stories that included several policies and gave the reader an idea of what the President as doing in the whole policy area but did not explain individual subjects in detail. The *New York Times* and CBS News, however, gave almost no space to general stories, exploring instead foreign and domestic stories in detail.

While both the *New York Times* and CBS News gave a great deal of attention to specific policy stories, the role of their White House correspondents was different. CBS News imposed stringent limits on the length of a White House story; each generally ran no more than two minutes. In that time the reporter could do little more than tell what it was the President did that day relating to the policy. The *New York Times* correspondent, however, had a different function. While the emphasis on CBS News was on the President and what he did, in the *New York Times* the emphasis was on explaining the policy itself. The White House correspondent would choose subjects based on White House involvement in them. Once a subject was chosen, the correspondent had to look into the policies as legislative and administrative programs.

The *New York Times* is a newspaper of record, and because of that emphasis, its stories reflect an interest in recording presidential events and actions and providing a complete treatment of what happened, who was involved, and what it means. CBS News, on the other hand, tries to present the highlights of what happened, but, realizing its own time limitations, does not seek to cover stories completely or give attention to all of the events that its reporters regard as news. *Time* magazine gives a general treatment of the week's events with an emphasis on who was involved in them.

Each of the news sources reflects its own interest, but the most striking finding that a comparison shows is how similar to each other they are. They pay attention to the same general kinds of stories and give their articles a similar tone. While each news source presents different pieces of information on a subject, the overall tone of the articles is quite similar. Knowledge of these patterns over the years has led presidents and their staffs to develop strategies based on the predictability and the uniformity of the press coverage of the White House.

Notes

1. Memo, Dan Rather to George Reedy, forwarded to President Johnson, marginal notes on the Rather letter are in Johnson's handwriting, April 20, 1964, EX FG 11-8-1, WHCF, LBJ Library.

2. Memo, Marvin Watson to President Johnson, Johnson marginal notes, April 27, 1965, EX PR 18, WHCF, LBJ Library.

3. Transcript, interview with Lyndon Johnson by Walter Cronkite, CBS News Special, "LBJ: Why I Choose Not to Run," December 27, 1969, p. 4, LBJ Library.

4. In order for a story to qualify as a White House story, both coders had to agree that its central focus was on the actions and programs of those physically part of the White House or the Executive Office of the President. Stories about other people with a personal or political connection to the President were not included unless their actions affected the White House in a fundamental way.

The coders were given general instructions relating to story tone. They were asked to categorize a story as favorable, unfavorable, or neutral, based on the overall impression the story gave them. What we (the authors) were looking for was the average reader's or viewer's first response to a story. The favorable and unfavorable categories contained stories that the coders found left a clear impression. The neutral category contains those stories that both found to be neutral and those that contained positive and negative elements that tended to balance each other off. It also contains a small number of cases in which one coder classified a story as negative and the other as positive. Because judgments on tone are subjective, we did not give extensive instructions in order to avoid losing the spontaneous responses of the coders. In spite of the subjective nature of the task, their responses were quite similar and provide a clear impression of the direction of White House press coverage.

The coders working on CBS News had the same evaluation in 87 percent of the stories, while the coders for *Time* agreed on 77 percent of the articles and those for the *New York Times* had the same findings on tone in 86 percent of the stories.

5. The nine subjects contained the following subcategories. Program and policy: general, foreign, domestic, budget. Activity: speech, news conference, ceremony, business trip, meeting, message to Congress, appointments, bill-signing. Personal: personal, philosophy, with family, family, health. Vice President: vice president, vice president during election. Congress and administration: president and Congress, president and administration. The remaining categories—Watergate, staff, president and press, and election—had only one heading. They contained no subcategories.

 # Chapter Seven

The President
and the Vice President

Throughout most of our political history, the office of vice president has been an object of derision, even by vice presidents themselves. Indeed, the litany of ridicule directed at the office by its occupants has probably done more to secure their memory in history than anything they did while serving in the role.

The longstanding criticisms made of the vice presidency may be subsumed under two general indictments: the lack of adequate care taken in choosing its occupant and the paucity of responsibilities that attach to the office. The selections appearing in this chapter bear upon these indictments.

While Michael Nelson acknowledges the relevance of both *governance* (competence and loyalty) and *election* (broadening appeal and party unity) criteria in choosing a vice president, he believes the former should be given stronger weight. Noting that, in the past, election criteria have clearly dominated the decision-making processes in choosing vice presidents, Nelson contends that since 1945 governance criteria have gained in importance. He considers why this change has occurred.

In addition to how he is chosen, some critics have questioned the necessity of having a vice president. His only major constitutional responsibility, after all, is to wait for the president to die or become incapacitated. Moreover, even though a president is free to delegate significant responsibilities to the vice president, few have been inclined to do so. Small wonder, then, that Harry Truman characterized the office "as about as useful as a cow's fifth teat." The second selection, however, suggests that consigning the office to a status of permanent irrelevancy may be premature. In it Paul Light shows how and why the vice presidency has become a much more important office in the last decade or so and suggests what presidents and vice presidents can do to ensure that this trend continues.

Notes

1. See, for example, Arthur Schlesinger, Jr., "On Presidential Succession," *Political Science Quarterly*, 89 (Fall 1974), p. 500; Eugene McCarthy, "No More Veeps," *New York Times*, August 28, 1988, p. E23.
2. Cited in Donald Young, *American Roulette: The History and Dilemma of the Vice Presidency* (Viking Press, 1965), p. 5.

Michael Nelson

Choosing The Vice President

Michael Nelson is the author and editor of numerous books and articles on the presidency and associate professor of political science at Vanderbilt University. Nelson suggests that the considerations weighed in selecting a vice president may be subsumed under two general categories: election *and* governance *criteria. He explains why the latter have gained in importance since 1945, although not always to the degree we might like.*

How—and how well—does the modern process of vice presidential selection work? What can be learned by considering the nominations of Texas Sen. Lloyd Bentsen by the Democrats and Sen. Dan Quayle of Indiana by the Republicans in 1988?

Most students and practitioners of American politics agree as a matter of principle that vice presidents should be chosen with their constitutional role as presidential successor uppermost in mind. Nine vice presidents, more than a fifth of those who have held the office, have succeeded to the presidency. (They served as president for forty-two years, twenty-nine of them in this century). During one recent period from 1945 to 1977, vice presidents who became president by succession occupied the Oval Office fully half the time. Illnesses, impeachment proceedings, and assassination attempts have made succession an active possibility during twenty of the nation's forty presidencies (Goldstein 1982, 207–08). Every postwar vice president except Walter F. Mondale has become the subject of unusual public concern because of some event or condition that raised the possibility that he would succeed to the presidency.

To the extent that the concern for presidential succession is taken seriously, it implies two *governance* criteria for evaluating the vice presidential selection process. The most important governance criterion is the competence of nominees for vice president to be president. Historically, six of the nine successions have occurred during the vice president's first year in office, suggesting that even the best on-the-job training is no substitute for a wise initial choice.[1] The second governance criterion for vice presidential selection is loyalty to the president's policies, so that some measure of continuity in the administration the voters elected is likely to be maintained after a succession.

In practice, governance criteria for vice presidential selection may or may not conflict with constitutional and democratic values that the public prizes. This

From *PS* 21 (Fall 1988). Reprinted by permission.

fundamentally important *legitimacy* criterion was the source, for example, of some debate within both parties in 1988 about the right of the presidential nominees to select their running mates effectively on their own. Governance criteria also may or may not accord with the operation of the two *election* criteria that traditionally have dominated the process of choosing vice presidents. The first, and the more important, election criterion is that the vice presidential nomination should unite the party in the aftermath of the presidential nominating contest.

By these standards, the ideal vice presidential selection process would fulfill the governance and legitimacy criteria and would accommodate the election criteria. Stated more plainly, the process would foster the selection of competent and loyal vice presidents by constitutional and democratic means, while helping the parties to unite and presidential candidates to win the general election.

The history of vice presidential selection in this century, especially since 1945, is a history of progress toward (but not attainment of) this ideal. For all the controversy over Quayle, the 1988 nominations suggest that such progress as has been made has not been reversed. Indeed, the outcry at Quayle's nomination was a useful reminder of how seriously the public—political journalists, activists, scholars, and voters—now regards the governance criterion of competence.

Vice Presidential Selection In Historical Perspective

During the nineteenth and early twentieth centuries, party leaders, not presidential candidates, chose the parties' nominees for vice president.[2] Election criteria invariably drove their decisions. Vice presidential nominations were used almost exclusively to balance the ticket, partly to heal the party's divisions, partly to win additional support in the general election. If elected, the vice president could look forward to being replaced four years later, when, in an altered political setting, election criterion were likely to indicate the choice of a different vice presidential candidate who could provide the ticket with a revised set of electoral balances. Until 1912, when James S. Sherman was chosen to run again with William Howard Taft, no vice president was nominated for reelection by a party convention.

Not only were governance criteria neglected in this procedure, the extreme application of election criteria actively discouraged competence and loyalty in the vice presidency. Old-style ticket balancing usually paired candidates from different and often opposing factions of the party—North-South, hard money-soft money, Stalwart-Progressive, and the like. Seldom did the president feel much trust or affinity for the vice president. The prospect of spending four years presiding over the Senate, only to be replaced at the end of the term, dissuaded most talented political leaders from accepting vice presidential nominations in the first place. (Daniel Webster, declining the second spot on the Whig party ticket in 1848, said "I do not propose to be buried until I am dead.")[3] Politicians who hoped someday to run for president shunned the office: except for Martin Van Buren in 1836, no nineteenth century vice president was nominated for the presidency by a major party convention.

Not surprisingly, the early vice presidents make up a virtual rogues gallery of personal and political failures. Because the office was so unappealing, an unusual number of the politicians who could be enticed to run for vice president were old and in bad health. Six died in office, all of natural causes. Some vice presidents became embroiled in financial, others in personal, scandal. Several vice presidents publicly expressed their dislike for the president. Others did not bother to live in Washington—one actually left for Kentucky to run a tavern, another took the oath of office in Cuba, then died there (Nelson 1988, 30).

The price for ignoring governance criteria in the selection of vice presidents (admittedly small at a time when Washington was home to arguably the nation's least important level of government) was paid when they succeeded to the presidency, which four of them did. The administrations of John Tyler, Millard Fillmore, Andrew Johnson, and, to a lesser degree, Chester A. Arthur, were marred by debilitating disagreements with their parties, especially in Congress and the cabinet. None is regarded by historians as having been a successful president.[4] Nor were any of them nominated for a full term in their own right, much less elected.

TR to FDR: The rise of national news media (specifically mass circulation magazines and newspaper wire services), a new style of active presidential campaigning, and some alterations in the vice presidential nominating process moderately enhanced the prestige of the vice presidency during the first half of the twentieth century. So, because of the vice presidency's constitutional status as the successor office, did the emergence of the presidency as the central institution in American political life.

In 1900, Theodore Roosevelt became the first vice presidential candidate (and, other than William Jennings Bryan, the first member of a national party ticket) to campaign vigorously around the country. The national reputation and political stature within the Republican party that Roosevelt established through travel and the media (he delivered 673 speeches to three million people in twenty-four states) stood him in good stead when he succeeded to the presidency after President William L. McKinley's assassination in 1901. Roosevelt was able to reverse the earlier pattern of successor presidents and set a new one: he was nominated by his party for a full term as president in 1904, as were Calvin Coolidge in 1924, Harry S Truman in 1948, Lyndon B. Johnson in 1964, and Gerald R. Ford in 1976. (All but Ford, who lost narrowly, were elected, most of them by a landslide). In addition, Roosevelt was the first of 15 (out of 19) twentieth century vice presidents to later run for their party's presidential nomination, nine of them successfully.[5]

The political debts that Roosevelt and subsequent vice presidents accrued through active partisan campaigning also help to explain the emergence of another new pattern that contrasts sharply with nineteenth century practice. Starting with Sherman in 1912, every first-term vice president who has sought a second term has been nominated for reelection, often at the behest of party activists grateful for the vice president's grassroots political assistance. Because the election criterion of uniting the party militated their renomination, competent politicians in this century no longer were discouraged from running for vice president by the promise of a humiliating dismissal four years later. It remained unusual during the early twentieth century, but no longer was unheard of, for leaders of stature like Charles Dawes, who had held office in three administrations and won a Nobel Prize; Charles Curtis, the Senate majority leader; and Speaker of the House John Nance Garner to accept the second spot on a ticket.

An even more significant alteration in vice presidential selection came in 1940, when Franklin D. Roosevelt seized from party leaders the right to choose his running mate. Roosevelt had long felt that presidents should make good use of their vice presidents and had entrusted unprecedented responsibilities—as liaison to Congress, cabinet member, goodwill ambassador abroad, and personal adviser—to Garner, his first vice president (Roosevelt, 1920). But Roosevelt and the conservative Garner (whom party leaders had placed on the ticket in 1932) had a falling out in 1937, convincing the president that he had to pick his own vice president if he were to use the office as fully as he desired. Roosevelt accomplished his goal by threatening to refuse the Democratic convention's nomination for a third term if it rejected his choice for a running mate, Henry A. Wallace.[6] Although the circumstances of Roosevelt's precedent-setting power grab—his extraordinary standing in the party and unrivaled concern for the vice presidency as an office—were unusual, the transfer of the effective power to select vice presidential candidates from party leaders to presidential nominees probably was bound to occur eventually, as part of the more general rise of the twentieth-century presidency as a political institution and the simultaneous decline of the parties.

Modern Vice Presidential Selection

Just as Theodore Roosevelt helped make the vice presidency a more appealing office to talented political leaders and Franklin Roosevelt enhanced the prospects for affinity between the president and vice president, Harry Truman's succession to the presidency in 1945 prompted further improvements in the vice presidential selection process. The combination of Truman's woeful lack of preparation (he was unaware of the existence of the atom bomb and postwar plans), the subsequent development of an ongoing cold war between the United States and the Soviet Union, and the proliferation of nuclear-armed intercontinental ballistic missiles heightened public concern that the vice president should be a leader who was ready to step into the presidency at a moment's notice and serve ably and faithfully.[7]

One thing the modern presidents have done to meet the new expectations about vice presidential competence is to entrust the vice president with greater duties and resources. The goal has been to convince the public that the president is preparing responsibly for a possible succession, but an added consequence has been the virtual "institutionalization" of the vice presidency (Light 1984). The office is significantly larger and more complex than in the past: the vice president's staff, for example, has grown from twenty in 1960 to around seventy today, including many more professionals. Again, in contrast to 1960, the vice president now has an office in the White House and a suite of offices in the Old Executive Office Building, a separate line item in the executive budget, an official residence, even a more impressive seal of office. But the vice presidency also has become institutionalized in the broader sense that certain kinds of vice presidential activities now are virtually taken for granted. These include: regular private meetings with the president, a wide ranging role as senior presidential adviser, membership on the National Security Council, full national security briefings, frequent and sometimes substantive diplomatic missions, public advocacy of the president's leadership and programs, party leadership, attendance at cabinet meetings, and congressional and other liaison activities. Most of these resources and duties exist at the pleasure of the president, but precedents do take on a life of their own: it would now be politically difficult to deny a vice president, say, a West Wing office or a sizable staff. And as the attractiveness of the modern vice presidency to a better class of political leaders has grown, so have the chances that the vice president will be someone on whom the president actually wants to rely.

The other, more obvious strategy that most modern presidential candidates have used to meet the new public expectations about vice presidential competence has been to pay considerable attention to experience, ability, and political compatibility in selecting their running mates. Winning votes on election day still is the goal, but most presidential nominees realize that voters now care more about a vice presidential candidate's competence and loyalty—the ability to succeed to the presidency ably and to carry on the departed president's policies faithfully—than they do about having all religious faiths or party factions represented on the ticket. In a sense, governance criteria have been brought into conformity with at least the more important of the two election criteria, namely, winning in November. Hamilton Jordan stated the situation well in a 1976 memo to his candidate, Jimmy Carter: "the best politics is to select a person who is accurately perceived by the American people as being qualified and able to serve as president if that became necessary" (Witcover 1977, 361).[8]

Results: The fruits of the new emphasis on governance criteria can be seen in the roster of postwar vice presidential nominees. The era has been marked by an almost complete absence of ideologically opposed running mates, and those vice presidential candidates who have differed even slightly on the issues with the heads of their tickets (as George Bush, who once described Ronald Reagan's supply-side tax proposals as "voodoo economics," did in 1980 and Bentsen, and as Bentsen, generally more conservative than Michael Dukakis, did in 1988) have hastened to gloss over past disagreements and deny that any would exist in office. In all cases, vice presidents have defined their role to be faithful lieutenant to the president. Bentsen told reporters that he would vote his own convictions as long as he was a senator, but would publicly advocate only the president's policies if he became vice president.

The record is compelling not just for loyalty, but for competence. From 1948 to 1988, the vice presidential candidate as often as not has been the more experienced member of the ticket in high government office, including John Sparkman in 1952, Estes Kefauver in 1956, Johnson and Henry Cabot Lodge in 1960, Mondale in 1976, Bush in 1980, and Bentsen in 1988. Around half the vice presidential nominees in this period already had sought or been prominently mentioned for the presidency at the time they were picked (Goldstein 1982, 72–75, 84–88). Historians actually rate the twentieth century's five successor presidents higher on average than the 11 elected presidents.[9]

Process: Not much is purposely left to chance in modern vice presidential selection, at least not when the presidential nominating contest is settled, as is typical nowadays, well in advance of the convention. The obvious lessons of the hasty, causally screened, and (when evidence of his undisclosed treatments for mental illness was uncovered by the press) politically disastrous selection of Sen. Thomas Eagleton in 1972 by Sen. George McGovern, the Democratic nominee for president, were particularly instructive in this regard. In 1976, Carter set a precedent of sorts for Democrats when he conducted a careful, organized, and unusually public preconvention search for a running mate. From a list of roughly 400 Democratic officeholders that aides compiled for him in June, followed by polling, further staff research, and personal conversations with around sixty prominent Democrats in Congress, business and labor, Carter narrowed the pool of contenders to seven. In early July, the finalists were interviewed by Carter adviser Charles Kirbo; asked to provide detailed answers to written inquiries about their finances, health, and personal and political lives; and, eventually, summoned to Plains, Georgia, to meet with Carter, who finally tapped Mondale at the convention (Witcover 1977, ch. 24). Mondale followed a similar procedure as the Democratic presidential candidate in 1984, erring mainly in the execution: he selected finalists whose competence to be president was less obvious than their symbolic representation of the most vocal interests in the party, notably blacks, Hispanics, and women. Mondale also neglected to evaluate adequately the financial records of his eventual choice, Rep. Geraldine A. Ferraro of New York.

In 1988, hours after the last primaries were over, Dukakis and his close friend and adviser Paul Brountas formally launched a search that was designed both to preserve the best of the Carter process and to avoid the mistakes made by Mondale.[10] The goal was to find a vice presidential nominee who had extensive experience in Washington (starting with Eisenhower and Stevenson in 1952, all nine non-Washington presidential candidates have picked Washington politicians as running mates), a spotless personal and financial background, the respect of Dukakis, and a political base that would broaden the ticket's appeal in the general election. The search involved wide ranging but inconclusive polling, teams of lawyers and accountants poring over the thousands of pages of personal and financial information that was requested from prospective nominees, hundreds of phone calls, dozens of face-to-face interviews by Brountas, and, as it turned out, several less than secret meetings between Dukakis and the finalists. (Jesse Jackson, who invoked legitimacy arguments to insist that his second-place finish in the primaries entitled him to an invitations to join the ticket, also was interviewed and treated publicly as a serious contender, but was never in the running). Some potential nominees asked not to be considered. A week before the convention, Bentsen, whose personal manner, experience as a powerful three-term senator, and a strong political base in Texas impressed Dukakis, was chosen at a late night meeting of the governor and his closest aides.

Republicans, who suffered their own vice presidential embarrassment when Spiro T. Agnew, the party's victorious nominee in 1968 and 1972, resigned in October 1973 as part of a plea bargain that enabled him to avoid prosecution on political corruption charges, also have adopted the new-style search process, albeit less publicly and, sometimes, less thoroughly than the Democrats. In 1976, Ford asked thousands of Republican leaders for their recommendations for vice president, assigned White House chief of staff Richard Cheney and presidential counsel Philip Buchen to request financial and other personal information from two dozen prospective nominees, and reviewed his options in several staff meetings before selecting Kansas senator Robert Dole as his running mate. Four years later, Reagan confined his choice to three men— former ambassador Bush, Senate minority leader Howard Baker, and Ford—who had long records in public life and who already had undergone intense scrutiny as presidential candidates, thus obviating any need for detailed background examinations (White 1982, ch. 11). Bush, Reagan's choice in 1980, was renominated in 1984.[11]

Bush began his own formal search for a vice presidential nominee in July 1988 by appointing his close associate, Washington lawyer Robert Kimmitt, to explore the personal and financial backgrounds of those being considered. Bush started a very long list of prospects, partly because he canvassed the views of Republican senators, representatives, governors, and national committee members and partly because his Washington experience freed him to consider governors as well as legislators for the ticket. Offended by Dukakis's "marching arm in arm around" in public forums with his own prospective running mates and insisting that "I know most of these people very, very well," Bush designed a search procedure that was deliberately protective of the candidates' privacy. Among other things, Bush eschewed face-to-face interviews and told Kimmitt to report the results of the background checks directly to him, without allowing his political staff to probe the findings for potential problems.

Bush pared down his long list of candidates to six names at a freewheeling meeting with his staff on August 12, the Friday before the convention; a few candidates already had withdrawn their names from consideration. He was looking not just for electoral appeal in November but for a vice president much like himself—personally compatible, loyal, and grateful for the honor of serving. After concluding from polling evidence that no running mate could deliver a region or even an important swing state, Bush chose the agreeable Quayle (whom he did not know very well), hoping that the young, handsome senator would broaden the ticket's demographic, if not its geographic, appeal. Shortly after making his decision, Bush announced it on August 16.

Thus, in most of the recent instances in which a vice presidential nomination had to be decided, the presidential candidate undertook a search that was generally well-designed, although hardly guaranteed, to result in a reasoned, responsible selection that was sensitive to the public desire for a worthy presidential successor. Those candidates who did not paid a price. A recent study indicates that in the general election campaign, vice presidential nominees have been most likely to make the front page for bad things, such as scandals or blunders (Goldstein 1982, 123–27). To select a running mate whose competence and loyalty are less than certain is to invite such coverage, as Bush learned after choosing Quayle. (It also is to hand the other party a potent issue. Democratic attacks on Quayle found precedent in a commercial the party ran in 1968, which displayed the words "Agnew for Vice President?" Differences in the qualifications of the candidates may also (and, in 1988, did) become apparent in the vice presidential debate, televised on all the networks, that has become a regular feature of the presidential campaign. Ultimately, the price of slighting governance criteria when choosing a running mate is votes: surveys from various elections—including CBS/*New York Times*, ABC/*Washing Post*, and other 1988 pools—indicate that a poor vice presidential candidate can harm a ticket's chances on election day (Goldstein 1982, 130–32).

Imperfections: With the political cost ignoring governance criteria in the selection of a vice presidential nominee potentially so high, why don't presidential candidates do better not just ordinarily, but consistently? Five sets of circumstances may impede a sensible choice. First, politicians do not always see their interests clearly. Nixon was too clever by half when, acting on the theory that a relatively unknown running mate would have few enemies and cost the ticket few votes, he chose Agnew in 1968. Bush was fanciful in thinking that Quayle's youth and physical attractiveness would add support from "baby-boomers" and women. Second, conventions still select the candidate for vice president within hours of the presidential nomination. A presidential nominating contest that is unresolved going into the convention, like the McGovern-Humphrey battle in 1972, tends to consume the time and attention of the candidates, making a hasty choice of a running mate in an atmosphere of frenzy and exhaustion all too likely.

Third, even a leisurely, reasonably thorough search into the background of prospective vice presidential nominee may not reveal everything. Only after questions were raised by the press (a day after Bush's announcement of his selection) about whether Quayle had pulled strings to get into the National Guard during the Vietnam war did Bush realize that simply taking Quayle's explanation of his service record at face value may not have been enough. The controversy revived painful memories for Democrats, who faced a similar problem in 1984 when the press uncovered information about Ferraro's family finances. Fourth, party activists can make it difficult for a president even to consider removing a vice president they especially like, such as Nixon in 1956 or Agnew in 1972.

The final, potentially most serious problem of vice presidential selection is that one election criterion—uniting the party—continues to bear little relation to the governance criteria for vice presidential selection. Threats from the National Organization of Women and other feminist groups to oppose a male nominee for vice president at the 1984 Democratic convention forced Mondale's hand—he feared that with a fractured party he had no hope of winning the general election. (It is hard to imagine that Mondale would have picked any other third-term member of the House of Representatives without notable foreign affairs experience than Ferraro.) In 1988, similar fears were raised about Jackson and his large coalition of mainly black and liberal delegates at the Democratic convention. Jackson, who had told Brountas that he actually wanted the vice presidency only hours before Dukakis chose Bentsen, and then learned about Dukakis's decision from a reporter, threatened as late as the eve of the convention to allow supporters to nominate him for vice president.

Yet it was not Jackson and the Democrats, but Sen. Gorden Humphrey of New Hampshire and other arch conservatives in the Republican party (the self-styled "Coalition for a Winning Ticket") whose saber-rattling turned out to be more potent. They threatened Bush, who always has been regarded as a closet liberal by the right, with at best minimal enthusiastic support in the fall election, and at worst vocal dissent on the convention floor, if he did not choose one of them as his running mate. In Quayle, Bush tapped a "New Right" loyalist.

Conclusion

Vice presidential selection, for all its imperfections has improved greatly in this century, especially in recent decades. The main purpose of the selection process—namely, to choose vice presidents who, if needed, will be worthy successors to the presidency—is being achieved more successfully than at any time in history. Remaining problems are, for the most part, soluble, minor, or both. The Bentsen and Quayle nominations affirm these developments in a number of ways, some of them ironic.

To understand the reasons why the vice presidential selection process has improved is as important as to mark the improvement itself. The first is that presidential candidates are looking to a better class of political leaders for running mates. It is not that politicians have put aside the election criteria—uniting the party and winning votes for the ticket—that traditionally have animated vice presidential choices for the sake of accommodating the governance criteria—competence and loyalty—and the legitimacy criterion—constitutional and democratic values—that the public prizes. It is rather that, ever since the importance of having an able and faithful vice president available to assume the presidency became unmistakably clear with the birth of the nuclear age, the public has demanded that governance criteria be served in vice presidential selection, lest electoral consequences be paid. Most politicians, notably presidential nominees, have come to realize that good government and good politics are not that different when it comes to choosing vice presidents.

Second, the vice presidency itself is attractive to a better class of political leaders. This development, which began in the early part of the century, has accelerated in recent years—not just because the office has become more substantial in its own right, but also because its standing as the leading steppingstone to the presidency has grown. The vice president is the presumptive frontrunner for the party's presidential nomination: starting with Nixon, every vice president has led in a majority of the Gallup surveys that measure the rank-and-file's preferences for president (Nelson 1988, 91). Six of the eight most recent vice presidents (Nixon, Johnson, Humphrey, Ford, Mondale, and Bush) have been nominated for president, including all three who served presidents who did not or could not run for reelection. (One of the wholly unanticipated consequences of the Twenty-second Amendment is that it freed the vice presidents who serve with second term presidents to run for the presidency without giving offense.) Even a vice presidential nomination now is a steppingstone of sorts: five of the seven losing vice presidential candidates since 1960 (Lodge, Edmund Muskie, Sargent Shriver, Dole, and Mondale) later showed support in nominating contests.[12]

Much has been made of the "Van Buren jinx": no incumbent vice president has been elected president since Martin Van Buren in 1836. To be sure, vice presidents face certain strategic difficulties in presidential campaigns, notably to overcome the image of loyal subservience they may have developed during their tenure and to substitute one of strength and independent vision, which voters seem to prize in their presidents. But the vice presidency's political liabilities can be overstated. Of the 34 incumbent vice presidents who served between Van Buren and Bush, only seven ran for president.[13] The 1988 election aside the two vice presidents who preceded Bush (Nixon in 1960 and Humphrey in 1968) nearly were elected. Certainly the vice presidency draws an ambitious political leader closer to the presidency than does any other office.

The best lesson about how to address remaining problems in the vice presidential selection process may be that changes in rules and procedures or exhortations to act in the public interest are less important than changes in electoral incentives. If the public continues to criticize presidential nominees who choose inferior running mates, whatever the motive for choosing them, then future nominees will adapt or risk defeat. If ambitious political leaders who are offered the second slot on the ticket fail to recognize the unrivaled steppingstone status of the modern vice presidency, they will reduce their chances of becoming president.

Notes

1. Assassination attempts almost ended the lives of President-elect Franklin Roosevelt less than a month before his inauguration in 1933 and of two of the three most recent presidents, Ford and Reagan, shortly after they become president.

2. The vice presidency of the original Constitution was the prize awarded to the runner-up in the presidential election. As such, it was an office of considerable prestige, despite its minor responsibilities. John Adams and Thomas Jefferson, the nations's first and second vice presidents, were elected its second and third presidents.

Within a very short time, however, vice presidential selection became the province of the Twelfth Amendment. The original electoral college floundered on the shoals of national political parties, which, having nominated complete tickets for the presidential election, had no other way for their electors to express their partisan preferences than to cast both of their two votes for president for the party's presidential and vice presidential candidates. In 1800, the victorious Republican, Jefferson, was tied in the presidential election by his running mate, Aaron Burr, prompting weeks of Federalist mischief making the House of Representatives before Jefferson was elected president. When the Twelfth Amendment, enacted in 1804 in time for the election, separated the voting for president and vice president, it robbed the vice presidency of its presumptive claim to presidential stature and left it nothing but its rather feeble constitutional power to preside over the Senate, voting only to break ties.

3. Ironically, as vice president, Webster would have succeeded to the presidency when President Zachary Taylor died in 1850.

4. In the most recent and extensive round of historians' rankings, Johnson was rated a failure, Tyler and Fillmore as below average, and Arthur as average (Murray and Blessing, 1983).

5. Roosevelt, Coolidge, and Johnson won landslide elections. The nine vice presidents-turned-presidential-nominee were Nixon, Humphrey, Mondale, Bush, and the five successor presidents. The four vice presidents who did not seek a nomination were the sort of exceptions who demonstrate the rule: criminal conviction accounts for one (Agnew), age or ill health the others (Charles Curtis, Alben W. Barkley, and Rockefeller).

6. The abolition in 1936 of the Democratic party's two-thirds rule for presidential nomination also enhanced the presidential nominee's discretion in choosing a running mate by reducing the need to bargain for the nomination Roosevelt ran for vice president in 1920.

7. A concern for competence and loyalty in the vice presidency also characterized the solution Congress invented to a recurring problem of the executive that the challenges of the postwar era had made seem urgent: vice presidential vacancies. The Twenty-fifth Amendment, which established a procedure for selecting vice presidents in unusual circumstances, was passed in 1965 and ratified in 1967. Prior to then, the vice presidency had been vacant for parts of sixteen administrations, leaving the president without a constitutionally designated successor. The amendment authorized the president to fill vacancies in the vice presidency by appointment, with the advice and consent of both Houses of Congress. It also made the vice president the central figure in addressing presidential disabilities.

8. Governance criteria even can accommodate, at least, some traditional forms of ticket balancing that still are practiced. Specifically, Protestant presidential candidates often choose Catholic running mates, candidates without extensive experience in the federal government usually pair themselves with Washington insiders, and, almost invariably, presidential candidates limit their choice for a vice president to political leaders from other parts of the country (Goldstein 1982, 70-72). Dukakis and Bentsen revived the "Boston-Austin" axis that Kennedy and Johnson forged in 1960. Quayle, a midwesterner, was from one of the few regions of the country where Bush has never lived.

9. Calculated from data in Murray and Blessing (1983), Roosevelt and Truman were rated near-great; Johnson, above average; Ford, average; and Coolidge, below average.

10. The descriptions of the Bentsen and Quayle nominations are based mainly on newspaper accounts in the *New York Times* and *Washington Post*.

11. Republicans clearly have considered a wider range of possibilities concerning vice presidential nominations than Democrats. In 1976, Reagan, a close challenger to Ford for the party's presidential nomination, announced the name of his running mate (Sen. Richard Schweiker of Pennsylvania) weeks before the convention, and tried unsuccessfully to persuade

the delegates to require Ford to do the same. In 1980, Reagan and Ford considered, but ultimately rejected, a number of suggestions to enhance the powers of the vice presidency as a way to get Ford on the ticket. A proposal in the same spirit was bandied about among some Democrats in 1988: they suggested that Sen. Sam Nunn of Georgia be invited to run for vice president by promising also to appoint him as secretary of defense.

12. In 1988, Bush demonstrated the benefits that vice presidents derive from their affiliation with the president in the nominating contest: even in the early, contested primaries, he won well over three-fourths of the support of the primary voters who approved of Reagan's performance as president.

13. Eight vice presidents died or resigned in office, nine became president when the president died or resigned, and eleven either chose not to run for president or lacked the opportunity to do so. Only George Dallas (1848), John C. Breckinridge (1860), Charles Fairbanks (1908), Garner (1940), Nixon (1960), and Humphrey (1968) sought the presidency from their position as vice president. See Sirgiovanni (1988).

References

Goldstein, Joel K. 1982. *The Modern Vice Presidency*. Princeton: NJ: Princeton University Press.

Light, Paul C. 1984. *Vice-Presidential Power: Advice and Influence in the White House*. Baltimore: The Johns Hopkins University Press.

Murray, Robert K., and Tim H. Blessing. 1983. The Presidential Performance Study: A Progress Report. *Journal of American History* 70, No. 4 (Dec.): 535–55.

Nelson, Michael. 1988. *A Heartbeat Away*. New York: Priority Press.

Pika, Joseph. 1987. In Michael Nelson, ed., *The Presidency and the Political System*, 2nd ed. Washington: Congressional Quarterly Press, pp. 462–81.

Roosevelt, Franklin D. 1920. "Can the Vice President Be Useful?" *Saturday Evening Post* (16 Oct.): 8.

Sirgiovanni, George. 1988. The 'Van Buren Jinx': Vice Presidents Need Not Beware. *Presidential Studies Quarterly* 18, No. 1, Winter: 61–76.

White, Theodore H. 1982. *America in Search of Itself: The Making of the President. 1956–1980*. New York: Harper and Row.

Witcover, Jules. 1977. *Marathon: The Pursuit of the Presidency, 1972–1976* New York: Viking.

7.2

Paul C. Light

Making the Most
of the New Vice Presidency

Paul C. Light is guest scholar at the Brookings Institute and author of Vice-Presidential Power: Advice and Influence in the White House. *In this selection he shows that the vice presidency has gained in importance in recent years, even though it has been viewed as an innocuous office throughout most of our political history. He offers suggestions as to what presidents and vice presidents could do to ensure that this trend continues.*

Every four years, the American vice presidency emerges from the shadows. Before and at the Democratic and Republican nominating conventions, the choice of vice presidential candidates becomes a focus of intense speculation and bargaining.

What makes the hoopla all the more intriguing is the fact that the vice presidency has always had such a bad reputation; it has been derided for nearly two hundred years, even—or perhaps especially—by those who have held the office. John Adams called it "the most insignificant office that ever the invention of man contrived or his imagination conceived," and John Nance Garner declared, with some feeling, that the job was "hardly worth a pitcher of warm spit."

The choice of a vice presidential candidate has traditionally been viewed as having more symbolic than substantive significance. Consequently, the selection has typically been made on the basis of political considerations, be they matters of intraparty import (the desire to propitiate a rival faction) or electoral strategy (the hope of balancing a ticket in an advantageous way).

This article argues that in the last decade or so the vice presidency has become a much more important office than it once was—more important in its impact on policy as well as politics—and that the criteria used to pick vice presidential candidates ought to reflect that transformation. Presidents these days need and can receive valuable help from their vice presidents—but only if, as presidential nominees, they select their running mates with the realities of governing in mind. The closing section of the essay discusses what presidents and vice presidents can do to ensure that the potential of the new vice presidency—for both of them—is realized.

From Paul C. Light, "Making the Most of the New Vice Presidency." *The Brookings Review* (Summer 1984).

A Metamorphosis of the Vice Presidency

The title has not changed, but the job certainly has. The vice presidency has become—at long last, against all odds—a very good place for a political figure to be. Three changes are especially striking.

First, the vice president's position description has been rewritten. At one time, vice presidents were relegated to ceremonial functions: cutting ribbons, attending funerals, chairing backwater White House commissions, serving on the Board of Regents of the Smithsonian Institution, and occasionally visiting Capitol Hill. Alben Barkley, vice president under Truman, had this recollection of his days as second in command: "I seemed to be much in demand as a crowner of 'queens' at various celebrations—Apple Blossom festivals, Cherry Blossom festivals, and just about every sort of festival that one can think of." While vice presidents are still conspicuous by their presence at a goodly number of ceremonies, they now have extensive political and policy roles as well. They are key players in midterm and reelection campaigns; preeminent congressional lobbyists; and senior presidential advisers on all manner of policy issues. It is no exaggeration to say that there is a new vice presidency; Barkley would not recognize the job today.

Second, there has been a dramatic increase in the resources and institutional support accorded vice presidents. In 1961, Vice President Lyndon Johnson had fewer than twenty staff positions under his control; George Bush now has about seventy. The office of the vice president has become the fifth largest unit in the Executive Office of the President. Once a makeshift aggregation of detailees and others whose salaries depended on the generosity of strangers, the vice president's office now has its own budget line and an annual appropriation of $2 million. What is more, the last two vice presidents have had offices in the West Wing of the White House, just down the hall from the Oval Office. In addition, they have been given ample allotments of space in the Old Executive Office Building, next door to the White House, in which to house their sizable staffs. (In the old days, staff assistants to the vice president were scattered around Washington; this was not conducive to a strong sense of institutional identity). The vice president also has an official residence now, located on Washington's Embassy Row, and even—courtesy of Nelson Rockefeller—a new seal and flag. The old seal showed an eagle at rest; the new one pictures an eagle in flight, armed with a full claw of arrows.

The vice president's office is a microcosm of the White House staff structure, complete with press, foreign policy, domestic policy, administrative, and political aides. Vice presidents are now equipped to carry real weight in the White House policy process. For example, Mondale was able, with the help of his domestic policy shop, to become the manager of the Carter administration's agenda-setting process; in that capacity, he was able to exercise a good deal of influence over the administration's legislative priorities.

Third, presidents have finally come to realize how helpful vice presidents can be to them—as allies and advisers on the campaign trail, in negotiations with Congress, and in the development of policy. While it is difficult to be very precise about the origins of this recent advance in the presidential valuation of vice presidents, one critical factor has been a series of changes in the context in which presidential business is conducted. For example, the decline of the national party organizations has increased the usefulness of vice presidents as campaigners, spokesmen, and public liaison specialists. The diffusion of power in Congress—due to the proliferation of subcommittees, the decline of seniority, and the weakening of party leadership—has enhanced the importance of whatever clout and skill vice presidents can bring to bear in lobbying for the passage of administration initiatives. Finally, the sheer complexity of the world that presidents have to contend with—the crush of issues and programs—has made them more receptive to assistance from vice presidents and their staffs.

The Watergate scandal played a key role in the emergence of the new vice presidency. In 1973, President Nixon, under increasing fire from the press and the Congress, asked House Minority Leader Gerald Ford to bring his good name and his Capitol Hill connections to the White House as the successor to Vice President Spiro Agnew, who had resigned. Ford, who knew that he was in a strong bargaining position under the circumstances, demanded as a condition of his coming on board more staff and independence than had previously been afforded vice presidents. After Nixon himself resigned and Ford succeeded to the presidency, he realized that he needed a strong vice president to shore up his administration. Nelson Rockefeller—who had turned down offers in 1960 and 1968 of the vice presidential spot on the Republican ticket—extracted, as his price for relenting this time around, chairmanship of the Domestic Council, access to the Oval Office, and further expansion of the vice presidential staff.

It remained for Walter Mondale to consolidate and build on the gains that had been made and, in so doing, to establish a powerful precedent for future vice presidents. Mondale was clearly a member of President Carter's inner circle, and, as such, had more impact on presidential decisions than any vice president in history. He was a key force on behalf of numerous Carter initiatives—among them the appointments of Joseph Califano and Robert Bergland to cabinet posts; creation of the Department of Education; admission of the Shah of Iran to the United States for medical treatment; the attempt to rescue the American hostages in Iran; electoral reform; expansion of the CETA job training program; and hospital cost containment.

Mondale did suffer his share of defeats, having opposed the Soviet grain embargo, the MX "racetrack" design, the 1979 firings of cabinet officials, the sale of F-15s to Saudi Arabia, and budget cuts in social services. But whatever the exact tally of victories and setbacks, the central point is that Mondale's influence in the Carter administration raised expectations about the role to be played by future vice presidents—and made it more difficult for future presidents to turn back the clock. He was the first vice president to maintain regular access to the president, becoming more of a senior adviser and less of a figurehead. He had a standing invitation to all meetings and full access to information, including the President's Daily Brief on foreign policy. Finally, he was the first vice president to have an office in the West Wing of the White House; it has come to be known as the vice president's office and appears to have become a permanent endowment of the vice presidency.

The vice presidency is now a more attractive position than ever before. It is a job for all reasons; it can further a politician's presidential prospects, enhance his or her influence on policy, or simply satisfy a craving for perquisites.

For someone who wants to be president someday, what better job to have for the time being than the vice presidency? First, the job involves considerable contact with state and local officials, who could become valuable allies in a future bid for the presidency. Mondale's liaison work as vice president led to countless endorsements of his 1984 presidential candidacy from the very state and local officeholders he had once dealt with on behalf of Jimmy Carter. Second, the job entitles the occupant to advanced on-the-job political training. Not only does campaigning increase a vice president's national visibility and enhance his or her political network, it also helps to refine, through constant practice, a vice president's speaking and gladhanding skills. Third, the job gives a vice president many opportunities to heal old wounds and to demonstrate loyalty to the president's wing of the party. Fourth, the vice presidency ensures a politician four years of free and extensive media coverage. The job has been known to transform relative unknowns into household names and putative frontrunners for future presidential nominations.

For someone who wants to shape national policy, what better position to be in, short of the presidency itself, than the vice presidency? As Mondale demonstrated, a vice president can have a substantial impact on how both foreign and domestic issues are addressed. Vice President Bush has carried forward this legacy of influence; inside sources indicate that he has been a powerful force for moderation in the Reagan White House—arguing forcefully for withdrawal of American troops from Lebanon, for example.

Finally, for a politician who savors the spoils of victory, what better circumstance for pomp than being in the second-highest office in the land? Vice presidents are like most politicians; they like red carpets and limousines, jet airplanes and first-class accommodations, bands and salutes. The vice presidency now offers more perquisites, and its incumbents are treated with more dignity and greeted with more effusion, than ever before. Gerald Ford, when he was vice president, mused on the trappings of the office: "I am now surrounded everywhere by a clutch of Secret Service agents, reporters and cameramen, and assorted well-wishers. When I travel, I am greeted by bands playing 'Hail, Columbia' and introduced to audiences with great solemnity instead of as 'my good friend Jerry Ford'." Thus, even if the job does not work out in terms of politics or policy—even if, for whatever reason, the president shuns and isolates the vice president—there are perquisites attached to the office that can help ease the pain.

Balance and Compatibility

The new vice presidency is an appealing job, but it comes with no constitutional guarantees of access and influence. It is true that presidents now have strong incentives to utilize their vice presidents for more than ceremonial duties and that vice presidents now have the resources they need to play major roles. But much still depends on the compatibility—both personal and political—of a president and vice president.

Unfortunately, vice presidential nominees are often chosen so hastily that the chances of a mismatch are high. Carter in 1976 was an exception to this pattern. Having wrapped up the Democratic presidential nomination well in advance of the convention, Carter had the time—and took the time—to be more deliberate in his selection of a running mate. He and his staff assembled a list of twenty or so possible nominees and ranked them on leadership abilities, voting records, constituency connections, campaign skills, and geographic strength. After narrowing the list to seven (Mondale, Edmund Muskie, John Glenn, Henry Jackson, Frank Church, Adlai Stevenson, III, and Peter Rodino), Carter interviewed the candidates and decided on Mondale.

Clearly, choosing a running mate is—and will continue to be—a political decision. Presidential candidates are understandably concerned, first and foremost, with getting elected. Nevertheless, the qualities that make for an appealing running mate may not make for a smooth working relationship in office. Indeed, if there is a pattern in vice presidential nominations over the past two decades, it is that opposites attract. The theory seems to have been that the key to a strong ticket is balance, whether on the basis of geography, ideology, or, it is now being argued, gender.

Whether these balancing acts lead to strong vice presidencies depends on the most important balance of all, the one between Washington insiders and outsiders. Presidents who are new to national politics and government tend to rely more heavily on their vice presidents than do presidents who have spent the bulk of their political careers in Washington. Because outsider presidents enter office with fewer resources, their vice presidents have more opportunities for input and impact. The most recent outsider presidents (Eisenhower, Carter, and Reagan) picked insiders as their vice presidents (Nixon, Mondale, and Bush)—and all three vice presidents expanded the role of their office. Nixon took on extensive political responsibilities; Mondale played an active and central policy role; and Bush has become more heavily involved in foreign affairs than any of his predecessors.

The opposite combination—insider presidents with outsider vice presidents—is the least likely to succeed. This pattern has appeared only once in recent years: Nixon's selection of Agnew as his running mate. Agnew was the least prepared of the modern vice presidents and was quickly frozen out of the policy process in the Nixon administration. In fact, Nixon was so unhappy with Agnew's performance in office that he considered replacing him on the ticket in 1972. Like Agnew, most outsiders simply do not have enough information or expertise to fight for influence in an insider's White House.

The balance with the most uncertain outcome is also the one that has occurred most frequently over the past four decades: an insider president with an insider vice president. That pattern has appeared seven times during this period: Roosevelt-Wallace, Roosevelt-Truman, Truman-Barkley, Kennedy-Johnson, Johnson-Humphrey, Nixon-Ford, and Ford-Rockefeller. The first and last of these teams involved significant policy roles for the vice president (Wallace as chairman of a major wartime agency and Rockefeller as head of the Domestic Council); the others did not. Insider presidents—and Kennedy and Johnson were prime examples of this—have tended to see their vice presidents as irritations and impediments to quick action. With stronger incentives to use their vice presidents and the increased resources that vice presidents now enjoy, future insider presidents are more likely to draw on their number twos. But the plain fact is that they do not need help of even insider vice presidents as much as outsider presidents do.

Presidential nominees are not likely to abandon political criteria in selecting their running mates. What they need to do, however, is supplement political considerations with a second set of questions. Within the pool of politically acceptable possibilities, presidential candidates should assess the compatibility, leadership qualities, experience, intellect, and savvy of each potential candidate.

The strength of the Carter system in large part was that it incorporated these additional factors. Having winnowed his list of potential running mates down to a group of politically strong candidates, Carter then considered other characteristics—and, while Muskie and others on the short list were certainly qualified, Carter picked a running mate with whom he felt he could work comfortably.

Effectiveness in Office

It is in the vice president's best interest to start building a working relationship with the president and White House staffers as early as possible. Looking back at the Mondale and Bush experiences, there seem to be four somewhat distinct periods in forging that partnership.

The first is the series of conversations leading to acceptance of the vice presidential nomination itself. It is important at this stage to gain the presidential candidate's support for an active vice presidency. Even if that support is ambiguous, obtaining it is a necessary first step in what might be called "presidential consciousness-raising." Conventions are hardly the time and place to outline detailed plans for a future administration. The ticket must win first. Nevertheless, the vice presidential nominee should try to elicit some general commitments—to access, for example. During the convention-time press conferences regarding his or her nomination, the vice presidential candidate should make clear his or her conceptions of the office. Occasional references to the Mondale precedent (for Democrats) or the Bush precedent (for Republicans) should suffice for this purpose.

The second phase comes during the campaign. In 1976, for example, Mondale decided to merge his campaign staff with Carter's and to move it to the presidential candidate's Atlanta headquarters. As one Mondale aide later recalled, "When we got to Washington after the election and the principal Carter campaign workers became the core of the White House staff, our relationships were established. It was easy to continue the cooperative working relationships that had been established in Atlanta."

The campaign also offers a chance for the vice presidential candidate to prove his or her mettle. Mondale's performance in the 1976 campaign, particularly in his debate with Republican Robert Dole, boosted his reputation with Carter and the future White House staff. Given the closeness of the 1976 election, Mondale could claim at least some of the credit for Carter's victory. The campaign is even more important to future harmony if the vice presidential nominee happens to have been a defeated candidate for the presidential nomination. Old comments have a habit of popping up. In 1980, Bush's oft-quoted remarks about "voodoo economics" had to be erased. His bruising campaign schedule and repeated demonstrations of loyalty helped rebuild his image with Reagan and his advisers.

The third phase of the relationship-building process comes immediately after the election. The vice president-elect should prepare a detailed memorandum outlining his or her ideas about the job and its responsibilities. This is the time to hammer out some specific understandings with the president-elect—for example, agreement that the two will have a weekly private meeting and that the vice president will be given a West Wing office and access to all information and meetings. If not now, then when?

The transition also offers an opportunity for the vice president-elect to participate in the appointments process. The vice president-elect can contribute to the list of potential appointees for the 2000 or so political positions to be filled; if his or her people are chosen, they become valuable allies within the new administration. Moreover, if the vice president-elect can participate in the selection of cabinet officers, he or she can influence the course of the administration from the very start. Mondale's role in the appointments of Califano, Bergland, Blumenthal, and Vance to cabinet posts surely created a measure of indirect influence over the Carter agenda. Further, Mondale's willingness to lend several of his own top aides to the Carter staff created back-channels for influence and information. In particular, Mondale's former aides Bert Carp and David Aaron emerged as key deputies on the Domestic Policy Staff and National Security Council staff respectively. On one level, they were simply conduits for briefings and papers. On another, they served as powerful signals to other senior White House officials that Mondale could not be ignored. "Every Cabinet secretary, every policy-maker in the executive branch knew these two people would keep Mondale and his staff informed on any issue in which Mondale had or should have an interest," a top Mondale aide later reported. "Any executive branch policy-maker inclined to exclude Mondale from the process was quick to learn that it wouldn't work." Bush's willingness to lend James Baker III, to Reagan as chief of staff had a similar effect, giving the vice president an important source of leverage and information.

The fourth and final phase of the process involves the inauguration and the early days in office. The most important step to take at this stage is to secure a West Wing office, close to the action. This move is central to a more general strategy of filling vacuums early in an administration. As a presidency ages, the vacuums always close: White House staffers learn the ropes, knowledge expands, new people arrive. The legislative and election calendars clearly point to the first year of an administration as the critical period for influence both inside the White House and on Capitol Hill. Presidents set their policy agendas early in the term. If presidents often "move it or lose it," so must vice presidents. They must set their agendas early also, so that they can take advantage of the opportunities for impact that are open in the first few months of a term.

There are other lessons for vice presidents from the Mondale and Bush successes. First among them is that it is crucial to the effectiveness of vice presidents that the presidents they serve are willing to listen. After all else is said and done, a vice president's job depends on the president's commitment to their relationship. Each hour that the president spends in private conference with the vice president is an hour not spent with someone else. That is why what the vice president can bring to those conversations in the way of knowledge and experience is so important.

Carter, whose lack of Washington experience gave him all the more incentive to listen to Mondale, clearly wanted an active vice president. Carter believed in using all of his staffers, and he was determined to make the vice presidency work. First, Carter repeatedly instructed his staff to include Mondale in the White House policy-making process. Second, Carter's own operating style helped Mondale. Carter preferred to be pulled and pushed on most issues, telling his staff only that they were to "be bold" in their presentation of options and analyses. As part of this process of give-and-take, Carter and Mondale met frequently. Third, Carter had an expansive policy agenda, which gave Mondale more room for influence.

As Jordan later recalled, "Mondale took advantage of the opportunity and tried to influence administration policy, and that was just how Carter wanted it. To the extent people blame Mondale for pursuing his own 'agenda,' he was only doing what he had been urged to do from the outset by the president."

Vice presidents fare best under presidents who have open staffing systems; they do not thrive in hierarchical systems. The more people there are guarding the president, the fewer opportunities there are for vice-presidential impact. Vice presidents have had more success in "collegial" or "spokes-of-the-wheel" systems, taking advantage of the chances to work one-on-one with the president. Vice presidents have more freedom to move in and out on the issues in such systems, avoiding conflict with gatekeepers.

There are ways that vice presidents can make themselves more attractive as advisers and confidants. In the first place, Mondale suggested, an "adviser must be ready to advise." It helps to have occupied a national office before joining the ticket; senators and representatives have more exposure to national issues and politics than governors do. Once in office, however, the best assurance of being prepared is access to all of the paper moving in and out of the Oval Office. "That might sound like a little matter," Mondale said, "but you cannot possibly imagine the tremendous volume of paper that flows into and from the president's personal office. You cannot possibly imagine, unless you have been part of it, the tremendous flow of secret classified information on defense, the political situation in other nations, on assessments and appraisals by our intelligence communities." Without access to this information, the vice president cannot compete with other White House advisers. How could Agnew advise Nixon on China policy when he did not even know the issue was being discussed? When asked whether he had told Agnew about his dramatic trip to China, Nixon replied, "Agnew? Agnew? Oh, of course not."

Vice presidents can also help themselves by being connected to key constituency groups with which the presidential relationship is not strong. Much of Mondale's value inside the Carter White House came from his political connections to liberals, labor, and Jewish organizations. As Carter moved leftward to meet Edward Kennedy's challenge in the 1980 primaries, Mondale's ties proved to be extremely useful, balancing Carter's Southern strength. Moreover, Mondale's links to the Capitol Hill establishment helped when Carter's legislative program became tangled in the congressional system.

Vice presidents also enhance their own effectiveness by becoming team players and assuming a low profile once in office. As a Bush aide commented, "Bush earned Reagan's respect by working hard, not making mistakes, and proving that he was a 100 percent, solid team guy. The first time that Bush went into the Oval Office and the conversation came out in the papers, we'd find ourselves with a job that wouldn't be worth having." There are four basic rules for vice presidents to follow in order to build trust inside the White House:

1. *Never complain to the press.* One of Rockefeller's continuing problems in the Ford administration was his high profile in the media. Leaks were easily and often traced to the vice president's office.
2. *Never take credit from the president.* The vice president must constantly be mindful of who is president—and who is not.

3. *Fall in line.* No matter how much the vice president opposes a presidential decision, he or she must support the final policy. The vice president does not have to become a vocal supporter or lobbyist on the particular issue, but must fall in line like any other staffer.
4. *Share the dirty work.* Though the vice president may not like endless travel, for example, it comes with the territory; it is part of being a team player. Mondale was on the road 600 days during his term.

What works best is working diligently outside the White House and quietly within it. Unlike Rockefeller, Mondale preferred to operate through hidden channels, avoiding open positions. Mondale learned this style during his long service as a protege of other politicians. According to his closest campaign aide, James Johnson, "On the fundamental question of being the junior partner, he was schooled beyond anyone else in American politics." Whereas Rockefeller's motto had once been "I never wanted to be vice president of anything," Mondale's might have been "patience is a virtue." This is not to say Mondale was a passive player in the White House—he was very active. But he knew he was not president, and he acted accordingly.

Finally, vice presidents should avoid line assignments. Such duties generally involve administrative chores and absorb a great deal of time and energy. Every hour spent in line responsibility is an hour *not* spent with the president. And, as Mondale once observed, if line assignments were truly important, they would be "assigned to some cabinet or key executive officer and why should I handle them? Or, if they weren't significant, they would trivialize the vice presidency."

Chapter Eight

The President and the Policy-making Process: Domestic and Foreign Policy

While presidents perform a variety of functions for our political system, in the final analysis we elect them to make decisions. Indeed, how presidents are judged by history ultimately depends on the policy decisions they make in addressing the key foreign and domestic issues of their day.

The first two selections that follow examine the role of the presidency in the formulation of domestic policy. In this connection, Ben Heineman rejects the view that the structure and operation of the policy-making process should be largely determined by the personal style of each president. He argues, instead, that the domestic policy-making process can function effectively only if organized in accordance with certain general principles—principles that relate to goals, priorities, politics, and participants. In the next article, Roger Porter focuses more narrowly on the role of the president in economic policy-making. Examining the administrations of the last seven presidents, he evaluates those structural arrangements created to provide each president with the information and advice needed to make informed economic decisions.

The second pair of articles addresses two problem areas widely discussed in connection with the making of foreign policy: the president's relationship with the State Department and with Congress. Zbigniew Brzezinski, himself a national security advisor under President Carter, chronicles the longstanding tension between the president's national security advisor and the secretary of state over the formulation of American foreign policy. Given the fact that the conduct of foreign relations cuts across several departments in the executive branch, he insists that coordination in this area can only come·from the White House. In order to reflect this reality, he calls for restructuring the roles of both the national security advisor and the secretary of state. Dick Cheney addresses tensions between the president and another foreign policy actor—the Congress. Focusing upon the Reagan years, he cites numerous occasions when Congress injected itself into matters related to diplomacy, covert operations, and war powers. These actions, in his judgment, not only exceeded the constitutional authority of Congress and its institutional competence, but also seriously comprised the president's ability to conduct foreign policy.

8.1

Ben W. Heineman, Jr.

Some Rules of the Game:
Prescription for Organizing the Domestic Presidency

Ben W. Heineman, Jr., is senior vice president and general counsel for the General Electric Company. In the Carter administration he was assistant secretary for planning and evaluation at the Department of Health, Education, and Welfare. He is the coauthor of Memorandum to the President. *Rejecting the view that the structures and processes of the presidency should be determined by the personal style of each president, Heineman insists that certain fundamental principles must be incorporated into the domestic policy-making process if it is to function effectively.*

The Supreme Court has well-established, clearly articulated procedures for conducting its business. So does the Congress, and its Committees and Subcommittees.

But a new Presidency starts with a clean slate and without any well accepted guide on how to structure and operate its key internal processes. A new administration often assumes that it must alter the way its predecessor organized the Executive Office of the President (EOP), and the relations between the EOP and the Cabinet Departments.

Indeed, a number of scholars and former officials believe that the structures and processes of a presidency should be largely, if not wholly, dependent on the personal style of the incumbent.[1] I disagree.

This essay argues that any Chief Executive in the late Twentieth Century should follow certain principles in structuring and organizing his domestic presidency. These prescriptions arise both from the experience of modern Presidents and from the social, economic and political environment in which future Presidents must operate. These organizing principles were set forth in detail in 1980 in a book Curt Hessler and I wrote after refracting the domestic failures of the Carter Administration through the lens of central writings on the post-New Deal Presidency,[2] and seemed valid in 1984 when I reflected on the first Reagan term.[3] Although necessarily general, I think these essential rules of the domestic presidential game will have a practical, beneficial effect if followed by the man who succeeds Ronald Reagan—regardless of his party or his personal style.

From *The Presidency in Transition*, ed. Pfiffner and Hoxie, 1989. Permission granted by Center for the Study of the Presidency, publisher of *The Presidency in Transition*.

Like many others, of course, I believe that the key determinants of a successful presidency will be the President's personality and his substantive vision of how the federal government can influence the trajectory of national life. Strong presidential leadership will also turn on other key factors which can be identified but not prescribed, such as the chemistry between key appointees, the tides of history and simple good luck. Thus, I would only claim that the prescriptions which follow are necessary not sufficient conditions of an effective presidency.

1. *The need for a Strategic Presidency.* The paramount task of the modern domestic presidency is to develop, and consistently test against a changing reality, a sophisticated strategy of governing that systematically incorporates and vigorously integrates in a realistic time frame the four fundamental dimensions of executive government: substantive policy (where to go); practical politics (how to get there); administrative structures (how power is distributed within the executive branch); and action-forcing processes (how to run executive government to get things done). Indeed, the nature and degree of presidential power in this era turns on the ability of the Chief Executive to forge and execute such a strategy.

A strategic approach is necessary to understand and then resolve the painful dilemmas within and between these four dimensions of the domestic presidency: for example, between the expectation that the President can effect sweeping change and the reality of multiple constraints on presidential action; between economic and social policy; between domestic policy and defense policy; between the politics of governing, renomination and the next general election; between high risk-high reward initiatives and lower risk efforts; between centralization and delegation. Most importantly, the strategy must reconcile the often contradictory demands of policy and politics—must find that marriage between them which is the acme of presidential leadership.

If properly articulated, the presidential strategy has the paradoxical effect of increasing the President's reach (by making clear to his Administration and the rest of the political world what he wants), while conserving his time (if he has made big decisions many smaller ones should follow without his intense involvement). Surely the truth of this paradox is illustrated by contrasting Carter's term with Reagan's first four years.

2. *Making the Strategy Clear From the Start.* Obviously, the first year of an Administration is crucial: Carter never recovered from 1977, while Reagan rode the successes of 1981 for a long time. For maximum effect, the strategy of governing must be developed immediately after the election and then communicated forcefully in the months after the inauguration. Thus, although this rarely happens, key personnel decisions must be made in November if at all possible, leaving two full months for strategic thinking with the new, senior members of the incoming administration. Perhaps the greatest power of the presidency—the ability to set the national agenda—is never so potent as after the initial election to office, yet that power must be wielded at a time when the new President, especially one without Washington experience, is ill-prepared for the task.

Setting the strategic course early not only influences the outside political world, but it is crucial for running an effective administration immediately. Substantively, it communicates what is the "presidential interest," and thus reduces (though it could hardly eliminate) the inevitable intra-administration disputes about what the President wants. Procedurally, establishing the rules of the game at the outset should also avoid the often debilitating, intra-administration warfare about how decisions get made.

3. Priority-Setting to Demarcate Presidential From Sub-Presidential Decision-Making. A key element of the strategy of governing is the division of domestic issues into first, second and third order initiatives. If the Reagan Presidency has shown anything, it has demonstrated the importance of having the President focus on a few key issues.

- On first order issues, which should be limited to five or so in domestic affairs, the President should be deeply involved and make all significant decisions. his performance, and success, on this small percentage of issues will have a disproportionate impact on how he is perceived in Washington and in the nation.
- On second order issues, which should number about 25, the President should make the basic decisions on the shape of the policy and the strategic directions. But subsequent decisions about details and implementation should be made at the sub-presidential level, with further presidential involvement limited to large problems which may arise or to select political maneuvers.
- On third order issues, the President should indicate that he regards the issue as important to the record of the administration, and may approve a general policy direction but he should leave virtually all decision-making to the sub-presidential system. These third order issues might number 100 or so, and would be specially tracked in the EOP because of their potential importance to the administration's record.

Given his foreign affairs responsibilities, his general political obligations, the time he will spend managing crises and his duties as head of state, it is not realistic to expect any greater involvement of the President in domestic affairs. Unless we are at one of those rare moments like the mid-30s or the mid-60s, when a President must race to keep up with historic change, I believe the imperative of a slimmed down agenda applies whether a President is a high-energy person like Carter, or a low-energy person like Reagan. There is, of course, nothing magic in the 5–25–100 numbers for first, second and third order issues, but it would be surprising to me if the variance of those guidelines would be great. Time—both the demands of the daily schedule and the difficulty in changing deeply rooted historical patterns and practices—has the President in its vise.

4. The Need for a Strong Chief of Staff. Given the need for a system of sub-presidential decision-making to make executive government work, there must be a person who can, in fact, oversee this system. This person should be the chief of staff, who is the President's most important appointment. The chief of staff must have an aptitude for both policy and politics. He or she must be able to develop the strategy of governing, ensure that policy is consistent with that strategy and mediate disputes that arise within the EOP or between the EOP and the Departments on second and third order issues. The chief of staff must also make the strategic and organizational connections between domestic and foreign policy (which are beyond the scope of this essay).

Mediation is desirable because the senior members of the EOP and the Cabinet will be reluctant to accept a decision-maker short of the President. Nonetheless, to make a system of delegation and sub-presidential decision-making work, the chief of staff must be able to resolve intractable conflicts when mediation fails on these second and third order issues. The President will need to make clear to his administration—first in words and then in practice—that, once he has set policy on second order issues or announced a general direction on third order issues, he expects the chief of staff to compose subsequent differences within the administration.

5. The Need for Three Substantive Policy Channels. The first, second and third order issues should be coordinated in one of three policy channels. First, economic affairs should be coordinated by the Treasury Secretary, as chair of an EOP economic policy group comprised of relevant department heads and the heads of relevant EOP units. Second, the OMB Director will, of course, direct budget and program coordination. Third, a top presidential aide should coordinate activities within a "domestic affairs" channel. Issues in the domestic affairs channel should be limited (10–20 first and second order issues) to avoid creating inevitable conflict between the OMB and domestic affairs staffs on virtually every issue. They should be the major domestic affairs issues—such as social policy or legal or environmental matters—which are important but which cannot be given appropriate, high level attention in the economic and budget channels.

The significance of the channels is that the lead person—the Treasury Secretary, the OMB Director, the head of domestic affairs—has the responsibility for *coordinating* the *process* of policy development or implementation. Given the overlapping responsibilities of various EOP offices and cabinet departments, advice on those issues will come from a variety of sources which must be represented fairly by the office with the process responsibility. Although it sounds small and bureaucratic, anyone who has been in the belly of the executive branch beast knows the central importance of clarity on the simple question of who is coordinating development of an issue.

The chief of staff should decide what issue belongs to which channel (and who should be part of the intra-EOP, inter-agency process), if it is not clear.

6. The Need for a Political Director. A senior presidential assistant for political affairs should oversee relations with Congress, state and local governments, the interest groups, party officials and the media (although there will be separate EOP officials with specific responsibility for each set of relationships). The complexity of the political world faced by the President requires a senior aide with an overview of all the key political relationships who can creatively see how to create coalitions and political energy for innovative policy.

This person must participate extensively in the work carried on in the three substantive channels. Policy development—and policy implementation of controversial decisions—should be a continual dialogue between those with substantive and those with political responsibilities. Once again, it will be the special responsibility of the chief of staff to ensure that the political and policy officials are working closely together.

7. The Cabinet: The Need for Access on Presidential Decisions. Mercifully, the cry for "cabinet" government has abated since the Carter years. Proper use of cabinet officers does not lend itself to easy generalizations. The "don'ts"—don't try to use the cabinet as a whole very much, don't pretend that the cabinet is free of important issues to operate in isolation from the EOP—are easier to state than the "do's."

Simply put, the cabinet officer's role should vary depending on whether the issue is of first, second or third order importance to the President. On first and second order issues, when the President will be making the key decisions himself, the fundamental role of the cabinet officer will be to give analysis and advice. His will be an important voice, but not the only voice. Most presidential issues will implicate other cabinet departments and various EOP units. All need to be heard before the President decides, although a President is obviously going to give deference (but not automatic acquiescence) to his Defense Secretary on defense matters, to his Attorney General on legal matters.

A more complicated question is whether the EOP or the cabinet officer manages the process of policy development on these presidential issues. As noted above, all presidential issues should be *coordinated* through one of the three policy channels. Under this general principle, there are two broad alternatives. The EOP policy channel can provide a *process check* by ensuring that other views are fairly represented in any decision papers or presentation going to the President.

8. The EOP and the Cabinet: The Need for a (Relatively) Clear System of Sub-Presidential Decision-Making. An even more difficult issue than who manages the process of issue development or presidential-order questions is how the system of sub-presidential decision-making on second and third order issues operates. I believe this one of the hidden areas of the presidency which could benefit from increased historical and scholarly inquiry. The focus on the President himself obscures the vast web of sub-presidential decision-making which drives so much of the work of the Executive Branch—or causes the gears of government to lock.

Because of the potential for debilitating conflict, defining some system of sub-presidential decision-making on second and third order issues that is understood by the EOP and the cabinet officers is probably more important than any particular system. In defining roles, any system must distinguish between process management, advice-giving and decision-making. The following is one possibility.

- *Process management.* Depending on whether the issue is heavily inter-departmental in character or largely confined to a single department, the process can be managed by the head of the EOP policy channel (*e.g.*, OMB Director or head of the Troika) or by the cabinet officer with an EOP process check.
- *Advice-Giving.* EOP units and cabinet departments implicated by the issue should have the fair opportunity to provide analysis and advice.
- *Decision-Making.* Given the importance of the second and third order issues to the record of the presidency, and given the inevitability that no issue is wholly the interest of a single department, the heads of the EOP policy channels should have decision-making authority on these issues, short of the chief of staff (and the president). Obviously, however, when an issue is predominantly located in a single department, a substantial

degree of deference should be given to the cabinet officer's views. This proposition has greater applicability to third order issues than the roughly 25 second order domestic issues.

Given the ineluctable tension between the Cabinet and the EOP and within the EOP itself, the chief of staff, under clear direction from the President, must make this system of sub-presidential decision-making work with techniques which range from "schmoozing" to arbitrating, as indicated above. There will be lots of play in the joints, and exceptions to every rule (as the President discovers that not all his appointees are of sterling quality). But a general approach to the difficult question of sub-presidential decision-making is essential if an Administration is not to tear itself apart.

9. Delegation to the Departments: Cabinet Level Issues. Beyond the first, second and third order issues which constitute the essential strategic thrust of the presidency, there are, of course, a host of other issues which often are confined to a single department. Often these involve implementation of policy, as opposed to policy development. On these, a Cabinet Secretary should not be too closely monitored by the EOP. He or she should be judged by results—but not nitpicked to death by EOP review processes. As has been noted on many occasions, executive government is simply too vast to be run out of the White House or the EOP.

If the EOP can effectively coordinate the 125–150 first, second and third order issues, it will be doing wondrous well. Recognizing the need to give discretion to the Cabinet officers on many others (when they are not very heavily inter-agency in character) is a bedrock principle of EOP wisdom. The President should insist on this—and make sure that junior members of the EOP are not mucking about in these cabinet level issues. On these, departmental performance, not polite involvement in interadministration process, is key to the decision about whether a cabinet officer should be commended—or fired.

10. The Vice President: Senior Advisor Without Portfolio. The innovation of the Carter years—followed generally by President Reagan and Vice President Bush—should be continued. The Vice President should have access to all the President's memoranda, briefings, decision meetings—and to the President himself. He should ask questions, use his political antennae, and give the President his best judgment on important issues based on the work flowing from others to the President. In so using the Vice President, the President is not only getting something very important—the seasoned, inside view of a senior person who has no bureaucratic ax to grind—but he is giving the Vice President the best possible training in the event that he must assume the highest office after presidential death or disability. One of the many problems with giving the Vice President major, substantive responsibilities beyond the "senior advisor" role recommended here is that it necessarily implies an expanded, separate vice presidential staff. The last thing that the invariably overblown EOP needs is yet another large staff.

Some might argue that these prescriptions are too broad. I would hope, instead, that they are powerful and interrelated organizing ideas, which reflect the complexity of executive government and which have significant practical implications. Recognizing that presidential "strategy" involves linking policy, politics, structure and process in a realistic time frame implicitly asks a set of interrelated questions which must be answered. Recognizing that priority setting has enormous implications for executive branch processes, and for the respective roles of the President, chief of staff, EOP and cabinet officers, can shape the whole internal governance of the Executive Branch.

Some might argue that these prescriptions are too narrow and will promote legalistic disputes, rather than dampen conflict, within the Executive Branch. In my view, it is naive to think that an institution as complex as the Executive Branch can function without a shared understanding of some broad organizing ideas. The potential for acrimonious disputes—all in the name of "The presidential interest," of course—is simply too great. If all issues are treated in an ad hoc fashion, then the wheel has to be reinvented on a daily basis. Better, I believe, to have an approach which applies generally, but which is flexible enough to allow for special situations. If the President indicates early and clearly the rules of the game in his Administration, including the chief of staff's role in administering those rules, then conflict will be minimized to the extent possible in executive government, a vast, sprawling and unwieldy institution which has conflict embedded in its very structure and which operates in a fish bowl under enormous pressures.

With the wrong people, even the right rules of the game won't work. But, the right people, with no rules or the wrong rules, can fail just as well. Appropriate structures and processes are not glamorous. They are simply essential.

Notes

1. Fred Greenstein ed., *Leadership in the Modern Presidency* (Cambridge: Harvard University Press, 1988), p. 352.

2. Ben W. Heineman, Jr. and Curtis A. Hessler, *Memorandum for the President· A Strategic Approach to Domestic Affairs in the 1980s* (New York: Random House, 1980).

3. Ben W. Heineman, Jr., "Marrying Politics and Policy," in Lester M. Salamon and Michael S. Lund eds., *The Reagan Presidency and the Governing of America* (Washington, D.C.: Urban Institute Press, 1984).

Roger B. Porter

Economic Advice to the President:
From Eisenhower to Reagan

Roger Porter is the director of the White House Office of Policy Development. He identifies the economic policymaking patterns that have emerged over the last four decades and critiques reform proposals (i.e., Department of Economic Affairs, economic czar, National Economic Council Staff, Cabinet Council) designed to enhance the president's ability to achieve policy coherence in this area.

Economic advice to the president over the last thirty years has varied widely, reflecting the decision-making styles of the president and his leading administration officials. Any brief survey can, at best, only suggest broad characteristics and trends. A comprehensive study, rich in the details of economic policymaking over the past seven administrations, awaits presidential scholars and economic historians.

A description and assessment of the substantive economic policy advice provided the president and its contribution to the decisions presidents ultimately have made are also beyond the scope of this article. The purpose of this article is two-fold: first, to review the development of three entities or types of institutional arrangements that have characterized economic policy advice to the president over the past thirty years; and second, to discuss three organizational issues concerning the president and economic policy decision-making.

This article draws from scores of interviews conducted over the past four years with senior economic policy officials in the Eisenhower, Kennedy, Johnson, Nixon, Ford, Carter, and Reagan administrations and from research in the Eisenhower, Kennedy, and Johnson presidential libraries.[1] Its focus is on structural arrangements for providing economic policy advice to the president. It necessarily includes only brief summaries of each administration.

The concentration here on structural arrangements should not obscure the fact that all advice ultimately comes from people, not institutions. The positions officials hold have a certain legitimacy attached to them and provide a foundation on which to build. Likewise, decision-making processes and institutional arrangements influence the access of policymakers and the opportunities available to

Reprinted with permission from *Political Science Quarterly* 102 (Fall 1989): 229–250.

them. But in the end, individual competence, personality, and prior relationships also weigh heavily in the balance. Individual effort, excellence, and entrepreneurship are as important as systems and structure.

The Council of Economic Advisers

The Employment Act of 1946 created a three-member Council of Economic Advisers (CEA) to advise the president, and a newly created Joint Economic Committee of Congress, on economic policy matters.[2] President Truman did not request creation of the council, and it rates only passing mention in one of his two-volume memoirs.[3] The three members were equal in authority over the council's operations and over a small professional staff.

Reorganization Plan No. 9 of 1953 reconstituted the Council, establishing the chairman as preeminent.[4] Responsibility for employing staff, specialists, and consultants was transferred from the Council to the chairman, as was the formal function of reporting to the president on the Council's views and activities.[5]

There was a modest increase in the size of the Council staff under Walter Heller at the onset of the Kennedy administration, but the characteristics and functions of the CEA have remained remarkably constant. The three council members and the staff of twelve to twenty professionals are drawn disproportionately from academia. There is a high turnover among staff members. Most remain with the council no more than two years.[6] This high turnover rate limits the institutional memory of the staff. However, many of the Council members previously served as a junior or senior economist on the staff. Arthur Okun, for example, was successively a senior staff member, a council member, and finally chairman of the Council. Of the thirteen CEA chairmen, eight previously served with the Council in some capacity before their appointment as Chairman.[7] Party affiliation has had little influence in the selection of the staff. The Council has been extremely successful in attracting well-trained and highly motivated professional staff.

The CEA has avoided assuming operational responsibilities and instead has served exclusively as a staff arm to the president. While its members regularly testify before the Joint Economic Committee and other congressional committees, it is clearly the servant of the chief executive and not of the Congress. It has had three principal functions. First, it forecasts trends and the future pattern of overall economic activity. Second, it provides an economic analysis of issues for the president. (In the past two decades, microeconomic issues have consumed more and more of the CEA staff time and the staff has become somewhat more specialized.) Finally, it prepares an annual economic report to the Congress.[8]

Presidents have sought the advice of the CEA with varying frequency over the post–World War II period. While the principal function of the CEA has been expert analysis, it has, from time to time, served as a coordinator of views for the president. In almost every administration, the CEA has participated in many, and has chaired some, interagency committees. But the CEA was not originally intended or designed to serve as a coordinator or broker. Executive departments and agencies view the CEA as an advocate, not as a broker. It is viewed not as an advocate for a constituency, such as farmers or labor unions, but as an advocate for the view of professional economists—it usually favors markets and opposes subsidies. It has no "constituency"; rather, it has a "client," the president. This is true for both Democratic and Republican administrations. In interagency discussions, CEA members take positions and press for particular policies as avidly as other department or agency representatives.

There is general agreement among former CEA chairmen that the Council should stay small and avoid administrative responsibilities. They generally oppose a more active role for the CEA in coordinating or brokering. A highly qualified expert staff has served the Council well in the past and presumably will continue to do so in the future.

Interdepartmental Committees

Interdepartmental committees, councils, and groups (formal and informal) have played a central role in marshalling analysis and coordinating views on economic policy issues. Almost every president, usually early in his administration, talks of reviving the cabinet as an institution and indicates his intention to hold regular and frequent cabinet meetings. Yet most presidents eventually regard the full cabinet as an unsatisfactory forum for considering major policy issues. Few problems engage either the interest or the expertise of all cabinet members. The sheer work volume and time demands suggest the wisdom of focusing their expertise rather than using the entire cabinet for serious deliberation of policy issues.

Regular participants in cabinet meetings held by the last six presidents uniformly describe them as mainly exercises in exchanging information and getting direction from the president.[10] Reports on how the administrations' program is faring in the Congress, an account of the latest foreign mission of the secretary of state or the prospects for successfully concluding current negotiations with foreign countries, a description of the current state of the economy and the principles underlying the administration's economic program, are representative of the agenda items that are standard fare at cabinet meetings.

The most systematic use of the cabinet as a body occurred during the Eisenhower administration, when the cabinet met 230 times during his eight years as president (an average of nearly 29 meetings each year). This compares with 366 National Security Council meetings during the Eisenhower years.[11] Both Gerald Ford and Jimmy Carter indicated that they planned on weekly cabinet meetings. This fairly soon shifted to every other week and then to once every four to six weeks. Carter held 74 cabinet meetings in his four-year presidency.[12]

Ronald Reagan, drawing from his experience as governor of California, came to the White House committed to holding regular and frequent cabinet meetings. During the first two years of his presidency, Ronald Reagan held cabinet meetings fairly frequently. He held 27 cabinet meetings in 1981 and 20 in 1982.

During the Eisenhower years, a small cabinet secretariat was established with responsibility for the cabinet meeting agendas, papers, and minutes, and for overseeing the implementation of any decisions made.[13] While the Eisenhower administration likely generated more documents relative to cabinet meetings than most administrations, one does not get the feeling from reading the papers and minutes that full cabinet meetings were where the most important decisions were made. Options were not seriously discussed. The papers prepared were more for informational purposes than to help structure a debate. Cabinet meetings were occasions for setting a general tone—conveying what was going on, what the general philosophy on budget matters was, and so on.

The cabinet itself has generally not had committees under the direction of a cabinet secretariat or cabinet office. In the Reagan White House, the Office of Cabinet Administration (which, along with the Office of Policy Development, coordinates the activities of the cabinet councils), is an exception to this pattern. Most presidents have established various independently operating cabinet-level committees and councils. Some councils have been created by statute (the National Security Council, the Energy Resources Council, and the Council on International Economic Policy);[14] others by executive order (the Economic Policy Board);[15] others by presidential memorandum (the Council on Economic Policy, the Agricultural Policy Committee);[16] or letter (the Council on Foreign Economic Policy);[17] or by mention in a presidential message (the Advisory Board on Economic Growth and Stability).[18]

The evolution of councils and committees dealing with economic policy issues reveals some interesting patterns. Early in his administration, Dwight D. Eisenhower, at the urging of Arthur Burns, created the Advisory Board on Economic Growth and Stability (ABEGS) as "essentially a committee advisory to the Council." It was designed as "a forum at which thinking on economic policy of the various departments and agencies . . . [could] be compared and coordinated."[1] It originally consisted of eight cabinet-level departments and agencies and was subsequently expanded to ten.

A year and a half later, ABEGS was joined by another high-level interagency body, the Council on Foreign Economic Policy (CFEP), which also met regularly to discuss and coordinate foreign economic policy issues. These two bodies remained active for the remainder of both Eisenhower administrations. They were supplemented by many other committees—such as the Cabinet Committee on Small Business, the Trade Policy Committee, the Committee for the Rural Development Program, the Committee on Government Activities Affecting Prices and Costs, the Cabinet Committee on Price Stability for Economic Growth (chaired by the vice president), the President's Special Committee on Financial Policies for Post-attack Operations, and the Interdepartmental Committee to Coordinate Federal Urban Area Assistance Programs—to name just a few.

John F. Kennedy, who considered the Eisenhower decision-making process too highly structured, not only quickly dismantled the National Security Council apparatus, but also abolished ABEGS and the Council on Foreign Economic Policy. In their places he encouraged less formal arrangements. Several new committees were created in 1961 to deal with specific economic problems. These ranged from an ad hoc committee on housing credit to a White House committee on small business; from an advisory committee on labor-management policy to "new machinery for interagency cooperation in formulating fiscal estimates and policies"—later referred to as the "Troika," consisting of the chairman of the CEA, the secretary of the treasury, and the director of the budget bureau.[20] An Interdepartmental Committee of Under Secretaries on Foreign Economic Policy and informal arrangements under the direction of Carl Kaysen, deputy special assistant to the president for national security affairs, handled most foreign economic policy issues other than monetary affairs.

On the domestic side, the Troika was joined by the broader Cabinet Committee on Economic Growth established in August 1962 and including the secretaries of the treasury, commerce, and labor, the budget bureau director, and the chairman of the CEA.[21] In June 1962, President Kennedy asked Douglas Dillon, his secretary of the treasury, to chair a Cabinet Committee on the Balance of Payments, that would consider broad policy issues and monitor overseas expenditures. The Committee originally included the secretaries of the treasury, defense, and commerce, the under secretary of state, the administrator of the Agency for International Development (AID), the director of the bureau of the budget, the chairman of the council of economic advisers, and a member of the senior White House staff, initially Carl Kaysen.[22] Since the president wanted the committee to operate informally, he issued no executive order or other formal document to create it. The committee reported to the president, usually two or three times a year, on the U.S. balance of payments and the gold situation.

Under Lyndon Johnson, the relatively informal set of institutional arrangements that prevailed during the Kennedy years continued. The Troika and the "Quadriad" (the Troika plus the chairman of the Federal Reserve Board) met regularly, formally preparing an economic forecast every three months that was sent to the president and personally reviewed with him if the Troika members felt some action was needed.[23] Interestingly, these were consensus memoranda hammered out so that all three members could feel comfortable signing them.

Soon after he became president, Lyndon Johnson established the Long-Run International Payments Committee (LRIPC), which prepared the U.S. position papers for the Group of Ten discussions regarding the General Agreement to Borrow and other aspects of the international monetary system. In 1965, a group of high-level subcabinet officials from the Treasury and State Departments, the CEA, the Federal Reserve Board, and the White House staff began meeting regularly to discuss reforms of the international monetary system. The group, chaired by Frederick Demming, under secretary of the treasury for monetary affairs, was known as the Demming Group and was soon acknowledged as one of the most effective small interagency groups in Washington.

While the CFEP had served as a focal point for foreign economic policy issues in the Eisenhower administration, the National Security Council became the central focus of coordination during the Kennedy and Johnson years. A deputy assistant to the president for national security affairs, first Carl Kaysen and later Francis Bator, shaped the work of the various interagency groups dealing with an immediate staff of two professionals and became the key White House staffers on such issues as the balance of payments, trade negotiations, foreign aid, and international monetary problems. Both supplemented their own modestly sized staff by drawing on specialists in the Bureau of the Budget, the Council of Economic Advisers, the Office of the Special Trade Representative (STR), and the Departments of the Treasury and State. Both soon developed independent access to the president and worked directly with cabinet officers on many foreign economic issues.

At the end of the Johnson administration, the NSC's dominant role on foreign economic policy questions waned. The title of deputy was abolished with Bator's departure, and the job was divided between two officials. One dealt with foreign aid, the other with trade and monetary affairs. Other White House officials, the assistant secretary of state for economic affairs and the STR, played stronger roles.[24]

Richard Nixon brought to the White House a preference for formal interagency mechanisms and for increased staff capabilities at the center. He enlarged the

National Security Council staff and expanded the committee structure that supported it. He also created the Urban Affairs Council, the Rural Affairs Council, and the Cabinet Committee on Economic Policy (established by executive order on 24 January 1969) chaired by himself and including the vice president, the secretaries of the treasury, agriculture, commerce, labor, and housing and urban development, the counselors to the president (Arthur F. Burns and Daniel Patrick Moynihan), the director of the budget bureau, the deputy under secretary of state for economic affairs, and the chairman of the CEA.[25] These committees were to serve as the principal mechanisms for shaping administration policies. In January 1971 they were joined by another cabinet-level body, the Council on International Economic Policy (CIEP).

But Nixon was never very happy with this phalanx of committees and, over time, met with them less and less frequently. His appointment of John Connally in December 1970 as secretary of the treasury marked the second phase in Nixon economic policymaking. Nixon selected Connally in part because he wanted an economic "czar" to whom he felt comfortable delegating most economic policy decisions. In Connally, he found the czar he wanted. Formerly the meetings of the Troika, held roughly every other week, rotated among the offices of the three leading officials. Connally announced shortly after his arrival that henceforth they would be held at the Department of the Treasury.

Connally was succeeded as treasury secretary in the spring of 1972 by George Shultz, formerly secretary of labor and director of the Office of Management and Budget (OMB). Shultz held the same title as Connally, but was by temperament more collegial in his approach.

In January 1973, Shultz was appointed assistant to the president for economic affairs (in addition to his Treasury portfolio) and made chairman of a cabinet-level Council on Economic Policy (CEP) designed to coordinate all economic policy decision-making.[26] While the Council formally met infrequently, Shultz personally succeeded in presiding over a process that involved most senior administration officials in issues that affected their interests.

As Shultz prepared to leave government in the spring of 1974, Nixon faced the choice of his successor. William Simon, Shultz's deputy of the Treasury and the energy czar, and Roy Ash, director of the Office of Management and Budget, were both anxious to succeed Shultz as the administration's leading economic figure. Rather than choose between them, Nixon selected Kenneth Rush, deputy secretary of state, as his counsellor for economic affairs, making him chairman of most of the interagency economic committees.

But within weeks after the appointment, Nixon had resigned and Gerald Ford had replaced the Nixon machinery with a new Economic Policy Board (EPB), chaired by the secretary of the treasury, but managed by an assistant to the president for economic affairs. It was designed to coordinate both foreign and domestic economic policy.[27]

Two overriding objectives guided the EPB's creation. First, Ford, anxious to differentiate his administration from his predecessor's, wanted visibly to enhance the role of departmental officials and reduce the public role of White House aides. By establishing a new high-level entity chaired by the secretary of the treasury, he sent a clear signal that he intended to elevate the role of his cabinet officers. Second, the EPB replaced a plethora of specialized committees and councils with a single entity responsible for domestic and international economic policy. The board and its executive committee (the secretary of the treasury, the director of the OMB, the chairman of the CEA, the executive director of the CIEP, and the assistant to the president for economic affairs, later expanded to include the secretaries of labor, commerce, and state) soon established itself as the primary conduit for advice to the president on economic policy issues and maintained its central role throughout the Ford years.

Two and a half years later, Jimmy Carter abolished the Economic Policy Board and created an Economic Policy Group (EPG), initially cochaired by the secretary of the treasury and the chairman of the CEA. While the EPG existed throughout the Carter administration, its influence at the White House and with the president waxed and waned. Frequently, it struggled unsuccessfully with the Domestic Policy Staff for control of issues having a major impact on the economy. The EPG, with no firm White House base, was seldom a match for the relatively large Domestic Policy Staff—approximately seventy total staff members including twenty-five to thirty professionals. A regular channel and predictable pattern for handling major economic issues never emerged.

Fashioning an economic recovery program was at the top of Ronald Reagan's agenda as he took office in January 1981. During the transition period, an Economic Policy Coordinating Committee, headed by David Stockman, the OMB director-designate, was established. It included the administration's senior economic officials, as they were designated, and concentrated on developing a major series of spending and tax reduction proposals, which were initially announced on February 18 and supplemented on March 10.

From the outset, the Economic Policy Coordinating Committee (later frequently referred to as the Budget Working Group) was viewed as temporary. Stockman, and his quickly assembled OMB team, would initially have the lead, but Treasury Secretary-designate Donald Reagan was promised that he would head a cabinet-level interagency council responsible for domestic and foreign economic policy that would emerge once the budget proposals were completed.

By the end of February the White House announced the creation of five cabinet councils chaired by the president with a cabinet secretary designated chairman pro tempore:[28]

Cabinet Council on Economic Affairs
(Secretary of the Treasury)
Cabinet Council on Natural Resources and the Environment
(Secretary of the Interior)
Cabinet Council on Commerce and Trade
(Secretary of Commerce)
Cabinet Council on Food and Agriculture
(Secretary of Agriculture)
Cabinet Council on Human Resources
(Secretary of Health and Human Services)

Each council is managed by an executive secretary who is a member of the White House Office of Policy Development. The Cabinet Council on Economic Affairs (CCEA) includes the secretaries of the treasury, state, commerce, labor, and transportation, the director of OMB, the chairman of the CEA, and the U.S. Trade Representative. Other cabinet officers are invited to attend CCEA meetings when issues involving their departments' interests are under discussion.

The first two years of the CCEA's operation suggest that it has established itself as a viable entity. Its regular meetings (two to three times weekly) are attended by cabinet-level officials; it handles a steady stream of domestic and foreign economic policy issues; and it has established a phalanx of subcabinet level working groups to develop these issues for cabinet-level consideration.

The Role of Interdepartmental Committees

This brief sketch of economic policymaking arrangements in the last seven administrations highlights a number of important features regarding the role of interdepartmental committees. For example, there has been no real analog in economic policy to the National Security Council staff. The CEA, which was established at approximately the same time, is not an interdepartmental council, nor does its charter include coordinating advice to the president on economic policy issues.

Most councils or committees have not survived from administration to administration. The narrowly focused National Advisory Council on International Financial and Monetary Problems (NAC) and the informal Troika and Quadriad arrangements are exceptions.

Moreover, virtually every administration has created a number of cabinet committees to deal with specific issues. They have tended to proliferate over time for several reasons. By creating a new council or cabinet-level committee reporting directly to the president, a president may demonstrate concern and action, both to the participants and to the public. A president may establish such groups to help assuage the bruised feelings of a specific constituency. (The March 1976 creation of the Agricultural Policy Committee, chaired by the secretary of agriculture, was a symbolic action calculated to improve President Ford's sagging popularity in the farm community.) Most presidents view such groups as inexpensive ways of building political support and demonstrating some movement in addressing a problem. In addition, they are often the work of a skillful entrepreneur within an administration.

These committees have operated with little overall direction. When Gerald Ford succeeded Richard Nixon, he instructed William Seidman, his assistant for administration, to attend any cabinet-level meetings related to economic policy. Seidman set about trying to find out what committees existed and where they were meeting. After asking OMB and Treasury independently to prepare lists of cabinet-level committees dealing with economic policy issues, he discovered that there were more than a score of such committees.

Most of these committees have been chaired by the department or agency that has lead responsibility for the problem. The U.S. trade representative chairs the Trade Policy Committee, Treasury chairs the NAC, and OMB chairs the interagency committee on PL-480 allocations of concessionary agricultural exports to developing countries.

Few of these committees have had direct access to the president. Most have quickly become in effect subcabinet-level committees with cabinet officers not attending the meetings. The Economic Policy Board (which met 520 times at the cabinet level in two and a quarter years, averaging almost 5 meetings each week, and which President Ford used to make virtually all his economic policy decisions), was an exception to the pattern of most committees.

In the place of genuinely effective formal structures, most administrations have evolved a set of informal relationships among the leading officials. A version of the "Troika" has existed in every administration over the past quarter century. A rough division of labor between the three principal agencies has generally held. The Treasury Department has provided revenue estimates, OMB federal spending estimates, and the CEA has forecasted future patterns of economic activity.[2] For the most part, other agencies within the federal government have been, or were for many years, effectively excluded from Troika deliberations and from macroeconomic policy issues. The Departments of Labor, and Commerce, and others viewed as "constituency-oriented" by Troika members, did not play a major role. But in the 1970s this pattern began to shift as departments and agencies throughout the executive branch developed new internal capacities. The number of professional economists increased in virtually all departments. One recent senior administration official, who returned to government after more than a decade, described the change that had occurred:

> In the 1960s there were a lot of people who would have liked to get into the game but just did not have the staff. They were unsupported and when you weren't supported, you couldn't carry the issue. Nobody had a group of economists to evaluate all these issues for them. CEA had a monopoly on it along with a few people at the Treasury. What has changed today is that every agency has an economic policy and planning group and it is not easy to tear their arguments apart. CEA cannot blow people out of the water with the depth of its analysis like it could in the 1960s. Few people understood what the term "multiplier" meant in the 1960s much less were able to argue with CEA's arguments about a tax policy to stimulate the economy. When CEA said the effect of a specific tax action on investment was such-and-such there wasn't any other agency doing its own empirical work to argue with it. But now, Treasury may say, "No, it's Y." And Labor, "It's Z." The Labor Department has turned their economic policy planning group into a mini-CEA. There is no issue that they don't regard as absolutely vital.[30]

Finally, in surveying economic policymaking patterns over the past thirty years, one finds that interagency committees and groups have played a major role in organizing advice to the president on specific issues, but that most presidents have generally not relied principally on general purpose, formal entities. More frequently, presidents have relied on a trusted adviser or group of advisers settling many issues bilaterally with the interested parties. The increasing complexity of the economic policy arena and the growing interest and capability of departments and agencies to influence a wide range of economic policy issues, foreign and domestic, represent a challenge to this traditional pattern. The challenge is particularly acute for those concerned with developing a coherent and integrated administration program.

A White House Assistant for Economic Policy

The existence of senior White House aides with responsibility for economic policy has varied greatly from administration to administration. The Eisenhower White

House had first Arthur Burns (before the Council of Economic Advisers was reconstituted and Burns was named as its chairman), then Gabriel Hague and Don Paarlberg. The Kennedy administration had no senior official whose principal duties were economic policy matters, although Theodore Sorensen, as White House counsel, coordinated some economic policy issues and attended the sessions of the Troika with the president. On the foreign economic policy side, Carl Kaysen coordinated several issues as McGeorge Bundy's deputy at the National Security Council. In the Johnson administration, Joseph Califano played a similar role to that Sorensen had played in the Kennedy years, and Francis Bator a similar role to that played by Kaysen.

Richard Nixon did not initially appoint a senior White House official to deal with economic policy issues, although Arthur Burns, as counselor to the president with cabinet rank, actively participated in White House economic policy discussions. In February 1970, Burns was appointed chairman of the board of governors of the Federal Reserve System. It was not until January 1973 that a small White House economic policy office was established and Treasury Secretary George Shultz was given a second hat and a small West Wing outpost as assistant to the president for economic affairs. Following Shultz's departure in the spring of 1974, Kenneth Rush was appointed counsellor of the president for economic affairs and chairman of most of the major economic policy committees, including the Council on International Economic Policy and the Council on Economic Policy.

When Gerald Ford became president, he appointed L. William Seidman as assistant to the president for economic affairs and as executive director of the Economic Policy Board. Other than Rush's brief tenure, this was the first time that a White House economic assistant had been given responsibility for managing the process of policy development on economic issues. Hague and Paarlberg during the Eisenhower administration had responsibility for handling many day-to-day issues for the president, but they did not principally coordinate interagency processes.

Jimmy Carter made the explicit decision at the outset of his administration not to appoint a White House assistant for economic policy (a precondition for Charles Schultz accepting the CEA chairmanship). The Economic Policy Group replaced the Economic Policy Board. The secretary of the treasury and the chairman of the CEA were named cochairmen; and the executive director who was ultimately appointed had neither a White House office nor a title. Subsequently, Carter named first Robert Strauss and later Alfred Kahn as his inflation adviser and as chairman of the Council on Wage and Price Stability. They were not given responsibility for managing an interagency process, although they were given membership on the Economic Policy Group Steering Committee and did have reasonable access to the president.

Ronald Reagan has divided responsibility in his White House between a chief of staff, James Baker, with responsibility for overall administration and coordinating White House relations with constituencies outside the executive branch (the Congress, the press, interest groups, state and local government officials) and a counsellor to the president, Edwin Meese, with responsibility for policy development within the executive branch.

In practice, the division of labor is more apparent than real. Meese, Baker, and Michael Deaver, deputy chief of staff and a long-time Reagan confidant, are in almost constant contact and work closely as a team. (They are popularly referred to as "The Big Three" or "the Triumvirate.") The cabinet, councils, and overall policy development fall under the "Meese side" of the White House.

A somewhat different pattern has existed for dealing with foreign economic policy issues, which have frequently been treated apart from domestic economic policy problems. Joseph Dodge and Clarence Randall served as chairman of the Council on Foreign Economic Policy during the Eisenhower administration and also simultaneously held the title of special assistant to the president. Likewise, Carl Kaysen and Francis Bator held the title of deputy special assistant to the president for national security affairs while serving on the staff of the National Security Council under Bundy and Walter Rostow. Peter Peterson and Peter Flanigan also held White House staff titles while serving as executive directors of the Council on International Economic Policy. During the Carter administration, Ambassador Henry Owen managed preparations for the annual international economic summit conferences and coordinated some other foreign economic policy issues. He and his small staff were technically part of the larger National Security Council staff.

In summary, presidents have generally not relied heavily on White House economic policy assistants to organize the pattern of economic advice and decision-making to the same degree that they have for national security affairs or domestic affairs. Most have handled day-to-day concerns rather than overseeing a policy development process.

Developing Coherent Economic Policies

The Council of Economic Advisers has performed a valuable function for the president by introducing the viewpoints of professional economists, detached from departmental perspectives or operational responsibilities, into his deliberations concerning issues related to the economy. There is general consensus that the CEA should remain relatively modest in size (three members and fifteen to eighteen professionals), that it should continue to avoid administrative responsibilities, and that it should not have the principal responsibility for policy coordination. The review here of economic policy making patterns during the last three decades, however, raises three issues concerning the president and economic policy decision-making that merit consideration.

The first issue concerns the means for coordinating policy advice and achieving policy coherence. The president must seek to integrate policy. He wants the parts to bear some relationship to the whole since he is uniquely accountable for the comprehensiveness and coherence of his administration's policies. The aggregate of microeconomic and sectoral decisions can have a tremendous impact on the president's ability to influence the pattern of overall economic activity. Some machinery is needed to mesh macroeconomic and microeconomic concerns. There are at least four broad alternative ways of achieving such coordination and integration.

Creating a Super Department

Many countries have a Department of Economic Affairs or a Finance Ministry that combines in one what is normally performed by the U.S. Treasury Department, the Office of Management and Budget, and the Council of Economic Advisers. Similarly, one of the central criticisms made by students of federal organization is that departments are too closely tied to particular constituencies and special interests. The recommended solution is creating "super departments" with comprehensive interests that will be able to resist the pleas of special interests. In 1964, the President's Task Force on Government Organization recommended creating a Department of Labor and Commerce. In 1967, the Heineman Task Force made a similar proposal. In 1970, the President's Advisory Council on Executive Organization (the Ash Council) recommended that four main executive departments that handle highly interdependent economic matters (Commerce, Labor, Agriculture, and Transportation) be combined into a Department of Economic Affairs. Richard Nixon, in his State of the Union address on 22 January 1971, proposed a sweeping reorganization of the executive branch that called for four new super departments to join the four "inner cabinet" departments—State, Defense, Treasury, and Justice.[31]

Proponents of the large department concept point to several potential advantages. To the extent that those at the top of such departments exercise effective control of the department's activities, such a department would aid in the integration of policy. Those "who deal with common or closely related problems would work together in the same organizational framework." The department "would be given a mission broad enough so that it could set comprehensive policy directions and resolve internally the policy conflicts which are most likely to arise."[32] As the Ash Council pointed out: "The present organizational structure encourages fragmentation when comprehensive responses to social and economic problems are needed. Problems are defined to fit within the limits of organizational authority, resulting in piecemeal approaches to their solutions by separate departments and agencies."

Second, large departments would help the president provide overall direction to economic policy development. In Nixon's view: "As this single new Department joined the Treasury Department, the Council of Economic Advisers and the Federal Reserve Board in shaping economic policy, it would speak with a stronger voice and would offer a more effective, more highly integrated viewpoint than four different departments can possibly do at present."[33] Moreover, when the responsibility for realizing basic objectives is clearly focused in a specific governmental unit, that department can be held accountable for achieving them.

Finally, a large, comprehensive department could also ease the president's decision-making burden. Nixon noted: "Decisionmaking responsibility is often shifted to the Executive Office of the President because no official at the departmental level has the authority to decide the issues."[34] Thus, large departments may help in pushing some problems away from the president. As one seasoned executive office veteran remarked: "Our difficulty is that we clutch tightly to us every problem that appears on the horizon."

While there are several potential advantages—concentrating authority to resolve problems without the intervention of the president, focusing responsibility and thereby enhancing accountability, increasing the likelihood of comprehensive rather than piecemeal approaches to policy problems, and easing the decision-making burden on the president consistent with the concept of an "economizing presidency"—the concept of a super economic department has several limitations.

Many who press for larger and more comprehensive executive departments do so in the belief that consolidation will undermine narrow departmental perspectives. Yet there is reason to question whether aggregating responsibilities within larger entities will produce the desired effect. Few would argue that the size and scope of the Department of Defense or the Department of Health, Education, and Welfare eliminated, or even significantly reduced, the power of special interests and specific constituencies. Aggregating functions into larger departments may transfer the resolution of certain disputes and the weighing of certain trade-offs from the White House to the office of the departmental secretary, but the competing narrow interests would still remain. Consolidations may result in fewer major decisions naturally flowing to the White House with no guarantee that the president's interests will prevail in those decisions made at the departmental level. From the president's vantage point, even large consolidated departments will have different outlooks, perspectives, and constituencies than his own. Moreover, as problems become more complex, it is increasingly difficult to concentrate authority in one place without the entity soon looking like the entire executive branch.

Designating a Super Secretary or Czar

As an alternative to the creation of a comprehensive Department of Economic Affairs, the president might either designate one cabinet official as a super secretary for economic affairs or effectively delegate responsibility for economic policy decisions to a czar.

John Connally, as Nixon's treasury secretary, had a public and private mandate from the president that extended well beyond his Treasury portfolio. Connally used this grant to dominate economic policy decision-making. As Connally explained their relationship:

> Most of the meetings that I had with the President were one-on-one. In the economic field, he made it clear that I was his chief economic adviser. Throughout my entire time there, it was a situation in which he clearly delegated the authority to me. I kept in constant contact with George Shultz, with Paul McCracken, with Arthur Burns. When we had all these meetings in Rome and London and Washington on the international monetary currency exchange rates, we were the only people who had any authority to do anything. There wasn't a finance minister in the room in any of those meetings, in my judgment, that could commit to anything. But the President had clearly said to me, "Just go ahead and do what you think you have to do." He just gave me almost unlimited authority and delegation of authority. Of course, I kept him fully informed all the way along.[35]

Later, unable to obtain favorable congressional action on his departmental reorganization proposals, President Nixon briefly instituted a system of super secretaries. Four cabinet secretaries were designated as super secretaries to have offices in the Old Executive Office Building and to coordinate the activities within jurisdictions that were similar to the four major departments proposed earlier. The experiment was short-lived. One of the super secretaries related that within three months after his designation, following a cabinet meeting the day after the resignations of H.R. Haldeman and John D. Ehrlichman, he was told that the concept had been scrapped.

The "czar" approach has many of the same potential advantages as the super department approach—resolving disputes without the intervention of the president, concentrating responsibility and hence accountability, and clarifying the public perception of who speaks for the administration. Moreover, it may be congenial to a president who has limited interest in economic policy questions and is anxious to delegate authority to an individual.

But there are also problems. Just as it is difficult to effectively consolidate power under a super department, it is perhaps even more difficult to concentrate power in a czar. Bits and pieces of economic policy responsibility are scattered throughout the federal government because they are linked to other important governmental responsibilities. Decentralization of operating responsibilities will remain a central fact of life. This characteristic presents a formidable challenge to concentrating authority in any one set of hands. Moreover, the czar approach depends heavily on the individual selected. If such an official is to have any opportunity for success he or she must not only enjoy the confidence of the president, but must also be perceived by other department and agency heads, external groups, the press, and the Congress as having the clout and the powers of persuasion to be truly first among equals.

Thus far several difficulties have been identified with the super department and super secretary approaches. But a capacity for central oversight is badly needed. There is a need to raise issues to the presidential level when a personal decision is desirable. There is a need to assure that the president receives the views of the senior advisers whose responsibilities are most relevant to the issue.

Creating a National Economic Council Staff

One response to the frequently alleged parochialism of executive branch departments would be to create a centralized White House staff similar to the Nixon-Kissinger National Security Council or the Nixon-Ehrlichman Domestic Council staffs. Such a staff would be large enough—consisting of perhaps forty or fifty professionals—that it would not only manage the flow of day-to-day communications between executive departments and the president, but would also pull the strands of a policy problem together and provide an assessment of relevant information and alternatives.

As Alexander George has pointed out, a centralized management approach sees the president as a "unitary rational decision maker, shielded from raw disagreements over policy."[36] This approach gives primary responsibility to the Executive Office of the President and to the immediate White House staff. It emphasizes careful, systematic examination of policy questions with control vested in individuals familiar with the president and his views. Executive branch departments and agencies might have substantial input on particular issues, but they would generally play a distinctly secondary role, since centralized management is designed to overcome what is viewed as departmental parochialism and inertia.

While such a staff can increase the president's control over the policymaking process, raise issues for his attention that might not necessarily reach the White

House otherwise, and increase his likelihood of controlling the timing and announcement of a new policy or initiative, a large centralized management staff also involves substantial costs and risks for the president. A heavy reliance on the president's immediate staff will inevitably undermine morale and initiative in departments and agencies. Moreover, the objectivity of a presidentially oriented staff may be an illusion if the staff ends up mirroring and reinforcing perceived presidential inclinations. It cannot mobilize the same resources or reflect the range of concerns that exist in departments and agencies. Implementing a large number of issues requires the cooperation of departments and agencies who will withhold it if they feel alienated. Thus, centralized management widens the gulf between policy formulation and implementation, and the gulf between the president and the executive branch.

Establishing a Cabinet-Level Multiple Advocacy Council

A fourth alternative would be to establish a cabinet-level body designed to bring together regularly the leading economic policy officials within the administration to advise the president on a broad range of economic policy issues. The core of such a collegial enterprise would be the three elements of the Troika (Treasury, OMB, and the CEA), but its mandate would extend well beyond the issues traditionally considered by the Troika. It would include, as part of the core group, other leading administration officials—the secretaries of state, commerce, and labor, for example. Whatever the size of the "core group," its deliberations would include representatives from all departments and agencies that have a legitimate interest in an issue under discussion. This group of officials would have collective responsibility for advising the president on all major economic policy issues. Its emphasis would be to help departments see their responsibilities in a broader setting. It would mobilize the resources of departments and agencies rather than transcend them. Such an approach would involve combining the principles of multiple advocacy (that the president is exposed to competing arguments and viewpoints made by the advocates themselves rather than having viewpoints filtered through a staff) and collegiality (a continuity among advisers who share responsibility with the president for policy development over a broad area).

There are many limitations of such a system in practice. Disparities in resources, talent, and abilities among the advocates can distort the process. As Theodore Sorensen has observed: "The most formidable debater is not necessarily the most informed, and the most reticent may sometimes be the wisest."[37] A genuine competition of ideas may be undermined by one or more advocates consistently dominating the process because of superior skills and resources. Moreover, there is no guarantee the advocates will represent all viable policy alternatives rather than lowest common denominator recommendations. Group norms stifling creativity and reflecting a single ideology may emerge. Such a system could consume enormous amounts of time, run the risk of leaks on sensitive issues, force a large number of decisions to the top, and weaken the ability of senior executives responsible for particular policy areas to "deliver" on commitments to their constituencies and to the Congress.

No structure can consistently transcend the abilities and limitations of its individual actors. But many of the collegial experiments on providing policy advice to the president have been undermined by structural deficiencies. Several organizational guidelines can help minimize the potential limitations of such a system in practice.

Unquestionably, the council's or committee's effectiveness depends on its having the president's imprimatur. Departments and agencies must perceive it as the president's vehicle. If the president permits individual officials consistently to circumvent the collegial process, departments will cease to take it seriously. Thus, such a system depends heavily on the president's commitment to it.

Equally important, an "honest broker" or process manager should control the council's operations. Such a manager must be perceived as dispensing due process and should not have other, competing responsibilities. He or she must be intelligent enough to be considered a peer by his or her colleagues and also must enjoy the president's confidence. The manager should find satisfaction in pulling the strands of a problem together rather than in driving the process toward a particular outcome. In seeking a balanced presentation to the president, he or she must be willing and able to reach for advocacy as an instrument of brokerage rather than undertaking brokerage because of orders from superiors. The honest broker should have what the Brownlow Committee called "a passion for anonymity."

The staff for such a council should be small and consist of generalists. A large staff can exercise greater quality control, but invariably such staffs have become specialized, have tended to ignore departments and agencies (and are viewed as competitors by departmental staffs), and have been tempted to circumvent the process themselves.

Such a council should meet regularly and operate at the cabinet level. The clout of such a council will depend on the capacity of its members to speak authoritatively for their department or agency. If given responsibility for advising the president over a broad policy area, the council could help insure that a comprehensive approach is taken to a wide range of policy problems, that the president is not left to integrate interrelated issues on his own, and that senior departmental officials are likely to view problems in the framework of a context that transcends their own departmental responsibilities.

Multiple advocacy is a difficult system to operate. Its success depends on consistent presidential support. Powerful officials with access to the president may attempt to circumvent the collegial process to advance a particular interest. Multiple advocacy depends on having the "right" people to manage it. The other participants must view them as fair and even-handed in their coordination of policy development. The necessary combination of skills that an honest broker needs are frequently not found in those people most closely associated with presidential candidates. There are often powerful personal factors and political forces that guide a president-elect in the selection of his immediate staff. These people will have the most decisive influence on organizing the pattern of advice the president receives. In short, such a system depends on the president recognizing its value, appointing individuals with the requisite abilities (and temperament) as the managers of his policy development process, and demonstrating a clear commitment to such a system by not allowing individual officials to circumvent it.

The Relationship Between Foreign and Domestic Economic Policy Formation

For most of the past thirty years, different processes have existed for considering foreign and domestic economic policy issues. Parallel cabinet-level committees have often existed—the Council on Foreign Economic Policy and ABEGS, the Council on International Economic Policy (CIEP) and the Cabinet Committee on Economic Policy. The most continuous informal arrangements—the Troika and the Quadriad—have concentrated almost exclusively on domestic economic policy questions. Not until the Council on Economic Policy under George Shultz during the Nixon administration and the Economic Policy Board under William Simon during the Ford administration have foreign and domestic economic policy questions been considered regularly by a single entity.

The creation of such bodies as the Council on Foreign Economic Policy and the Council on International Economic Policy has been the result of the conviction that international economic policy questions are important, merit high-level attention, and are being insufficiently addressed under the current machinery.[38] While Carl Kaysen and Francis Bator were with the National Security Council (NSC) during the 1960s, they effectively coordinated a host of foreign economic policy questions. But they were trained economists who were given the mandate to do so by their superiors, McGeorge Bundy and Walter Rostow, and Presidents Kennedy and Johnson. Under the Kissinger and Brent Scowcroft National Security Councils there was less interest in economic policy questions and on Kissinger's part a reluctance to delegate authority. Moreover, CIEP never acquired the clout to fill the gap adequately. With the abolition of CIEP, international economic policy coordination was once again partially returned under the NSC umbrella in the person of Henry Owen, who played a role similar to the Kaysen-Bator model. In the Reagan administration, responsibility has been shared by the Cabinet Council on Economic Affairs, the Cabinet Council on Commerce and Trade, and the National Security Council.

The attraction of reestablishing a formal entity to advise the president on foreign economic policy questions remains strong. But there are two principal arguments for not establishing a separate foreign economic policymaking channel to the president. First, it is increasingly difficult to distinguish issues as either foreign policy, domestic economic, or foreign economic problems. The distinctions have blurred with the growing complexity of considerations and interests that presidents must weigh.

Second, the experiments with entities established to address foreign economic policy issues suggest that they have not succeeded in consistently engaging the president's interest and attention, largely because they have not been tied to a regular work flow with which he must deal.

However, a decision against creating a separate channel to advise the president on foreign economic policy issues still leaves open the question of whether foreign economic policy issues, to the extent they can be identified, should be tied to the national security or economic policy machinery. There are good arguments in support of both positions, and an excellent discussion of them is found in I. M. Destler's *Making Foreign Economic Policy*. Destler argues convincingly that the substance and politics of current foreign economic issues "encourage the conclusion that it is more realistic to build their coordination around economic policy officials and institutions."[39] The substance of most foreign economic policy issues relates more closely to domestic economic policy concerns than to foreign policy ones. Moreover, senior foreign policy officials have generally been able effectively to influence economic policymaking processes more easily than economic officials have been able to penetrate foreign-policymaking processes.

A White House Economic Policy Assistant

A third issue meriting consideration is whether the president should appoint an assistant for economic affairs. While the positions of assistant to the president for national security affairs and assistant to the president for domestic policy now have a tradition extending back through at least four administrations, a White House assistant for economic affairs is less solidly entrenched. The pattern over the past thirty years is for Republican presidents generally to favor the idea and for Democratic presidents to consider the position unnecessary, although there is nothing partisan in the concept.

There is no compelling need for such an assistant to handle the president's day-to-day concerns related to economic policy issues. Several administrations have demonstrated that a national security assistant and a domestic policy assistant, aided by adequate staffs, can handle most of the day-to-day responsibilities of keeping the president apprised of current developments.

The issue of a White House economic assistant hinges in large part on the type of integrating machinery, if any, the president should establish. The creation of a super department or the delegation of most economic policy decision-making authority to a czar reduces the need for a White House economic assistant. The establishment of a National Economic Council staff or a cabinet-level economic policy entity would create a need for such a White House assistant. A relatively large centralized staff to shape alternatives for the president on economic policy issues would obviously need a senior official to oversee it. Experience with cabinet-level coordinating mechanisms suggests the usefulness of a White House-based assistant to manage the process unencumbered by departmental or agency responsibilities.

There is the potential for tension between a White House economic assistant and the chairman of the council of economic advisers, but conceptually there is no necessary conflict. To the extent that the process works well, it provides the CEA chairman and council members with the opportunity to become involved in presidential deliberations across a broad range of issues that transcend macroeconomic policy. A White House economic assistant can also share the work load and help reduce CEA involvement in many activities that are not central to its mission, such as personnel appointments, dealings with special interest groups, and handling numerous small, but nondeferable items, that the president cannot ignore.

The role of the CEA is to provide substantive economic advice and analysis. A White House assistant, responsible for managing the process of providing the president advice, has a coordinating, facilitating role. He or she need not become a major adviser with regard to substantive questions, and indeed doing so may well reduce his or her effectiveness as a coordinator. There is the risk that a White

House economic assistant may acquire a taste for shaping policy outcomes to the extent that the assistant becomes a regular competitor with the CEA chairman and other administration economic officials for the president's ear. But a White House assistant, who tends to managing the policy development process, can prove a great asset to his or her colleagues.

Presidents are inclined to devote their time and energies to those areas where they have the greatest interest and where they feel they have the greatest opportunity to influence events. Most presidents have spent disproportionate time on foreign policy matters, in part because of fewer domestic and congressional constraints, but also because their national security policymaking machinery has been relatively well developed. The National Security Council apparatus, for all its limitations, has generally produced good quality products—issue papers and options memorandums—for presidential consumption.

The consistent engagement of presidential interest in shaping major economic policies requires machinery that can effectively identify alternatives and generate quality analysis across a wide range of issues. The challenges of an unfavorable economic environment and the intertwining of foreign and domestic economic policy interests make it more crucial than ever that the president have the benefit of a structure that will enhance the prospects for developing coherent policies to address the economic problems facing the nation.

Notes

1. The list of interviewees included Arthur Burns, Walter Heller, the late Arthur Okun, Alan Greenspan, Paul McCracken, William Simon, John Connally, and Herbert Stein. These interviews were conducted over the period from 1977 to 1981.

2. Employment Act of 1946 (60 Stat. 23), Section 4.

3. Harry S. Truman, *Year of Decisions* (Garden City, N.Y.: Doubleday, 155), 493–94. The council is not mentioned in the second volume of his memoirs, *Years of Trial and Hope* (Garden City, N.Y.: Doubleday, 1956). The relatively modest role of the council during its early years is reflected in the sparse references to its activities found in the major works to date on the Truman years. See Merle Miller, *Plain Speaking: An Oral Biography of Harry S Truman* (Berkeley, Calif.: Berkeley Publishing Corporation, 1973); Barton J. Bernstein and Allen J. Matusow, eds., *The Truman Administration: A Documentary History* (New York: Harper and Row, 1966); Bert Cochran, *Harry Truman and the Crisis Presidency: The History of a Triumphant Succession* (London: MacMillan Co., 1966); Margaret Truman, *Harry S. Truman* (New York: William Morrow and Co., 1973), 308, 449, 451; Robert J. Donovan, *Conflict and Crisis: The Presidency of Harry S. Truman, 1945–1948* (New York: W. W. Norton and Co., 1977), 170, 339–41.

4. Reorganization Plan No. 9 of 1953 (67 Stat. 644). See also Special Message to the Congress Transmitting Reorganization Plan 9 of 1953 Concerning the Council of Economic Advisers, June 1, 1953, *Public Papers of the Presidents: Dwight D. Eisenhower, 1953* (Washington, D.C.: Government Printing Office, 1960), 355–359. The chairman of the Council of Economic Advisers is an Executive Level II official. The other two members of the council are Executive Level IV officials.

5. The position of vice chairman of the council was abolished.

6. See the Annual Report to the President on the Activities of the Council of Economic Advisers published with the *Economic Report of the President* that is transmitted to the Congress each January in accordance with the Employment Act of 1946.

7. Leon Keyserling, Raymond Saulnier, Gardner Ackley, Arthur Okun, Paul McCracken, and Herbert Stein had all served as council members before their designation as chairmen. Charles Shultz and Murray Weidenbaum had previously served as staff members at the council

and had held significant posts elsewhere in the executive branch as director of the Bureau of the Budget and assistant secretary of the treasury for economic policy respectively.

Edwin Nourse was the first chairman and Arthur Burns the first Republican appointee. Only Walter Heller, Alan Greenspan, and Martin Feldstein were appointed chairmen without previous Council service after it had become an established entity.

8. See Edwin G. Nourse, *Economics in the Public Service* (New York: Harcourt Brace, 1953), 107.

9. See Robert B. Semple, Jr., "Nixon Rules Out Agency Control by Staff Aides," *New York Times*, 14 November 1968; James Reston, "Half-Speech Ahead, *New York Times*, 15 December 1976; Dom Bonafede, "The Carter White House—The Shape Is There, But No Specifics," *National Journal* 8 (1976): 1799.

10. Emmet John Hughes, *The Living Presidency* (New York: Coward, McCann and Geoghegan, 1972), 335; Theodore Sorensen, *Decision Making in the White House* (New York: Columbia University Press, 1963), 58.

11. Minutes, Cabinet Meetings, Dwight D. Eisenhower Presidential Library, Abiline, Kansas.

12. Edward Walsh, "Carter's Cabinet Holds 'Emotional' Farewell Session," *Washington Post*, 4 December 1980.

13. Bradley H. Patterson, Jr., *The President's Cabinet: Issues and Answers*, Special Publication, American Society for Public Administration, May 1976, 106–11; Fred I. Greenstein, *The Hidden-Hand Presidency: Eisenhower As Leader* (New York: Basic Books, 1982), 113–124.

14. The National Security Council was established by the National Security Act of 1947 (61 Stat. 496; 50 U.S.C. 402), amended by the National Security Act Amendments of 1949 (63 Stat. 579; 50 U.S.C. 401 et seq.). The Energy Resources Council was established by the Energy Reorganization Act of 1974 (88 Stat. 1241; U.S.C. 5818). The Council on International Economic Policy was established by statute in the International Economic Policy Act of 1972 (86 Stat. 646). This statutorily authorized the council, which had been created by presidential memorandum the previous year. See Memorandum Establishing the Council on International Economic Policy. January 19, 1971, *Public Papers of the Presidents: Richard M. Nixon, 1971* (Washington, D.C.: Government Printing Office, 1972), 41.

15. The President's Economic Policy Board was established by Executive Order 11808 on 30 September 1974. See *Public Papers of the Presidents: Gerald R. Ford, 1974* (Washington, D.C.: Government Printing Office, 1975), 207.

16. The Council on Economic Policy was established by presidential memorandum on 2 February 1973. The Agricultural Policy Committee was established by presidential memorandum on 11 March 1976. See *Public Papers of the Presidents, Gerald R. Ford, 1976* (Washington, D.C.: Government Printing Office, 1979), 606.

17. The Council on Foreign Economic Policy was established by a letter from President Eisenhower to Joseph M. Dodge, 11 December 1954, Dodge Series, Correspondence Subseries, Box 1, Eisenhower Presidential Library, Abiline, Kansas.

18. Dwight D. Eisenhower, in his message to the Congress transmitting Reorganization Plan No. 9 of 1953, stated: "In order to make the work of the Council of Economic Advisers more effective at the top policy level of the executive branch, I am also asking the heads of several departments and agencies, or the representatives they may designate, to serve as an Advisory Board on Economic Growth and Stability, under the chairmanship of the Chairman of the Council of Economic Advisers. . . . It is contemplated that the Advisory Board on Economic Growth and Stability, supported by the existing staffs of the various departments and agencies, will meet frequently, and through its Chairman will keep me closely informed about the state of the national economy and the various measures necessary to aid in maintaining a stable prosperity." Special Message to the Congress Transmitting Reorganization Plan 9 of 1953 Concerning the council fo Economic Advisers, June 1, 1953, *Public Papers of the Presidents, Dwight D. Eisenhower, 1953*, 358.

19. *Economic Report of the President, 1954* (Washington, D.C.: Government Printing Office, 1954), 122.

20. *Economic Report of the President, 1962* (Washington, D.C.: Government Printing Office, 1962), 197.

21. Presidential memorandum on Establishment of a Cabinet Committee on Economic Growth, August 21, 1962. Presidential Office Files, Box 89A, Department of the Treasury File, John F. Kennedy Presidential Library, Boston, Massachusetts.

22. The Cabinet Committee on the Balance of Payments was later expanded in the spring of 1963 to include the special representative for trade negotiations, in the fall of 1965 to include the secretary of agriculture, and in November 1967 to include the secretary of transportation. See

Henry H. Fowler, Memorandum for the President on the Addition of the Secretary of Transportation to the Cabinet Committee on Balance of Payments, November 3, 1967, Lyndon B. Johnson Library, Austin, Texas.

23. Arthur Okun, "The Formulation of National Economic Policy," *Perspectives in Defense Management* (December 1968): 9–12.

24. For example, the key decision changing U.S. policy on trade preferences for developing countries was made through a White House assistant rather than the NSC staff. See President's Advisory Council on Executive Organization, "Organization for Foreign Economic Affairs," mimeographed, 17 August 1970, Appendix C, "Some Previous Attempts to Coordinate Foreign Economic Policy," 269–271.

25. Executive Order 11453, *Public Papers of the Presidents: Richard M. Nixon, 1969* (Washington, D.C.: Government Printing Office, 1971), 16.

26. See *Public Papers of the Presidents: Richard M. Nixon, 1973* (Washington, D.C.: Government Printing Office, 1975), 3–4.

27. For an account of the creation of the Economic Policy Board, see Roger B. Porter, *Presidential Decision Making* (New York: Cambridge University Press, 1980), 30–44.

28. Statement by the Press Secretary on the Formation of the Cabinet Councils, February 26, 1981, *Public Papers of the Presidents: Ronald Reagan, 1981* (Washington, D.C.: Government Printing Office, 1982), 166–167.

29. Okun, "National Economic Policy," 9–12.

30. Quoted in Roger B. Porter, "Organizing Economic Advice to the President: A Modest Proposal," *American Economic Review* 72 (1982): 357.

31. See *Papers Relating to the President's Departmental Reorganization Program* (Washington, D.C.: Government Printing Office, 1971).

32. President's message, 25 March 1971, in ibid., 11.

33. Ibid., 18.

34. Ibid., 235.

35. John Connally, interview with the author, Cambridge, Mass., November 1979.

36. Alexander L. George, "The Case for Multiple Advocacy in Foreign Policy Making," *American Political Science Review* 66 (1972): 752.

37. Sorensen, *Decision Making in the White House*, 62.

38. See Joseph M. Dodge, Report to the President on the Development and Coordination of Foreign Economic Policy, November 22, 1954, CFEP Office Series, Box 2, History CFEP (1), Dwight D. Eisenhower Presidential Library, Abiline, Kansas; President's Advisory Council on Executive Organization, "Organization for Foreign Economic Affairs," mimeographed, 17 August 1970.

39. I. M. Destler, *Making Foreign Economic Policy* (Washington, D.C.: Brookings Institution, 1980), 220.

Dick Cheney

Congressional Overreaching in Foreign Policy

Dick Cheney served as White House Chief of Staff under President Ford. From 1979 to 1989 he served in Congress, representing Wyoming. He is currently Secretary of Defense. Here he argues that by meddling in diplomacy, covert actions, and the commitment of troops abroad, Congress has not only exceeded both its constitutional authority and institutional competence but also compromised the president's ability to conduct the nation's foreign policy.

The eight years of President Reagan's Administration were a rocky period for legislative-executive relations in foreign policy. Broadly speaking, the sharper the disagreement between congressional Democrats and the Republican President over substantive issues, the more likely were those disagreements to spill over into procedural and constitutional turf battles. The procedural fights in turn would raise institutional jealousies that would feed back to harm substantive policies.

In the early months of President Bush's Administration, as these words are being written, it appears that players on both ends of Pennsylvania Avenue are trying to tone down the institutional rhetoric. The President, Speaker of the House and Majority Leader of the Senate all have been talking about the need for bipartisanship. Far be it for me to dissent here from this salutary tone. Nevertheless, one does have to prepare for eventualities. Sooner or later, under this President or a future one, some foreign policy issue is bound to provoke a sharp disagreement between the White House and Congress. Before that day comes, it is important to reflect on the institutional issues raised by the clashes just past.

This essay is about patterns of Congressional overreaching during the years of the Reagan Administration. By choosing that subject, I do not mean to suggest that overreaching was limited to Capitol Hill. Anyone who followed the Iran-Contra affair knows that not to have been so. However, congressional aggrandizement does seem less generally understood, more systemic and more institutionally ingrained, than does its White House counterpart. Members of Congress may be asking for bipartisanship, but they have not given up what I would consider to be some of the more problematic aspects of their institutional self-understanding.

This is a draft of a chapter which will appear in a book to be published in 1990 by the American Enterprise Institute. Reprinted with the permission of the American Enterprise Institute for Public Policy Research.

Posing the Issue

Congress and the President both have important roles to play in shaping the conduct of U.S. foreign policy. Both will have to be involved for any major policy to be successful over the long term. But this does not mean that all forms of joint participation work equally well. The odds for success become much worse if either branch steps beyond its institutional competence. It is crucial, therefore, to understand: (1) just what is the institutional competence of each branch: (2) what is the connection between institutional competence and constitutional authority; and (3) how has Congress, in an attempt to force joint participation, overstepped the bounds of its competence and authority with harmful effects.

I am posing these questions because I want to get beyond the usual legal arguments to look at the practical consequences of abusing the separation of powers. (For readers interested in the legal and constitutional history, I refer them to the relevant chapters in the Iran-Contra committees' minority report.[1]) The problem with most legal arguments is that they tend to become debates about the precise application of this or that group of words. In too many judicial opinions, the Constitution appears almost as if it were a collection of disembodied clauses, each with its own legal history, parceling power every which way. But individual clauses are not the best prisms for viewing the separation of powers, a subject suffusing the whole Constitution.

The Constitution does not really distribute powers at random. It does give the separate branches distinct levers for influencing the same set of policy decisions. But the powers are separated, and the levers of influence conferred, according to a consistent set of underlying principles. Broadly speaking, the Congress was intended to be a collective, deliberative body. When working at its best, it would slow down decisions, improve their substantive content, subject them to compromise, and help build a consensus behind general rules before they were to be applied to the citizen body. The Presidency, in contrast, was designed as a one-person office to insure it would be ready for action. Its major characteristics, to use the language of *Federalist* No. 70, were to be "decision, activity, secrecy and dispatch."[2]

I am convinced that the history of the past few years once again confirms the Framers' wisdom. When Congress stays within its capacities, it can be a helpful participant in formulating policy. In a wide range of recent disagreements with the President, however, the Congress has used policy levers that go well beyond the ones the Constitution intended for the legislative branch. The issue is not limited to a formal violation of a parchment document. When Congress steps beyond its capacities, it takes traits that can be helpful to collective deliberation and turns them into a harmful blend of vacillation, credit-claiming, blame avoidance and indecision. The real world effect often turns out, as Caspar Weinberger has said, not to be *transfer* of power from the President to the Congress, but a *denial* of power to the government as a whole.[3]

The following pages examine three policy areas: diplomacy, covert operations and war powers. In all three, congressional overreaching has systematic policy effects. It is important to be clear at the outset that my argument is about *systematic* effects, not individual policy disagreements. For example, Congress's efforts to dictate diplomatic bargaining tactics, as well as the efforts by individual members to conduct back channel negotiations of their own, make it extremely difficult for the country to sustain a consistent bargaining posture for an extended time period, whomever the President and whatever the policy. In intelligence, the problem goes beyond consistency to a more basic conflict between action and inaction. One proposal made in the wake of Iran-Contra would have required the President to notify Congress of all covert actions within 48 hours, without any exceptions. By refusing to allow the President any leeway, no matter how urgent the circumstances, that proposal would have set up a direct conflict between Congress's procedural requirements and the President's constitutional obligation to act. The War Powers Act combines both of these problems in one statute. Just as congressional diplomacy tilts the balance away from patient diplomacy, so does the War Powers Act tilt the balance away from a patient, measured application of force toward either a quick strike or inaction. And just as requiring 48 hour notification for all covert operations favors inaction over action in rare but important circumstances, so does the War Powers Act favor inaction over measured action in the more common circumstances in which that act might be applied. In all of these cases, the underlying issues are the same: the relationships between deliberation and action, and between procedure and substance. To explain why, let us begin with congressional diplomacy.

Congressional Diplomacy

Congressional diplomacy has two different aspects: (1) Congress's attempts to tie the President's negotiating hands, and (2) back channel negotiations conducted by some leading members of Congress with foreign governments. The first is familiar and therefore will be treated more briefly. I shall concentrate on one major bill to illustrate, but any of a dozen would do just as well.

Instructing the President: In 1987 and 1988, the House of Representatives added provisions to the Defense Authorization bill that would have required the President to abide by provisions of the unratified, decade old strategic arms limitation treaty between the United States and Soviet Union (SALT II). Although the House bills did not mention SALT II by name, they tried to prohibit the President from deploying weapons that would have taken our nuclear arsenals above three of the treaty's "sublimits" for submarines, missiles and bombers. The Senate rejected the House's sublimits in both years, but House and Senate conferees required the President to retire old submarines to keep the United States warhead total near the overall SALT II limit.

President Reagan opposed the restriction in both years because (1) the Soviet Union was violating other aspects of the SALT II treaty, (2) the Soviet Union was deploying 30 per cent more multiple warhead missiles (820) than the United States (550), (3) the President was in the midst of trying to negotiate a 50% reduction of nuclear arms in a Strategic Arms Reduction Treaty (START) and (4) unilateral adherence to SALT II would have undercut the President's negotiating position in the START talks. For tactical reasons, the President was willing to sign a bill in 1987 that required him to retire one old submarine. But in 1988, he decided to veto the authorization bill to make a principled defense of his position during an election year. House Democrats backed down, but they did not change their views about the propriety of the original bill.

No one can dispute Congress's constitutional power to determine what weapons should be funded and deployed. The issue therefore is not one of constitutional law, but of Congress's willingness to second guess the President's bargaining tactics. To put the point bluntly, liberal Democrats doubted the President was telling the truth when he said he was trying to negotiate a verifiable arms treaty that would involve major reductions. They seemed to believe that the best way to negotiate a treaty was to place limits on our side and then politely ask the Soviet Union to follow.

At least they were consistent. The framework almost exactly paralleled 1982, when liberal Democrats in the House failed by two votes to pass a nuclear freeze resolution that would have prevented us from deploying intermediate range missiles in Europe, even though the Soviets had already deployed similar missiles of their own. At that time, House Democrats said that deployment would make the Russians angry and break up Intermediate Nuclear Force (INF) negotiations. The President replied that we had to deploy—that is, we had to assure our defenses would be strong even if there were no agreement—before the Soviets would have a reason to talk. President Reagan's view prevailed, narrowly. The missiles were deployed, the Soviet Union returned to the bargaining table, and in 1988 a treaty was ratified that for the first time banned a whole class of nuclear weapons from the arsenals of both major superpowers.

There is an important lesson here that goes beyond the specific predispositions Republicans and Democrats have about military strength. Congress does have the constitutional power to prevent missiles from being built or deployed. When it makes those decisions based on its budgetary and strategic priorities, it is making the kind of decision a legislature is equipped institutionally to make. But trying to dictate bargaining tactics is another matter. President Reagan's record on INF shows that negotiating success with the Soviets requires a willingness to stick patiently to a tough strategy. But patience, the willingness to stand pat, is in reality a form of decisive action—the kind of action a single person is better able than a collective body to deploy over time. Congress, made up of 535 people most of whom have to stand for reelection every two years, finds it difficult to speak with one voice for a sustained time period. A significant number of its members at any given moment, on any given issue, are looking for quick results—something to show the voters before the next election.

It would be the better part of prudence, therefore, for Congress to maintain a collective silence in its formal lawmaking capacity about ongoing negotiations. Presidents do need, of course, to consult with members of Congress. Any negotiation that proceeds without paying attention to the need for Senate ratification, or the participation of both chambers in passing implementing legislation, is a negotiation that is headed for trouble. But consultation, advice and influence are far removed from binding instructions conveyed through formal legislative acts. There is time enough for formal action after a negotiation is finished, when Congress can deliberate responsibly and collectively about a real product.

Members as Diplomats

As troubling as congressional negotiating instructions may be, they pale when compared to the disturbing tendency of some members to conduct their own back channel negotiations with foreign leaders. Increasingly, members of Congress have set themselves up as alternative Secretaries of State. Senators and Representatives from both parties have crossed the line separating what I would consider to be legitimate legislative fact-finding from the realm of diplomatic communication. Some recent examples will show how serious the problem has become.

The Speaker and Nicaragua: The Speaker of the House symbolically represents the House's self-understanding of its role. The first example, therefore, will be about his actions at one of the many potential turning points in negotiations between the Communist government of Nicaragua and the Nicaraguan Democratic Resistance. To place the events in context, the Organization of American States was scheduled to meet in Washington in the middle of November, 1987.

On November 9, a few days before the OAS sessions, President Reagan announced for the first time that the United States would be willing to negotiate security issues with Nicaragua, but only if the representatives of four other Central American countries were also involved. The question of direct U.S.-Nicaragua talks had been a sticky one for some time. The Sandinistas were trying to portray the Resistance as puppets of the United States. Their aim was to negotiate a deal that would cut off U.S. support for the Contras in return for a promise that the Nicaraguan government would not export arms to the Communists in El Salvador and elsewhere. Left out of the Sandinista equation would have been any limitations on the military support Nicaragua had been receiving from the Soviet Union and Cuba, or any meaningful reforms that would move the Managua regime toward genuine political freedom.

President Reagan's November 9 statement was a carefully measured response to the ongoing stalemate. The President was saying that we are, and always have been, open to discussing some issues directly with Nicaragua and the other countries of Central America. But Nicaragua's main dispute is not with us, the President was saying. The Sandinistas still ought to begin direct talks with the Contras to negotiate a domestic political settlement conducive to pluralism and political freedom.

At this point, the Speaker of the House, Jim Wright, entered the picture. Here is *Congressional Quarterly's* description of the next few days.

> At his ornate office in the Capitol, Wright met with [Nicaraguan President Daniel] Ortega for more than an hour on Nov. 11. The next day, he met with Ortega again for nearly an hour, then spent about 90 minutes with three members of the Contra "directorate," the civilian leadership of the guerrilla force. Wright talked later in the day with Cardinal [Miguel] Obando [y Bravo] after he arrived in Washington from Managua.
>
> On Nov. 13, Wright travelled to the Vatican Embassy in Washington for a final 90-minute session between Ortega and Cardinal Obando. At that session, Ortega gave the Cardinal a copy of his government's multi-point plan for a cease-fire . . .
>
> [Rep. David E.] Bonior [D-Mich.], the House chief deputy majority whip, was the only other member of Congress at Wright's sessions with the Nicaraguans.
>
> In his sessions with Ortega, Wright apparently discussed in detail the Nicaraguan's proposal for implementing a cease-fire. Sources said the plan originally contained nearly 20 points but was eventually reduced to 11 points, partly as a result of the Wright-Ortega discussions.[4]

These three days of meetings clearly were a series of negotiations, under any ordinary understanding of that term. Interestingly, they were conducted in secret, without including or adequately informing the State Department. After the sessions were over, the Sandinista leader crowed to the press on November 13 that his dealings with Wright would "leave the Administration totally isolated."[5]

Other Members and Nicaragua: Speaker Wright's November 1987 meetings were not isolated examples. Unfortunately, they built upon, and helped lend a sense of legitimacy to, a growing pattern of legislative branch intrusions into a field that was clearly intended to be executive in character. Consider the following examples, all of which also involved Nicaragua.

In April 1985, the House decided against Contra aid by two votes. The next week, Ortega took a trip to Moscow. His trip was a public relations fiasco for House Democrats who had voted against the Contras. Shortly afterward, Reps. Bonior and George Miller (D-CA) visited Managua, where they reportedly held a series of meetings with government officials and barred U.S.embassy officials from attending. According to one unnamed House Democratic leader who was quoted in a press account, the meetings were "dangerously close to negotiations." The point, according to one report, was to inform the Sandinistas that unless their government took steps toward pluralism, some congressional Democrats would be likely to switch votes and support Contra aid.[6]

At least Miller and Bonior gave the embassy a summary of their meetings after the fact. Sometimes, not even that much occurs. The same press account said, for example, that shortly before the same 1985 House vote, Senator John Kerry of Massachusetts and Tom Harkin of Iowa made a similar trip to Managua. That time, the two Senators not only kept embassy officials out of the meeting, but they did not even give a report to them afterwards.

Members of Congress do not need a personal meeting to intrude in the realm of diplomacy. On March 20, 1984, while the U.S. was still legally aiding the Contras, 10 House Democrats—including then Majority Leader Wright, Michael Barnes, chairman of the Western Hemisphere subcommittee of the Foreign Affairs Committee, and other prominent members—sent the famous (or infamous) "Dear Commandante" letter to Ortega. After declaring their opposition to Contra aid, the signers said, "we want to commend you and the members of your government for taking steps to open up the political process of your country." Although those steps were barely visible and clearly opportunistic, the signers went on to urge Ortega to continue what he had started to "strengthen the hands of those in our country who desire better relations."[7] In other words, the letter was telling Ortega how to behave to strengthen the legislative position of those members of Congress who were opposed to official U.S. policy.

More Members, Other Countries: The following year, a different group of 13 non-leadership Democrats delivered a letter to Prime Minister Wilfried Martens of Belgium during the Prime Minister's state visit to the United States.[8] That letter mistakenly praised a (non-existent) "recent announcement by your Government to delay the initial deployment of Cruise missiles in your country." In fact, as one newspaper column noted, Martens strongly supported deployment against strong domestic political opposition.[9] As it turns out, the missiles were deployed, and their deployment was an essential building block in negotiating the INF

Treaty with the Soviet Union. The point, however, is not that these members of Congress were wrong. The point is that they stepped beyond the normal and fully legitimate realm of domestic political debate about foreign policy, to communicate directly with another government in an attempt to influence that government to behave in a manner that was contrary to U.S. foreign policy.

The problem, as I said earlier, is not limited to one party. One former Republican House member who stepped over what I think are appropriate lines was George Hansen of Idaho. Hansen made a ten day visit to Teheran in November 1979, two weeks after more than 60 Americans were taken hostage in the U.S. Embassy. His aim, Hansen said at the time, was to "get in on an unofficial basis and do business."[10]

Neither is the problem confined to the House. During the Iran-Contra hearings, the House and Senate investigating committees' received a series of 1986 State Department cables about American citizens who allegedly were visiting Eden Pastora "at [the] request of Sen. Jessie Helms." Pastora at that time was a Contra leader based south of Nicaragua. According to one of the cables (from Central America to Washington), the Americans agreed that *the United States* would send supplies to Pastora in return for his willingness to undertake specific activities on behalf of the Nicaraguan Resistance. In reply, the State Department fired back that it was "astounded" because the private citizens were "not in a position to commit the U.S. government."[11]

A Recurring Problem: The problem of private diplomacy is not new. In 1778, a Dr. George Logan was accused of meddling in negotiations betwen the United States and France. Although there was dispute over the facts, he was suspected by many Federalists of having been a secret envoy sent to France to represent the Jeffersonian Democrats. In response, Congress passed a law the next year that made it criminal for any citizen of the United States, without the permission of the U.S. government,

> Directly or indirectly [to] commence, or carry on, any verbal or written correspondence or intercourse with any foreign government, or any agent or officer thereof, with an intent to influence the measures or conduct of any foreign government, or of any officer or agent thereof, in relation to any disputes or controversies with the United States, or defeat the measures of the government of the United States.

The only exception in the act was for individuals seeking to redress a personal injury to themselves.[12]

The Logan Act is still a part of the U.S. Code, with only minor grammatical changes.[13] Although aimed at the most obvious level against private citizens, congressional debate at the time made it clear that the function belonged to the *executive* branch, and outrage was expressed not only at Dr. Logan's own role, but at the alleged support he received from members of the opposition political party who did not have the President's blessings. It is significant, as the noted constitutional historian Charles Warren wrote when he was Assistant Attorney General, that the more than two hundred pages of debate about the act are printed in the *Annals of Congress* under the heading, "Usurpation of Executive Authority."[14]

Unfortunately, political and legal difficulties have made the Logan act all but a dead letter in practical terms. As a result, it is important to find a less confrontational, more enforceable way to restore the President's constitutional role as the sole organ of diplomacy. To meet that objective, some of us drafted a measure in 1988 that would have required members of Congress to report any communications with foreign representatives within 48 hours after they occur. This modest proposal may not prevent individual members from overstepping the bounds, but at least it would insure that the government's only official channel knows what is going on.

The basic issue is not about a reporting requirement, however. Congress's diplomatic interventions undermine the country's ability to act effectively in the international arena. Domestic disputes over foreign policy are fully legitimate, but the Constitution's Framers were explicit about the dangers of projecting our internal disputes externally. Their debates referred to situations that almost exactly parallel the one in the 1984 "Dear Commandante" memorandum. Every foreign leader in a dispute with this country has an incentive to play upon divisions inside the United States. To the extent that we let members of Congress behave as if they are diplomats, we guarantee foreign opportunism under all future Presidents of either party. The United States needs to speak to other countries with one voice. Congress, by its nature, cannot do so. That is why the Framers separated the foreign policy powers as they did. While some other constitutional issues may be in dispute, there can be no doubt that the President was meant to be the "sole organ"—the eyes, ears and mouth—of this country's diplomacy.[15]

Covert Operations

The idea of a 48-hour "reverse notification" for members of Congress was originally proposed as an amendment to an ill advised 1988 attempt to revise the Intelligence Oversight Act of 1980. Under the 1980 law, all agencies and entities of the United States involved in intelligence activities are required to notify the House and Senate intelligence committees (or, under special conditions, the chairmen and ranking minority members of the two committees, and four leaders of the House and Senate) before beginning any significant, anticipated intelligence activity. The law also contemplated, however, that there might be some conditions under which prior notice would not be given. In those situations, it required the President "to fully inform the intelligence committees in a timely fashion."

Under this law, the intelligence committees have become significant players whose support any prudent Administration would do well to encourage. The 1980 law did not challenge the President's inherent constitutional authority to initiate covert actions. In fact, that law specifically denied any intention to require advance congressional approval for such actions. Nevertheless, Congress does have a very strong lever for controlling any operation that lasts more than a short period of time.

Operations undertaken without prior approval have to be limited to the funds available through a contingency fund. Constitutionally, Congress could abolish that fund and require project-by-project financing. Of course, such a decision would be suicidal because it would deprive the country of the ability to react quickly to breaking events. But because Congress does have this draconian power in principle, the intelligence committees can and do use the annual budget process to review every single ongoing operation. Any time Congress feels that an operation is unwise, it may step in to prohibit funds in the coming budget cycle from being used for that purpose. As a result, all operations of extended duration have the committees' tacit support. Considering how many people in Congress and the general public have reservations about all covert operations, this is an important political base for any Administration concerned about the country's long-term intelligence capabilities.

Proposed 48-Hour Rule: The intelligence committees can only review covert operations if they know about them, however. President Reagan did not notify the intelligence committees of his Administration's 1986 sales of arms to Iran for almost eleven months after signing a formal finding to authorize them. I do not think anyone in Congress believes this was timely. The important question for the future is, how should   Congress respond?

In 1988, the Senate passed and two House committees reported legislation that would have required the President under all conditions, with no exceptions, to notify Congress of all covert operations within 48 hours of their start. Early in 1989, Speaker Wright announced that the bill temporarily would be shelved "as an opening gesture of good faith on our part" toward the new Administration. However, the Speaker also specifically reserved the option to reintroduce the bill if the situation calls for it.[16] Therefore, the underlying theoretical issues remain to be addressed.

At the heart of the dispute over requiring notification within 48 hours was a deeper one over the scope of the President's inherent consitutional power. I believe the President has the authority, without statute, to use the resources placed at his disposal to protect American lives abroad and to serve certain other important foreign policy objectives. The range of the President's discretion does vary, as Justice Jackson said in his famous concurring opinion in the *Steel Seizure Case.* When the President's actions are consonant with express congressional authorizations, discretion can be at its maximum. A middle range of power exists when Congress is silent. Presidential power is at its lowest ebb when it is directly opposed to congressional mandate.[17] What is interesting about this typology, however, is that even when Congress speaks, and the President's power is at its lowest, Jackson acknowledged that there are limits beyond which Congress cannot legislate.[18] Those limits are defined by the scope of the inviolable powers inherent in the Presidential office itself.

Let me now apply this mode of analysis to the sphere of covert action. Congress was legislatively silent about covert action for most of American history, knowing full well that many broad ranging actions had been undertaken at Presidential initiative, with congressionally provided contingency funds.[19] For most of American history, therefore, Presidents were acting in the middle range of the authority Jackson described. Congress does have the power, however, to control the money and material resources available to the President for covert actions. The 1980 oversight act, and its predecessors since 1974, were attempts by Congress to place conditions on the President's use of congressionally provided resources. Those conditions, for the most part, have to do with providing information to Congress. Because Congress arguably cannot properly fulfill its legislative function on future money bills without information, the reporting requirements can be understood as logical and appropriate extensions of a legitimate legislative power.

The constitutional question is: what are the limits to what Congress may demand as an adjunct of its appropriations power? Broadly speaking, Congress may not use the money power to achieve purposes that it would be unconstitutional for Congress to achieve directly. It may not place a condition on the salaries of judges, for example, to prohibit the judges from spending any time (i.e., any part of their salaries) to reach a particular constitutional conclusion.[20] In the same way, Congress may not use its clearly constitutional powers over executive branch resources and procedures to invade an inherently Presidential power. For example, Congress may not use an appropriations rider to deprive the President of his authority as the "sole organ of diplomacy" to speak personally, or through any agent of his choice, with another government about any subject at all.

How would this reasoning apply to the proposed 48-hour rule? Congress properly justified the 1980 notification requirement in terms of the need for information as a necessary adjunct to the legislative power to appropriate money. By using this justification, Congress stood squarely within a line of cases upholding Congress's contempt power. In the 1821 case of *Anderson* v. *Dunn* the Supreme Court upheld the use of contempt as an implied power needed to implement others given expressly by the Constitution. In a statement that applies to all of the government's branches, the Court said: "There is not in the whole of that admirable instrument, a grant of powers which does not draw after it others, not expressed, but vital to their exercise; not substantive and independent, indeed, but auxiliary and subordinate."[21]

Using this reasoning, the Court argued though courts were vested with the contempt power by statute, they would have been able to exercise that power without a statute. For the same reason, the court held, Congress must have inherent authority to exercise a similar power.[22] Later cases tried to circumscribe Congress's contempt power, but the power itself was always held to be an adjunct to Congress's legislative functions and therefore to rest on an implied constitutional foundation.[23]

The Court's argument might seem to support Congress's implied right to demand information. But what happens if one branch's right to demand information confronts another implied power, equally well grounded on an explicit constitutional foundation, claimed by another one of the government's branches? That was the issue in the executive privilege case of *U.S.* v. *Nixon*. In that case, we learned that the decision in any specific case will depend upon the competing claims of the two branches at odds with each other.

The proposed 48-hour bill explicitly recognized the President's inherent power to initiate covert actions. The 1980 oversight act and the 48-hour bill both took pains to say that by requiring notification, Congress was not asserting a right to approve Presidential decisions in advance. But if the President has the inherent power to initiate covert actions, then the same rule about implied powers that gives Congress the right to demand information, also gives the President the implied powers he may need to put his acknowledged power into effect.

In most cases, there is no conflict between the President's power to initiate an action, and requiring the President to notify the intelligence committees (or a smaller group of leaders) of that operation in advance. In a few very rare circumstances, however, there can be a direct conflict. Consider a clear cut example from the Carter Administration.

According to Admiral Stansfield Turner, who was the Director of Central Intelligence at the time, there were three occasions, all occurring while Americans were being held hostage in Iran, in which the President Carter withheld notification during an ongoing operation. In each case, Turner said, "I would have found it very difficult to look . . . a person in the eye and tell him or her that I was going to discuss this life threatening mission with even half a dozen people in the CIA who did not absolutely have to know."[25] Of the three cases mentioned by Turner, the one that raised the key issue most directly occurred when notification was withheld for about three months until six Americans could be smuggled out of the Canadian Embassy in Teheran. In that operation, the Canadian government—whose own embassy was being placed at extreme risk—apparently made withholding notification a condition of their participation.[26] Since Congress cannot tell another government what risks that government should be willing to take with the safety of its own personnel, the decision to go forward had to be made on Canada's terms or not at all. Under these conditions, the President could not have fulfilled his constitutional obligation to protect American lives if he insisted on notifying Congress within 48 hours.

The Iranian hostage examples show that the situations under which notification may have to be withheld depend not on how much time has elapsed, but on the character of the operations themselves.[27] There can be no question that when other governments place specific security requirements on cooperating with the United States, the no-exceptions aspect of the proposed 48-hour rule would be equivalent to denying the President his constitutionally inherent power to act.

Leaks: Supporters of the 48-hour bill tried to respond to the concerns about foreign government cooperation by sidestepping the precise issue and describing the concern about congressional leaks as being ill founded. I wish that were so. It is true that President Reagan gave timely reports to the Intelligence Committees about every operation during his Administration (except the Iran arms sales), and that most of the information was kept secure. It is wrong to suggest, however, that Congress is leak proof. An entire chapter of the minority report of the Iran-Contra investigating committees was devoted to congressional leaks.[28]

It is bad enough when any member of Congress or staff person discloses classified information. It is far more serious when a leak comes from the so-called Gang of Eight (House and Senate Intelligence Committee chairmen and ranking minority members, Speaker and Minority Leader of the House, Majority and Minority Leader of the Senate).[29] This is the select group the oversight act designates for notification of operations considered too sensitive to be shared with the full committees. But the most remarkable situation of all comes when a member of this group tries to justify leaks as a matter of policy.

That is exactly what happened during the closing weeks of the 100th Congress. The 48 hour bill never came up for House floor debate because of the public outcry over a possible leak by the Speaker of the House. At his September 20 daily press briefing, Speaker Wright told reporters: "We have received clear testimony from CIA people that they have deliberately done things to provoke an overreaction on the part of the government in Nicaragua."[30] Based on the press reports, Minority Leader Robert Michel and I sent a letter the next day to the House Select

Committee on Standards of Official Conduct (the "ethics committee"), asking it to investigate whether the Speaker had violated Rule 48 of the House, governing the disclosure of classified information.[31]

It would be wrong of me at this stage, before the Ethics Committee concludes its investigation, to comment on or speculate about whether a leak did occur. Whatever the conclusion on this matter, however, the Speaker's immediate public response to the issue was troubling. "The fact that a matter is classified secret, doesn't mean it's sacrosanct and immune from criticism," Wright told a group of reporters. "It is not only my right but my responsibility to express publicly my opposition to policies I think are wrong."[32] The premise underlying this statement is not new. At least one Senator and one former member of the House have been quoted as saying similar things.[33] But familiarity in this case does not breed acceptance. If Congress is to have any role in overseeing covert operations, it must take seriously its responsibility to protect the information it receives. What Wright asserted was that it might be acceptable for a single member of Congress to "blow" a covert action, with all the danger that implies, by discussing it overtly.

Now consider the Speaker's stated position in light of (1) the characteristic differences between a legislature and an executive, and (2) the fact that a decision to leak in effect is a decision to kill an operation. Virtually no policy of any consequence will have unanimous support in a democratic legislature. That may be good for deliberation, but makes it very tough to maintain operational security. If more members took the Speaker's position, maintaining secrecy after congressional notification would not just be hard: it would be literally impossible.[34] There would be a direct conflict between notification and the country's ability to do anything covertly. That is one reason—however important reporting and consultation may be—why the final decision about when to notify Congress about unusually sensitive cases is a decision that ultimately must rest with the President.

The Constitutional Balance: So, on the one side of the scale, we see from the Canadian example, and from the problem of leaks, that the President's implied power to withhold notification may, in rare and extraordinary cases, be a *necessary* adjunct to the inherent power to act. What is on Congress's side of the constitutional scale to warrant notification within 48 hours, without any exceptions? The best argument, to quote the Senate Intelligence Committee's 1988 report, is that notification is needed "to provide Congress with an oportunity to exercise its responsibilities under the Constitution."[35] The problem is that there is no legislative power that requires notification under all conditions during any precisely specified time period. All Congress needs to know is whether to continue funding ongoing operations. We have had that information in every case, with the exception of President Carter's and President Reagan's hostage-related Iran initiatives.

I suppose you could argue that failure to notify might, in the extreme, deprive us of our ability to decide about continuing to fund a particular operation. Iran-Contra was such an extreme. But the choice is not one-sided. The price of assuring notification about all operations within a specific time period is to make some potentially life-saving operations impossible. On the scale of risks, I am more concerned about depriving the President of his ability to act than I am about Congress's alleged inability to respond. I feel this way not because I am sanguine about every decision Presidents might take. Rather, it is because I am confident Congress eventually will find out in this leaky city about decisions of any consequence. When that happens, Congress has the political tools to take retribution against any President whom it feels withheld information without adequate justification. President Reagan learned this dramatically in the Iran-Contra affair. It is a lesson no future President is likely to forget.

Underlying Issue—Substitution for Public Debate: Underlying the dispute over notification is a more basic issue. Congress insists on notification because the executive's consultations with the intelligence committees substitute for the open debate and deliberation available in other policy arenas. The committees thus serve as a forum for mediating the tension between the Constitution's two-sided concern for security and informed consent. On the whole, the committees are not simply barriers for Presidents to overcome. They can help Presidents build needed political support when the normal public tools cannot be used.

But what happens if there is no consent? That is, what if the committee, or a significant proportion of its members, thinks a particular covert operation is a bad idea? Sometimes, the committee can persuade the executive branch to change its mind. But what if persuasion does not work?

One answer offered by some of my colleagues is that no covert action should be undertaken unless it is suported by a bipartisan consensus. It is a good idea to begin from a presumption in favor of bipartisanship, but wishing for consensus provides no guidance about how to behave when there are real disagreements. To insist upon consensus as a precondition for action is equivalent to saying the President should not act in the face of disagreement. In effect, it is equivalent to taking the President's power and giving it to Congress. In fact, demanding consensus could be worse than requiring an up or down vote. If taken seriously, the President would need the support of a super-majority before he could do anything. He might even need unanimity, if more members come to accept the view that leaking is legitimate. A consensus requirement, therefore, would be a decision rule weighted heavily toward the inaction side of any action-versus-inaction dispute. In the real world of breaking events, it is important to recognize that inaction *is* a form of action or decision.

To require or expect a consensus before action, in other words, is only one possible answer to questions that should be articulated more clearly and openly. Some of the questions are: Who should hold what levers at what stage of the process? Under what political and legislative conditions should the presumption be weighted toward the President or toward Congress? That is, what rules should decide who prevails under conditions of stalemate? These questions apply not only to covert operations, but to national security more generally. To broaden the discussion, therefore, I turn now to the War Powers Act.

War Powers

Like the proposed 48 hour bill, the War Powers Resolution [36] is a classic example of the problems with "never again" legislation. The act was written to insure that the United States would "never again" be drawn into a war without a specific congressional declaration authorizing U.S. participation.* The main "teeth" consisted of four provisions. (1) The President was required to submit a report to the Speaker of the House and President pro tempore of the Senate, within 48 hours, describing the reasons for introducing U.S. armed forces into hostilities, or into situations in which imminent involvement in hostilities was clearly indicated by the circumstances, or under certain other conditions. (2) The President was required to terminate the involvement of U.S. forces within 60 calendar days, unless Congress specifically declared war or extended the time period. (3) Congress may require the President to withdraw U.S. forces at any time by passing a concurrent resolution—a form of congressional action that does not require a Presidential signature. (4) Neither appropriations acts nor treaties count as congressional authorizations to use force, even if the use of force is clearly required by the terms of a previously ratified treaty.

The third provision needs little discussion because it involves a legislative veto of the sort the Supreme Court declared unconstitutional in 1983.[37] The others have never been tested authoritatively in court, but the entire framework strikes me as being unworkable and of dubious constitutionality. The War Powers Resolution explicitly assumes, and states, that the President may not constitutionally use force without a formal declaration of war or statutory authorization unless the country is under attack.[38] Only upon this assumption does the act's most essential feature—its use of the clock—make any sense. In the view of the act's main sponsors, the sixty day clock was granting the President authority that it was fully within Congress's constitutional power to withhold. That authority was set to expire after two months because that should be enough time for Congress to reauthorize. If Congress fails to so reauthorize, the sponsors concluded that the Constitution requires withdrawal because the President has no independent authority to act without Congress.[39]

I cannot accept such a limited view of the President's inherent constitutional powers. When the Constitutional Convention debated the war power on August 17, 1787, it decided to change draft language that would have given Congress the power to *make* war to the power to *declare* war. James Madison and Elbridge Gerry defended the change in the congressional power by saying it was necessary for "leaving the Executive the power to repel sudden attacks." Because of this statement, the advocates of a weak executive have claimed that the convention intended to limit the President's inherent power to that single situation. What these advocates fail to note, however, is that in the very next speech of the same debate, Roger Sherman said that the new language giving Congress only the power to declare war would mean that the President would have the power "to commence war" and not simply defend against invasion.[40] It is no wonder, therefore, that the narrow view of the President's power has been rejected throughout American history. From the earliest years, Presidents have deployed force without statutory authorization for purposes well beyond a defense against sudden attacks.[41]

I believe the Constitution gives the President not only the power, but the obligation to protect American lives, to enforce valid treaties and to defend other vital U.S. national interests. But the precise boundary of the President's inherent

---

*Let us put aside, for the moment, the historical fact that the Tonkin Gulf Resolution, authorizing the Vietnam War, clearly would have satisfied the terms of the War Powers Act.

power is not crucial to my argument. Once one accepts the idea that there is *any* inherent Presidential power to act, the framework of the War Powers Act collapses of its own weight. Whatever the boundary, if the President's power to act comes directly from the Constitution, and not from Congress, then the same conditions that make an action valid on the first day of a crisis, would make the same action valid on the sixty-first day. The Constitution talks about who may exercise what power. It does not talk about how long. Congress *cannot* constitutionally set up a framework that declares an inherent Presidential power to be inoperative after a specific date.

I promised earlier, however, that I would not let my argument rest solely on legal abstractions. If the United States has to use force for an extended period, it clearly would be better for the country if the President were to show the world that he had support for what he is doing. Unfortunately, the War Powers Act paradoxically seems to make effective interbranch cooperation more difficult instead of less. It grates against the underlying logic of the separation of powers and brings Congress's institutional proclivities to bear in exactly the ways the Framers understood would be harmful.

To understand why this is so, it is worth thinking about what a sixty day deadline could mean. The ticking clock could have at least three dangerous effects. It could easily encourage Presidents to escalate the use of force in the hope of obtaining a quick victory. In addition, it declares to our allies that our treaties express wishes, not dependable obligations. Finally, it tells any adversary that rather than negotiate, it should wait us out for sixty days to see whether we are serious.

These dangers arise from the way Congress works. By forcing a withdrawal in the absence of a specific congressional authorization, the act gives the political advantage to those members who oppose the President. Because bills have to go through a multi-stage process—House committee, House floor, Senate committee, Senate floor, conference committee, and then back to the House floor and Senate floor—it is always easier for opponents to derail a controversial bill than for supporters to pass it. The War Powers Resolution tries to get around this with expedited procedures to guarantee an initial House and Senate vote within a prescribed time period. But one vote cannot ensure that Congress will reach a conclusion. Because the act rests on the assumption that the power at issue comes from Congress, it preserves the constitutional right of both chambers to amend whatever resolution it may choose to discuss. As a result, the act, as a matter of principle, cannot assure an agreement between the two chambers. That is more than enough of a wedge for a determined set of opponents or fence straddlers.

The opponents and fence straddlers will be abetted by Congress's institutional tendencies. Several recent studies of the act have shown that Congress typically tries to avoid responsibility for a clear decision, avoids confrontation when Presidents refuse to invoke the Act's terms, and prefers instead to praise successful Presidential actions or criticize unsuccessful ones after the fact.[42] In 1987, for example, the Senate spent a long time debating whether the War Powers Act should have been triggered by the President's decision to have the U.S. Navy escort reflagged Kuwaiti oil tankers in the Persian Gulf. The net result was a resolution that did nothing more than promise a future debate and decision. When it became apparent in 1988 that the President's policy was bearing positive fruits—largely because our allies and the Gulf countries finally became convinced we were not going to cut and run—the issue was dropped.

The War Powers Act's supporters say that the Senate's non-decision was possible only because President Reagan, like all of his predecessors, refused to submit the kind of report that would have triggered an expedited vote. But who can have any doubt, after debates over the order of battle, and after the Senate's final action, that a formal use of the act probably would have produced only a short term extension of the deadline to allow more second guessing in the next round? Formally invoking the act would not have changed the political realities and therefore would not be likely to have changed the result.

The root question raised by the War Powers Act is not about the desirability of consultation, deliberation, or formal resolutions of congressional support. The more basic question, as I said in connection with intelligence oversight, is about finding an appropriate balance that will encourage deliberation without destroying the ability to act. I am firmly convinced that Congress would be no less likely to deliberate if there were no War Powers Act than when there is one. If anything, the absence of a sixty-day crutch would be more likely to force Congress to find a common denominator with the president. Meanwhile, as Congress goes through its normal bargaining gyrations, the nation's adversaries would at least be aware that the country's highest elected official is empowered to maintain a predictable course.

The War Powers Act therefore should be repealed. The idea of a ticking clock is based on wrongheaded constitutional assumptions that produce mischievous and dangerous results. Congress has plenty of constitutional and political power to stop a President whenever it wants to. Anyone who doubts this should look at the long list of foreign policy limitation amendments to the appropriations acts of the past decade. If Congress does not have the will to support or oppose the President definitively, the nation should not be paralyzed by Congress's indecision.

Conclusion

At its best, Congress is a deliberative body whose internal checks and balances favor delay as a method for stimulating compromise. At its worst, it is a collection of 535 individual, separately elected politicians, each of whom seeks to claim credit and avoid blame. Whichever of these faces Congress may put on at any given moment, the legislative branch is ill equipped to handle the foreign policy tasks it has taken upon itself over the past 15 years.

The purpose of the United States Constitution is to protect and promote liberty. But protecting liberty has at least two facets. In domestic policy, it has to do with insuring that proposed changes in law receive a proper airing to guard against minority or majority factional tyranny. The emphasis, therefore, is on forcing compromise and coalition, with the constitutional preference—albeit not always the practice—weighted toward inaction until compromise has been achieved.

The other aspect of liberty has to do with preservation and protection. According to the Declaration of Independence, governments are instituted not to create rights (which are "inalienable") but to secure them. Securing rights means, among other things, preserving the government's ability to react internationally to countries that may want to harm us. In the face of danger, a tilt toward inaction would have just the opposite effect from a tilt toward inaction in domestic law. Instead of helping secure our liberty, it would help those foreign powers who want to endanger it. That is why the Constitution allowed a much greater scope for executive power in foreign than in domestic policy.

Underlying all this was the Framers' hard headed view of the tough world of international politics. They saw a world, much like today's, in which at least some states would work actively against our interests. They saw a world in which we would have adversarial relationships as well as friendly ones, a world in which force might have to buttress reason, a world in which there would always be some nation eager to exploit an inability to respond. Their world was different from ours in some important ways. Technology has shrunk the globe, making the need for quick response and predictability of purpose all that much more important. But the fundamentals of human nature—from the motivations of sovereign states to the proclivities of domestic politicians—remain unchanged. We would do well, therefore, to reinvigorate the Framers' understanding of the separation of powers as we head toward the 21st century.

Notes

This is a draft prepared for a March 14-15, 1989 American Enterprise Institute conference, "Foreign Policy and the Constitution." It was written before Mr. Cheney was nominated to be Secretary of Defense. It should be read, therefore, as a statement of his personal views.

1. U.S. House of Representatives, Select Committee to Investigate Covert Arms Transactions with Iran and U.S. Senate, Select Committee On Secret Military Assistance to Iran and the Nicaraguan Opposition, 100th Congress, 1st Session, *Report of the Congressional Committees Investigating the Iran-Contra Affair, With Supplemental, Minority, and Additional Views*, H.Rept. 100-433, S.Rept. 100-216 (Washington, D.C.: 1987), *Minority Report*, chap. 2-4, pp. 457-79.

2. Alexander Hamilton, James Madison, and John Jay, *The Federalist* (Jacob Cooke, ed., 1961), No. 70, p. 471-72. Herafter cited as *Federalist*.

3. "Contrary to the political maxim that power abhors a vacuum, it is simply *not* the case that powers removed or stripped away from one branch will find a home in another. Power can be dissipated and lost. There are some tasks that one branch can perform that others simply cannot." Caspar Weinberger, "Non-Partisan National Security Policy: History, War Powers and the Persian Gulf," remarks prepared for delivery by Secretary of Defense Weinberger to the Naval Postgraduate School, Monterey California, November 2, 1987, as printed in U.S. Department of Defense, News Release 564-87, of the same date.

4. John Felton, "Nicaragua Peace Process Moves to Capitol Hill," *Congressional Quarterly*, November 14, 1987, p. 2791.

5. *Ibid.*, p. 2789.

6. Rowland Evans and Robert Novak, "Dash to Managua," *The Washington Post*, May 15, 1985.

7. Letter from Jim Wright *et al.* to Commandante Daniel Ortega, March 20, 1984.

8. Letter from Ronald V. Dellums *et al.* to Prime Minister Wilfried Martens, January 11, 1985.

9. Rowland Evans and Robert Novak, "Message to Martens," *The Washington Post*, February 6, 1985, p. A19.

10. John Felton, "Iran: Tensions Mount as Crisis Continues," *Congressional Quarterly*, December 1, 1979, p. 2704.

11. U.S. Congress, 100th Congress, First Session, Joint Hearings Before the Senate Select Committee on Secret Military Assistance to Iran and the Nicaraguan Opposition and the House Select Committee to Investigate Covert Arms Transactions with Iran, *The Iran-Contra Investigation*, Vol. 100-5, pp. 571-75. See also Vol. 100-3, pp. 92, 387 and Vol. 100-5, pp. 26-27.

12. 1 Stat. 613 (1799).

13. 18 U.S.C. 953.

14. Charles Warren, Assistant AttorneyGeneral, *History of Laws Prohibiting Correspondence With a Foreign Government and Acceptance of a Commission,* U.S. Senate, 64th Congress, 2d Sess., S.Doc. 64–696 (1917), p. 7. See also, *Annals of Congress,* Fifth Congress, 3d Sess., (Dec. 3, 1798 - March 3, 1789), pp. 2487–2721.

15. See Iran-Contra *Minority Report,* chap. 3, pp. 463–66 and chap. 4, pp. 472–73.

16. John Goshko, "Wright, in 'Good Faith,' Delays Legislation Requiring Fast Notice of Covert Acts," *The Washington Post,* February 1, 1989; Bill Gertz, "House Won't Ask 48-hour Disclosure of Covert Operations," *The Washington Times,* February 1, 1989; Michael Oreskes, "Wright in Gesture to Bush, Shelves Bill on Covert Acts," *The New York Times,* February 1, 1989.

17. *Youngstown Sheet and Tube Co.* v. *Sawyer* 343 U.S. 579, 635–38 (1952).

18 *Ibid.* at 645.

19. For a summary, see U.S. House of Representatives, 100th Congress, First Session, Select Committee to Investigate Covert Arms Transactions with Iran and U.S. Senate, 100th Congress, First Session, Select Committee On Secret Military Assistance to Iran and the Nicaraguan Opposition, *Report of the Congressional Committees Investigating the Iran-Contra Affair,* H.Rept. 100–433, S.Rept. 100–216 (November 1987), pp. 467–69.

20. For a somewhat analogous but less absurd case, see *Brown* v. *Califano* 627 F. 2d 1221 (1980).

21. *Anderson* v. *Dunn,* 6 Wheat. 204, 225–26 (1821).

22. *Ibid.* at 628–29.

23. *Kilbourn* v. *Thompson,* 103 U.S. 168 (1881) read the power narrowly, but *McGrain* v. *Dougherty,* 273 U.S. 135 (1927) and *Sinclair* v. *U.S.,* 279 U.S. 263 (1929) in turn read *Kilbourn* narrowly. Later cases have tended to involve conflicts between the contempt power and the First Amendment, *Watkins* v. *U.S.,* 354 U.S. 178 (1957) and *Barenblatt* v. *U.S.,* 360 U.S. 109 (1959).

24. *U.S.* v. *Nixon* 418 U.S. 683 (1974).

25. U.S. House of Representatives, Permanent Select Committee on Intelligence, Subcommittee on Legislation, 100th Cong., 1st Sess., *Hearings on H.R. 1013, H.R. 1371, and Other Proposals Which Address the Issue of Affording Prior Notice of Covert Actions to the Congress,* April 1 and 8, June 10, 1987, p. 45. See also 46, 49, 58, 61.

26. *Ibid.,* p. 158. Also see: Letter from Secretary of Defense Frank Carlucci to David Boren, chairman of the Senate Select Committee on Intelligence, August 8, 1988.

27. It is worth emphasizing that the proposed bill would have required notification within 48 hours of an operation's start—that is, when the U.S. began putting people in place, not when the operation is finished.

28. Iran-Contra *Iran-Contra Minority Report,* ch. 13, pp. 575–80.

29. The Iran-Contra Minority Report indicated two occasions when there apparently were inadvertent, unauthorized disclosures from past Senate committee members in this group of eight. *Ibid.,* p. 577.

30. "Wright Says CIA Operatives Aim at Provoking Sandinistas," by Jim Drinkard, Associated Press wire service, September 20, 1988; "CIA Attempted to Provoke Sandinistas, Wright Asserts," by Joe Pichirallo, *The Washington Post,* September 21, 1988, A1 and A28; "CIA Tied to Nicaragua Provocations," by Susan F. Rasky, *The New York Times,* September 21, 1988; "Wright Draws Fire for Spilling Secrets," by Bill Gertz and Peter LaBarbera, *The Washington Times,* September 21, 1988, A1 and A11.

31. See also H.Res. 561, 100th Congress, 2d Session, filed September 30 by the six Republican members of the House Select Committee on Intelligence.

32. "Wright's Confident House Panels Will Drop Complaints About CIA Disclosures," by Jim Drinkard, Associated Press wire service, September 26, 1988; "Congressmen Have Right to Reveal Secrets, Wright Says," by Bill Gertz and Peter LaBarbera, *The Washington Times,* September 27, 1988, A1.

33. (1) "The late Rep. Leo Ryan told me (in 1975) that he would condone such a leak if it was the only way to block an ill conceived operation." See Daniel Schorr, "Cloak and Dagger Relics," *The Washington Post,* November 14, 1985, A23. (2) Senator Joseph Biden, then a member of the Intelligence Committee, told a reporter he had "twice threatened to go public with covert action plans by the Reagan Administration that were harebrained." See Brit Hume, "Mighty Mouth," *The New Republic,* September 1, 1986, p. 20.

34. In the 1970s, when operations had to be reported to many more committees, former Director of Central Intelligence William Colby said that "every new project submitted to this

procedure leaked, and the 'covert' part of CIA's covert action seemed almost gone." See William Colby, *Honorable Men* (1978), p. 423.

35. U.S. Senate, 100th Congress, 2d Session, Select Committee on Intelligence, *Intelligence Oversight Act of 1988*, S.Rept. 100–276 (Jan. 27, 1988), p. 21.

36. P.L. 93–148 [H.J.Res. 542], 87 Stat. 555, 50 U.S.C. 1541–48, passed over the President's veto November 7, 1973.

37. *Immigration and Naturalization Service* v. *Chadha* 462 U.S. 919 (1983).

38. P.L. 93–148, Sec. 2 (c).

39. See, for example, U.S. Senate, Committee on Foreign Relations, 92nd Congress, 2nd Sess., *War Powers*, S.Rept. 92–606, to accompany S.2956 (Feb. 9, 1972), pp. 4, 12.

40. Max Farrand, *The Records of the Federal Convention of 1787*, (New Haven, Conn.: Yale University Press, 1937), 4 vols., Vol. II, pp. 318–19.

41. See Abraham D. Sofaer, *War, Foreign Affairs and Constitutional Power* (1976), *passim*. Also see J. T. Emerson, "War Powers Legislation," 74 *W. Va. L. Rev.* 53, 88–119 (1972). Emerson's article ends with a long listing of the occasions on which force was used without a declaration of war. A revised version of the list appears in U.S. House of Representatives, Committee on Foreign Affairs, 93rd Cong., 1st Sess., *War Powers*, Hearings Before the Subcommittee on National Security Policy and Scientific Developments, Exhibit II, pp. 328–376 (1973).

42. See Pat M. Holt, *The War Powers Resolution* (Washington, D.C.: American Enterprise Institute, 1978), p. 33; Robert F. Turner, *The War Powers Resolution: Its Implementation in Theory and Practice* (Philadelphia, Pa.: Foreign Policy Research Institute, 1983), pp. 119–25.

Zbigniew Brzezinski

Deciding Who Makes Foreign Policy

Zbigniew Brzezinski was the head of the National Security Council under President Carter. In this article he details the long-standing tension between the State Department and the national security advisor over the formulation and coordination of American foreign policy. Given the fact that there are diplomatic, intelligence, and military components to foreign policy, Brzezinski insists that the coordination of these three must of necessity be achieved above the department level. Accordingly, he proposes that the national security advisor be upgraded to Director of National Security Affairs, subject to confirmation by the Senate, and that the Secretary of State's responsibilities henceforth be confined exclusively to managing the diplomatic dimension of foreign policy.

If one thing should have been made clear by George P. Shultz's current stewardship as Secretary of State, it is that the besetting problem of who makes foreign policy is not the product of a conflict of personalities. [This article was written in 1983, when Shultz was Secretary of State—ED.] The issue, as posed in recent years, is whether primacy in the area belongs in the State Department or in the National Security Council (N.S.C.). When Henry Kissinger headed the N.S.C. in the Nixon White House, it was alleged to be his ego and his taste for the Machiavellian that kept the Secretary of State, William P. Rogers, out of the center of things. When I occupied the same White House post under President Carter, it was said that my instinct for the jugular gave the N.S.C. an excessive share of foreign-policy initiatives, at the expense of Secretary of State Cyrus R. Vance.

Yet in Mr. Shultz and the current N.S.C. chief, William P. Clark, we have two men who, to all appearances, enjoy a relationship untroubled by ego trips in either direction. Indeed, Mr. Clark is generally perceived as not deeply involved in the complex substance of key foreign issues. Nonetheless, in recent months, the press has noted that influence has been gravitating away from the experienced Mr. Shultz to the able but relatively inexpert Mr. Clark. Surely that speaks for itself, suggesting that the problem that has bedeviled a succession of Presidents is not one of individuals but of organization.

What is the proper arrangement for the shaping of United States foreign policy? The traditional answer—that the policy should be molded by the Secretary of State—seems to have been proving increasingly inadequate. It would appear that the old formula can no longer cope either with the challenges we face abroad or with the distribution of power in Washington among key agencies involved in promoting national security—of which foreign policy is a part.

This institutional difficulty has, in fact, been perennial in the modern age. For many years, the main struggle over foreign policy was between the Secretary of State and the Secretary of Defense. It was only later that public attention shifted to the conflicts between the Secretary of State and the national security adviser.

Of course, the personal element does enter into it, as it does into every human endeavor. A reading of the various relevant memoirs of recent years leaves little doubt that personal conflict did affect the relationship between Mr. Kissinger and Mr. Rogers, although one cannot discern very profound policy differences between them. There was also evidence of conflict, occasionally intense, between Secretary of State Alexander M. Haig Jr. and the former national security adviser Richard V. Allen; again, policy disagreements do not seem to have played a significant role. During the Carter years, the situation was somewhat different. I have denied many times that there was any personal conflict between me and Mr. Vance. But there were occasions when we had rather dissimilar views on policy issues.

These differences, personal or substantive, tend to spill over and produce wider interagency conflicts. And recent years have seen a full measure not only of the traditional conflict between the State and Defense Departments but of the newer conflict between State and the N.S.C. for pre-eminence in the making of foreign policy.

Control over turf is a very important bureaucratic asset. Institutions tend to fight over areas of responsibility as much as over policy. And policy differences or personality conflicts between principals tend to intensify and accentuate institutional conflicts over turf. Currently, there is a new phenomenon in the area of foreign policy. I call it "parcelization," a term used in rural economics to describe the dividing up of land holdings into smaller parcels—and, progressively, into still smaller ones.

Today, the making of foreign policy involves a pronounced degree of parcelization. Take the Middle East. There was a period when the State Department had preeminence in this region, but lately the initiative seems to have passed to the White House. A new Presidential negotiator for the Middle East, Robert C. McFarlane, has been plucked out of the N.S.C. to assume more direct personal responsibility for this area of nonactivity.

On Central America, policy is apparently under White House control, exercised primarily by the national security adviser, Mr. Clark, though he does not have any extensive experience in the Central American problems. The State Department appears increasingly to be playing a secondary role, while the Defense Department and the C.I.A. actively promote their own special ventures.

On Far Eastern questions, and particularly in the relationship with China, the action seems to be primarily dominated by the Defense and Commerce Departments, with the State Department playing a secondary role.

On Europe, the State Department appears able to maintain its traditional predominance in the more conventional areas of United States-European relations, such as diplomacy and defense policy. At the same time, however, the shaping of our relations with Europe is being increasingly shared with the Commerce Department and the President's special trade representative.

On arms control, there appears to be a three-way split. The State Department seems to be playing a major role in shaping our proposals and defining our negotiating strategy on secondary levels, for the Secretary of State does not seem to be too interested or well versed in the intricacies of this problem. Lately, even this secondary responsibility has come to be shared increasingly with the Defense Department. On a higher conceptual level, the job of framing some long-term consensus on our arms-control and strategic policies has been given to a special bipartisan commission of experts drawn from public life.

In the making of national security policy, we have, in effect, a chaotic non-system. And that nonsystem, I think, reflects some of the persistent institutional problems that have eluded solution in recent years. Where, then, does the solution lie?

To start with, it is important to remember that the position I had the privilege of holding in the White House carries two titles. The formal one is Assistant to the President for National Security Affairs. The informal title, not to be found in any Governmental document or legislative act, and yet widely used by the press and by Presidents themselves, is that of national security adviser. And these two titles encapsulate the two roles that these close associates of the President have tended to perform.

As Assistant for National Security Affairs, the incumbent is meant to be an objective and detached processor of key issues. He is supposed to define these issues and present them for Presidential decisions, integrating for the President the views of the State and Defense Departments and the C.I.A. He is also called upon to prepare the basis for an objective analysis of the problems involved if there is dispute between the affected agencies.

But the second and unofficial title—national security adviser—implies something more. It means that the occupant of this post is indeed an adviser to the President, and thus a subjective participant in this allegedly objective process. He is supposed to make choices and influence the President's decisions.

There is bound to be some conflict between these roles, and some occasional confusion. And there are bound to be situations in which the national security adviser steps on other people's toes. You will recall that at different times in recent years, national security advisers have acted as spokesmen for the President—even, occasionally, as secret negotiators.

It should be borne in mind, however, that when they did so, whether it was Mr. Kissinger or myself, it was with a Presidential mandate, at the President's specific request. This is explicitly stated in Mr. Nixon's and Mr. Carter's memoirs. Yet the performance of these tasks by the national security adviser inevitably generated public dispute and was, by and large, perceived in Washington as an illegitimate usurpation of the rightful prerogatives of the Secretary of State.

This view of the national security advisers' activities was personally damaging not only to the advisers but, sometimes, to the Presidents they served. Mr. Nixon resolved the dilemma by appointing Mr. Kissinger as Secretary of State. Mr. Carter's similar dilemma was resolved by the American electorate. Yet the issue remains.

There are three basic reasons why certain tasks dealing with foreign policy in its national security context can best be carried out by the national security adviser. First, there is the increasing intermeshing of diplomacy, intelligence and defense. You cannot reduce national security policy only to defense policy, or only to diplomacy. Secretaries of State all too often confuse diplomacy with foreign policy, forgetting that diplomacy is only a tool of foreign policy, and that there are other tools, including the application of force.

Thus, integration is needed, but this cannot be achieved from a departmental vantage point. No self-respecting Secretary of Defense will willingly agree to have his contribution, along with those of other agencies, integrated for Presidential decision by another departmental secretary—notably, the Secretary of State. And no self-respecting Secretary of State will accept integration by a Defense Secretary. It has to be done by someone close to the President, and perceived as much by all the principals.

Second, decision making in the nuclear age is almost inevitably concentrated in the White House. So many of the issues have an ultimate bearing on national survival, so many crises require prompt and immediate response, that a Presidential perspective on these matters has to be maintained and asserted. It cannot be done from the vantage point of a department.

Third, foreign policy and domestic politics have become increasingly intertwined. The time when foreign policy could be viewed as an esoteric exercise by a few of the initiated is past. Today, the public at large, the mass media, the Congress, all insist on participating in the process, and that makes coordination at the highest level all the more important.

In searching for a remedy to the problem in all its aspects, we must recognize that the elimination of conflict is an idle dream. Conflict is bound to exist whenever a number of individuals are engaged in a decision-making process, whenever a number of institutions project different institutional perspectives. So some conflict is unavoidable and is bound to be with us, enlivening and, one hopes, enlightening our lives. But some tempering of conflict is possible. And, in that respect, it would be useful to look at our national experience in two other areas of decision making.

The first is national defense. In fighting World War II, we managed without formal, institutional integration of decision making. The war was conducted by the War Department and the Navy Department on the basis of some informal institutional arrangements—notably committees established by the Army Chief of Staff, Gen. George C. Marshall, with President Roosevelt's approval.

But the war taught us that this situation could not endure; the response was the coordination of civil and military decision making under the National Security Act of 1947. That act created a body, the National Security Council, with statutory membership limited to the President's immediate associates. In practice, attendance was somewhat wider, and initially included the Secretaries of the Army, Navy and Air Force, as well as the three service chiefs of staff, along with the Secretary of State and the holder of the newly created post of Secretary of Defense—all under the chairmanship of the President.

Additional reforms over the next few years centralized the system further. The service secretaries and the service chiefs were removed from the N.S.C. That left the Secretary of Defense and the Chairman of the Joint Chiefs of Staff, another new post, as the only authoritative voices in the N.S.C. on defense matters. The service secretaries were removed from the Cabinet as well, leaving the Secretary of Defense as the sole authoritative voice on defense matters at that level. A unified approach was adopted in defense budgeting.

These moves toward more centralized control evoked enormous opposition. Yet who today would suggest that the position of the Secretary of Defense be abolished, and that we go back to a situation in which defense policy was shaped by three secretaries, each representing a different service, each fighting for his own budget, each shaping that budget and its strategic priorities within his own department?

There has been a similar evolution in the area of economic and fiscal policy. Until 1921, all departments and agencies of the United States Government made special, separate requests for funds to Congress. They did so directly, with copies to the President. It was only in 1921 that the Bureau of the Budget was made an agency, within the Treasury Department, responsible to the President, and the various departments were forbidden to ask Congress directly for money.

In 1939, on the eve of World War II, the Bureau of the Budget was transferred from the Treasury Department to the Executive Office of the President. In 1970, the Bureau of the Budget became the Office of Management and Budget in order to support the President in the exercise of managerial control over all Government departments. And in 1974, the appointment of a Director of the Office of Management and Budget was made subject to confirmation by the Senate.

Would anyone claim today that the existence of such a director inhibits the effective shaping of our national economic policy? Would anyone argue that the Secretaries of Commerce or of the Treasury cannot perform their functions because of the existence of such an arrangement?

I believe we must face up to the need for similar reforms for better coordination and integration of our national security policy. The first step, in my judgment, ought to be to upgrade the office of Assistant to the President for National Security Affairs by redesignating it as the office of the Director of National Security Affairs, comparable to the post of Director of the Office of Management and Budget. This would give it the status and authority it requires for the coordination of national security recommendations as they emanate from the State and Defense Departments and from the C.I.A.

Second, the appointment of the Director of National Security Affairs should be made subject to Senate confirmation. Only such a process would create a formal position fully legitimized in its functions. In such a setting, it would be clear that the Secretary of Defense is responsible for defense, that the head of the C.I.A. is responsible for intelligence, that the Secretary of State is responsible for diplomacy, while integrating the work of these three agencies into comprehensive national security policy is the responsibility of the Director of National Security Affairs.

Indeed, the clarification of the role of the Secretary of State as specifically responsible for diplomacy could, in time, open the way to yet another highly desirable step—the appointment of the first Secretary of State from the ranks of the professional Foreign Service. For then the Secretary of State would be clearly seen as professionally responsible for the task of managing our diplomacy, but would not be mistakenly perceived—as he has been in recent years—as a would-be architect of overall foreign policy, with its large security dimension.

Last but not least, I believe that such an arrangement would permit a more reasonable and effective relationship between our national security policy and our legislative branches. Under existing arrangements, the Assistant to the President for National Security Affairs is inhibited from appearing before Congress, since his testimony is viewed as an intrusion on the rightful prerogatives of the Secretaries of State and Defense. Once his appointment is subject to Senate confirmation, his appearance before legislative bodies would be normal and customary. He would be in a position to articulate our national policy on the President's behalf.

In effect, in the area of national security, we would be adopting an arrangement analogous to the arrangements developed earlier for national defense and the national economy. It would not resolve conflict altogether; it would not prevent divisions; but it would create a structured and orderly system in the central area of policy making—that of national survival.

Index